Focus on Women's Rights

State of the World's Minorities and Indigenous Peoples 2011

Events of 2010

Edited by Joanna Hoare

Minority Rights Group International

Acknowledgements

Minority Rights Group International (MRG) gratefully acknowledges the support of all organizations and individuals who gave financial and other assistance to this publication, including CAFOD, the European Commission, the Finnish Ministry of Foreign Affairs, and Matrix Causes Fund.

For further information please contact MRG. A CIP catalogue record of this publication is available from the British Library.

ISBN 978 1 907919 02 2

Published July 2011
Production: Kristen Harrison
Copy editing: Sophie Richmond
Design: Tom Carpenter, Texture
Printed in the UK

PEFC
PEFC/16-33-287

Minority Rights Group International
54 Commercial Street, London E1 6LT, United Kingdom. Tel +44 (0)20 7422 4200, Fax +44 (0)20 7422 4201, Email minority.rights@mrgmail.org
Website www.minorityrights.org

Getting involved

MRG relies on the generous support of institutions and individuals to further our work. All donations received contribute directly to our projects with minorities and indigenous peoples.

One valuable way to support us is to subscribe to our report series. Subscribers receive regular MRG reports and our annual review. We also have over 100 titles which can be purchased from our publications catalogue. In addition, MRG publications are available to minority and indigenous peoples' organizations through our library scheme.

MRG's unique publications provide well-researched, accurate and impartial information on minority and indigenous peoples' rights worldwide. We offer critical analysis and new perspectives on international issues. Our specialist training materials include essential guides for NGOs and others on international human rights instruments, and on accessing international bodies. Many MRG publications have been translated into several languages.

If you would like to know more about MRG, how to support us and how to work with us, please visit our website www.minorityrights.org

This document has been produced with the financial assistance of the European Union. The contents of this document are the sole responsibility of Minority Rights Group International and can under no circumstances be regarded as reflecting the position of the European Union

Front cover: Women from the pastoralist Gabbra community, in the Chalbi desert of northern Kenya, perform a traditional dance. *Eric Lafforgue.*
Inside front cover: Two Guatemalan women *Julio Etchart.* **Inside back cover:** A girl from the pastoralist Karrayyu minority in the Awash Valley, Ethiopia. *Eric Lafforgue.*

To the memory of Kevin Boyle
and Kristina Hedlund Thulin,
former Chair and Member of
the Council of Minority Rights
Group International, who
dedicated their careers to the
advancement of human rights.

Introduction

Part 1 Thematic essays

Part 2 Regional overviews

Part 3 Reference

Foreword
Gay J. McDougall
United Nations Independent Expert on minority issues

Minority groups are not monolithic, but the diversity within minority communities is often overlooked, both by those who are guided by prejudice, and by those who, with well-meaning intent, want to 'accommodate' the 'culture' of minority groups as a whole. Meanwhile, the aspirations of minority women are often sacrificed by internal group dynamics to demands for loyalty to broader community struggles, before issues of feminism and women's rights can be advanced. And so women's self-realization may be surrendered for notions of group culture and solidarity, into which women have had little input.

My mandate as United Nations Independent Expert on Minority Issues explicitly requires me to apply a gender perspective in my work. This has led me to seek out women in minority communities around the world on my country visits; to convene them in separate forums, as well as to sit with them in their kitchens, places of work and agricultural fields. I have listened to their issues and concerns.

I have found two concerns among women in all the minority communities that I have visited, regardless of the region of the world. First, within each community, there is activism among minority women to address the condition of women and that of their larger community. In many cases, they are leading their community struggles, sometimes by default, always by their vision and the force of their determination. But their leadership role comes at greater cost than that of their male compatriots, who need not also defeat general negative notions about the appropriateness of female activism.

Second, there is a common struggle for recognition and voice within the broader movement for women's rights. The feminist movements of majority women in both developed and developing countries are fraught with hierarchies and disregard for minority issues. They have not made space for the full empowerment of minority women within the movement.

Women members of minority and indigenous groups in all regions of the world are struggling to be recognized and heard. They are hidden behind walls of prejudice, patriarchy, paternalism, traditions, culture and the boundaries of the home. They are easy and common targets of violence in the home, their communities and the larger society. Many strive to knit families together in communities fractured by conquest, colonization, slavery, imperial domination, and armed conflict. Poverty, ethnic prejudice and gender-based restrictions can weigh heavily on women and girls. And marginalized women bear the most severe negative consequences of the modern globalized economy.

In developed countries, I found women struggling for personal autonomy in the context of either debates about banning the *burqa* in some countries, or 'multicultural' policies in other countries. Immigrant women in Europe are dealing with the consequences of male-centered immigration laws that deny wives separate status, thereby creating added vulnerabilities of deportation in situations of domestic violence or divorce. Or they may face immigration regimes that deny them the right to work, regardless of their own professional credentials.

I talked to Roma women who lowered their voices to a whisper when the subject of domestic violence was raised, but let me know that it was out of the question to seek assistance from police, because of the general antagonism between the police and all Roma.

In Canada, single black mother-led families have three times the poverty rate of mother-led families of the majority population. Even in the fast moving economy of Brazil, where upwards of 50 per cent of the population is now considered to be of African descent, Afro-Brazilian women are largely seen as either maids, or cultural icons of the tourism trade. As one indigenous Colombian women recently said to me: 'Indigenous women are tired of being projected in romantic notions'.

Minority women in rural or remote areas in some developing countries must cope with profound isolation, exacerbated by lack of education and language barriers. Their workload is made heavier by a lack of basic amenities such as clean water and sanitation, cheap and clean cooking fuels, the availability of child-care support, and protection against domestic and societal violence. Entrenched gender roles leave women highly vulnerable, particularly in regard to ownership of land or property, inheritance rights, and access to credit, technology or markets.

In India I heard the testimony of scores of Dalit women who had been beaten, raped or had their families threatened because they were serving on

Right: Dalit women work to collect recycling at an illegal dump near the Gujarati village of Kalol, India. *Andy Martinez.*

local governing councils. I also had the privilege to stand with nearly 1,000 Dalit women as they rallied to declare themselves 'free' of the degrading work of 'manual scavenging'; that is, cleaning the excrement from dry toilets by hand —a task reserved for women of the lowest caste, despite the practice having long been banned in India. Those women were raising their voices to claim their rights and dignity and had symbolically burned their manual scavenging baskets. I was struck by their bravery. Many of them had known no other way of life and had no guarantee of an alternative source of income for their families - yet they were making a stand.

Several of the Afro-Colombian women that I met had taken leadership positions in the Community Councils that have authority to make decisions regarding collective lands. They were in fear for their lives, faced with credible death threats. But they complained that their leadership positions were being discounted by sexist national security forces that refused to provide them the protective measures that were warranted because they were women and they were black. Others pulled me to the side after a day-long community meeting to plead for help for their children—the offspring of gang rape by marauding ex-paramilitary forces—who were unable to attend school because of the bullying and rejection they were suffering from their neighbors.

Each one of these stories presents challenges that must be addressed to unlock the full potential of individuals and societies. They are challenges to the United Nations system for the promotion and protection of minority rights, and the larger framework of human rights. They are challenges confronting every nation, since in today's world, all nations have populations with ethnic, racial and religious diversity. And they are challenges to the global feminist movement.

This volume of *State of the World's Minority and Indigenous Peoples* seeks to highlight many of the barriers and issues that must be tackled for minority and indigenous women to realize full economic, social and political equality. ∎

Preface

Yakın Ertürk

Former United Nations Special Rapporteur on violence against women, its causes and consequences (2003–2009)

Patriarchal violence affects women from all walks of life, in every country, and every community. It is the ultimate manifestation of gender inequality, committed by family members, partners, state and non-state actors. It also serves to sustain women's subordination to an unequal gender order, and violate their right to bodily integrity and the enjoyment of the full range of their human rights. Violence directly or indirectly limits women's and girls' freedom of movement, access to employment, education and healthcare, and participation in political, civic and economic life. Women in all societies continue to under report the physical, sexual and emotional abuse they experience because of shame, fear of reprisal or of being blamed for the abuse (as they know all too well that the police will do little to help them), or because they do not recognize that what is happening to them constitutes violence and a violation of their human rights.

While gender-based discrimination and violence occur universally, gender relations do not exist in a vacuum. Intersections of various systems of inequality and domination create diverse subject positions for women whose experiences are shaped by their ethnic, religious, and linguistic identities, as well as by other factors such as age, (dis)ability, geographical location, HIV status, and sexual orientation, therefore, creating layers of discrimination for some women. *State of the World's Minorities and Indigenous Peoples 2011* includes compelling depictions of the experiences of women belonging to marginalized and dispossessed populations, who are often uprooted from their lands and communities due to discriminatory government policies, the impact of armed conflicts, and the actions of private social, political and economic interest groups.

During my fact finding missions to different countries as the UN Special Rapporteur on violence against women, its causes and consequences, I all too often witnessed how 'minority', including indigenous and in many instances migrant women, faced high risk of multiple forms of violence with little or no access to support services and justice. Minority women stand at the intersection of gender and racial/ethnic inequality; they are discriminated against because they are women and because they are members of a marginalized group. As members of a minority group, they may be assaulted by members of the majority population, and / or by

agents of the state.

In my discussions with women in the North Caucasus in the Russian Federation in 2006, I heard accounts of Chechen and other minority women being targeted by the authorities, as they assumed more prominent roles in their communities (as men were increasingly absent, due to forced disappearances or terrorist activity). Muslim women wearing headscarves were particularly stigmatized and subjected to strip searches and arbitrary detention. In the North Caucasus and other conflict zones, reports of rape and sexual assault of minority women and the impunity with which it occurs is alarming. Similarly, the treatment of women in detention because of their group affiliation or alleged involvement in terrorist activity often amounts to ill-treatment and torture. Such assaults, in turn, leave women in danger of further abuse and ostracism from within their own communities, where due to a rigid, patriarchal morality code they are accused of having 'dishonoured' themselves and their families.

In other instances, where women are not specifically targeted on the basis of their minority or indigenous identity, the social, economic, political and often geographical marginalization of a particular minority group can leave women belonging to such a group disproportionately vulnerable to exclusion, exploitation and abuse. For example, some hill tribe populations in northern Thailand have no legal status, meaning they cannot access education and employment opportunities, or make use of pubic health services. Lack of citizenship rights combined with socio-economic marginalization makes women and girls from these hill tribes easy prey for sex traffickers. Elsewhere, female migrant domestic workers are often extremely vulnerable to physical, sexual and psychological abuse at the hands of their employers, due to their isolation, and because their employment and immigration status are dependent on their employers. In Canada, indigenous women are found to be three times more likely to be HIV positive than non-indigenous women, in part as a result of the high levels of sexual violence experienced by indigenous women.

Minority women are also at risk of violence from within their own communities. Such violence is often justified on the basis of 'culture' or 'tradition', ignoring both that certain harmful practices may in fact be recent developments to subdue women, and that they serve the interests of dominant members of the group. This risk is compounded by the fact that redress and support services for these women may not be available or accessible. In Guatemala, despite being a numerical majority, the indigenous population is excluded from the mainstream institutions and denied access to the resources of the wider society. Indigenous women in particular face multiple exclusions and discrimination. During my visit to the country in 2004, women's rights activists told me that levels of gender-based violence within indigenous communities are very high. Yet, the remote, rural locations of many indigenous settlements and language barriers make it difficult for indigenous women to escape abusive relationships and lead independent lives. Women in the North Caucasus reported that pressure to maintain community cohesion, as well as total lack of trust in the authorities made it virtually impossible for women to report domestic abuse, despite its high prevalence levels. Similarly in Sweden, Saami women rarely report violence or seek help from mainstream Swedish institutions, as they see such institutions as alien to their culture. Immigration policies may also make it difficult for minority women to access help if they are victims of gender-based violence. During my missions to Sweden and the Netherlands, I found that some migrant women remained trapped in violent relationships, either because they were undocumented migrants and feared deportation if they went to the police, or because their immigration status was dependent on their spouse.

Empirical and anecdotal evidence from around the world, including testimonies I have personally received as the UN Special Rapporteur reveal that minority women confront many challenges, which by their nature are intersectional and multifaceted. As a result, these women face a dual task. They may be seeking to defend their rights as members of an excluded group within a dominant society with its repressive or indifferent state apparatuses, discriminatory laws and institutions and prejudiced public opinion. At the same time, they may be questioning and resisting static, patriarchal perceptions of culture and tradition within their own communities, which are used to justify gendered subordination and violence. Ultimately, minority and indigenous peoples' struggle for social

justice on a human rights platform will only be legitimate and therefore successful, if human rights problems within these communities, in particular violence and discrimination against women, are also acknowledged and addressed.

Minority women have not been passive in the face of these challenges. They have been developing strategies to counter public and private forms of discrimination individually and collectively. Awareness-raising programmes and other projects implemented in remote communities are making an impact in supporting women's empowerment and their mobilization for concerted action in their quest for equality, security and dignity for themselves as well as for their communities. In so doing, these women are facilitating dialogues between the various human rights movements and the global women's movement, linking their particular concerns with other struggles.

Failure to recognize the intersectional nature of systems of oppression and integrate a racial and gender perspective when analyzing indigenous women's status will ultimately result in further reinforcing their subordination to both patriarchy and racism. Evidence shows that greater autonomy for minority/indigenous communities does not necessarily result in enhancing the rights of women in these communities, and that gender equality strategies designed in a vacuum do not work. Therefore, in addressing the status of indigenous and minority women it is essential to identify racial elements of gender discrimination, as well as the gendered elements of race discrimination. The recently established United Nations entity for gender equality and women's empowerment – UN Women –provides an opportunity for revisiting our vision for gender equality to better respond to both the universality and the particularity of women's realities.

It is with great pleasure that I present this volume to the reader. I am confident that it will enhance our understanding of the intersectional nature of gendered discrimination and violence, and contribute to the ongoing struggle for their elimination. ∎

Why focus on minority and indigenous women?

Kathryn Ramsay

A Batwa woman is raped by a non-Batwa man because he believed a local myth that sex with a Batwa woman cures backache; a Roma woman complains to the authorities about domestic violence she suffered and is criticized by Roma men for giving the authorities another reason to attack the community; a pregnant Dalit woman is forced to give birth in the street because the doctors refused to admit a Dalit to hospital; a Pastoralist woman candidate in local elections is told by other women in her community to run for councillor because being a Member of Parliament is too big a job for a woman; a Muslim girl is sexually assaulted by majority boys in her class who targeted her because as a member of a minority, they thought she would be less likely to report them than a girl from their community ….

These examples show the complexity of the multiple problems facing minority and indigenous women. They may face discrimination and violence from majority communities and from within their own community, and often cannot get access to the justice and support services to which they are entitled. But minority and indigenous women are not only passive victims of violations of their human rights. As discussed in the thematic articles and regional and country updates included in this year's *State of the World's Minorities and Indigenous Peoples*, many are actively fighting for their rights as women, for the rights of their communities and for their rights as minority or indigenous women. And by challenging the status quo – both in terms of acceptable gender roles, as well as confronting the discrimination that they face as members of minorities – many face difficulties or violent reprisals from the majority community, or even from within their own families.

Minority and indigenous women are entitled to all human rights – civil, political, economic, social and cultural – as set out in various universal and regional legal instruments, such as the International Covenant on Civil and Political Rights (ICCPR) and International Covenant on Economic, Social and Cultural Rights (ICESCR). As women, they are entitled to specific rights on the basis of their gender, such as those included in the Convention on the Elimination of All Forms of Discrimination Against Women, or in regional instruments such as the Protocol to the African Charter on Human and Peoples' Rights on the Rights of Women in

Africa. As members of minorities and indigenous peoples, they are also entitled to minority rights and indigenous rights, set out in relevant United Nations (UN) Declarations (UN Declaration on the Rights of Persons Belonging to National or Ethnic, Religious and Linguistic Minorities [UNDM] and UN Declaration on the Rights of Indigenous Peoples [UNDRIP]) and regional instruments. These instruments recognize the unique (and frequently more vulnerable) situations of minorities and indigenous peoples, and provide additional guarantees to ensure they can enjoy their human rights equally with others.

The problems experienced by minority and indigenous women have many strands, and initially may seem complex, with tensions between different rights. One example of this tension is that between the rights of minorities and indigenous peoples to maintain their cultural identity and practise their culture, and the rights of women to be free from harmful cultural practices, such as female genital mutilation and child marriage. In such instances, it is essential to remember that minority and indigenous cultures are not homogeneous, and harmful practices that are presented as integral to the cultural identity of a minority group may not necessarily be supported by every member of that group. It is highly likely that there will be women within the community who are challenging them.

In other cases, tension may emerge over prioritization of which rights to fight for first. For instance, leaders of an ethnic minority community suffering from entrenched discrimination may prioritize securing rights for the community and ending ethnic discrimination, before looking at gender discrimination affecting minority women. This may also be the case where minority women have taken part in wider social movements or armed struggles, as discussed in the chapter on conflict included here.

Minority and indigenous women may face gender-based discrimination and violence in common with women from majority communities, and they may face discrimination because of their minority or indigenous identity, shared with minority and indigenous men. Moreover, discrimination on the basis of minority or indigenous status may work together with or intersect with gender-based discrimination to result in unique disadvantages for minority and indigenous women, because of their status as women belonging to minority or indigenous communities. Other forms of disadvantage such as on the basis of age, disability, sexuality or socio-economic status may further intersect to create overlapping and entrenched marginalization. Minority and indigenous women activists have drawn attention to the fact that, in some cases, mainstream feminist movements have treated women as a homogeneous group, and have often ignored the particular concerns and experiences of minority women. Sometimes majority women's groups even perpetuate discrimination on the basis of minority or indigenous status against minority or indigenous women, for example by rejecting their participation in International Women's Day events. Minority women's rights activists have also on occasion felt uncomfortable when they have felt pressured by calls for feminist solidarity into 'choosing' between solidarity on the basis of gender, or on the basis of ethnic or religious identity. Equally, minority women activists promoting the rights of women within their own communities may be labelled as traitors by others within those communities, and raising issues of, for instance, the racist violence experienced by ethnic minority men, can lead to the same condemnation within feminist activist circles.

Many of these tensions can be resolved through an examination of both minority rights standards, women's rights standards and the reality for minority and indigenous women, keeping in mind the diversity which exists within all minority and indigenous communities, and among minority and indigenous women.

Discrimination

The following chapters outline many ways in which minority and indigenous women and girls experience discrimination as a result of their sex and their status as members of minorities or indigenous communities. This discrimination may be direct, for instance where women from a minority group are specifically targeted for sexual violence during conflict. Discrimination may also be indirect, where an apparently neutral provision has a disproportionately negative impact on minority or indigenous women. An example of this is where restrictions on the type of clothing that can be worn in schools or places of employment

apply to everyone, but the negative impact is disproportionately felt by minority or indigenous women.

Human rights instruments place obligations on states to eradicate discrimination against women. This includes eradicating discrimination against minority women. Obligations on states to remove discrimination against minorities and indigenous people also include removing discrimination against women from those communities. Comprehensive domestic legislation which defines and outlaws direct and indirect discrimination in line with international principles is essential, but not sufficient. To effectively remove discrimination, states must understand how and why it negatively affects minority and indigenous women. This requires data showing their specific socio-economic situation. Frequently, data disaggregated by sex *as well as* ethnicity, religion or language is not collected; however, it is impossible to produce policies and programmes which effectively improve the lives of minority and indigenous women if their situations are not fully understood. Chapter 2 on the Millennium Development Goals (MDGs) examines the need for disaggregated data in more detail.

Once a thorough analysis of the problems faced by minority and indigenous women and their causes has been completed, effective policies and programmes designed to tackle these problems can be established. International standards on eradication of racial discrimination and discrimination against women clearly set out that 'special measures' (e.g. specific programmes to boost the skills of certain groups, or quotas in political representation, education and employment) to benefit previous disadvantaged groups are not privileges for those groups and do not discriminate against other sections of society as long as they meet certain conditions. Special measures must aim to address specific discrimination, they must not be continued after the aim has been met and they must not lead to maintenance of different rights for different groups. Where minority and indigenous women have been marginalized, implementation of special measures is likely to be necessary in order to enable them to enjoy their rights on an equal footing with others in society.

Identity

The issue of the rights of minorities and indigenous peoples to maintain and develop their identity and cultural practices, versus the individual rights of members of those groups to be free from harmful cultural practices, is often highlighted as a problem for the concept of human rights. In many cultures – indigenous, minority and majority – women have primary responsibility for raising children, including teaching them about the culture. In effect they become the custodians of cultural traditions and are viewed as such by other members of their communities. For example men may no longer wear traditional clothes every day, whereas women may do so. This means that tensions associated with cultural practices are more likely to affect women and girls. This can be the case if restrictions and pressure limiting rights to cultural expression in this way come from the state or from the majority population. But it can also be the case when women from within a particular group question what they see as an obligation to follow certain practices or styles of dress, in their capacity as 'cultural custodians'.

States have an obligation under human rights standards to protect women and girls from cultural practices which violate their rights, whether they are carried out by a majority or minority. It is important to remember that harmful cultural practices are not only found in minority or indigenous communities. The main minority rights standard, the UNDM, provides guidance on how this can be balanced with the right of minorities to cultural identity. The UNDM, although not legally binding, was adopted by consensus at the UN General Assembly, which means that no state objected to its contents. The UNDM grants minorities the right to protect and develop their culture except under two named circumstances. These are: when specific practices are 'contrary to international standards', and where they are 'in violation of national law'. The first provision, 'contrary to international standards' means states are required to prohibit practices which also contravene standards such as those set out in the Convention on the Elimination of All forms of Discrimination Against Women or the Convention Against Torture (for example early marriage or female genital mutilation [FGM]). The second provision, 'in violation of national law', is more problematic. The provision would be rendered meaningless if

states could adopt any law they wished against any cultural practice of minorities. Prohibitions must be based on reasonable and objective grounds. States may not use the existence of a harmful cultural practice as a reason for prohibiting a range of cultural actions or a whole culture. Restrictions must relate only to the specific harmful practice. States must also not act in a discriminatory manner either, for instance focusing on eradication of early marriage in a minority community but ignoring the same practice in a majority community. For governments that *are* keen to meet their legal obligations to uphold both the rights of women and those of minorities, getting this balance right can be a difficult task. In a case study included in the Southern Africa update, this is discussed in the context of the South African government's approach to certain Zulu cultural practices that are harmful to women.

Legislation is necessary to restrict the specific harmful practice; however, it is not sufficient to ensure the practice is ended, especially if sections of the community are against the measures. For example, a number of states have laws which set a minimum age for marriage or prohibit FGM, but early marriage or FGM still occur. The most effective methods for the eradication of harmful practices require cooperation from the affected community. Cooperation is more likely when measures to be taken to eradicate the harmful practice are seen to be non-threatening to the overall cultural identity of the community. Minority or indigenous communities that have experienced systematic discrimination or marginalization may perceive legitimate state concern over a particular harmful cultural practice as another attack on them. However, no culture (minority or majority) is homogeneous or unchanging, and even where there may be a negative reaction from community leaders (who are often men), there may be others within the community who are already working to eradicate the practice.

Many minority and indigenous women (and men) who reject harmful cultural practices and/or work to eradicate them frequently face criticism, hostility or outright violence from others in the community (both men and women). They may be accused of aiding the destruction of their community identity because they are willing to see a cultural practice change, or of giving the government and the majority another reason to attack them by airing internal community issues in public. Arguments used are often that the rights of the community need to be prioritized and secured first; once that has been achieved, other areas, such as women's rights can be addressed. The implication of this argument is that women's rights are less important and can be left until later. However, the opposite argument also holds: failure to address the rights of women within a community undermines overall efforts to hold governments to account for securing the rights of the community.

State efforts to eliminate a harmful practice are more likely to be effective if they work with those in the community already engaged in its eradication, or sympathetic to their aims, to design a culturally relevant approach which includes addressing the reasons for the opposition within the community. It is important that such support allows community activists to take the lead, and does not put them in a position where they may face further hostility for receiving assistance and money from 'outside'.

Participation

In many countries, minority and indigenous women are under-represented in state decision-making processes at both national and local levels. They may also face difficulties or restrictions in exercising their political rights, such as their right to vote. For example, women from linguistic minority or indigenous communities may be less fluent in the language used in political life than minority or indigenous men, making it more difficult for them to access information about electoral processes, understand the positions of different candidates and make an informed choice. They may also be pressurized into supporting the candidate chosen by their family or others in the community. Those minority or indigenous women who would like to take part in such processes, or stand for elected office, may face criticism from within their own communities or their family for overstepping the boundaries of acceptable gender roles by trying to enter the 'male' world of politics, or scepticism at their ability to take on such roles. Political parties may refuse to have them stand as candidates, fearing that a minority or indigenous woman would be likely to lose the election. Where they do stand for election they may face prejudice from the electorate regarding their ability as women to assume leadership positions, compounded by negative bias

on the basis of their ethnic or religious identity. Practical barriers may also present themselves, such as lack of access to funding to support their campaigns and, as with majority women, difficulties of balancing the demands of their office with child care and domestic work may hinder them (seldom a consideration for male elected officials). In the face of these obstacles, it is perhaps not surprising that where parliamentary or local assembly quotas on the basis of ethnicity have been introduced, minority and indigenous women have not always benefited significantly; likewise, gender quotas have also not necessarily resulted in an increase in the numbers of women from minority and indigenous communities in elected office (as discussed in the Americas update, in the context of the low numbers of indigenous women in political office in the region). Few quotas relate directly to minority or indigenous women's participation. Even where quotas do lead to minority or indigenous women taking up governance positions, they may face additional barriers to exercising the role effectively. They may have been selected to fill the quota without understanding what the position means or to be a proxy for a male from their community or the majority. They may face discrimination from other elected officials who do not allow them to fulfil their duties, or a backlash if they are perceived to be 'too effective'. In the Indian context (as mentioned in the South Asia update), in 2010 this led to calls for a 'quota within a quota' at the national level for Dalit and religious minority women.

Minority and indigenous women are frequently also under-represented in traditional community decision-making processes or leadership structures, which can help to perpetuate gender-based discrimination against them (for instance in regard to community-level decisions relating to land rights or inheritance). This also means that they are seldom called upon to represent the community to outsiders. When governments want to find out what a community thinks about an issue or policy, they frequently look for representatives or community leaders to speak to. These are men. Often it may not be clear how these 'representatives' became spokespersons for the community or how representative their views are of the community as a whole. Even where there are calls to increase the participation of women, for example in conflict resolution and peace-building, minority and indigenous women's participation is frequently overlooked. However, it is important to ensure that the diverse viewpoints of those belonging to minorities and indigenous peoples are heard.

Minorities – including minority women – have the right to participation in decisions affecting the minority, in all aspects of public life, as well as in economic progress and development. For each of these areas, governments need to ensure that the participation of minority women is effective rather than tokenistic, and that they have a meaningful opportunity to influence the outcome of the decision or process. Government efforts to increase participation of women also need to include minority women.

Indigenous peoples have the right to self-determination under the UNDRIP. This includes the right to autonomy or self-government in their internal and local affairs, and the right to maintain their own institutions as well as to choose to participate fully in the life of the state. International standards impose obligations on states to ensure the rights of women, including indigenous women, to participate in political and public life. This includes the obligation to ensure that indigenous women can participate equally with men in indigenous-run institutions.

The following thematic chapters – on the MDGs, gender-based violence, reproductive health, and armed conflict – explore some of these issues and tensions in more depth. They are also discussed in the regional and country updates, all of which include coverage of events from 2010 and information significant to minority and indigenous women, where available. But as many of the authors of our updates this year have found, it is often difficult to obtain accurate, up-to-date information about the status of minority and indigenous women in a given country. In addition, in accounts of humanitarian disasters and wide-scale human rights violations, the specific experiences of minority and indigenous women are often invisible. ■

Joanna Hoare also contributed material to this chapter.

Minority and indigenous women and the Millennium Development Goals

Corinne Lennox

D olores Fernandez is a leader among the Roma community in Spain. She has struggled for decades alongside other Roma across Europe to secure dignity and equality. But she has carried more weight on her shoulders than her male counterparts. In her words:

'Our fight has two fronts: at home, we are fighting to get [Roma] women to study and have freedom. We also have to raise awareness about our problems and needs with different government bodies so that these are taken into account. In addition, we have to continue carrying out our family obligations (i.e. caring for our husbands, parents and children) that we know we cannot abandon. [...] We have fought a lot, many times on our own. We have had little support from non-[Roma] women's organizations, institutions in general, Romani organizations and sometimes even our own families.'

Her words, recorded in a 2007 report by the European Roma Rights Centre, are echoed by minority and indigenous women activists across the continents, and show clearly that women and girls from minority and indigenous groups face challenges on several fronts. Discrimination, domestic expectations and cultural or religious constraints are among the major factors that have resulted in lower levels of education, lower wages and employment, higher rates of maternal mortality, and greater poverty for these women and girls.

The Millennium Development Goals

Goal 1: Eradicate extreme poverty and hunger
Goal 2: Achieve universal primary education
Goal 3: Promote gender equality and empower women
Goal 4: Reduce child mortality
Goal 5: Improve maternal health
Goal 6: Combat HIV/AIDS, malaria and other diseases
Goal 7: Ensure environmental sustainability
Goal 8: Develop a global partnership for development

These elements conspire to diminish the chances that minority and indigenous women and girls have to benefit from the Millennium Development Goals (MDGs). Although development actors will sometimes acknowledge such challenges exist, there is an assumption that general or gender-specific measures will offer solutions. The evidence presented here will show that assumption to be misguided, and will present some suggestions for urgently needed reform, to ensure the full realization of the MDGs for minority and indigenous women and girls.

Gender and the MDGs

The MDGs were adopted in 2000 at the United Nations (UN) Millennium Summit. They are a set of commitments by states to address pressing development concerns by the year 2015. There are eight goals, 21 targets and 60 indicators. Although many of the issues included in the MDGs are relevant in both Northern and Southern states, broadly speaking, Southern state actors are implementing domestic MDGs plans, while Northern states are prioritizing the MDGs in their overseas development assistance, but not domestically. All states are invited to submit regular reports on progress towards realizing the goals.

The particular challenges faced by women and girls in achieving development outcomes are given special attention in the MDGs. Most prominent is Goal 3, to promote gender equality and empower women, followed by Goal 5, to improve maternal health. The true measure of the MDGs, however, is in the concrete targets that states have set, and the indicators used to assess progress. In examining the targets within each goal, there is evidence of a gender-aware approach, but also of limited aspirations. For example, Goal 3 has far-reaching intentions, but only one target is set specifically to eliminate gender disparity in primary and secondary education preferably by 2005, and at all levels by 2015. The indicators for Goal 3 include measuring the proportion of seats held by women in national parliaments, and yet no commitment was agreed to make this an official target for achieving gender equality. Moreover, of the 60 indicators, only 4 explicitly call for collection of disaggregated data by sex: 2.3, 3.1, 3.2 and 3.3 (5.1 on rates of maternal mortality has been excluded because it only requires data collection on women). The official list of

State of the World's Minorities
and Indigenous Peoples 2011

Minority and indigenous
women and the Millennium
Development Goals

21

MDG indicators states that 'all indicators should be disaggregated by sex and urban/rural as far as possible', although this practice is not strongly evidenced in the MDG reports.

From the perspective of women's human rights, the MDGs fall far short. Key issues like violence against women, lack of equal political participation and non-discrimination in access to land, financial services and inheritance rights are among the many human rights obligations of states that do not get full or even partial attention. Goal 5 on maternal mortality is reportedly the MDG where global progress has been slowest. Global crises in the financial sector and affecting the environment have increased women's hardship: as unemployment and food prices have risen, many women have had fewer resources to realize their own and their families' basic economic and social rights. The disproportionately low number of women in political and financial decision-making positions has given them less power to oppose these harsh realities and inequalities.

Minority and indigenous women and girls and the MDGs

Minority and indigenous women and girls across the world experience many of the same forms of discrimination, violence, abuse, exclusion and vulnerability that women and girls from majority groups face. Their identity as minorities or indigenous peoples and as minority or indigenous *women*, however, creates a number of particular barriers to equality that need to be addressed, including within MDGs programmes.

Minority and indigenous women and girls face intersecting discrimination, that is: discrimination on the basis of their national, ethnic, religious or linguistic identity; discrimination on the basis of their sex; and, in many cases, discrimination on the basis of their low economic status. They face discrimination from both outside and within the various identity groups to which they belong. For example, minority women can face discrimination from some women's organizations led by women from majority groups. Minority and indigenous women also face gender discrimination from members of their own cultural or religious communities. Discrimination can also manifest itself in different spheres of activity for minority and indigenous women: for example, women may not face discrimination in the home but may at the village level or the national level, as regards their participation in society or governance and decision-making. These various aspects of discrimination compound to put minority and indigenous women into deeper levels of poverty and exclusion.

Overcoming poverty

Goal 1 is to eradicate extreme poverty. Although it is increasingly common to find gender-disaggregated poverty figures, further disaggregation by minority or indigenous identity is less visible. Poverty surveys consistently show disproportionately higher levels of poverty for minority groups but women can experience further disparities. One dataset (used in an article by Suzanne Duryea and Maria Genoni published by the Inter-American Development Bank) for Bolivia, Brazil, Guatemala and Peru shows that indigenous or Afro-descendant women consistently earned less than their male counterparts and considerably less than non-indigenous, non-Afro-descendants, even among the poorest workers (measured as those earning less than US $1 per hour). For example, 67 per cent of Afro-Brazilian women earned less than US $1 per hour, compared to 60 per cent of Afro-Brazilian men and 43 per cent of white women; in Guatemala, 81 per cent of indigenous women earned less than US $1 per hour, compared to 59 per cent of non-indigenous women and 70 per cent of indigenous men.

High rates of poverty among minority groups are influenced greatly by the precarious nature of minority and indigenous women's employment opportunities. Goal 1, target 1b aims to 'Achieve full and productive employment and decent work for all, including women and young people.' Minority and indigenous women are more prevalent in low-wage and informal sector work where labour rights are not enforced and where social security safeguards rarely exist. They commonly rely on jobs as domestic workers or agricultural labourers and/or migrate in search of work. A study by the Open Society Institute quoted in a recent Plan International report found that '54 per cent of Roma women in Romania worked informally in jobs that provided no benefits or formal work agreements'. In Guatemala, the World Bank reports that the proportion of indigenous and Afro-descendant women in non-agricultural wage labour is only one-fifth of that recorded for women from the majority groups. In Peru, only 4 per cent

Minority and indigenous
women and the Millennium
Development Goals

of indigenous female workers have social security coverage compared to 10 per cent of indigenous male workers, 19 per cent of non-indigenous female workers and 26 per cent of non-indigenous male workers, as reported by Duryea and Genoni.

Securing wage labour outside the home can be particularly difficult for minority and indigenous women who often face greater burdens of 'time poverty' than other women. Research in South America by Claudia Piras, also published by the Inter-American Development Bank, shows that poor indigenous and Afro-descendant women 'have lower levels of schooling, higher rates of fertility and are more likely to lack access to electricity or running water, making child rearing and housework responsibilities more time consuming'. A study on pastoralist women in Tanzania indicates that the effect of declining viability of pastoralism as a livelihood has forced more men to migrate for work, leaving women as effective heads of household. This entails more work and responsibility, but rarely means increased rights and decision-making power, because, for example, they lack inheritance rights and have only limited rights regarding livestock.

Unequal access to land and inheritance rights severely limits the economic independence of women, making them more vulnerable to economic or social shocks. In many communities, customary law has governed the allocation of such resources, to the detriment of women. Irene Naguda, a representative from the Uganda Coalition for Crisis Prevention and a pastoralist from Karamoja speaking at the UN Forum on Minority Issues (December 2010), reported that women, 'are economically discriminated [against] within their community due to cultural domains of power limiting them from inheriting resources and assets despite national legislation enforcing equitable inheritance of property'. Men within communities express understandable fears that granting inheritance rights to women would make it easier for outsiders to appropriate land through marriage. In response, women advocate for a community-based solution and legislation to protect traditional lands that do not depend on gender-discrimination in inheritance or land rights. For example, one study from South Africa showed how indigenous women used appeals to custom and provisions of the Constitution in combination to assert claims to land under customary law that had traditionally

been allocated only to men, suggesting that shifting patterns to more female-headed families justified women's claims to these rights. The results varied, with some communities recognizing such rights *de facto* but only when a male relative retained customary title of the land, while others had made allocations to older women with children.

Accessing education

Education is widely seen as a tool for overcoming women's poverty and for improving health and education outcomes for children. Two of the MDG targets are focused on gender parity in access to education (Goal 2, target 2 and Goal 3, target 3). Girls from minority and indigenous groups often have less access to education and experience more marginalization and even abuse at school.

Data on educational attainment appears to be the most readily available data disaggregated by gender and minority or indigenous status. The MDG Report from Laos, for example, indicates that 'compared with boys, girls from the Sino-Tibetan group [of minorities] are much less likely to be in school than those from the Lao-Tai group'. Similarly, the MDG Report for Iran shows that in three regions where marginalized minorities predominate – the provinces of Kurdestan, Khuzestan and Sistan Baluchestan – the ratio of girls to boys in education lags behind other regions. In China, girls from minority groups have experienced much lower rates of secondary school enrolment than Han girls, according to a 2010 article by Emily Hannum and Meiyan Wang, published by the World Bank. By the year 2005, Han girls had increased secondary enrolment by 46 per cent since 2000 and 82 per cent since 1990 (the MDG base rate), whereas minority girls had achieved improvements of only 29 per cent since 2000 and 54 per cent since 1990. Some 30.1 per cent of minority girls in 2005 were not in secondary school, as compared to 8.8 per cent of Han girls. Even where girls are overcoming gender barriers, discrimination on the basis of their minority identity can hold them back: for example, the MDG report from Brazil finds that 'the advantageous situation enjoyed by females in education is minimized when the color/race element is taken into account; Afro-descendent girls are almost always in a worse situation than white boys'.

The figures are helpful but they do not explain the

complex and intersecting causal factors of exclusion and inequality in access to education experienced by minority and indigenous girl children Discrimination in the classroom is a common problem, manifest in various forms. Minority girl (and boy) children can experience harassment, teasing and insults from pupils and teachers. Teachers can have lower expectations of minority or indigenous girls, offering them less attention and fewer incentives to succeed. Curricula in general often do not mention minorities (or do so in negative or stereotypical ways) and positive images of minority or indigenous women will likely be even less visible. Overt discrimination can dissuade parents from enrolling children or cause children to drop out. Access to mother-tongue education is also lacking in many countries, making it difficult for minority and indigenous children to integrate and stay enrolled in primary school. This may be particularly difficult for girls who, because of domestic obligations and cultural norms, will have less contact outside the community before starting school than boys, and thus less exposure to the majority language(s). Minority and indigenous girl children may be particularly vulnerable to physical, sexual or other abuse by teachers or other students because they have less power to challenge authority and seek justice for crimes committed against them. For instance, Dalit girls at one school in India were particularly targeted for repeated rape by teachers. In this case, the case was heard and won in favour of the girls.

Minorities who are poorer than other groups will struggle to pay for school fees and related costs. Given the poor employment prospects for minority and indigenous women in many countries, this expense means that the girl child's education may not be prioritized when family income is limited, pushing girls into informal economy jobs before they can complete their schooling. There may be religious or cultural preferences of minority groups that impede equal access to education for girls: for example, gender-biased practices of early marriage or preferences for girl children to work and be educated in the home according to cultural or religious traditions. Parents of minority and indigenous girl children often do not have the chance to work with school authorities over such concerns; in Bangladesh, the non-governmental organization (NGO) Zabarang Kalyan Samity reports that most indigenous parents and community members in the Chittagong Hill Tracts region 'are not empowered to participate in school affairs and the local institutions are not fully authorized to deal with the context specific education situation'.

Improving health and reproductive health care
The MDGs give particular attention to the field of health care, with a focus on reduction of rates of HIV, AIDS and other diseases (Goal 6) and on maternal mortality (Goal 5). Cultural practices, geographic location and discrimination can lead to differential levels of health and maternal mortality for minority and indigenous women. For example, research on pastoralist communities in Tanzania points to increasing rates of HIV infection, particularly among adult women, estimated for pastoralists at 15–18 per cent as compared to a national average of 8.8 per cent. Among the contributing causes are polygymy and strong cultural resistance to condom use The government has failed to respond with targeted policies: for example, national education campaigns are only in the dominant language of Swahili and anti-retrovirals, although free, are not easily accessible in several districts where pastoralists live.

The topic of reproductive health is given specific attention elsewhere in *State of the World's Minorities and Indigenous Peoples 2011*, but suffice it to say here that living in remote regions where maternal health services are poor, and the lack of cultural awareness among maternal health practitioners, are among the factors that increase maternal mortality among minority and indigenous women. In Guatemala, maternal mortality for indigenous women is three times higher than for non-indigenous women, and while 68 per cent of non-indigenous women have had professional prenatal care, only 45.6 per cent of indigenous women report similar. In India, figures for 2005 show that only one-third of women from Scheduled Tribes received prenatal care, compared to a national average of 49 per cent. The disparity between these figures can be the result of inadequate service provision in minority regions, poor nutrition, limited access to clean water and adequate housing, cultural beliefs around maternity and childbirth, poor communication and intercultural understanding of health practitioners, and also the higher levels of poverty among minorities and indigenous peoples who are then less able than other women to pay for antenatal services.

Minority and indigenous
women and the Millennium
Development Goals

Better access to services

Geographic location, including urban/rural divides, impact strongly on access to social services for minority and indigenous women. According to the MDG Report for Nepal, among Dalits in Nepal, girls living in mountainous areas have less access to schooling than those living in Kathmandu. In China, research by Emily Hannum for the World Bank shows that ethnic minorities living in urban areas faced lower disparities on socio-economic indicators compared to the Han majority than do rurally based ethnic minority groups. Two things are important here: first, disparities still existed even in urban settings, suggesting that geographical location is not the only explanatory variable of inequality. The same study, for example, showed that in both rural and urban settings, minority children were three times as likely to be excluded from primary education as the Han majority children. Second, the chronic underinvestment in social services in regions where minorities and indigenous peoples live is contributing to disparities, a pattern repeated in many countries.

It is not uncommon for governments to misguidedly employ resettlement schemes to increase access to services for remote communities. The impact of such schemes on various indicators of health, income and food security has been shown to be negative, but the burden can be particularly harsh for minority and indigenous women. For example, women's role in food production can be undermined when displacement moves families away from traditional forms of agriculture and food gathering into unfamiliar environments. This decreases the value of women's knowledge on these issues and also seriously impedes their ability to feed their families and earn income from traditional agricultural products. One study from Laos reports that 'being in charge of collecting the daily firewood, fetching water and gathering forest food products, [Mon-Khmer women] are the first to be affected by increased competition over resources due to resettlement'. The same report found that increased poverty post-resettlement was making minority women more vulnerable to commercial sexual exploitation, abuse and HIV.

Protection from harm

Due to the nature of contemporary conflicts, often built upon inter-ethnic or sectarian grievances, minority women can be particularly at risk of targeted violence during conflict, or as they deal with the effects of conflict, such as displacement and widowhood. The use of rape as a form of ethnic cleansing or humiliation of male combatants makes minority women extremely vulnerable to such acts. Prejudices and taboos around rape within minority communities can mean that women are ostracized or dissuaded from reporting these crimes. For example, in her report on her 2006 mission to the Russian Federation, the UN Special Rapporteur on violence against women, Yakın Ertürk, reported on 'Operation Fatima' in Chechnya, where Muslim women wearing headscarves are targeted for searches by security forces under anti-terrorism policies. There have been reports of rape and other sexual violence during searches and detention, but many women have been fearful to step forward, for fear of reprisals by authorities or ostracization by their family.

In periods of economic crisis, minority or indigenous women and men may be the first to lose their jobs because of discrimination in the workplace, decreasing household income and placing greater care burdens on women. The effects of climate change and environmental degradation can impact greatly on the traditional food production practices of minorities and indigenous peoples, much of which is often done by women. For example, grazing and water for animal husbandry can dramatically decline, or biodiversity and forest resources can become less available, all impacting on traditional livelihoods, fuel sources and food production. The net effect for minority and indigenous women is that they have less household income, higher costs for fuel and greater burdens regarding food security. This has been the experience of pastoralist women in East and Horn of Africa; among the effects of increasing drought are greater labour to find water, reduced availability of wild foods to supplement the family diet, and greater frequency of dismantling and rebuilding houses to migrate in search of viable pasture.

Policy responses: a human rights-based approach to the MDGs for women and girls

Urgent efforts are needed to ensure that minority and indigenous women and girls are not excluded from MDG gains. A handful of MDG reports acknowledge this fact, but few show evidence of

State of the World's Minorities
and Indigenous Peoples 2011

Minority and indigenous
women and the Millennium
Development Goals

25

concrete steps to address the situation.

As a first step, recognition is needed that the situation of minority and indigenous women and girls requires special measures to achieve inclusion. The 'invisibility' of minority and indigenous women is a major contributing factor in their continued marginalization. Governments and those working towards the MDGs need to acknowledge the particular barriers faced by women from minority and indigenous groups.

Disaggregated data
Reforms in data collection, research and reporting can expedite this recognition. MDG reports and indicators should be expanded to include data that measures change by gender and minority or

26   Minority and indigenous
                      women and the Millennium
                      Development Goals

State of the World's Minorities
and Indigenous Peoples 2011

Left: A Karenni girl at school in the Thai village of Ban Nai Soiy, close to the Thailand-Burma border. *Eric Lafforgue.*

Elimination of All Forms of Racial Discrimination (ICERD) and other domestic legislation to ensure non-discrimination.

More research is needed on the specific obstacles minority and indigenous women are experiencing in all sectors of development policy. It is not too late for governments and other development actors to commission baseline studies on the position of minority and indigenous women vis-à-vis MDG attainment, in order to help guide further intervention policies that will meet the needs of the most marginalized. Data collection also needs to be part of a wider impact assessment process for MDG initiatives, to measure the potential and actual effect of interventions on the status of all women. Project proposals that include provisions that are directly or indirectly discriminatory must be ruled out before initiatives are approved.

It is also vital that data collection is undertaken with the full participation of minority and indigenous groups. Conventional indicators like household income may not reflect fully the aspirations of groups for whom poverty is measured also in terms such as loss of traditional livelihood, access to natural resources, or other aspects of cultural life. Minorities and indigenous peoples should be engaged in the data collection process to safeguard against misuse of data and violations of privacy, to avoid inaccuracies in data due to lack of cultural awareness or discrimination, and to ensure that data collected is useful for identifying the needs and concerns of minority and indigenous groups.

Protecting rights and preventing discrimination
Applying a human rights-based approach (HRBA) to the MDGs requires particular attention to non-discrimination, participation and accountability; minority and indigenous women have struggled to secure all three. HRBA efforts need to be adapted to meet the needs and rights of minority women if they are to tackle the structural causes of poverty and marginalization. There are important international standards to draw from, including ICERD, and the Convention on the Rights of the Child. The UN Declaration on the Rights of

indigenous identity. Gathering this information may be more time-consuming and more costly, but it will help to identify those populations most at risk, where minority and indigenous women often can be found. Such data also helps states to meet their obligations under the Convention on the Elimination of All Forms of Discrimination Against Women, the International Convention on the

State of the World's Minorities
and Indigenous Peoples 2011

Minority and indigenous
women and the Millennium
Development Goals

27

Persons Belonging to National or Ethnic, Religious and Linguistic Minorities holds that 'States should consider appropriate measures so that persons belonging to minorities may participate fully in the economic progress and development in their country' (Article 4 (5)). The recently adopted UN Declaration on the Rights on Indigenous Peoples makes specific reference to indigenous women (see Articles 21, 22 and 44), as well as numerous provisions relating to indigenous peoples' right to development (e.g. Article 23). National legislation can further extend these commitments.

Mechanisms for preventing and remedying discrimination need to be effective and accessible for women. Domestic legislation should take into account intersecting forms of discrimination and consider new safeguards for addressing such discrimination. For example, legal aid could be targeted at women from minority groups, including through outreach and providing translation services. National human rights institutions (NHRIs) could designate a programme of work to analyse the implementation of non-discrimination legislation for minority women, and recommend the adoption of policy or legislation reforms in cooperation with minority women. NHRIs can also support government actors in training on non-discrimination in provision of public services and awareness of cultural or religious identity issues that relate to service provision and national development strategies. In Brazil, the UN Country Team is working closely with the Special Secretariat of Policies for Women (SPM) and the Special Secretariat of Policies to Promote Racial Equality (SEPPIR) under the auspices of the MDG Achievement Fund to launch a series of initiatives on gender and race. These will include training government managers on the introduction and implementation of gender and racial equality projects; reforming disaggregated data collection practices; targeting the media to better examine issues of gender and race; and aiming to achieve greater gender and racial parity in decision-making at all levels.

Accountability

Accountability goes hand in hand with non-discrimination mechanisms. Because of their position of marginalization, minority and indigenous women will typically find it much harder to access existing accountability mechanisms. Ministries with responsibility for women, for example, should develop specific programme lines aimed at empowering minority and indigenous women to claim their rights, including through the justice system. All women must have equal protection from the law, including protection against domestic violence, all forms of abuse or labour rights violations by employers, and violence or abuse stemming from inter-communal tensions. Surveys can be conducted on how accessible key social services are to minority and indigenous women, to ensure that women are not facing discrimination at the point of contact. Civil society actors are starting to engage governments in gender budgeting; involving minority and indigenous women in such processes can further ensure that resources are used to the best effect in reaching the most marginalized. Minority and indigenous women are also highly concentrated in the informal economy. Trade unions can reach out to such women to build their capacity to defend themselves against exploitation, and seek protection of their labour rights.

Ensuring participation

Participation of minority and indigenous women at various levels is vital for improving MDG strategies. Minority and indigenous women are often under-represented in governance structures, excluded from traditional decision-making processes, or ignored in civil society consultations. Many will not have the resources or capacities to form strong organizations to give themselves a voice. MDG interventions could usefully address this by ensuring that women from minority groups are active in consultations and decision-making for MDG projects that will affect them. For example, meetings can take place in regions where minorities and indigenous peoples live, child care facilities can be provided, translation can be offered into minority languages, and incentives like beginning meetings only when a sufficient number of minority or indigenous women have arrived can be adopted. Access to information by women will often be low, so extra measures will need to be taken to build their capacity to contribute their views at meetings, and to make well-informed decisions on proposed activities. The NGO Sidreh works to empower Bedouin women in Israel, and has established a number of innovative

Minority and indigenous
women and the Millennium
Development Goals

initiatives for strengthening women's participation. These include literacy training and adult education programmes, the creation of women's committees in villages, taking women on excursions outside their home and village to build confidence and awareness, and publishing a feminist newspaper to promote positive images of Bedouin women.

At a political level, much can be done to open up opportunities for minority and indigenous women. Political parties and legislatures can adopt quotas or other structures to increase participation of women. In Vietnam, for example, the National Assembly has made efforts to prioritize greater representation for women and non-Kinh ethnic minorities, according to a 2009 Inter-Parliamentary Union study. Some 30 per cent of deputies are women from minority groups and 14 of the 33 minority groups present are represented only by minority women. In New Caledonia, indigenous Kanak women mobilized to secure the adoption of a parity law (requiring 50 per cent men and 50 per cent women in alternating order on election ballots) and have achieved (with non-indigenous women) a near gender parity in political representation at different levels of governance. Parliamentary committees established by minorities or by women can ensure full participation by minority women. Because of their starting position of marginalization, minority women representatives in government can benefit from extra support to assert their authority. The Navsarjan Trust, a Dalit NGO in Gujarat, India, has worked to bring together at state level all Dalit women *sarpanches* (elected village heads) and hundreds of Dalit female *panchayat* (village assembly) members, to help them find strength in networking and the confidence to raise Dalit women's issues in their roles.

Women's participation in traditional decision-making structures can often be weak or non-existent. Such male-dominated institutions are nevertheless important tools for securing the free, prior and informed consent of communities to development interventions that will affect them or the regions in which they live. It is also necessary to work with male leaders to transform harmful practices against minority and indigenous women, and traditional laws that discriminate against women and girls, for example on land and inheritance rights. The involvement of male leaders in workshops intended to develop the skills of indigenous women leaders helped to change the men's perceptions of indigenous women for the better. Support to women's organizations can also help to elevate their status in decision-making. In Tanzania, Maanda Ngoitika created the Pastoralist Women's Council in 1997 to empower women in such processes: '[W]e bring pastoralists together to give each other encouragement and to break the cycle of silence and oppression.' In Kenya, Amina Zuberi, a District Convenor in the Mombasa Regional Women's Assembly, reports that her organization is working with Muslim leaders to increase school enrolment among Muslim girls, by showing how securing education for girls can decrease the poverty rates of entire families. It is through such processes of engagement, women's empowerment and persuasion that traditional structures can be utilized and transformed.

Adopting targeted approaches

Measures targeted specifically at minority and indigenous women are one tool of an HRBA. While mainstream approaches to achieving the MDGs may help some minority women, and gender-mainstreaming approaches potentially could reach even farther, the effects of intersecting discrimination mean that many minority and indigenous women will still not benefit fully from general social inclusion initiatives. Targeted approaches include creating specific projects for minority women, creating quotas for participation of minority women in general projects, and creating mechanisms that ensure the equal participation of minority women in decision-making that affects them. For example, recognizing low levels of education among minority children, the government of Nepal has made targeted efforts to increase recruitment of women teachers and teachers from minority groups; figures have been gradually increasing. Further intersecting these goals, that is, to recruit minority women teachers and particularly Dalit women, would help to break down both gender and minority identity barriers in the classroom.

Targeted measures can be introduced within the MDG framework. In Thailand, the MDGs report records that the government elaborated additional targets under Goals 4 and 5, namely between 2005 and 2015, to reduce by half the under five mortality rate and the maternal mortality rate 'in

State of the World's Minorities
and Indigenous Peoples 2011

Minority and indigenous
women and the Millennium
Development Goals

29

highland areas, selected northern provinces and three southernmost provinces', all regions where minorities predominantly live. The Romania MDGs Report states that the government has created Roma Community Health Mediators to make improvements on ethnic disparities in health, including maternal mortality. In the Philippines, the 2003 MDG report discusses:

'alternative nonformal education systems for indigenous communities such as Magbasa Kita (Let Us Read) that teaches women and girls and parents of working children to read. School-based child-minding centers were also set up in the [indigenous] cultural communities so older children, mostly girls of school age who take care of younger siblings, can attend classes despite baby-sitting chores.'

Among the key outcomes of the most recent MDG Summit was the commitment to a new Global Strategy for Women's and Children's Health, recognizing the significant lack of progress on the related goals. There is an important opportunity within that strategy and fund to design specific interventions targeted at minority and indigenous women and girls, given that issues of culture, poverty, residence and discrimination intersect to create specific barriers to realizing the health-related MDGs.

A specific focus on minority and indigenous women can yield far-reaching results. It is widely recognized in the development field that a focus on women produces better returns because women are more likely to invest their income in their families and communities. With greater capacities, minority and indigenous women are able to improve the prospects for themselves and their children, but also the wider community, becoming generators of well-being and wealth. For example, one literacy and basic skills project in Laos, reported by Lorraine Corner for the UN Development Programme, targeted over 3,000 minority women, but estimated that 'another 16,000 people will benefit indirectly, including children and other family members, as well as villages'. By investing in social enterprise schemes targeted at minority and indigenous women, for example in handicrafts, small land holdings or livestock breeding, women can build new business-related skills and increase their decision-making power in household budgeting, the economic status of the community can grow,

and the public and private status of women can increase. It is important as well to look beyond these traditional gendered occupations, investing in women's and girls' education, literacy (including in dominant languages), vocational training, land rights, and credit and market access so they can realize their economic rights, and both seek and *create* new forms of employment within and beyond their community. Opportunities for technology transfer can focus on minority and indigenous women to alleviate their often higher time poverty burdens, freeing them to be more active in the education of their children and to participate equally in social, cultural and political life.

In any such targeted interventions, it is important to respect the cultural, ethnic, religious or linguistic identity of minority and indigenous women and girls. Minority and indigenous women's empowerment does not come from assimilation into dominant cultures, not least because gender discrimination will equally be a feature in the dominant culture. Examples of good practice could include curricula reform that gives special attention to empowering the girl child from minority and indigenous groups. This could be done by integrating intercultural education that is sensitive to the expectations of minority culture or religion, but which also helps to transcend gender discrimination. Moreover, a good understanding of cultural and religious identity issues can lead to better development interventions. On HIV prevention, for example, understanding the social and cultural norms around sex in minority communities can identify the higher socially determined risk factors for infection by minority women, and help to devise prevention programmes that are culturally relevant. Finally, it is important to state that minority and indigenous women and girls may not share dominant or conventional views on development priorities, either for themselves or for their community. Alternative forms of economic and social life should be respected in line with the right to self-determination, and women and girls should have the equal right to determine freely what 'development' means for them.

Conclusions
As the pressure builds on governments and other actors to achieve the MDGs in the next five years, they will need to reconsider whether

their interventions are achieving the best possible results. The most recent MDG Summit produced an outcome document that reiterates the need to address the particular situation of indigenous peoples, and to take account of culture in development. Regrettably, other ethnic, religious and linguistic minorities are not mentioned explicitly. Minority and indigenous women and girls often have farther than most to come before they reach the MDG targets and, consequently, there is a great risk that they will be left out.

Adopting a human rights-based approach to the MDGs can help avoid such negative outcomes, by drawing from the human rights obligations of states to address key structural barriers, such as discrimination on the basis of gender and ethnic, religious, linguistic or cultural identity. All MDG interventions need to be analysed with appropriate disaggregated data. Understanding and responding to the particular factors in the exclusion of minority and indigenous women and girls will improve development outcomes. Minority and indigenous women and girls need to be at the centre of policy and programme development geared towards the MDGs. They have a right to participate in this decision-making and to participate in development with dignity and respect for their contributions. The challenges of achieving equality and non-discrimination are great, but investing in minority and indigenous women and girls yields better results for families, communities and societies as a whole. ■

With thanks to Anna Horvai, Charlie Hoyle and Bobbie Mellor for assisting with research for this chapter.

State of the World's Minorities
and Indigenous Peoples 2011

Minority and indigenous
women and the Millennium
Development Goals

31

Violence against women in indigenous, minority and migrant groups

Claire Rowland and Michelle Carnegie

Gender-based violence refers to violence that targets individuals or groups on the basis of their gender. In much policy and programme work, the term is used interchangeably with 'violence against women', as the majority of this violence is directed against women, although it would be more accurate to class violence against women as a *form* of gender-based violence. The violence may involve physical, mental or sexual harm or suffering, or the threat of such acts; coercion; and other deprivations of liberty. The high personal, psycho-social and economic cost of violence, however, not only affects women themselves, but also their husbands and partners, children, extended families, communities and wider society. As such, it is a major public health issue, with implications for economic and social development.

Despite actions by international organizations and governments, violence against women continues to affect women in all parts of the world. At its most basic level, it is both symptomatic of, and active in, sustaining gender inequality, but it can also serve to sustain other forms of inequality, based on minority or other social status. Minority and indigenous status are recognized by the United Nations Entity for Gender Equality and Women's Empowerment (UN Women) as compounding factors in cases of violence against women, while the 2010 report on the 54th Session of the Commission on the Status of Women, states that:

'in the design, planning and monitoring of laws, policies and programmes to achieve gender equality, it is important to address fully the multiple forms of discrimination and marginalization that particular groups of women continue to face, in particular rural, Indigenous and older women, women belonging to ethnic minorities and women with disabilities.'

This chapter focuses on violence perpetrated toward indigenous, minority and migrant women. While indigenous peoples reside in many countries, we explore indigenous women in a postcolonial 'settler' society context (Australia). The chapter addresses violence against women in the context of ethnic, religious and linguistic minority women, but we acknowledge that, within these groups, there may be women who constitute minorities within a minority, on the basis of their (dis)ability, HIV status, sexual identity, occupation or marital status.

In addition, we recognize that women in indigenous, minority and migrant groups experience a whole spectrum of violence, perpetrated by those within their community groups, as well as by outsiders. This includes violence either perpetrated and/or condoned by the state and/or military; violence arising from wars and conflicts; and violence in post-conflict settings.

In general, there is a lack of disaggregated data on prevalence rates of violence towards women based on minority and indigenous status, and this remains a barrier to effectively addressing violence against these groups of women. Insufficient data is in part due to the difficulties of collecting robust and comparable data on such a sensitive issue, as Denise Hines and Kathleen Malley-Morrison pointed out in a 2007 article in the *Journal of Interpersonal Violence*. Compounding this is the fact that indigenous and minority women are much less likely to report violence voluntarily, due to their marginalized status in society.

In addition, the low prioritization and resources given to promoting gender equity in many national budgets inhibits the collection of data on gender-based violence disaggregated by gender and ethnicity. For example, while most Pacific Island countries and territories have signed the Convention on the Elimination of All Forms of Discrimination Against Women, only 6 out of 21 had a policy in place to promote gender equality in 2010. The Beijing+15 review process (to assess the implementation of the Beijng Platform for Action) found that national women's machineries are typically under-resourced and marginalized in government structures, relying heavily on donor support to implement programmes. With limited resources for gender equality programming overall, the needs of minority women, including with regard to the violence they experience, are likely to be overlooked entirely. As a result, many initiatives to combat gender-based violence in minority communities in the global South come from local organizations, many of which are funded via bilateral aid and small grants programmes. While their work contributes significantly to promoting equality, its scope is inevitably limited by agency size and funding availability.

The level of public awareness of gender-based violence and the commitment shown by governments towards combating such violence influence how much is known and documented about the issue. As Lenore Manderson and Linda Rae Bennett pointed out in their 2003 volume *Violence against Women in Asian Societies*, research is more likely to exist in countries that encourage open discussion on sexual and reproductive health and human rights, and where enabling government frameworks exist to address violence.

This chapter uses four case studies to illustrate a diverse range of issues relating to violence against minority and indigenous women, and to provide insights into both global North and global South perspectives. The case studies are: family violence within indigenous communities in Australia; violence against Indonesian women in Malaysia as a migrant worker minority; violence against Dalit women from outside the community in India due to their position in the caste system; and violence against Muslim women in the United Kingdom as a religious minority.

Family violence and indigenous women in Australia

Violence against women is considered to be a widespread problem within many indigenous communities in postcolonial 'settler' societies, including First Nations peoples in Canada, Native Americans and Alaska Natives in the United States, Māoris in Aotearoa/New Zealand, and Australians of Aboriginal or Torres Strait Island descent. Domestic or 'family violence' – that is, violence from women's intimate partners and other family members – is arguably the most widespread form of violence that women from these indigenous groups experience, as opposed to violence from outside groups.

The apparent 'normalization' of family violence within these indigenous communities is a product of the past and present impacts of colonization. In these settings, family violence is in part a function of the stress, isolation from mainstream society, and disempowerment experienced by these communities, driven and compounded by loss of lives, identity, health, land, family and community structures over time. Monique Keel, writing in a 2004 report for the Australian Centre for the Study of Sexual Assault, argues that violence has become a mechanism to compensate for a perceived lack of control over life and future options, and consequent low self-esteem. As such, it reflects the wider ongoing struggle of indigenous peoples in settler communities and elsewhere, over dispossession, marginalization and disempowerment.

In Australia, although accurate and robust data on family violence, including the sexual abuse of indigenous children, are difficult to obtain, all available studies indicate that the level of violence among the indigenous population 'is disproportionately high in comparison to the rates of the same types of violence in the Australian population as a whole' (as stated in a 2001 report by Paul Memmott, Rachael Stacy, Catherine Chambers and Catherine Keys). In its Concluding Comment on Australia (adopted on 30 July 2010), the UN Committee on the Elimination of Discrimination Against Women (CEDAW committee) noted with concern that indigenous women were hospitalized as a result of intimate partner violence at 35 times the rate of non-indigenous women. The data contained in the Australia Productivity Commission 2009 *Report on Government Services* on rates of hospitalization also indicate that alcohol is a key factor in family violence in indigenous communities.

Attempts made to address family violence in indigenous communities in Australia through the mainstream social welfare and criminal justice systems have to date had limited impact. In addition, Kyllie Cripps (in a 2010 book on mental health issues in the indigenous community) reported that several indigenous academics and human rights activists have claimed that 'women's refuges, criminal justice responses, and therapeutic programs have mostly been culturally inappropriate and ineffective'.

Indigenous people in Australia have a complex relationship with the state due to the legacies of colonialism. This includes a welfare state that has a chequered history in 'protecting' Aboriginal people in post-colonial times, most notoriously in regard to systematically removing Aboriginal children from their families in a policy that continued until the 1960s. Today, indigenous women are less likely than non-indigenous women to apply for protection from the state, and alongside indigenous men, are much less likely to attend court to respond to protection orders than non-indigenous women and men, according to Chris Cuneen, writing on responses to domestic violence in Queensland's indigenous communities in 2009.

Criminal justice responses to family violence have tended to emphasize addressing the behaviour of the perpetrator, by separating or removing them, without simultaneously addressing the historical and cultural context of violence. While removing the perpetrator can ensure the safety of victims, in some situations inter-community conflict and violence has ensued, with retributive measures taken by either a perpetrator's family or a victim's family, potentially placing the victim at further risk of violence. In the event that women want to continue living within their community and extended family, it is essential for responses to violence to restore family and wider community relationships, while at the same time ensuring the safety of victims.

As reported by Heather Nancorrow in a 2006 study, the views of influential indigenous women support this approach. In their role as members of a government taskforce on violence in indigenous communities, indigenous women felt that public responsibility for addressing violence should be located within affected communities rather than in state institutions, except in the case of homicide, child sex abuse and serious assaults.
They also expressed preference for restorative justice approaches as the primary response to violence, prioritising the restoration of relationships and increased awareness that violence is wrong over holding men accountable for wrong doing.
Their reasons related to the historically oppressive and violent role of the state in indigenous communities, and of the criminal justice system that had reinforced control over, and separation of, indigenous families.

In work on domestic violence within indigenous communities in Australia, it is increasingly accepted that responses must be developed that go beyond dealing with the behaviour of the individual perpetrator, and take into account the wider community and family-level responses and implications. Additionally, halting violence in these communities appears most effective when framed within indigenous understandings of violence, taking into account both the capacities of communities to act, as well as the barriers for action. In Australia, holistic responses to family violence are beginning to take shape, based on the existing successes of community-run men's groups, men's spaces, time-out spaces and healing centres. The common approach used within these spaces is healing, which recognizes the interconnectedness of racial and gendered oppression, and not only

addresses the impacts on the survivor and her family, but also takes steps to heal the perpetrator, maintain family relationships and address the impacts of violence across the community.

In 2009, the government appointed the National Council to Reduce Violence Against Women and their Children, and released a proposed national plan of action (POA) to address family and domestic violence. This POA broke ground by recommending national funding for a network of healing centres. Shortly afterwards, the indigenous-controlled national Aboriginal and Torres Strait Islander Healing Foundation was formed, followed by the National Aboriginal and Torres Strait Islander Women's Alliance (NATSIWA) in 2010, with the mandate 'to bring forward the concerns and issues from their communities, in their own words, with their own agendas, and their own solutions'. These changes reflect increasing national commitment to providing spaces for indigenous voices and approaches to inform solutions to gender-based violence. Continued government attention and financial commitment to improving socio-economic development outcomes, particularly in the areas of health, housing, employment and education, are arguably equally important.

Only time will tell whether or not these approaches are effective, and if so, how the lessons learned might be transferable to indigenous communities in Canada, the US and New Zealand.

Indonesian women migrants in Malaysia: violence on the basis of labour market position, gender and ethnicity

Migrant domestic workers in Malaysia (as elsewhere), the majority of whom are women, are at risk of abuse and violence on the basis of their gender, their nationality, and their dependence on their employers for accommodation and immigration support.

Recruited from relatively poorer states in the global South, foreign domestic workers or 'maids' can provide the low-cost, unregulated household labour that frees up middle-class women's time to participate in the formal economy, and thus contribute to national economic growth. Acquiring a maid can thus enable middle-class women greater opportunities for economic empowerment, as well as higher social status. However, the arrangement can simultaneously serve to reinforce poorer women's low status, as reproductive work such as care of the elderly and children, cooking and cleaning are often not valued as contributing to the 'real economy', and, as such, employment conditions are often not covered by state regulation and legislation. The invisibility of the work, its unregulated nature, and an unusual working environment which often requires living in the employers' home, combine to make domestic workers particularly vulnerable to psychological, physical and economic abuse. Racial stereotypes can compound these vulnerabilities. The country of origin has a strong bearing on a maid's potential wage and conditions, with racist stereotypes about work ethic, skills, commitment and intelligence enabling Filipino maids, for example, to earn twice as much as Indonesian maids in countries such as Malaysia and Singapore.

From 2009 to 2010, the Malaysian migrant advocacy agency, non-governmental organization (NGO) Tenaganita, documented over 1,050 cases of human rights abuses of domestic workers, ranging from rape to physical abuse and mental torture. This abuse is not new. In its 2004 report *Help Wanted: Abuses against Female Migrant Domestic Workers in Indonesia and Malaysia*, Human Rights Watch (HRW) interviewed recruitment agencies, employers, government officials and 51 domestic workers. The report detailed multiple cases of abuse, perpetrated by women and men, including that of Ani Rukmonto, a 22-year-old domestic worker:

'Every day something made [my employers] angry … Sometimes she said I was stupid, or like a bull. I didn't have anyone to turn to and I was afraid. I was beaten every day and swollen. I was beaten badly three times, and the third time, my head was bleeding and my body broke and then I lost consciousness.'

The report also provided examples of employers restricting maids' mobility and communication with outsiders, as well as starving and overworking them, depriving them of sleep and forcing them to sleep in uncomfortable places. The risks were not confined to the employment context; migrant domestic workers also faced risks of physical, sexual and emotional abuse during the recruitment, training, transit and return phase of their foreign work experience. In some cases, women are caught in situations of trafficking and forced labour.

At the time, HRW called on Malaysia to take decisive action to protect and monitor the treatment of migrant workers. A Memorandum of Understanding developed in 2006 between Malaysia and Indonesia has since been criticized for failing to create clear employment standards, penalties or enforcement mechanisms. Indeed, cases of abuse continue to be documented by NGOs and the trade union movement, and to be profiled in the media.

The issue of domestic-worker abuse is not only a human rights and women's rights concern; it also has implications for national economic growth. After a series of high-profile cases of the abuse of Indonesian maids by Malaysian employers in 2009, Indonesia suspended labour programmes to Malaysia and advised citizens to avoid seeking work as domestic helpers there. Negotiations with the Malaysian government have included establishing a compulsory day off per week and rights for workers to hold their own passports. At the time of writing, negotiations were stalled over the setting of minimum wages. Failure to negotiate acceptable conditions is likely to have significant economic implications, as Indonesian domestic workers represented almost 85 per cent of the more than 300,000 foreign workers in Malaysia's reproductive work sector in 2010, and media reports claim that 35,000 families are currently on waiting lists for maid services.

Dalit women in India: violence on the basis of caste, class and gender

Structural discrimination against Dalit men and women in India, Nepal and Sri Lanka stems from an entrenched hierarchical caste order in South Asian societies. Victims of the oldest surviving system of social stratification in the world, Dalits, or 'untouchables', are perceived as belonging to the 'lowest' social category, according to traditional caste values within the Hindu religion. They are also one of the most socio-economically marginalized groups in India, due to occupational discrimination.

Dalit women's oppression is deepened via ingrained patriarchal values and norms. Violence against Dalit women in India has thus been described as serving as 'a crucial social mechanism to maintain Dalit women's subordinate position in society, [that] is the core outcome of gender-based inequalities shaped and intensified by the caste system', according to a 2006 publication by the National Campaign on Dalit Human Rights, National Federation of Dalit Women and the Institute of Development Education, Action and Studies. As a minority, Dalit women are thus subject to a 'triple burden of inferiority' based on caste, class and gender. This combination of structural factors renders Dalit women vulnerable to some of the most abhorrent forms of physical violence. Beyond this, because beliefs about the low status of Dalits are pervasive among the general population in India, and more or less condoned by the state, the psychological violence that women (and men) experience is also severe.

Dalit women in India are vulnerable to murder, rape (including gang rape), custodial torture, and stripping and parading in public spaces. Upper-caste men are the main perpetrators of physical and sexual abuse, as well as members of the Indian police force and men in other societal positions of power and authority. Physical violence is often used as a method of dispelling dissent among the general Dalit population; or to force consent or confessions, or as a means of control and intimidation. According to the 2007 HRW report *Hidden Apartheid: Caste Discrimination against India's 'Untouchables'*, Dalit women are reported as being sexually abused during police raids or in custody, to 'punish Dalit communities as a whole' and 'as a means of exerting pressure on their male family members to surrender, give false evidence, retract their complaints, or silence their protests regarding police mistreatment'. The *State of Human Rights in India Report* 2010, produced by the Asian Human Rights Commission (AHRC), details a case of custodial violence and torture that occurred in Delhi, in May 2010. As stated in the report:

'the officers forced Mala [name changed] to strip naked in front of her minor son who was detained at the station, and ordered her to have sex with [her son]. Upon refusal, one of the police officers demanded Mala to have sex with him. Mala, a slum dweller had gone to the police outpost with her husband to enquire as to why her two sons were detained at the police station.'

Assisted by a local human rights organization, Mala lodged a complaint; to date, however, no charges have been laid.

Far from being an isolated incident, the authors of the report argue that this case reflects the ongoing abuse by police officers toward Dalit women in India today. In the 2006 study by the National Campaign on Dalit Human Rights et al. mentioned above, involving 500 Dalit women across four provincial states in northern India, in 40 per cent of violent incidents, women were unable to obtain either legal or non-legal recourse for the violence. In addition, perpetrators of violence against Dalit women were reported as being convicted by the courts in less than 1 per cent of all cases.

Legislation does exist in India to protect Dalits and other minority groups from discrimination, in the form of the Scheduled Castes and Scheduled Tribes (Prevention of Atrocities) Act 1989. Sadly, there is little effort on the part of the Indian state to implement this law via its judiciary and law enforcement agencies, and hence legal avenues of justice for Dalit women victims of violence are largely ineffectual. As stated in the 2007 HRW report, state and private actors enjoy virtual impunity for crimes against Dalit women. As a result of this situation, and according to its 2010 annual report, the National Campaign on Dalit Human Rights continued its efforts for the 'proper implementation of legislation and ... ensuring the effectiveness of future legislative measures'.

Many other bodies and organizations at the national and international level have spoken out on the issue of violence against Dalit women, urging the Indian state to take action, including the UN Special Rapporteur on violence against women. The Indian state, however, has refused to properly acknowledge and attend to the concerns raised by the Dalit rights organizations or international community. Meanwhile, many NGOs within India continue to work to secure Dalit human rights and dignity, and some focus specifically on Dalit women. For example, All India Dalit Mahila Adhikar Manch – an organization formed in 2006 by the National Campaign on Dalit Human Rights– aims to advocate for Dalit women representatives in local government, and to build the leadership skills of the few Dalit women who do gain seats, to ensure that their voices are heard in the effort to keep the multiple axes of discrimination against Dalit women on the political agenda.

Muslim women in the UK: violence against women on the basis of their gender and religion

According to data collected in the 2001 census, at approximately 3 per cent of the population, and from highly diverse ethnic and national origins, Muslims represented the second largest religious group in the UK after Christians. Of these, 46 per cent were born in the UK.

Muslim communities have long faced discrimination on the basis of race and religion in the UK. However, the events of 11 September 2001 and subsequent indiscriminate attacks elsewhere have served to compound existing Islamophobia. According to the 2005 report, *Intolerance and Discrimination against Muslims in the EU*, Muslim and minority rights organizations have criticized media agencies for spreading misconceptions about Islam and creating stereotypes of Islam as a 'monolithic and one-dimensional religion that is

'The media is responsible for the negative views about Islam – it's always attacking and stereotyping Islam, giving the impression that Muslim women are oppressed, suppressed and depressed!' The impacts of negative media and political representations of Islam are evident elsewhere in Europe. In Germany, for example, in an Allensbach polling agency survey in 2004, 93 per cent of survey respondents linked the word 'Islam' with 'oppression of women', and 83 per cent linked it to 'terrorism'.

Concurrent with increasingly negative perceptions, there has been an increase in seemingly paternalistic policy-making in Europe, focusing around the protection of 'helpless' Muslim women against oppression that is perceived to be sanctioned by and inherent within Islam, according to Jane Freedman, writing in 2007 in *Review of International Studies*. An example of this apparent paternalism is the French government's move to ban the wearing of veils that cover the face in public spaces (announced in September 2010), on the basis of promoting gender equality and a secular state.

Stereotypes of widespread violence against Muslim women within their communities are fuelled by broadcast incidents of forced marriages, domestic violence and crimes in the name of 'honour'. Some Muslim women have reported encountering service providers and criminal justice officials who have stated that violence against Muslim women is a part of their 'culture'. In response, there have been numerous calls from activists for a zero tolerance policy towards violence against Muslim women, and for recognition that cultural practice is the root cause of violence, rather than Islam.

Paradoxically, while public opinion may be largely opposed to the supposed oppressive and violent nature of Islam, some individuals and groups have used violence to intimidate and punish Muslim communities in the UK. A survey undertaken by ICM Research in 2004 indicated that out of 500 Muslims interviewed, 33 per cent said that they or their family members had experienced hostility and abuse because of their religion. Muslim women who wear the *hijab*, *niqab* or *burqa* are often at

fundamentalist and threatens western democratic values'. Political leaders and parties have also been criticized for contributing to negative stereotypes through misinformed public statements, and by undertaking anti-terrorism and security measures that stigmatize Muslim communities.

Stereotypes about Muslims in the UK extend to assumptions regarding gender roles. According to one female participant of the 'Listening to Muslim Women Consultations' held in the UK in 2006,

greater risk of Islamophobic attacks than Muslim men, due to their recognizable Muslim dress and perceptions of their perceived inferiority, passivity or vulnerability.

Ranging from insults and ridicule to verbal abuse and physical violence, attacks against women have been increasingly perpetrated in public spaces since 11 September 2001. During the 'Listening to Muslim Women Consultations' hosted by the UK Muslim Women's Network in 2005, many women told of experiences of assault and verbal abuse against themselves, family or friends:

'A car was driving past my friend and they opened the car door on her, just because she was wearing the hijab.'

'My mum wears the hijab. She's a little old lady in her sixties. She lives in a white area. Now young kids are throwing things at her – bottles and cans – every time there's something in the media about Muslim extremism.'

In Scotland, a Muslim woman participant in the Muslim Women's Resource Centre 2007 listening events said:

'Basically when they see the hijab, they know you are Muslim. Two girls attacked me in the town centre. It was in the evening. I am strong, but this girl just grabbed my hijab, she came towards me in a crowd. I snatched my bag and ran.'

Further cases were documented in 2010 in the report titled *Islamophobia and Anti-Muslim Hate Crime: UK Case Studies,* produced by the European Muslim Research Centre at Exeter University.

Despite ongoing verbal and physical assaults against women, levels of reporting of violent incidents have been low. Documented reasons include: the frequency of incidents; difficulty in proving the incident took place; concern that incidents are too small to worry about; and family and community pressure not to speak out for fear of compounding their social alienation. Fear about police responses is also a significant barrier to reporting, and is a particular concern for migrant Muslim women who have had negative experiences of police in their country of origin, or women who have perceived police approaches to addressing security concerns in the UK as prejudicial to Muslim communities.

Consultations indicate that these so-called hate crimes have created a significant sense of fear and vulnerability in Muslim communities, which has affected women's sense of well-being, freedom of movement, safety, belonging and their sense of control over their lives. Many Muslim women have taken active steps to reduce the daily risk of violence, intimidation and abuse by limiting their movements, travelling with friends and family when outside of the house, and avoiding travel at certain times of day or in what they perceive to be dangerous areas. For some, risk-mitigation strategies have meant reluctantly removing Islamic dress all together in public places.

There remains some concern that, in an effort to minimize further public violence, Muslim women may become increasingly silent on the issue of domestic violence. Writing in the Australian context for the Women's Studies International Forum in 2007, Christina Ho states that by revealing cases of domestic violence, survivors of violence may be concerned that they will contribute to negative stereotypes about their culture and their men, which could result in increased racism and hardship for the Muslim community, and for Muslim women in particular.

Demystifying Islam in order to dismantle the public perception of it as an inherently violent religion will be an essential step in opening up spaces for women to talk about domestic violence, to ensuring a zero tolerance approach towards violence in Muslim communities, and to reducing violence perpetrated by strangers. In order to promote reporting of domestic and hate-motivated violence, poor relationships between the police force and UK's Muslim communities need to be addressed, and processes created to ensure sensitivity to Muslim experiences. Ensuring diverse Muslim women's representation in media reports and government consultations is also necessary to challenge misconceptions of passive and submissive women, and to raise awareness of the diversity of Muslim women's perspectives and experiences. As Shabana Mahmood, one of three Muslim women to be elected to the British parliament in 2010, stated: 'The image of the voiceless Muslim woman who cannot leave the house is just not true.'

Conclusion
The case studies profiled in this chapter highlight

some of the key contemporary trends and issues facing indigenous, minority and migrant women who are subject to violence, as well as some of the justice strategies, and challenges in achieving justice. What is clear across the four cases is that structural factors drive much physical and psychological violence. For indigenous, minority and migrant women, some of these factors include legacies of colonialism, racism, religious and caste-based prejudices, unequal economic relations in the global economy, and patriarchy. Structural factors are difficult and complex issues to address. Change requires political will, creative and flexible approaches to justice and in some cases social transformation on behalf of the majority community. The struggle to overcome these barriers will continue to be an important and essential part of achieving justice and eliminating violence against women in the long term. There is clearly much good work being done on the ground, and much more work to be done. State and non-state actors must be involved in redressing violence and working toward generating social change. Our case studies highlight some examples of responses to redressing violence that demonstrate that indigenous, migrant and minority women themselves are not passive victims of violence. In many cases it is activism by these minority women that is creating awareness and revolutionising approaches to addressing violence in minority communities. Minority women's views, opinions and experiences must be taken into account in strategies to both prevent violence and to create effective pathways for justice for survivors of violence. ■

Reproductive rights:
a long way to go

Tanya Saroj Bakhru

W omen's reproductive health needs and desires – as well as their very understanding of what constitutes reproductive health – are shaped by nationality, race, class, ethnicity, religion and culture. For ethnic, religious and linguistic minority and indigenous women, there is often a wide gap between how they would best like their self-identified reproductive health needs to be met and the services that they receive, thanks to the intersecting and overlapping discrimination that they face as women, and as members of minority and indigenous groups. This can range from poor or culturally inappropriate provision of services in the areas that they live, to outright denial of access to reproductive health care. Poverty further compounds this discrimination for many minority and indigenous women, leading to high rates of maternal and infant mortality, and other poor reproductive health outcomes, in comparison to majority groups. In addition, in some cases minority and indigenous women have been specifically targeted for programmes aimed at reducing the number of births in a given community.

These systematic violations of minority and indigenous women's reproductive rights occur despite the emergence over the past 20 years of a global reproductive rights movement. This movement has linked women's health movements in different contexts, and has pushed for acknowledgement of the relationship between the social, economic, and political empowerment of women and their ability to control their own fertility and sexuality, with minimal risk and maximum decision-making power (as Rosalind Petchesky argued in 2003).

One of the key events in regard to the emergence of the global reproductive rights movement came in 1994 when the United Nations Population Fund (UNFPA) convened the International Conference on Population and Development (ICPD). The conference was attended by representatives from 179 nations and 11,000 individuals from non-governmental organizations (NGOs), international agencies, citizen activists and governments. At the conference, a 20-year Programme of Action (POA) was created, calling for a shift away from earlier focus on population control to improving women's lives; from demographic targets to individual needs; and relying on a rights-based approach to reproductive health. Minority women activists played an important role in drawing up the POA, particularly in regard to negotiating for the term 'reproductive rights' to be accepted and included in the POA. This followed the rejection of the proposed term 'sexual rights' by some conservative and religious constituencies, and led to a discussion addressing the link between individual rights and a community's conditions, which may limit or enhance those rights. This is a discussion that has particular relevance to minority and indigenous women, and is one that also contributed to the 1995 Beijing Platform of Action, and the UN Millennium Development Goals (MDGs).

The definition of reproductive health in section 7.2 of the ICPD POA is as follows:

'a state of complete physical, mental, and social well-being and not merely the absence of disease or infirmity, in all matters relating to the reproductive system and to its functions and processes. Reproductive health therefore implies that people are able to have a satisfying and safe sex life and that they have the capability to reproduce and the freedom to decide if, when, and how often to do so. [...] It also includes sexual health, the purpose of which is the enhancement of life and personal relations, and not merely counseling and care related to reproduction and sexually transmitted diseases.'

The input of minority women at the ICPD included the point that notions of reproductive and sexual rights must incorporate both personal freedom and social support, and affirmed that an individual's health is inextricably linked to her community's health. Further exploring this point, Sonia Correa and Rosalind Petchesky, writing in 1994, discuss the idea of 'enabling conditions' as a requirement for the full realization of all women's reproductive and sexual health. Enabling conditions include those 'material and infrastructural factors' that one needs to carry out the decisions one makes about one's reproductive health. Factors such as access to transportation, the means to economic subsistence, comprehensive and accessible services (including information in the appropriate language), protective laws, as well as freedom from discrimination (racism, sexism, xenophobia) are all part of those enabling conditions that must be present in order for minority and indigenous women to have control over their sexual and reproductive lives.

Minority and indigenous women's reproductive lives are shaped not only by such 'enabling conditions', and by forces from the dominant society based on their marginalization as part of a minority group, but also from within their own community, based on their status as women. This is because of the associations often made between women's bodies and the cultural and ethnic identity and integrity of a particular group, as Fareda Banda and Christine Chinkin argued in a report for

MRG in 2004. This can mean restrictions being placed on women's sexual and reproductive rights from within their own communities (e.g. pressure to abstain from using contraception, or to marry early), as well as discriminatory policies aimed at women from particular ethnic groups. Examples of this can be seen in instances of forced sterilization of women from minority and indigenous groups deemed 'undesirable', which are explored later in this chapter.

The potential for minority and indigenous women to be reduced to their biology as 'physical vessels for genetic messages' (a term used by Rosalind Petchesky in 1997) by both the dominant culture and within their own community is great. As Naila Kabeer writing in *Reversed Realties* in 1994 notes: 'For feminists, the issue of reproductive rights crystallizes in many ways the whole question of women's rights over their own bodies, a critical element to women's full participation in society'. In this way, denial of minority and indigenous women's reproductive rights (either from within or outside their communities) justifies and perpetuates gender, racial, ethnic and cultural discrimination, limits a woman's ability to realize her full reproductive health and marginalizes women within already existing social minority groups even further. In 1998, Dorothy E. Roberts pointed out that: 'Without the ability to determine their reproductive destinies, women will never achieve an equal role in social, economic, and political life and will continue to be politically subordinate to and economically dependent on men.'

Poverty, marginalization and maternal mortality

The social and political marginalization of minority and indigenous women – as well as the pressure and discrimination they face from within their own communities – is often compounded by poverty. Poverty remains one of the most significant barriers to the full actualization of reproductive health, and the link between health, income and minority status is well established (as argued by Alicia Armstrong and Yvonne Maddox, writing in 2007 for *Ethnicity and Disease*).

Women are not only the fastest growing portion of the world's most poor; they also lack the tools and resources necessary to recover from poverty in relation to men, according to Joni Seager (2009). For minority and indigenous women the challenge to overcome poverty is even greater, as systemic racism, ethnocentrism and xenophobia continues to be an endemic part of social institutions and results in barriers to economic autonomy, bodily

safety, or access to services including health and education. For example, findings from a 2009 comprehensive study by Cara James, Alina Salganicoff, Megan Thomas, Usha Ranji and Marsha Lillie-Blanton of health disparities among women in the United States show that in nearly every state, women of colour and Native American women are more likely to live below the poverty line than white women, have lower median household incomes than white women, earn less than white women, are less likely to hold a high school diploma, are more likely to be part of single female-headed households, and more likely to live in socio-economically disadvantaged neighbourhoods. These social factors greatly impact on minority and indigenous women's ability to realize full reproductive health, in that those living in poverty are less likely to have access to care, less likely to have routine care and more likely to delay care. Poverty also determines factors such as nutrition and stress that can exacerbate reproductive health problems. Outside the US, both within and between countries, the disparity in reproductive health care and reproductive health outcomes between rich and poor and along racial, ethnic and cultural lines is just as notable.

According to a 2005 study on maternal mortality undertaken by the World Health Organization (WHO), the UN Children's Fund (UNICEF), UNFPA and the World Bank, reproductive health issues are the leading cause of death for women worldwide. Complications during pregnancy and childbirth are the leading cause of death and disability among women of reproductive age, particularly among those living in the global South. While complications during pregnancy and childbirth are often fatal for poor women in general, they are, in the majority of cases, preventable.

For poor minority and indigenous women, barriers to safe pregnancy that can contribute to high rates of maternal mortality are exacerbated by circumstances specific to their racial, ethnic or cultural status, which can include geographical remoteness, lack of provision of services in the areas where they live and linguistic barriers. For example, the Karen ethnic minority group in Thailand has one of the highest maternal mortality rates in the country. This is due to poverty, their remote geographic location, and consequent inaccessibility of health clinics. In order to combat high maternal mortality, the Thailand Department of Health in conjunction with UNFPA began a programme to train village health workers to educate within their own community on maternal and child health, thereby providing resources in a culturally appropriate way that would reduce the negative experiences women endure during pregnancy and childbirth. A similar set of circumstances shapes the experiences of women of the Hmong minority group, who live in a mountainous region of north-western Vietnam. Poverty, remote geographic location, language barriers and cultural traditions that place traditional reproductive health practices in opposition to seeking mainstream medical attention characterize the obstacles to care that prevent Hmong women from accessing reproductive services. These circumstances result in high levels of maternal mortality. Acording to Maria Larrinaga, writing in 2009, campaigns to 'raise awareness about maternal health, to train local women in midwifery skills and to respect the local culture' have resulted in more Hmong women accessing reproductive health services, and a decrease in maternal mortality. Similar approaches have been taken to combat poverty, inaccessibility of services, and cultural traditions that hinder women to seek reproductive health services among Tai, Giay, Nung and Clao minority groups also living in Vietnam. Recruiting and training women locally and from the communities for which they serve has '[inspired] trust and [encouraged] more women to receive appropriate services'.

Another study of the challenges to maternal health care utilization among ethnic minority women in China (by Amanda Harris, Yun Zhou, Hua Liao, Lesley Barclay, Weiyue Zeng and Yu Gao, writing in *Health Policy Planning* in 2010) shows that maternal mortality rates are highest in the remote and impoverished areas where minority women live. This study took place in southern Sichuan Province, along the foothills of the Himalayan mountain range, where over 80 per cent of the population belong to Yi, Mong and Naxi ethnic minority groups. Services marked by poor accessibility and low quality as well as high costs proved to be detrimental to maternal health and service utilization. The study concluded that 'utilization of maternal health care services is associated with a range of social, economic, cultural, and geographic factors' specific to one's minority status.

The examples above illustrate how the existing socio-economic, political and physical marginalization of many minority groups can serve to perpetuate indirect discrimination against minority women in regard to access to reproductive health care (mainly as a result of poor or inadequate provision of health care services). But there are also instances where minority or indigenous women face direct discrimination. A 2009 report by Human Rights Watch (HRW) on reproductive health in Uttar Pradesh, in northern India, found that many of the Dalit and lower-caste women interviewed for the report had faced direct, caste-based discrimination from health workers. This had included nurses refusing to visit Dalit communities to provide ante- or postnatal care to women, or, in the event that they did visit, refusing to touch the woman or her baby. In another instance recorded in the report, a Dalit woman who gave birth in a state health facility was discharged without being properly examined by medical staff, meaning that health complications relating to her recent delivery were not picked up. As a result, she suffered serious and debilitating health problems, incurring US $1,000 in health care expenses, and she and her family experienced verbal abuse when they complained about the poor treatment that she had received. Other cases where Dalit women had received inadequate care as a result of caste-based discrimination were also not properly investigated. In other instances, reported by Healthwatch Forum Uttar Pradesh, scheduled caste women were physically abused by medical staff, or denied access to treatment because their families could not pay for medicines or refused to pay bribes to medical staff (antenatal, delivery and postnatal care are meant to be available free of charge). Such discrimination no doubt contributes to the fact that lower-caste and tribal women were found to make far less use of reproductive health services, and that they accounted for 61 per cent of maternal deaths in six north Indian states, according to a 2007 report by UNICEF.

At the global institutional level, the connection between poverty, gender inequality and minority status pervades international assessments of maternal mortality. Several United Nations (UN) resolutions parallel the findings noted above by acknowledging 'the unacceptably high global rates of preventable maternal mortality and morbidity'. For example,

Reproductive rights:
a long way to go

the UN Commission on the Status of Women passed a resolution (contained in UN Document E/CN.6/2010/L.6) in 2010 stating that these high rates:

'are directly related to poverty, the presence of persistent gender inequalities, including inequitable and unequal access to adequate health services and facilities, gender-based violence, harmful traditional practices, lack of education, lack of economic opportunity, [and] lack of participation in decision-making.'

Perpetuating cycles of disenfranchisement, the death of a mother due to pregnancy or childbirth can further entrench her children in poverty, according to UNFPA. Furthermore, there is a consensus in the international community that addressing maternal mortality will reduce poverty, improve overall health services and increase gender equity, as reflected in the fifth MDG to improve maternal health.

Coercive reproductive health practices
In addition to direct discrimination in regard to access to reproductive health care, minority and indigenous women in some contexts have faced coercive reproductive health practices, representing direct violations of their sexual and reproductive rights, and rights to bodily integrity. For example, in the United States, eugenicist ideology embedded in government policy tacitly sanctioned the forced sterilization of ethnic minority women throughout much of the twentieth century. Between 1929 and 1941 the US government funded over 700,000 involuntary sterilizations, including of women of colour, women who relied on federally subsidized clinics, and women who came into contact with the state through, for example, the prison system or state psychiatric facilities. Evidence reported by Jennifer Nelson in 2003 showed that in 1970 black women had been sterilized at over twice the rate of white women, while data from 1975–6 showed that women who used state-funded medical care were sterilized at a rate 2–4 times higher than those using other forms of health care. Based on this evidence, it has been argued that sterilization was pushed on women who were deemed unworthy to reproduce based on racist notions of the inferiority of people of colour. Alarmingly, documented cases of forced sterilization continued into the 1980s.

Discriminatory ideology regarding minorities has continued to inform coercive reproductive health practices in the contemporary era. For example, a Czech Public Defender of Rights report in 2005 documented and investigated 87 claims by Roma women in the Czech Republic of coercive sterilization practices in state-run hospitals. The women claim that they were specifically targeted for sterilization because of their race, and were either pressured at the time of giving birth into being sterilized or were sterilized without their full knowledge or understanding of the procedure. As reported by Dinah Spritzer for WeNews in 2005:

'Concerns that Roma women were sterilized without their consent in post-Communist Czech Republic were raised by Roma advocacy groups in the 1990s, but it was not until earlier this year that actual victims – encouraged by several Roma advocacy groups – began to talk publicly about their experiences and demand justice.'

The practice of sterilization of Roma women in the Czech Republic is embedded in ideology from the communist era to 'sterilize women the government deemed undesirables'. Similar cases were also reported in Hungary and Slovakia, where in 2004 eight Roma women lodged an application at the European Court of Human Rights (ECtHR) in order to gain access to their medical records. In 2009, the Court found in their favour, and requested that the Slovakian health authorities release the medical records.

Voices of reproductive health activists
Issues of the intersection of identity and barriers to reproductive health care provision, and advocacy around poverty, discrimination and social justice emerged in my own research with reproductive health NGOs in Dublin, Ireland, and San Diego, USA. The examination of reproductive health NGOs is significant, given the multifaceted roles they play simultaneously as advocates, educators and service providers.

In interviews with programme administrators from a reproductive health NGO in Dublin, issues of social justice for all members of society came to the fore. Several of my respondents noted the situation of refugee and asylum-seeking women (largely coming from the African continent) who were most marginalized in the Irish context. My interview respondents asserted that poverty and the invisibility of poor women in an economically prospering Ireland of the time, as well as racism, underpinned many of the problems the organization encountered in helping the women they worked with to gain access to reproductive health services. They also saw clear connections between poverty, migrant status, and the ethnic minority status of refugee and asylum-seeking women in Ireland. These elements linked in turn to the necessity of confronting racism and ethnocentrism within a greater reproductive health advocacy context. One NGO administrator, Sharon, said:

'In terms of poverty, I mean poverty is a huge issue … because it can be one of the biggest issues for separated women [or] refugee women. Then of course you're dealing with situations where you know because they are in [a] financial bind and there are a great many women in that position here and it's really escalated for the refugee women which of course, the added problems for getting visas etc. to get out of the country. There are no funds available to help those women. And with the refugee and asylum-seeking women it's very stressful. Because those women are in dire situations, they've often come into this country from you know desperate situations and are in awful positions, they're in hostels, they're overcrowded, they're lonely, they're isolated. They're in a perfect set of circumstances if they don't already arrive pregnant, for becoming pregnant here. I mean … for someone like me what the refugee women represent is the poor women in Ireland.'

In relation to accessing comprehensive reproductive health care, Sharon highlighted several key points by using the example of the situation of refugee and asylum-seeking women experiencing a crisis pregnancy. For her, the refugee women living in Ireland that she interacted with as a crisis pregnancy counsellor and reproductive health advocate were representative of poor and disenfranchised women across Ireland, both currently and historically. Issues such as lack of financial resources, limitation on travel, lack of privacy or confidentiality, encountering gender-based discrimination, the effects of violence both within one's personal life and wider society, were all matters that greatly influenced clients' decision-making about their reproductive (and wider) lives. Sharon also expressed her own frustration at how lack of financial resources and restrictive immigration policy

hampered her in helping women to navigate their decision-making under such circumstances.

In addition to the role that NGOs have increasingly come to play in providing reproductive (and other) health services as the state's role has decreased in many countries, they have also led advocacy efforts in relation to reproductive health, rights and justice. In speaking about her grassroots outreach activities, one respondent from San Diego, Renee, said:

'We get so many people that just say, why do I care about [reproductive] choice? And seeing the huge cross-connections between so many issues. You just can't separate issues like poverty, race, and sexuality, and gender from issues of reproductive choice.'

Similarly, when speaking about working with the Latina community in the border area of San Diego, Serena, an administrator from the Bi-National Affairs Department, said:

'It [poverty] also can limit choice to reproductive health. They keep saying how can you choose what to do with your life when you don't have the means to do it. You don't have education, food on your table, health care, insurance …'

Keeping issues of poverty, race, gender equity and sexuality interlinked was a growing part of the organization's policy and practice. At the heart of such an approach was the idea that people cannot have full access to reproductive health care when they face limitations concerning transport, funds and accurate information, as well as a lack of equity. Reproductive decisions cannot be made in any real and meaningful sense under such circumstances of deprivation and denial. Veronica, another respondent confirmed this, stating:

'if you think about the fact that a lot of the patients that we see, they don't have transportation, you know so, or can't even get to the clinics, so you have to address their basic needs in order for them to even think about getting birth control or whatever because they're thinking about how they're going to get food or where they are going to sleep.'

Conclusion
In order to address the challenging situation that many minority and indigenous women face around

the world, advocates – including policy makers, activists and scholars – must make an analysis based on 'both the experience of oppression and the strengths that individuals and communities bring to bear on particular issues by explicitly addressing the intersections of gender, race, class, and other identities and experiences that affect individuals and communities', as stated in a report by Asian Communities for Reproductive Justice (2009).

We must embrace the notion that women's control and right to take decisions over their own bodies is closely linked to equality and poverty reduction in general, and the empowerment of minorities and indigenous peoples in particular. Governments must repeal laws and policies that are discriminatory and enforce policies that aim at preventing violence against women and supporting the well-being of girls, as these are integral to the capacity of women to enjoy their full reproductive rights. In this way, we can move towards a global society in which all people have the economic, social, and political power and means to make decisions for themselves and their communities about their bodies and reproductive lives, and in which *all* women can participate in society as full human beings, regardless of geographic or social location. ∎

Women and armed conflict: from victims to activists

Deborah Eade and Morna Macleod

The motivations for armed conflict, and the means of achieving them, are diverse and affect specific population groups in different ways. Civilians are not simply caught in the crossfire, but are increasingly a deliberate target – sometimes even the main target. They are targeted in order to acquire or maintain power through terrorizing the civilian population, to (re)gain control over contested territory, or to define a state around a particular ethnic or religious identity. So during the war in El Salvador, the armed forces declared regions held by the Farabundo Martí National Liberation Front (FMLN) 'free-fire zones' – any civilians living there were military targets. In the Balkans, the Bosnian Serb Army and political leaders whipped up ethnic and religious identity in order to stake out exclusive territorial rights and 'cleanse' other populations. Burmese armed forces have conducted sustained campaigns against ethnic minorities: according to Human Rights Watch (HRW), there are an estimated half million internally displaced persons in eastern Burma, and 140,000 refugees remain in nine camps along the Thailand–Burma border, despite a large-scale resettlement programme by international agencies. More than 50,000 refugees from Chin state remain in eastern India, and 28,000 ethnic Rohingya Muslims live in squalid camps in Bangladesh.

Insofar as civilians have become the deliberate target of modern-day armed conflict, there are two common threads. One is the intentional exploitation of vulnerability. These vulnerable citizens are not only women and children, but include any group that suffers systematic discrimination, from ethnic minorities and indigenous peoples to the elderly and infirm or people with disabilities. The second thread, though one that international treaties and resolutions are designed to break, is that of impunity for mass rape and 'ethnic cleansing', crimes that deliberately target (primarily) women of the 'wrong' ethnic group, with the aim of traumatizing entire communities.

Following a consideration of the current international legal framework in regard to women in armed conflict, the remainder of this chapter focuses on two main issues, which are also the focus of its detailed case study of indigenous women in Guatemala:

■ How are minority and indigenous women involved in armed conflicts, both as active participants and as victims?

■ How are minority and indigenous women involved in peace and mediation processes?

Setting the international scene

Both international humanitarian law and international human rights instruments have increasingly focused on the protection of civilians during armed conflicts. In the past two decades, this focus has included a growing awareness of the gender-related impacts of armed conflict, and the role of women in conflict and post-conflict settings.

A significant development in humanitarian law was the two Additional Protocols (1977) to the 1949 Geneva Conventions, which together set out provisions for protecting civilians. These provisions specifically prohibit the targeting or terrorizing of civilians in non-international armed conflicts, even if there are non-civilians in their midst. The provisions for international armed conflicts also rule out any form of indiscriminate attack, including damage to the environment or to the means of subsistence. Populations should be displaced only if this is imperative for their own safety. In addition, desecrating religious symbols or attacking buildings used for religious worship is strictly off limits.

The sad reality, however, is that most modern warmongers either ignore the prohibition on indiscriminate attacks or deliberately target civilians. The civilian death tolls ('collateral damage') in Afghanistan and Iraq illustrate today that 'precision bombing' remains largely a fiction. There is no such pretence about landmines, which are deliberately strewn near water sources, along roadsides and in fields, and even around schools, with the sole purpose of maiming, killing and terrorizing civilians – which they will continue to do for many future generations. Thousands of people in conflicts from Liberia and Sierra Leone to Democratic Republic of the Congo and Rwanda have been literally hacked to death. But it was the break-up of the former Yugoslavia right at the heart of Europe that exposed once again the sheer brutality unleashed by a manipulated and re-politicized ethnicity. And the way this played out was to include systematic mass rape of ethnic minority women as a weapon of war.

Fifteen years after the drafting of the Additional Protocols, women's organizations at the 1993 United Nations (UN) World Conference on Human Rights rallied under the slogan 'women's rights are human rights'. The resulting Vienna Declaration and Programme of Action expressed 'dismay at massive violations of human rights especially in the form of genocide, "ethnic cleansing" and systematic rape of women in war situations, creating mass exodus of refugees and displaced persons', adding that while 'strongly condemning such abhorrent practices it reiterates the call that perpetrators of such crimes be punished and such practices immediately stopped' (Clause 28). Ironically, these 'abhorrent practices' were happening with apparent impunity in the Balkans, only a short distance away from Austria's borders, in conflicts that were egregiously flouting every one of the stipulations of the Geneva Conventions and Protocols regarding the treatment of civilians and respect for religious faiths.

Two years on, in line with the global objectives of empowering women and mainstreaming gender equality, the section on Women in Armed Conflict in the Platform for Action of the 1995 Beijing World Conference on Women listed six strategic objectives, among which were:

■ to increase the participation of women in conflict resolution and at decision-making levels, and protect women in situations of armed and other conflicts or under military occupation;

■ to promote non-violent forms of conflict resolution and promote women's contribution to fostering a culture of peace; and

■ to provide protection, assistance, and training to refugee women and women in comparable conditions.

Building on this growing momentum, the UN Security Council adopted a series of resolutions concerning gender-based violence as a war tactic *and* the need for women to play an active role in peace processes, noting that their marginalization can delay or undermine the achievement of durable peace, security and reconciliation.

■ Resolution 1325 (2000) on women, peace and security called on all parties to an armed conflict to take special measures to protect women and girls from gender-based violence, particularly rape and other forms of sexual abuse. It also calls for the equal participation and involvement of women in all efforts for the maintenance of peace and security

■ Resolution 1820 (2008) highlighted that the use of sexual violence against civilians as a tactic of war threatens international peace and security.

■ Resolution 1888 (2009) emphasized addressing issues of sexual violence from the very outset of peace and mediation processes and bringing its perpetrators to justice. The mandates for UN-sponsored peace negotiations and peacekeeping operations must include provisions for the protection of women and children.

On 16 December 2010, the 10th anniversary of Resolution 1325, the Security Council unanimously adopted Resolution 1960, which approves an annual publication listing armed groups that engage in deliberate campaigns of sexual violence – a public naming and shaming – and for sanctions to follow if the practice continues. Applauding the resolution, the Special Representative on Sexual Violence in Conflict, Margot Wallström, said:

'Instead of serving as a cheap, silent and effective tactic of war, sexual violence will be a liability for armed groups... The resolution may not bring justice to every victim throughout the history of war – but it will help to ensure that conflict-related sexual violence no longer goes unreported, unaddressed or unpunished.'

The growing number of standards, including other significant developments such as the International Criminal Court, which was inaugurated in 2003, put those who violate them under notice. These standards are a powerful expression of moral consensus even if they do not all carry the force of law. Taken together the international community has legal machinery and moral force (if not always the practical means or political will) to intervene in order to protect civilians, and to track down and prosecute those guilty of violating their rights.

What happens to women in armed conflicts?

At the launch of the 2010 *State of the World Population* report, Thoraya Ahmed Obaid, Executive Director of the United Nations Population Fund (UNFPA) said:

'When women and girls suffer deep discrimination, they are more vulnerable to the worst effects of disaster *or war, including the weapon and humiliation of rape, and less likely to contribute to peacebuilding, which threatens long-term recovery. If we're serious about preventing conflicts, recovering from war and natural disaster and building lasting peace, we need to empower women, as well as the young and the elderly, to become agents of positive change.'*

There is an implicit tension in the two principal goals of the UN Security Council resolutions discussed above. On the one hand, women and girls are cast as victims with no resources of their own, no autonomy and no voice. While not detracting from their courage and resilience, because of their vulnerability to sexual and other forms of violence and with their rights historically denied on multiple fronts, women's overarching need is for protection to stop these atrocities taking place. One aspect of preventing further atrocities is to ensure that the perpetrators are brought to justice, with the aim of making it clear to all, including survivors, that they will not enjoy impunity for their actions. The record here is not encouraging. As Margot Wallström, UN Special Representative of the Secretary-General, noted in a statement on 16 December 2010:

'The estimated 50,000 rapes that occurred during the conflict in Bosnia have resulted in just 12 convictions in national courts. The process has been painfully slow. Women describe being treated in the courtroom as just another exhibit from which evidence can be extracted, saying "It is better to be a criminal than a victim in this system". Most women who endured unspeakable brutality now endure the indignity of seeing their former assailant in the street, the bank, or supermarket, flaunting their impunity. I met with women who, 15 years after the peace agreement, still shake, sigh and weep; one described how the soldiers led her to the entrance of a rape camp, which she remembers as "the door to hell".'

On the other hand, as a country emerges from armed conflict, the resolutions emphasize the critical importance of women playing an active part in shaping the processes of mediation, demobilization and reintegration, and democratic peace-building. The resolutions stress that meeting the needs and perspectives of women and men in an inclusive and holistic manner is the key to preventing future conflicts.

Quite how women are meant to accomplish the rapid transformation from 'defenceless victims' to 'empowered subjects' remains unclear[1] – and it appears that those who are in a position to select the mediation processes also find it difficult to make the transition and actively ensure that women's voices are heard and are influential. Despite UN Resolution 1325, according to the UN Development Fund for Women (UNIFEM), women constitute only 6 per cent of peace negotiators and less than 3 per cent of signatories, and are completely absent from the chief mediating roles in UN-brokered peace talks. The mere fact of including women will not automatically ensure that women's interests will be properly reflected in the peace talks and subsequent processes. But their virtual absence makes it unlikely that their interests will feature at all.

The statistics and, more tellingly, the accounts of women sufficiently courageous to tell their stories, leave no room for doubt that women's predominant experience of armed conflict is indeed as the victims of atrocities and sexualized violence committed almost exclusively by men.[2]

But it is important to nuance the constant portrayal of women, including minority women, as 'innocent victims', and of minority populations as homogeneous and harmonious. In relation to the former, Cynthia Cockburn writes of how Serbian and Croatian journalists published articles featuring 'our' women, armed and in combat fatigues, standing up for the cause of politicized ethnicity. In reality, some 12 per cent of families were 'multi-ethnic', based on inter-ethnic marriage. In Sri Lanka, although the media focused on female suicide bombers, women were always active on the front lines in the Liberation Tigers of Tamil Eelam (LTTE) or 'Tamil Tigers' – which, incidentally, also forcibly evicted non-Tamils (including members of the Muslim minority) from areas under their control. In Eritrea, women constituted up to 40 per cent of the fighting force of the Eritrean People's Liberation Front (EPLF). As recounted by D. Parthasaraty in the journal *Manushi* in 2002, women increasingly participate in acts of communal violence in India, both in direct attacks on other religious communities or Dalit groups, and in the subsequent looting and destruction of their property. And according to Karen Kampwirth, writing in 2004, women also held high military office as well as being part of the rank and file in the liberation struggles in El Salvador and Nicaragua (30 per cent), and played a role as policy strategists in Guatemala (around 20 per cent), and providing logistical and moral support (60 per cent) in El Salvador. Women also constitute one-third of the predominantly indigenous Zapatistas in Mexico.

These examples by no means invalidate the obvious facts that the vast majority of fighters in both regular military forces and guerrilla movements are men, and that women combatants fight alongside men, and usually in junior roles. Nor is it to deny that armies and irregular forces alike sometimes engage in forcible recruitment. But they do somewhat complicate simplistic notions of what it means to be an 'innocent victim'. We know that it is specious to argue that women invite sexual attack because of what they are or are not wearing. By extension, if we believe in women's empowerment, it follows that women's agency in an armed conflict – whether in uniform, providing logistical or moral support, or engaging in international advocacy – does not detract from their experience as victims of atrocities. Indeed, women who step out of line, whether by taking sides in an armed conflict or by denouncing human rights violations, often face particularly cruel treatment. Women whose support over-steps the boundaries of their gender-submissive role face social as well as political sanctions.

The continuity of violence

Feminist groups in Belgrade and Zagreb were already working on issues of violence against women before the outbreak of armed conflict. As the war progressed they observed that domestic violence not only increased but also took on new and more militarized forms. More men were reported to be threatening or attacking their wives with guns, rifles, bombs or army knives. As Vesna Kesic recounted in an article published in 2002, local feminists therefore drew the link between 'ethnic chauvinism' and sexism:

'In both differences are exaggerated, "Others" are perceived stereotypically as of minor human value and as a threat to the nation and masculinity; domination and violence are perceived as natural and worth the infliction of cruelty and violence.'

But presenting the links between a patriarchal

culture and mass rape exposed these feminists to charges of being both traitors to the nation and of betraying women. By presenting mass rape as an extreme point on a continuum of misogyny and violence against women, their argument challenged the (patriarchal) discourse of ethnicity within which mass rape is part of a 'genocidal strategy'. This discourse treats women as a metaphor for the nation – 'a raped Bosniak or Croatian woman stands for a raped Bosnia or Croatia'. As Dubravka Zarkov puts it, the wars were not being fought between ethnic groups as is commonly understood, but were 'promoted to produce and deepen ethnic identities and obliterate the spaces in which choice might remain about who one feels oneself to be'.

In an analysis that goes well beyond the particularities of the Balkans, Vesna Kesic argues that:

'[M]ilitarized patriarchy and ethnic nationalism intersected and became enmeshed at the roots of the violence in these wars. This mix of ethnic and gender representations, symbols, and images has generated extremely violent practices, particularly in terms of the sexualization of war violence.… The question to answer is: How does sexual desire get invested into constructions of ethnicity and nationalism? How does it become "collectivized" and transformed into war violence?'

Throughout the former Yugoslavia, 'ethnic cleansing' was orchestrated on a vast scale – involving the mass murder of civilian men and the mass rape of civilian women – but rather than being an example of aberrant, 'out of character' behaviour, Kesic suggests a far more disturbing continuum between peace-time violence against women, and the sexualized brutality used against 'enemy' groups in war.

In Kenya, for instance, Peter Mwangi Kagwanja wrote in 2000 in *Forced Migration Review* of how, within the wider politicization of ethnicity, 'refugees from other Somali clans [from Somalia] were lumped together with Kenya's ethnic Somalis', who were already subject to multiple forms of discrimination. Non-governmental organization (NGO) health workers recorded that rape and beatings of refugee women were daily and nightly experiences. In a different case, this time involving Sudanese refugees in Kenya, Sudanese cross-border militias *and* male refugees, as well as members of the Kenyan security forces sexually assaulted, gang-raped, and kidnapped women and girls as young as 11 or

12. Most of the victims were from the Dinka community. The Kenyan authorities dismissed these reports, and few of the victims brought charges because of fear of reprisal by male refugees.

As these examples show, organized armed violence is not synonymous with war in its conventional sense. To take just two examples, from Colombia through Central America to Mexico, for instance, a violent death is more likely than not to be related to drug trafficking. And throughout much of Africa the illicit mineral trade both fuels and finances what the Kenyan Vice-President Kalonzo Musyoka calls 'the cause of incessant conflicts, environmental degradation but ultimately and sadly too, poverty'.

Waging war and claiming peace: the case of Guatemala

In March 2010, a Tribunal of Conscience against Sexual Violence towards Women during the Armed Conflict took place in Guatemala. Four 'judges' from other backgrounds and lands took part, as well as 35 witnesses of honour, including Mayan, *mestiza* and foreign women activists, several men and international academics. As UN Resolution 1325 passed its tenth anniversary, the Tribunal represented the culmination of a collective process to address and raise state and civil society awareness of sexual violence suffered by (predominantly indigenous) women during the armed conflict. Ugandan Judge of Conscience Teddy Atim comments that the Tribunal:

'is important for the local women, the indigenous women. For the first time they're talking about what they've gone through, and I think that the significance is that it helps them to discover who they are. The inner self destroyed by the war begins to open up through this kind of process.'

The Tribunal also brought to public attention the fact that rape of indigenous women continues to be commonplace as a reprisal against social organizing, especially in the forced evictions of indigenous *campesinos* in land conflicts. The fact that femicide (the gender-based murder of women) in Guatemala is higher than anywhere in the region was also noted.

Guatemala's 36-year internal armed conflict began in the eastern part of the country in the 1960s, shortly after the US-backed military coup overthrew President Jacobo Arbenz and the 'democratic revolution'. In the 1970s the conflict shifted to the mainly indigenous western highlands. Although half the Guatemalan population are indigenous, Mayans have always faced profound discrimination and marginalization, and inequalities in terms of class, ethnicity and gender run deep. Skewed land tenure (2 per cent of the population owns 60 per cent of the country's arable land) as well as grinding poverty, dire working conditions of indigenous *campesinos* in the large coffee, sugar and cotton export plantations, and next to no state services in health and education gave rise to mass indigenous incorporation into the rebel forces. Although more than 80 per cent of the rebel ranks were indigenous, and about 20 per cent were women, the guerrilla leaders were overwhelmingly *mestizo* men (of mixed Spanish and indigenous descent, also referred to as *ladinos*).

The army resorted to unprecedented levels of terror: after suppressing expressions of social organization and unrest in urban areas, it turned with a vengeance to the rural areas, using scorched earth operations and massacres, forced disappearance, selective and indiscriminate killings, accompanied by torture, mutilation and rape. Guatemala has one of the worst historic human rights records in Latin America: the 1999 UN Truth Commission documented 626 massacres, and more than 440 villages were destroyed as part of the armed forces' strategy to 'remove the water from the fish' (i.e. to isolate the rebels from their support base in the civilian population). More than 200,000 people were killed; 83.3 per cent of cases documented by the Truth Commission were Mayans.

The army sought to exterminate indigenous ways of life from the very roots, using symbolic as well as physical and material forms of destruction, as this Mayan woman testifying before the Tribunal stated:

'The soldiers burned all our houses, right in front of our eyes. They burned our millstones, our maize, our sacred life-giving maize ... they told us that by whatever means, they were going to make all Indians disappear.'

In her testimony presented at the Federation of the Relatives of the 'Disappeared' – FEDEFAM – conference in Mexico City (November 1983), Mayan catechist Carmelita Santos was one of the first indigenous women to denounce sexual violence:

'I think these massacres are worse for us women, because first the women are raped … and after raping her, they pull out her tongue, they put out her eyes, they tear away her breasts, and afterwards, they just leave her dying there. Many times we have said – witnessing such terrible suffering – that we'd prefer it if they simply shot us, but not be killed in this way.'

Scorched earth practices and indiscriminate repression led to the forced displacement of more than a million people from the indigenous highlands to cities and the coast, while hundreds of thousands of indigenous *campesinos* also sought refuge in neighbouring Mexico. Displacement was particularly painful for Mayan women, who had to change their traditional dress to hide their identity. Those captured were placed in militarized 'model villages' and 'development poles', similar to the strategic hamlets deployed in Vietnam. Others lived for more than a decade in 'communities in resistance' (*comunidades de población en resistencia*, or CPR), permanently on the move to avoid army persecution. A particularly destructive army measure intended to destroy the Mayan social fabric obliged all men in the highlands aged between 15 and 40 to join the 'civil patrols' to act as buffers between the army and insurgent forces.

Rape as a weapon of war

According to the Truth Commission, the most under-reported human rights violation was the rape of indigenous women. No overall estimates as to the number of women affected exist. Of the 1,465 cases of rape that were documented by the Commission, 88.7 per cent were of Mayan women and girls of all ages. As one survivor states: 'it's the *campesinos*, the Indians, who get raped because they used to say we were animals, that's why they did it to us, because they thought we were worthless'. In a 2009 report by Equipo de Estudios Comunitarios y Acción Psicosocial (ECAP) and Unión Nacional de Mujeres Guatemaltecas (UNAMG) (hereafter ECAP y UNAMG), indigenous women spoke of suffering sexual violence during the massacres and when the army captured their husbands and sons:

'I went to the military detachment based in the plantation to ask about my husband … I wanted them to

let him go because he hadn't done anything wrong … They raped me right there … five of those soldiers did it to me.'

Women were routinely raped in front of their children, often gang-raped, and others were forced into slave labour – cooking, washing clothes and providing sexual favours under duress – for the army or the civil patrol leaders.

The impact of rape, documented in the ECAP y UNAMG 2009 report, has been devastating. While young women were regarded by many in their own communities as 'damaged goods' and no longer 'suitable' for marriage, married women were treated as 'adulterers' and subjected to further sexual and physical violence. War widows have had an especially difficult time, often regarded by other women as 'loose' and potential 'husband-grabbers'. Community ostracism, particularly of women raped in public, led many widows to leave. Some women did receive support from their mothers and occasionally fathers, but others were rejected by their families. Most women, though, accepted the children they had conceived through violence:

'Well what that man did to me was against my will. But my son was born and grew up, and now he's 19. He's my consolation. He always leaves me a bit of money when he comes, and tells me not to worry. If it weren't for my son I would hang myself.'

Mayan spirituality has also been a source of solace and has contributed to reparation. One Mayan woman said that the cleansing powers of burning *pom* (resin) and lighting candles means: 'Now I don't feel dirty any more, I feel that my body is innocent, my body is all right because it is clean and I am clean.'

Organizing has promoted widows' mutual support and agency. Informal local widows' groups contributed to day-to-day living. Many of these joined the Mayan National Coordination of Widows (CONAVIGUA), protesting army violence and their sons' forced military recruitment. Participation, capacity-building and income-generation projects have contributed to their healing and well-being. Organized refugee women in Mexico participated in negotiations for their return to Guatemala, fighting for shared land tenure. While most refugee-returnee organizations disappeared once back in Guatemala, the women's organizations Mama Maquín, Madre Tierra and Ixmukane have continued to strengthen women's capacities and support rural women's demands.

Mayan women and the insurgency

Mayan women contributed to the rebel forces in different ways, many giving food and *tortillas* (handmade maize pancakes), sewing uniforms and acting as messengers. As the army killed their families, more Mayan women joined the guerrillas, as Lucía explains:

'They killed two of my sisters and two of my brothers, my father fell ill and died, and my other sister and I joined the guerrillas, first me and then she came later. We had to join because we thought that if we were captured by the army they would rape, torture and kill us. I asked my mother's permission and she had to agree. She was a lone parent and had to do all the manual labour, so she taught us how to use the machete and the hoe and cultivate our small plot of land.'

Some, like Margarita, joined the rebels to avenge the death of their loved ones: 'the armed forces should pay for killing my brother'. Others, as in Lidia's case, had nowhere to go: 'I made my own decision to join the rebels – after they had taken my dad, my mum and everyone else I was on my own. I must have been about 10 years old.' Wanting their voices to be heard and their testimony committed to history, these Maya Ixil ex-combatants sought the help of *mestiza* women in Guatemala City to get their story heard; these were eventually published in 2008 under the title *Rebel Memories Against Oblivion*:

'Some of the women who had joined the rebels dropped out of the organization afterwards, maybe because they are so overwhelmed with sadness that they hardly step outside the house. Others were killed in combat or fell sick and died. This is why we want to write a book recording our history, because we don't want to forget it. It's also important that young people know this history and so have some notion of how it all happened.'

Conditions in the rebel ranks point to greater equality between men and women in some aspects. Men washed clothes, cleaned dishes and cooked; however, these changes did not last after demobilization. As Morna Macleod argued in 2008, many Mayan intel-

lectuals and activists considered that the rebel forces prioritized the class struggle against poverty rather than indigenous or gender equality concerns.

While not remotely comparable to the scale of the violence committed by the armed forces, insurgents had raped 6 of the 54 Mayan women who testified in the 2009 ECAP y UNAMG study. A few indigenous women became captains and lieutenants, but had to excel more than men in order to be recognized. This contrasts with the Zapatista uprising 15 years later in neighbouring Chiapas, Mexico, when, to people's amazement, Maya Tzotzil rebel major Ana María headed the occupation of the town Ocosingo in January 1994.

While many indigenous women were driven to join the rebel forces in the face of repression in Guatemala, Mayan women in Chiapas joined the clandestine guerrilla organization as an option that freed them from the constraints of community life. The Zapatistas probably learned from the lack of gender and ethnicity-related demands on the agendas of their fellow Central American rebel forces, and on International Women's Day a year before the Zapatista uprising, a 'Revolution within the Revolution' took place: the Women's Revolutionary Law. The ten articles included the right to participate and occupy leadership roles, to work and receive a fair salary, to choose a marriage partner and have as many children as one wants and can look after, as well as the right to health and education, and the right not to suffer violence.

Peace without justice

Although rural Mayan women were among the most affected and most vociferous against ongoing army repression, no Mayan women were included in the UN-mediated peace negotiations between the government-army and rebel forces. The 1996 Peace Accords included an agreement on indigenous peoples' identity and rights, and specific provisions for women, including the creation of an Indigenous Women's Defence Commission (*Defensoría*). Implementation of the Accords has been patchy, and heavily dependent on international aid. While indigenous 'windows' (*ventanillas*) have been included in public social assistance programmes, these are notoriously underfunded. The Catholic Church and UN Truth Commissions brought to light much of the war atrocities, but dissemination of the reports and implementation of recommendations have been

scant. Monsignor Gerardi, president of the Catholic Church Truth Commission, was murdered just two days after presenting their findings in 1998, indicating the risks involved in revealing the toll of the armed conflict. Impunity runs rife, and human rights activists continue to risk their lives, as do key witnesses in cases of strategic litigation.

Armed conflict has had a devastating impact on Mayan community life, as a Kanjob'al ex-combatant explains: 'Our village never recovered. It was as if our communal heart had been cut out.'

One small gain is that Mayan women now have increased agency and visibility in Guatemalan society. Rigoberta Menchú set a precedent when she received the Nobel peace prize, and CONAVIGUA leader Rosalina Tuyuc and social activist Manuela Alvarado became a highly respected national congresswomen. For the first time in Guatemalan history, Mayan women have been appointed as cabinet (vice) ministers. But indigenous women continue to be deeply under-represented in local and national government. Many Mayan women's organizations have formed since the signing of peace, promoting their participation in public life and decision-making, and lobbying for culturally appropriate

public policy. In their struggle for culturally sensitive gender equity, many combine collective, individual and women's rights discourses with the Mayan principles of complementarity, duality and balance.

Various significant reparation initiatives are being carried out by civil society. For some years now several Guatemalan rights-based organizations, feminists and international academics, have been documenting cases of war crime rape and working with Mayan women survivors. The 2009 ECAP y UNAMG study is one such product. But writing in 2010, Alison Crosby and M. Brinton Lykes caution against the risk that rape survivors who speak out publicly become 'iconic representations of sexual violence'. They include in their collaborative research creative workshops with Mayan rape survivors that aim to:

'critically reflect upon what they are doing, who they are becoming and how to sustain these processes of change in the midst of the ongoing adversarial social and cultural conditions of violence and impunity.'

Despite the genocide, over the past two decades Mayan movements – and increasingly Mayan women – have gained a voice and are pushing for recognition of indigenous law, spirituality, languages and education. More recently, there is a growing movement around the defence of territory and natural resources, using International Labour Organization (ILO) Convention No. 169 (on indigenous and tribal people's rights) to carry out consultations on mining projects and dams. Given that these issues most affect the daily lives of Mayan women, many are spearheading these recent struggles.

What happens after war?

It is sometimes said that war and armed conflict can empower women, offering greater financial independence and thus building their confidence. True, women do take on many new roles – whether working in traditionally male-dominated jobs or being forced into survival activities such as sex-work. When Salvadoran refugees arrived in Honduras in 1981, there was not one teacher or health worker among them. By 1990, the returnees, mainly women, included 407 teachers and 358 health workers. Women had also become car mechanics, blacksmiths, carpenters, hammock-weavers, builders and shoemakers, as well as acquiring valuable administrative skills.

But the evidence on how far these new roles survive the peace is discouraging. While women's rights are seldom high on the revolutionary agenda – the Zapatistas in Mexico are the exception that proves the rule – women combatants understandably expect to play a part in shaping the new government or nation. Yet today few Eritrean women have jobs, and female illiteracy is high, as Ravinda Rena notes in a 2007 report published by the Eritrea Institute of Technology. A few years after their return to El Salvador, most of the refugee women had reverted to their pre-war gender roles and very few were actively using their new skills, as Norma Vasquez recounted in 1999. According to the international NGO International Alert, disarmament, demobilization, and reintegration (DRR) programmes commonly give precedence to men in terms of employment and job creation. Women fall back into the informal economy, as has happened in South Caucasus.

A common post-conflict discourse is that women should bear children – particularly if their community feels its survival is under threat. 'Pro-natalist' policies such as reduced tax and other inducements to encourage large families were common in parts of Europe as it emerged from two world wars. Following the liberation struggle in Nicaragua, women were also encouraged to have more children, as Julie Cupples wrote in a 2004 article for *Gender & Development*. Children may be seen to represent hope for the future, and perhaps a source of security. But as women from such different contexts as Eritrea and El Salvador found, rather than new beginnings, the post-war scenario can be far from liberating for women. As discussed in a 2004 report by Martina Fischer for the Berghof Research Center for Constructive Conflict Management, there may even be a backlash against freedoms enjoyed before or during the war as men return home and expect to resume their former roles, or as conservative 'traditions' are revived and imposed – as happened in the cases of Afghanistan and Iran. There is also some evidence to suggest that domestic violence increases in the post-war period. And, as the Guatemala case study showed, women who have survived rape and have no option but to bear any child they conceive may then be ostracized for dishonouring their family or community. Albanian women in Kosovo did not dare to confide in their husbands that they had been raped during the war, for fear of being divorced on these grounds.

Gender inequality is a reality in all societies. UN Women estimates that one woman in three will experience sexual violence over the course of her life. Globally, women have far fewer resources than men, including access to education, decent work, wealth and property. Consequently women are hugely under-represented in the upper echelons of institutions that are so relevant to peace processes, such as the military and security forces, the legal profession, religious authorities and government. Given that according to the Inter-Parliamentary Union, only 19 per cent of parliamentary seats are held by women worldwide, their power to shape formal political agendas even in peacetime remains extremely limited. The Beijing goals of women's empowerment and gender equality are just as valid today as they were in 1995.

So even when mediation processes do make genuine efforts to ensure that women participate equally with men, they face a difficult task in facilitating women's full engagement from such a low starting point, while at the same time convincing men – and women – that this is an integral part of the democratic process, not just an optional extra. While 'women's participation' certainly projects a stronger role than 'women as victims', gender inequality before – as well as during and usually after – conflict poses a colossal challenge to making it a reality. This is an even greater challenge when the women who might have most to contribute are also subject to discrimination on the grounds of their ethnic identity or language, as the Guatemala case study makes very clear. In view of donors' current demand for quick and tangible 'results' rather than investing in the long-term and messier process of supporting women's participation in building a democracy, international funding and UN interventions have focused far more on protecting women and girls in armed conflict than on promoting women-led peace. There is obviously an imperative to protect those who are in immediate danger, but it is short-sighted to neglect the investment in peace-building, which would in the long run aim to reduce the need for urgent protection interventions. And the failure to address major structural injustices, such as the systematic subordination of women, or the exclusion of particular ethnic or religious groups, seriously undermines the achievement of 'positive peace', as opposed to merely the absence of war. As Anwarul K. Chowdhury, UN Under-Secretary-General and High Representative for the Least Developed Countries, Landlocked Developing Countries and Small Island Developing States notes:

'Sustainable peace is inseparable from gender equality. In coming years, women could and should play a more significant and substantive role in making the transition from culture of violence to culture of peace. We should not forget that when women are marginalized, there is little chance for an open and participatory society.'

Can minority and indigenous women benefit from international agreements?
Without the material and political backing to act upon them in a comprehensive and disinterested manner, international agreements and resolutions are benchmarks, statements of principle rather than action plans. This does not detract from their importance. The history of human rights is one of gradual rather than spectacular gains. History also tells us that rights are never just handed down from above, but have to be simultaneously claimed from below.

Mary Robinson, the former UN High Commissioner for Human Rights, has underlined that the prevention of violence depends on linking up the women, peace and security agenda with human rights mechanisms. Minority women have also pointed out that international instruments, including UN Resolution 1325 and its successors, tend to be silent on ethnicity. There is no specific mention, for instance, of the need to ensure that minority women are involved in peace processes, recognizing the role they can play in building bridges across communities, taking on leadership roles in their own communities, and encouraging male leaders to commit to the peaceful pursuit of their collective claims.

Some minority communities have successfully used international instruments, including human rights, as a tool for demanding accountability, creating space for their participation in discussions on peace and security, and engaging in wider political action.

In Nepal, the Peace Women's Alliance, which represents indigenous, Dalit, Madhesi and disabled women, regards UN Resolution 1325 as a major step in ensuring their representation in the post-conflict parliament. So they requested that the UN Technical Assistance Mission (TAM) take UN Resolution 1325 as its point of departure in regard to security, reintegration, and elections, and take account of 'the differential needs and situation of minority women and men in all … deliberations'. The Alliance also pointed out that the TAM's composition should reflect a proper gender balance.

In the South Caucasus and Russian Federation, the NGO International Alert held a series of workshops with women on international standards, such as the 1979 Convention on the Elimination of All Forms of Discrimination against Women. They then elicited the participants' ideas on how to strengthen UN Resolution 1325. Women in the South Caucasus pointed out that the breakaway states (such as Abkhazia and South Ossetia) do not recognize previous commitments, and that women's political representation is almost non-existent. They also emphasized the largely ignored consequences of the conflicts for women: displacement, unemployment or the loss of career, the proliferation of small arms, ethnicity and gender inequality all restrict women's enjoyment of formal rights.

Women in Timor-Leste considered violence a part of family life, not a matter for police intervention. With UN support, the Police Development Programme prepared a manual for the Timorese National Police on violence against women, and conducted training sessions on domestic abuse. And in May 2010 the Timorese Parliament passed the Law Against Domestic Violence. Now deemed as a public crime, prosecution for domestic violence no longer depends on whether a complaint is filed.

There are some serious shortcomings, however. For one thing, not only are peace processes conducted largely without any substantive input by women, let alone minority women, peace agreements also often include amnesty clauses for the perpetrators of human rights abuses, including rape. This gives the message to survivors and violators alike that these crimes are not as heinous as other violations. It also means that women continue to live in fear.

In Rwanda, according to MRG's local partner organizations, criminal law against 'genocide ideology' has made it impossible to discuss ethnicity, which makes it hard for people to form groups that could bridge ethnic divides and ease tensions. In addition, HRW has reported that rape survivors have complained about the lack of privacy in Rwanda's informal *gacaca* courts, and observers have raised concerns about lenient sentences on the one hand and convictions based on flimsy evidence on the other.

Women excluded from post-war planning

'It is really amazing', said one Kosovar woman ... 'that the international community cared only about Kosovar women when they were being raped – and then only as some sort of exciting story. We see now that they really don't give a damn about us. What we see here are men, men, men from Europe and America, and even Asia, listening to men, men, men from Kosovo. Sometimes they have to be politically correct so they include a woman on a committee or they add a paragraph to a report. But when it comes to real involvement in the planning for the future of this country, our men tell the foreign men to ignore our ideas. And they are happy to do so – under the notion of "cultural sensitivity". Why is it politically incorrect to ignore the concerns of Serbs or other minorities, but "culturally sensitive" to ignore the concerns of women?'

As the above quotation (taken from a 2002 UNIFEM report, *Women, War and Peace*) indicates, where peace accords are silent on systematic exclusion and discrimination, it seems ingenuous to imagine that post-war governments will voluntarily address such structural inequalities, or be in a position to guarantee the full democracy that underpins 'positive peace', as opposed to regarding peace as merely the absence of war and armed conflict. The Millennium Development Goals, which have very much influenced, even dominated, the thinking, policy and practice of aid donors and international NGOs, are also silent on issues of conflict, human rights, ethnic discrimination and violence against women.

Human rights, as we have said earlier, have to be claimed from below in order for a culture of rights to take root. An important role for international cooperation – not just aid agencies, but also scholars and activists – is therefore to support grassroots and civil society organizations to articulate and press for their rights and to make sure that their interests are properly addressed in any reparations, transitional justice systems and, perhaps most important in terms of 'positive' and sustainable peace, the truthful recording of their history. ■

Notes

1. Thanks to Susan A. Berger (2006) *Guatemaltecas: The Women's Movement 1986–2003*, Austin, University of Texas Press, p. 45, for this formulation.

2. The term 'sexualized' rather than 'sexual' denotes that the violence encompasses a wide range of offences that are meant to humiliate and break down the victim's integrity and self-esteem as well as to cause pain and physical harm. Though few survivors talk about it, men and boys are also victims of such violence, usually inflicted by men but occasionally by women, such as the case of sexualized violence against Iraqi male prisoners at Abu Ghraib. In focusing on atrocities that are usually masterminded by a small minority, it is easy to forget that the vast majority of men do not benefit from war. Men are also brutalized, victimized, sexually abused, humiliated, mutilated, tortured and killed; boys and young men are forcibly recruited into one or another fighting force.

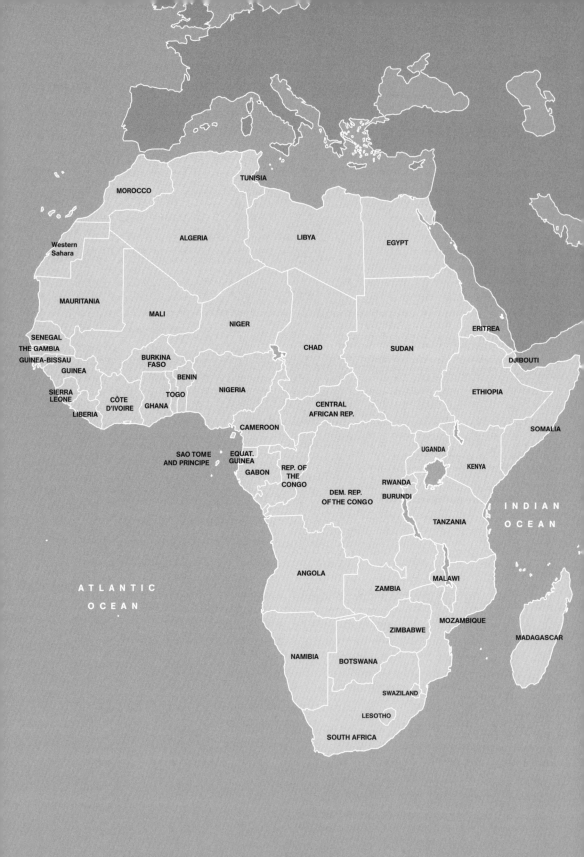

Africa

Rahnuma Hassan, Anna Horvai,
Paige Jennings, Bobbie Mellor and
George Mukundi Wachira

Central and West Africa

Paige Jennings

The year 2010 marked 50 years of independence for many countries in Africa. Elections, some unprecedented, were held in 22 countries, with others planned for 2011. While elections can be a positive indicator of the level of respect for fundamental freedoms, the region offered several examples of how electoral contests can also increase levels of violence, including that based on gender and ethnicity. In this context, women and girls from minority and indigenous groups can be at particular risk, as they may find themselves targeted on the basis of both gender and minority or indigenous identity.

Though the African Union (AU) declared 2010–20 the African Women's Decade, renewing commitments to gender equality and women's empowerment, events around the region demonstrated that the rights of women continue to be in need of particular protection. The newly-appointed UN Special Representative of the Secretary-General (SRSG) on sexual violence in conflict highlighted egregious abuses against women during the year, particularly in the Democratic Republic of Congo (DRC).

Across the region, human rights defenders and journalists continued their courageous work on the social issues of greatest concern in their countries. At times, this was at great risk to their own security, as highlighted in the country entries below. Attacks on human rights defenders as well as journalists have a devastating impact, not just on individual lives, but also on the fabric of societies as a whole, by shrinking the space available for free debate and hampering the outside world's ability to understand developments in their countries.

Concerns continue regarding significant cross-border issues. A number of non-governmental organizations (NGOs) and international bodies publicized findings regarding the practice of human trafficking, including of women and girls, within and through the region, while others drew attention to the effects of drug trafficking. The treatment of asylum-seekers and refugees, many of whom may belong to minorities in their countries of origin, was also a serious concern. In one example, in July a joint operation between the governments of Uganda and Rwanda saw the forced return of around 1,700 Rwandans from refugee settlements in south-western Uganda. Armed police officers reportedly surrounded them and forced them onto waiting trucks, which proceeded to drop them at a transit centre in Rwanda. The United Nations High Commissioner for Refugees (UNHCR) protested at the failure to respect international standards and reported that not only asylum-seekers but also recognized refugees were among those forcibly returned to their country of origin.

Efforts to address past human rights violations

The year 2010 also saw a range of positive efforts to address past human rights violations, including those targeted at minority groups.

Former president Charles Taylor of Liberia remains on trial before the Special Court for Sierra Leone. The Court was set up jointly by the government of Sierra Leone and the United Nations (UN) to address serious violations of international humanitarian and Sierra Leone law committed after November 1996. Taylor has pleaded not guilty to 11 charges of instigating murder, rape, mutilation, sexual slavery and conscription of child soldiers.

Efforts continue to bring Hissène Habré, the former dictator of Chad, to justice, following a 2006 recommendation by the AU to Senegal (where Habré lives in exile) that he should be prosecuted. The government of Senegal stated that the trial would proceed if donors funded it; in November they pledged to do so. The Court of Justice of the Economic Community of West African States (ECOWAS) also gave input.

The International Criminal Tribunal for Rwanda (ICTR), created in 1994 in the aftermath of the genocide, continued its work. Cases are currently in progress against 21 people, while two are awaiting trial and guilty verdicts against nine more are under appeal. Ten accused remain at large. The UN Security Council had recommended that the Tribunal

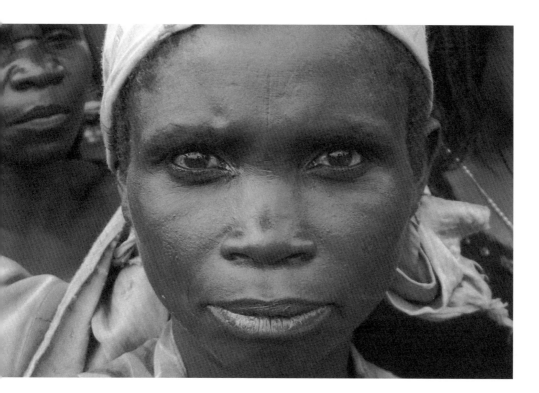

– reportedly over 1 million – have been prosecuted
in Rwanda before *gacaca*, or traditional community
tribunals that have been expanded in order to deal
with the significant caseload.

The International Criminal Court (ICC)
remained an important mechanism for bringing
perpetrators to justice, though its Review
Conference in Kampala in June heard calls for
more robust prosecution of sexual violence crimes.
It is currently hearing cases from four armed
conflicts, in the DRC, the Central African Republic
(CAR), Sudan and Uganda. In March it opened
an investigation into the post-election violence of
2007–8 in Kenya.

The arrest in October in France of Rwandan
Hutu rebel leader Callixte Mbarushimana of the
Democratic Forces for the Liberation of Rwanda
(Forces Démocratiques de Libération du Rwanda,
FDLR), on charges of crimes against humanity and
war crimes dating from 2009, brings to five the
number of alleged perpetrators of egregious human
rights abuses in the DRC with cases before the ICC.
Four are in international custody. The fifth, Bosco
Ntaganda, is a serving DRC army general.

Above: Internally-displaced Bambuti woman,
Kalehe, South Kivu, DRC. *Mark Lattimer/MRG.*

The trial of Jean-Pierre Bemba Gombo, leader
of the Movement for the Liberation of Congo
(MLC), opened in November; Gombo was
arrested in Belgium in 2008 and transferred to The
Hague to face charges of crimes against humanity,
including murder and rape, and war crimes allegedly
committed in the CAR. Since 2007 the ICC has
been investigating abuses against civilians reportedly
committed during armed conflict between the CAR
government and rebel forces in 2002 and 2003.

ICC arrest warrants issued in 2005 remain
pending against three surviving leaders of the
notorious Lord's Resistance Army (LRA) for abuses
committed in northern Uganda. After being forced
from Uganda in 2005, the LRA moved into the
Haut-Uele and Bas-Uele districts of Orientale
province in the DRC, the Central and Western
Equatoria region of Sudan and the Haute-Mbomou
province of the CAR. In May the UNHCR
reported an alarming rise in its attacks on civilians.

Finally, a UN 'mapping exercise' of a decade of
conflict in the DRC, published in October, reported
that the Rwandan army systematically killed tens

of thousands of Hutu civilians after it invaded the DRC in 1996 in pursuit of perpetrators of the 1994 genocide and subsequent attacks on the region's Tutsis. The report contained more than 600 alleged incidents of violence, including widespread rape and sexual assault by all sides. While the root causes of the high incidence of sexual violence in the DRC today (see below) are clearly complex, the report highlighted victims' lack of access to justice and the resulting impunity as significant contributing factors. The DRC welcomed the report's release but Burundi, Rwanda and Uganda reacted very negatively, with Rwanda calling it a 'dangerous and irresponsible attempt [...] to undermine the peace and stability attained in the Great Lakes region'.

Central Africa
Burundi
Burundi emerged in 2008 from over a decade and a half of civil war between the army, drawn predominantly from the minority Tutsi group, and militias from the majority Hutu. During the war, women and girls of all ethnic groups were systematically targeted for violence by both sides. This violence did not stop with the cessation of hostilities. In May the outgoing Independent Expert of the UN Human Rights Council on the situation of human rights in Burundi, Akich Okola, reported that gender-based violence had escalated year on year.

Also during the civil war, Batwa, caught in the middle between Hutu and Tutsi militants, both accusing them of loyalty to the other side, were killed in large numbers. They continue to face what the Independent Expert called 'systemic discrimination'. In October the UN Committee on the Rights of the Child (CRC) urged Burundi to 'elaborate a plan of action to protect the rights of Batwa children', particularly marginalized girls. In May MRG published the results of research into the reasons for low enrolment and high drop-out rates of Batwa girls in primary and secondary education in Burundi. The report indicated that Batwa boys and girls from other ethnic groups are twice as likely to go to school as Batwa girls. Drop-out rates for Batwa girls are also double those for Batwa boys. Factors contributing to Batwa girls' lack of access to education include poverty, the attitude of Batwa parents towards the education of girls, and early marriage. Finally, violence and discrimination towards albinos also continues to occur, with at least

three reportedly murdered in 2010.

Nevertheless, Burundi's Constitution does recognize 'minority groups', including ethnic, cultural and religious minorities. It also provides for proportionate ethnic representation in public enterprises, the National Assembly and the Senate. The explicit mention of Batwa as beneficiaries of this ethnic quota constitutes an important step forward for this ancient hunting and gathering community. Despite this, however, stereotyping and marginalization of Batwa people continues, restricting their involvement in political life.

Local, communal, legislative and presidential elections were all held in 2010. In the run-up to the elections, opposition parties reported intimidation and violence from both police and the youth wing of the party in power, the National Council for the Defence of Democracy – Forces for the Defence of Democracy (Conseil National pour la Défense de la Démocratie – Forces de Défense de la Démocratie, CNDD-FDD), which had been formed from one of the main Hutu rebel groups active in the civil war. Other parties organized their own youth wings in response, at times with disaffected young ex-combatants. These groups, including that of the CNDD-FDD's closest rival the National Liberation Forces (FNL), were involved in numerous violent clashes.

The communal elections, held in May, went off peacefully, although Human Rights Watch reported at least five politically motivated killings in the weeks running up to them. The international community officially recognized their results; however opposition parties accused the government of fraud and formed a coalition, ADC-Ikibiri. They pulled their candidates from the presidential race, leaving President Pierre Nkurunziza of the CNDD-FDD unopposed. The beginning of the presidential campaign saw an increased level of violence with grenade and arson attacks mainly on ruling party offices, and killings of both ruling and opposition party activists. Some of the opposition parties boycotted legislative contests as well. The government declared the boycott illegal and banned opposition meetings. Scores of opposition activists were reportedly arrested, and three of their leaders were prevented from leaving the country. President Nkurunziza was inaugurated for a second term in August. His party also won most legislative and local posts.

Democratic Republic of Congo (DRC)

The DRC is the scene of ongoing violent conflicts often driven by concerns relating to resources or ethnic identity and involving the military and numerous armed groups. An estimated 2 million people are internally displaced, and there are more than 200,000 refugees who have returned or are awaiting return to the eastern part of the country. Human rights abuses, including unlawful killings, torture, recruitment of children and sexual violence, are widespread in conflict areas. Minorities, including Batwa or Bambuti, are particularly vulnerable to attack.

Abuses can at times be fuelled, at least in part, by ethnic identity, as armed groups target communities or groups suspected of supporting opposing forces. Analysts believe that the widespread use of rape, inflicted by all sides and affecting all ethnic groups, has led to the 'normalization' of rape even among the civilian population and has resulted in greater levels of sexual violence generally.

North and South Kivu, in the east on the Rwandan border, is one of the most bitterly contested areas, with 1.4 million people internally displaced. While the roots of conflict in the area are deep and complex, the 1994 genocide in Rwanda served as a catalyst to the current displacement and violence. After the genocide, many Hutu extremist perpetrators joined hundreds of thousands of Hutu refugees who feared retribution in fleeing to the Kivus (among other areas) from Rwanda. From there, the militants launched attacks on the new Rwandan government, as well as on Congolese Tutsi. In 1996 Rwanda and Uganda sent their own forces into the area; in the course of their invasion they and their allies killed thousands of Hutus, both combatants and non-combatants alike. As conflict has continued and spread, all identity groups living in the area have been affected, including Batwa/Bambuti.

Ethnic tensions have been exacerbated by successive waves of conflict-driven displacement, and by the ensuing land disputes. UNHCR estimates that over 50,000 mainly Tutsi refugees from the DRC currently live in camps in Rwanda, but the Rwandan authorities claim that three times that number live outside the camps. The anticipated return of refugees, particularly in light of the February signing of a tri-partite repatriation agreement between UNHCR and the two governments, has further increased these tensions.

In a controversial move, in 2009 UN peacekeepers began providing support to DRC military operations in the Kivus against the predominantly Hutu rebels of the Democratic Forces for the Liberation of Rwanda, FDLR, in an effort to stabilize the region by military means. However, the DRC military is itself accused of committing violations with impunity, while the FDLR continues to carry out abuses undeterred. Both DRC military and rebel militias have been accused of rapes against the civilian population. All ethnicities have suffered in this regard, though UN and other sources have indicated that specific groups have at times been targeted for particularly vicious or widespread 'retaliatory' rapes and related killings due to the victims' perceived sympathies with rival factions.

The LRA, pushed out of Uganda in 2005, is now said to be operating in a remote border area between southern Sudan, the DRC and the CAR. Between January and April 2010, it reportedly killed at least 96 civilians around the town of Niangara, Orientale province, and abducted dozens more, in spite of the presence of UN peacekeepers there. The LRA has also been accused of forcibly recruiting civilians, particularly children, as porters, cooks and combatants, and of widespread mutilation and sexual violence against women and girls, including during revenge attacks on communities it perceives as supporting the state. By May 2010, the UN reported that the LRA had killed almost 2,000 people in Orientale province since December 2007. For their part, government soldiers have also been accused of serious violations against civilians, including unlawful killings and rape.

In Equateur province, over 100,000 refugees have reportedly fled across the Ubangui River to the Republic of Congo as a result of what began as an inter-ethnic clash between the Enyele and Munzaya tribes over fishing rights, with tens of thousands internally displaced.

During mass expulsions of Congolese from Angola in October, a large number of women and girls were reportedly raped by Angolan security forces. Special Representative of the UN Secretary-General (UN SRSG) on sexual violence in conflict Margot Wallström urged both governments to investigate.

Meanwhile, human rights defenders struggling to protect women and girls and to bring perpetrators to account are themselves under serious threat. Amnesty International reported that in October Clémence Bakatuseka, an activist working for victims of sexual violence in North Kivu, was reportedly attacked at her home by armed men in uniform demanding money.

In another case, the body of Floribert Chebeya Bahizire, executive director of one of the DRC's largest human rights organizations and of the national network of human rights groups, was found in June in Kinshasa, the day after he was summoned to meet with police officials there. His driver, Fidèle Bazana Edadi, is reported to be still missing.

Rwanda

The 1994 genocide, in which as many as 800,000 to 1 million people – a large part of the country's minority Tutsi population, along with Batwa and moderate Hutus – were killed, continued to shape Rwanda in 2010.

In marking the International Day of Reflection on the Genocide, UN High Commissioner for Human Rights Navanethem (Navi) Pillay praised Rwanda's 'remarkable progress towards gender equality', noting that more than half of parliamentarians and at least 30 per cent of postholders in the cabinet and the courts are women (no information was available as to the ethnic breakdown of these women MPs). She commended the opening of an independent Gender Monitoring Office to promote equal opportunity.

In August serving President Paul Kagame was elected to a second seven-year term. International observers reported that the elections were peaceful, but they expressed concerns about the stifling of dissent that preceded them. Numerous media outlets were closed in the months before the polls, some of them under a 2009 law restricting media freedom. None of the main opposition parties were able to participate on polling day. Some had been obstructed from holding the meetings required to register their parties while others were blocked by the detention of their leaders, along with key journalists, under a 2008 law criminalizing 'genocide ideology'. The law, like a similar one prohibiting 'divisionism', is ostensibly intended to outlaw behaviour encouraging ethnic hatred. Both texts, however, have been criticized for impinging on freedom of expression by failing to define clearly which specific acts they penalize. While

New technologies and 'Africa's World War'

ipod, Blackberry, DS, laptop … for some of us, luxuries, for others, seeming necessities. We certainly do not think of them as tangible links to 'Africa's World War', a ten-year conflict with the highest death toll since the Second World War. Its aftershocks continue, most recently in the form of brutal mass rapes in the DRC, planned and carried out with the aim of terrorizing defenceless communities.

Over four days in July and August, around 200 fighters from a loose alliance of three rebel groups systematically cut off and encircled 13 villages along a 21-km stretch of road in the mineral-rich Walikale territory in North Kivu, DRC. To isolate the population, the rebels took control of the one hill in the area from which telephone calls could be made. They approached mostly at night, on foot through the forest or by road. One group would enter the village while another spread out around it, to catch anyone who tried to run. In some places the men initially told villagers that they had come to protect them. Then, armed with AK-47s, grenades and machetes, they attacked, looting shops and houses. All told they raped or gang-raped at least 303 people, including women, men, girls and boys.

Local residents, most of whom belong to the Nianga ethnic group, told UN investigators that their communities had been targeted as punishment for suspected pro-government sympathies. They said that they believed rape was deliberately chosen as a weapon because of

the stigma traditionally attached to in their culture. There were no DRC army units in the region at the time. It was not until 13 August that UN troops stationed nearby substantiated rumours of attacks and began to respond; by then, it was far too late.

These horrific events have their roots in long-standing tensions over identity, citizenship, land rights and related issues in the region. These were exacerbated by the 1994 Rwandan genocide, in which up to 1 million people were murdered in just 100 days. Two and a half years later Rwanda invaded neighbouring DRC (then Zaire) in pursuit of those responsible.

Over time, nine African nations and up to 20 armed groups became involved in the conflict, in large part due to the vast natural resources in the region. These include coltan, a rare commodity essential to the global electronics industry; according to a December report by the NGO Global Witness, this industry 'accounts for much of the demand for

Above: A man holds Coltan (columbite-tantalite) in his hands, the precious metal used to make consumer electronic products, DRC. *Sven Torfinn/Panos.*

eastern Congo's minerals'.

When foreign armies withdrew, the militias remained behind, their allegiances largely fluid and their main motivation greed.

Leaders may grow extremely wealthy from the mines, but this does not necessarily trickle down. As an April report by Oxfam on sexual violence in the region pointed out, militias on the ground are poorly paid and supplied, relying on looting to get what they need. This brings them into direct confrontation with local communities. In this context, rape is an effective, inexpensive, low-tech way to terrorize and impose control on an entire population.

In the wake of the attacks, DRC authorities

established a commission of military, judicial and police officials to investigate the events and bring the perpetrators to justice. However in January UN authorities reported that the dozens of victims who had dared cooperate with these authorities had apparently received threats.

In a briefing to the UN Security Council on the Walikale attacks, the SRSG on sexual violence in conflict, Margot Wallström, drew special attention to the nexus between illegal mining, the presence of militias and attacks on civilians, particularly women. UN High Commissioner for Human Rights Navi Pillay reiterated this concern:

'so long as this free-for-all continues, with the mines and quarries controlled by armed groups or other rogue elements, the local population will be prey to attacks such as these.'

This issue is not new. Some mobile phone companies began trying to track their suppliers after a 2001 Security Council report of proceeds from the mines funding rebel attacks. In November the Security Council went further, adopting a resolution urging the use of due diligence guidelines for importers, processing industries and consumers. For its part, the US Congress in July passed a bill requiring companies trading in or using key minerals to report yearly on their sources and supply chain.

Sourcing of component elements for electronic equipment is not, of course, the only human rights issue facing the industry; if anything, it represents one end of the scale of concerns. At the other, 'user' end are concerns about the potential misappropriation of social networking technologies to spread messages of hate and mobilize ethnic or sectarian violence.

Sitting at the computer or sending a text, the forest of Walikale may seem a world away. It is closer than you think. ∎

government sensitivities regarding the mention of ethnic differences are understandable given the country's recent history, its stance risks concealing discrimination against vulnerable minorities such as Batwa and women from minority groups. The government announced a review of the 'genocide ideology' law in April.

Two prominent government critics were killed in the months preceding the election, contributing to a climate of tension and fear. These were André Kagwa Rwisereka, former supporter of the party in power who left in 2009 to help found the Democratic Green Party, and journalist Jean-Leonard Rugambage, who had been investigating the attempted murder a week earlier of a former military chief-of-staff who had become an increasingly outspoken critic of the government.

Uganda

The UN Committee for the Elimination of Discrimination against Women (CEDAW committee) noted some positive developments in Uganda, for instance in regard to new legislation prohibiting domestic violence, human trafficking, female genital mutilation and sexual violence against women during conflict. A law criminalizing female genital mutilation (FGM) was signed in March. Perpetrators can face sentences of up to ten years in jail, increasing to life in cases where the victim dies. The BBC reported that it is still practised by some Sabiny, some Karamojong sub-groups and Pokot in eastern Uganda, as well as Nubi of West Nile. In its October observations, the CEDAW committee welcomed the law but expressed concern at the 'continued prevalence of this harmful practice'. In addition, a number of other serious concerns relating to women's rights remained.

In May MRG published the results of research into violence against Batwa women in Uganda. One hundred per cent of Batwa women responding to individual interviews reported having experienced some form of violence; for the majority, the violence was ongoing or had occurred in the past 12 months. This is significantly higher than national averages.

Before it was pushed out of northern Uganda in 2005, 20 years of conflict involving the LRA had forced an estimated 1.5 million people to leave their homes. The Office of the UN High Commissioner for Human Rights (OHCHR) reported in June that 240,000 remain in camps.

Vulnerable people, including older women and those with disabilities, faced particular difficulties in returning home. Community support on which they would traditionally have relied has been disrupted, and their home areas lack security and health services. In the camps themselves, they are particularly at risk of sexual violence, the prevalence of which is 'inordinately high' in Uganda according to the CEDAW committee.

Karamoja in north-east Uganda is home to the Karamajong, a traditionally pastoralist ethnic group badly affected by the local impact of climate change. More frequent cycles of drought in an already harsh environment have led to ever greater competition for scarce resources, and cattle-raiding and the violence accompanying it have increased. Raids by armed bands of cattle rustlers have led to heavy security force responses in which civilians have been killed. In January at least 13 people, including children and women, were reportedly killed during a military operation against gangs in the area; in April at least half of the ten deaths confirmed by the OHCHR in similar circumstances were children.

In March a fire destroyed the Kasubi tombs, a world heritage site in Kampala and the burial site of the kings of the Baganda, Uganda's largest ethnic group. President Yoweri Museveni was met by protests when he tried to visit the scene, and his guards reportedly shot and killed at least three people.

Moves to begin exploiting oil reserves at Lake Albert fuelled tensions around the proposed distribution of the eventual proceeds from resource extraction. Most of the drilling is set to take place in zones belonging to the Bunyoro kingdom, and some of its members, as well as environmental activists, have demanded greater participation in the process and more transparency about the government's agreements with oil companies.

Bombs in a restaurant and in a crowd watching the football World Cup final killed at least 76 people in Kampala on 11 July. Somali Islamist group al-Shabaab claimed responsibility, reportedly in retaliation for Uganda's participation in the AU military force in Somalia. Following concerns about the impact of the attacks on relations between Uganda's Muslims and Christians, President Museveni publicly cautioned Ugandans not to collectively blame Somalis for the bombing. Two Kenyan activists working on the cases of suspects detained in relation to the events were themselves

arrested in September. One was released, but the other, Al-Amin Kimathi of the Nairobi-based Muslim Human Rights Foundation, remained in detention.

The 2011 presidential campaign opened in November, with President Museveni seeking another five-year term. He was returned to office in February 2011.

West Africa
Côte d'Ivoire

Côte d'Ivoire has over 60 ethnic groups, whose linguistic and cultural identities and interrelationships are complex. The five main cultural clusters are: the dominant Akan-speakers, who make up 42 per cent of the population; Northern Manding (Mandé); Voltaic peoples; Krou; and Southern Manding (Mandé). The Baoulé, an Akan sub-group, are the largest single ethnic group, comprising about 15–20 per cent of the total population.

Long-delayed presidential elections were held in Côte d'Ivoire, the first in a decade. The previous contest, in 2000, was followed by widespread violence. In 2002 a group of army officers attempted a military coup. They failed to overthrow then President Laurent Gbagbo but did take control of the country's largely Muslim north, arguing that northerners had been treated as second-class citizens by a largely southern government. A ceasefire in 2003 followed by political accords in 2007 eased tensions between the regions, but they remained effectively partitioned.

Xenophobic election campaign language heightened tensions between north and south. Gbagbo and his 'Young Patriot' supporters questioned the nationality of his main opponent, northerner Alassane Ouattara, playing on the perception among some of the public of northerners as descendants of economic migrants drawn to Côte d'Ivoire by its relative affluence over past decades.

Calls by Gbagbo's supporters for 'foreigners' – largely those with Muslim names – to be barred from the electoral roll were met by protests. The 10,000-strong UN Operation in Côte d'Ivoire (UNOCI), in the country since 2004, reported that 13 demonstrators and bystanders were killed by security forces in February following Gbagbo's decision to dissolve the government and the Independent Electoral Commission (IEC).

The first round of the presidential elections, in

October, went off peacefully, with an estimated turnout of over 80 per cent. The run-off between Gbagbo and Ouattara was held on 28 November. The UN Special Representative said that it had taken place in a democratic climate, and other international observers agreed. The IEC declared Ouattara the winner with over 54 per cent of the vote. However, Gbagbo appealed to the Constitutional Council, which overturned the IEC findings and declared him the victor. The UN, the AU, the ECOWAS, the European Union (EU) and individual governments recognized Ouattara's victory; but Gbagbo, with the backing of the army, refused to step down.

This refusal was followed by violence, including 'disappearances', extra-judicial killings, unlawful use of force and other violations. Most were attributed to security forces and militias loyal to Gbagbo. Francis Deng, the Special Adviser of the Secretary-General on the Prevention of Genocide, and Edward Luck, the Special Adviser of the Secretary-General on the responsibility to protect, expressed concern at indications that some leaders were 'inciting violence between different elements of the population so as to serve their political purposes'. By the end of December, the UN reported that 173 people had been killed in the violence, which was showing little signs of abating. UNHCR reported that over 15,000 people, including supporters of both camps, had fled to Liberia from western Côte d'Ivoire out of fear of political violence; others had arrived in Guinea.

Guinea

Presidential elections in 2010 offered Guineans their first real opportunity to choose their own leaders, after successive dictatorships following independence from France. When Lansana Conté, president for 24 years, died in 2008, a military coup followed. Its leader, Captain Moussa Dadis Camara, promised elections but then announced his intention to run. A peaceful demonstration by tens of thousands of opposition supporters at a Conakry stadium in September 2009 was brutally dispersed by security forces and militia. In several days of violence at least 150 people were killed and scores of women raped. More than 1,500 were wounded, and many others detained. The majority of victims were reported to be from the majority Peuhl (Fula) ethnic group.

The events were placed under preliminary

Right: A Haratine woman and her son, Sahara Desert, Mauritania. *Robert Moran.*

examination by the ICC. In February the deputy prosecutor Fatou Bensouda announced her belief that 'crimes constituting crimes against humanity were committed'.

In December 2009 Dadis left the country after being shot by an aide. His deputy, General Sékouba Konaté, joined with opposition groups to form an interim government. He announced elections for mid 2010 and promised that no serving member of government would be allowed to stand. The first round of the elections, in July, was predominantly peaceful. Former prime minister Cellou Dalein Diallo, a Peuhl, won 43 per cent of the vote in June, so he and the runner-up, opposition leader Alpha Condé, moved to a second round in November.

The contest between Diallo and Condé, a Malinké, fuelled existing tensions between their ethnic groups. Guinea's first president, Ahmed Sekou Touré, a Malinké, led the country from independence in 1958 until 1984, and those from his ethnic group held relatively favoured status during his tenure He distrusted the Peuhl, however, and they suffered disproportionately under what became an increasingly autocratic and brutal state. Though they represent the country's largest ethnic group, a Peuhl has never led the country, and many Diallo supporters felt that this situation was due to change.

The 15 November run-off was carried out fairly peacefully, and international observers said that it appeared free and fair. However, violence erupted after Condé was found to have won by a narrow margin. A state of emergency was declared, imposing a curfew and granting security forces extra powers. Inter-communal violence, as well as violations by security forces accused of systematic attacks against Peuhls, reportedly resulted in at least seven deaths and several hundred people injured. However, the new government was installed peacefully. At year's end President Condé named himself defence minister. He promised to reform the military and to organize a truth and reconciliation commission to address past human rights violations.

Mauritania

In August the UN Special Rapporteur on contemporary forms of slavery, Gulnara Shahinian,

reported that 'de facto slavery continues to exist in certain remote parts of Mauritania', despite the legal abolition of the practice in 1980 and its criminalization in 2007. She indicated that Haratine, or 'Black Moors', are the ethnic group most at risk. In this situation, she reported, women suffer 'triple discrimination: firstly as women, secondly as mothers and thirdly as slaves. They are viewed by their masters firstly as labour and secondly as producers of a labour force.' Among other violations, they are systematically denied the right to a family life, and have no rights in their children.

In December up to eight activists from the Initiative for the Resurgence of the Abolitionist Movement in Mauritania (Initiative pour la Résurgence du Mouvement Abolitionniste en Mauritanie), were said to have been arrested on public order charges, in the course of a police investigation into a case of possible slavery that they had reported.

The UNHCR repatriation programme for Mauritanian refugees in Senegal, begun in 2008, resumed in October after a 10-month break. Most of the refugees are black Africans from the Peuhl ethnic group. They were forced to flee in April 1989 following ethnic violence sparked by the alleged killing of two Senegalese farmers in a dispute over grazing rights with Mauritarian herders in the Senegal River valley border region. Returnees face a number of obstacles. Disputes over ownership of property are frequent, as other families have often occupied lands left vacant by the fleeing refugees. Some children of returnee families, born in Senegal, do not speak local languages.

In January a group of 34 Muslim clerics and scholars in Mauritania signed a *fatwa*, or religious decree, banning FGM. In 2009 the UN CRC reported that some 70 per cent of girls in Mauritania undergo the procedure, and all ethnic groups are affected; it is more prevalent in rural areas.

Nigeria

Nigeria opened 2010 with uncertainty, following the hospitalization outside the country of President Umaru Yar'Adua. In February the National Assembly named Vice President Goodluck Jonathan acting president. In May Yar'Adua, a northerner, died, leaving Jonathan, from the oil-rich Niger Delta in the south of the country, to finish the final year of his term. The dominant People's Democratic Party (PDP) named Jonathan as its candidate for April 2011 elections, in spite of an informal arrangement whereby northerners and southerners alternate every two terms in the Presidency.

The Middle Belt dividing the largely Muslim north and the largely Christian south has long been an area of tensions, in part due to a system whereby people are classified as 'indigenes' or 'non-indigenes' depending on where their parents or grandparents were born. 'Non-indigenes', in this region, generally Muslims from the Hausa group, are barred from competing for government jobs or academic scholarships, leading to resentment against 'indigenes', most often Berom Christians. While ostensibly intended to protect traditional cultures, the policy has served to divide communities, fuel identity-based politics and deepen existing disputes, for example over land.

These tensions reignited in Jos, the capital of Plateau State, on 17 January, between rival mobs reportedly armed with guns, bows and arrows, and machetes. At least 200 people were killed, with another 5,000 estimated to have been forced from their homes.

Violence spread to the town of Kuru Karama, 30 km away, where at least 150 Muslim residents were reportedly massacred by marauding gangs believed to be Christian. Some of the victims reportedly sought refuge in the local mosque. On 7 March, in what were said by police to be revenge attacks, several hundred Christians were reportedly massacred in the villages of Dogo Nahawa, Zot and Ratsat, 10 km from Jos. In this case the attackers were said to have been Muslim.

UN High Commissioner for Human Rights Navi Pillay called for:

'… a concerted effort to tackle the underlying causes of the repeated outbreaks of ethnic and religious violence which Nigeria has witnessed in recent years, namely discrimination, poverty and disputes over land.'

At year's end, however, violence flared again. Christmas Eve bombs in Jos reportedly killed at least 80 people, sparking more inter-communal violence. Around ten people were said to have been killed in a series of attacks in Maiduguri. The Islamic sect Boko Haram claimed responsibility; police arrested 90 suspects and were accused of excessive use of force and other violations in the process.

Armed groups based in the Niger Delta have long demanded more even distribution of government income from oil production, which over the last decades has caused environmental damage that has wiped out traditional livelihoods such as farming and fishing. An August 2009 amnesty brought a pause in their activities. However, in October the Movement for the Emancipation of the Niger Delta (MEND) claimed responsibility for two car bombs in Abuja during celebrations marking the 50th anniversary of Nigerian independence, though some members disputed its involvement. At least ten people were killed. By year's end sabotage of pipelines and kidnappings of workers had resumed. The Nigerian army said that six civilians were killed in mid-December when it attacked a suspected militant base near the Niger Delta community of Ayakoromo; local groups said the number was higher.

East and Horn of Africa

George Mukundi Wachira

Legal and institutional reforms and elections were key highlights of the year 2010 in East and Horn of Africa. The adoption of constitutional reforms in Kenya, and elections in Sudan and Ethiopia, were ostensibly aimed at improving and guaranteeing citizens' fundamental rights and freedoms, and promoting the rule of law and good governance. But ironically, in all three cases, minorities and indigenous peoples were left more vulnerable following these events.

In Kenya, the promulgation of a new Constitution on 27 August 2010 was hailed by many Kenyans, including those belonging to minority and indigenous groups, as promising a new start for the country. It may be too early to pass verdict, but so far that promise is yet to be realized. Already since August, the president has been compelled to withdraw a list of nominees to key constitutional offices – the Chief Justice, Attorney-General and

Director of Public Prosecutions – on the basis that he did not adequately consult the Prime Minister and did not follow the requirements laid down in the Constitution regarding gender parity and the processes requisite in such nominations. Such a development raises questions as to the extent to which ordinary citizens' views are being taken into account in processes and mechanisms to implement the new constitutional order.

Of equal if not greater significance in Kenya during the reporting period is the question of dealing with impunity with regard to the post-election violence in 2007–8. Following the failure of the state to prosecute those responsible for the violence – which particularly affected minorities and indigenous peoples in the Rift Valley – the International Criminal Court (ICC) issued summonses in 2010 for six suspects to appear before the Court. The possible indictment of the six suspects has serious ramifications, given that the suspects continue to occupy high leadership positions in the country. Indeed, the Kenyan government is seeking a deferral from the United Nations (UN) Security Council for these cases, ostensibly with the aim of according an opportunity for the domestic courts to proceed with prosecutions.

In Sudan, reflecting earlier patterns, minorities were again excluded from the general elections held in April 2010. The boycott by the main opposition parties, coupled with incidents of violence, intimidation and general insecurity, effectively denied most members of minority groups their right to vote. Minority women in Sudan continued to bear the brunt of the conflict and the seemingly elusive peace in Darfur, a situation that was often compounded by their exclusion from peace negotiations that are ongoing in Doha, Qatar and other world capitals. In the South, members of minority groups awaited the outcome of the referendum to choose between unity and secession which took place in January 2011, in the hope that the outcome would bring an improvement in their human rights situation.

Parliamentary elections in Ethiopia in May 2010 were marred by controversy and riddled with allegations of fraud, violence and intimidation, according to European Union (EU) and US election observers, who also concluded that the elections were not free and fair, and did not conform to international standards (a view disputed by election observers from the African Union [AU]). Critics, however, continue to accuse Western governments of condoning or turning a blind eye to Prime Minister Meles Zenawi's political repression of his opponents in return for his support in the fight against global terrorism in the region. This repression includes targeting of some minority political movements, such as the Ogaden National Liberation Front and the Oromo Liberation Front. Granted Zenawi is credited with reducing Ethiopia's reliance on development assistance. However, questions abound as to whether minorities and other marginalized groups are gaining from these economic advances, as wealth does not appear to be trickling down to poor people in general, and minorities in particular, particularly in the historically neglected southern, eastern and western border regions.

Eritrea has not held elections since the country seceded from Ethiopia in 1993. The human rights situation of Eritreans generally and of minorities in particular are compounded by UN sanctions imposed on the country in 2009 for allegedly backing Islamist insurgents in Somalia. Apart from the UN sanctions, the fact that relations over borders with all of its neighbours are either severely strained or completely blocked due to disputes, impacts on the human rights situation in the country. The regime has also clamped down on political dissidents, and continues to violate freedoms of religion, movement and expression, with private media outlets closed down and large numbers of journalists imprisoned. Meanwhile in Somalia, widespread human rights abuses and ongoing conflict continue to have a disproportionate impact on minority groups.

Eritrea

The year 2010 saw sanctions imposed on Eritrea by the UN, following a vote by the Security Council in December 2009. According to UN Security Council Resolution 1907, the sanctions include an arms embargo as a result of of Eritrea providing 'political, financial and logistical support to armed groups engaged in undermining peace and reconciliation in Somalia and regional stability'. In addition, the government of President Isaias Afewerki continued to suppress, detain and torture political opponents and prisoners of conscience.

Religious freedom was severely curtailed,

especially for Jehovah's Witnesses, who are opposed to compulsory military service on the grounds of conscientious objection. In 2010, the US Committee on International Religious Freedom (USCIRF) again recommended that Eritrea be classified a country of particular concern. Apart from Jehovah's Witnesses, USCIRF noted that the situation for evangelical and Pentecostal Christians remained very serious. The Eritrean government uses a registration requirement (and the withholding of permission) as a way of curtailing religious activities. Muslims at risk of repression included those who were viewed as radical or opposed to the government-appointed head of the Muslim community. Hundreds of members of unauthorized religious groups continued to be detained. Human Rights Watch (HRW) reported that a woman died in April 2010 following two years' detention in a cargo container for not renouncing her unregistered faith.

Women in Eritrea, including those from minority communities, face state harassment for their own political views and actions, but also as a result of the actions of their children and relatives. Indefinite military service is compulsory for all able-bodied young people, male and female. Each year, many young people leave the country to avoid this, and it appears that their mothers are then targeted. According to a 2009 HRW report on indefinite conscription in Eritrea, families and especially mothers are subject to retribution if conscripts desert and leave the country. In such cases, families are fined 50,000 Nakfa (approximately US $3,300). Several persons interviewed said that land would be taken or mothers would be imprisoned if the families could not pay the fine.

According to a woman interviewed by HRW, sexual harassment, serious death threats as well as inhumane treatment and conditions are the daily reality of women conscripts in the military in Eritrea. Because of their objection to military service on the grounds of conscientious objection, Jehovah's Witnesses are particularly targeted. HRW concluded that: 'Eritrea's extensive detention and torture of its citizens and its policy of prolonged military conscription are creating a human rights crisis and prompting increasing numbers of Eritreans to flee the country.'

Ethiopia

As highlighted in *State of the World's Minorities*

and Indigenous Peoples 2010, the adoption of the Charities and Societies Proclamation Act of 2009 (NGO Law) has severely restricted the activities of most human rights organizations working in the country. The law also prohibits international organizations from engaging in human rights advocacy and governance work in the country, which has seriously limited the resource capacity of organizations working with minorities, such as the Pastoralist Forum of Ethiopia. According to HRW, the government claims that the legislation:

'is mainly intended to ensure greater openness and financial probity on the part of nongovernmental organizations. But instead it places such severe restrictions on all human rights and governance-related work as to make most such work impossible, violating fundamental rights to freedom of association and expression provided for in the Ethiopian Constitution and international human rights law.'

The law appears to be part of a broader strategy to suppress political dissent, limit fundamental human rights and freedoms, and control the populace.

Wider political repression in 2010 continued

Above: A young Oromo woman in Central Ethiopia. *Eric Lafforgue.*

to affect minority communities, particularly those supporting the Oromo Liberation Front and the Ogaden National Liberation Front (ONLF), whose leaders were detained, harassed or went into exile. In addition, despite the withdrawal of Ethiopian government troops from Somalia, the Ethiopian National Defense Forces (ENDF) used force to quell dissent in its own Somali region (also known as Ogaden). Minority women bore the brunt of the repression, with Amnesty International reporting that there were 'cases of rape and extrajudicial executions by government forces of suspected supporters of the ONLF in the Somali Region of Ethiopia'. The struggle against international terrorism was given as the government's reason for cracking down on dissent, but the opposition insists that these actions are politically motivated.

It is worth noting that in June 2010, the Ethiopian government signed a ceasefire agreement in Germany with one faction of the ONLF. The ceasefire was expected to hold for three months to prevent further loss of life and facilitate a framework for future talks, and was renewed again in October 2010. However, given that the ceasefire was not signed by all the parties to the conflict, the hostilities continue.

Parliamentary elections held in May 2010 were won by Ethiopia's ruling party, the Ethiopian People's Revolutionary Democratic Front (EPRDF), with a large majority. The elections were judged free and fair by AU observers, but other international observers (such as EU observers) felt that they had fallen short of international standards, and had taken place within a 'narrowing political space', heavily skewed in favour of the incumbent. In such circumstances it is difficult for women from minority communities, especially those perceived to be from the political opposition strongholds of Oromo and Ogaden, to participate effectively, let alone be represented in national government and public affairs. For while women from those constituencies are likely to be targeted by security agencies for their assumed allegiance to opposition political movements, generally 'women are underrepresented in the Ethiopian political scene and within the electoral administration', as observed by the EU Election Observation Mission.

Kenya

The year 2010 presented significant promise and potential for minorities, while at the same time also witnessing continued derogation of the fundamental human rights and freedoms of some communities. Some significant positive developments included the promulgation of a new Constitution in August 2010, which followed the adoption of a Land Policy and transitional justice mechanisms in 2009, security sector reforms, legal and institutional reforms, and the launch of the 'Kenya Vision 2030' national development plan. The implementation of these processes – the outcome of the 2008 National Accord and Reconciliation Act – proceeded in earnest in 2010, despite some political, legal and capacity-related challenges.

These institutional and legal reforms present an opportunity for minorities and indigenous peoples in Kenya to participate in and influence the implementation of the new Constitution, in a way that could for the first time take into account their historical marginalization, exclusion, needs, special circumstances and aspirations. The new Constitution is progressive and includes provisions that have the potential to secure the rights of

minorities and indigenous peoples in Kenya. For instance, it stipulates national values and principles of governance (Article 10); expressly acknowledges the rights of minorities and marginalized groups (Article 56); protects community land ownership (Article 63); incorporates socio-economic rights (Article 43); guarantees access to justice for all persons (Article 48); guarantees the right to language and culture (Article 44); provides for an equitable share of the national revenue and resources (Article 202); and importantly, devolves power to the people at the local level (chapter 11).

Of key significance to minority and indigenous women in Kenya, the new Constitution provides for 'equal treatment of men and women including the right to equal opportunities in political, economic, cultural and social spheres' (Article 27 (3)). That means that women in Kenya, including those from indigenous and minority communities, have equal rights relative to citizenship, matrimonial property and inheritance. The new Constitution further outlaws any person from compelling another 'to perform, observe or undergo any cultural practice or rite' (Article 44(3)). This provision effectively protects women and girls from harmful cultural practices, which are common in some indigenous and minority communities. In addition, the Constitution calls on the state to 'take legislative and other measures, including affirmative action programmes and policies designed to redress any disadvantage suffered by individuals and groups because of past discrimination' (Article 27 (6); 20 (5)(b)). This can be construed as an express acknowledgment of the historical marginalization and exclusion of minority and indigenous peoples in Kenya.

As the new Constitution is implemented, it is expected and hoped that indigenous and minority peoples in Kenya will begin to enjoy the fruits of *uhuru* (independence). However, minority groups must remain vigilant, given past experiences where they have often been left at the margins of reform processes by elites and mainstream communities. Indeed, during the reporting period, one minority community – Ogiek – were threatened with eviction from their ancestral lands in Mau Forest. An application has since been filed (2009) at the African Commission on Human and Peoples Rights (ACHPR) on behalf of the community by Ogiek Peoples Development Programme (OPDP), Centre for Minority Rights Development (CEMIRIDE) and MRG, alleging various violations, including forced evictions from their territory and lands.

However, it is important to acknowledge the Ministry of Lands' intimations that it is looking to secure the land rights of indigenous communities. Indeed, responding to a question by a Member of Parliament, Ekwe Ethuro, the Minister of Lands, James Orengo, indicated that the ministry was 'seeking to secure land rights of marginalized communities especially the Endorois, Ogiek and Ilchamus by proposing geographical mapping of their areas and resources'.

In December 2009, the Kenyan parliament adopted a new National Land Policy, aimed at resolving land disputes and addressing historical injustices. Despite this, and promises that the state would implement the 2010 Endorois decision by the ACHPR, this has not yet happened. However, it is encouraging to note that the matter of the implementation of the Endorois decision has been raised in parliament. Ethuro (who is also the chair of the Pastoralists Parliamentary Forum) asked the Minister of Lands a question by Private Notice on the steps the minister had taken to comply with the ACHPR decision on the Endorois. The minister replied that he had yet to receive an authenticated copy of the decision, meaning that he could not proceed towards implementation. He has since received a sealed copy of the ACHPR recommendation.

Women, including those from minority communities, who suffered internal displacement and serious abuse including rape and grievous bodily harm during the 2007–8 post-election violence, are yet to receive legal remedy at the national level. The summons in 2011 by the ICC of six suspects – Former Police Commissioner Hussein Ali, Head of Public Service Francis Muthaura, suspended Higher Education Minister William Ruto, Deputy Prime Minister and Finance Minister Uhuru Kenyatta, Former Industrialization Minister Henry Kosgei, and Head of Operations and Kass FM Radio Presenter Joshua arap Sang – is a significant development, sending the message that impunity will not be tolerated by the international community. However, even if the suspects are formally indicted and arraigned, those indictments at the ICC are not likely to yield much if the Kenyan courts do not bring the thousands of people who perpetrated violence in the post-election period to justice, in particular those who committed acts of gender-based violence against women.

Inter-communal conflicts between pastoral communities also continued throughout the reporting period. According to the 2010 mission report of the African Commission Working Group of Experts on Indigenous Populations, the Kenyan government's response to such conflicts has often been harsh and one-sided. An example is the case of Samburus of Laikipia and Pokot pastoralists who were involved in conflicts over cattle in 2009. Government forces responded violently, and Samburus accused them of taking sides. Samburus of Laikipia say that they are not adequately represented and therefore lack state protection.

Somalia
Anna Horvai and Bobbie Mellor

Many Somalis regularly experience serious human rights violations, regardless of their ethnicity, religion or clan affiliation. These violations become more severe for both women and members of minority groups, resulting in the multiple discrimination that has come to characterize the lives of Somali minority women.

In September 2010, Prime Minister Omar Abdirashid Ali Sharmarke of the Transitional Federal Government (TFG) resigned and was replaced by Mohamed Abdullahi Mohamed. The year 2010 also saw the TFG lose more territory to insurgent groups, dominated by Islamist group al-Shabaab, who now control most of south-central Somalia. In mid August, the TFG's Constitutional Commission (IFCC) submitted a new draft Constitution to the Somali parliament and the cabinet for scrutiny. This was followed by a wider consultation process, with official launches in Galkayo, Galmudug, Garowe, Mogadishu and Puntland. However, by the end of the year minority communities remained largely unaware and excluded from the consultation process.

The '4.5' formula – designed to include minorities in political participation by allowing half a seat for all minorities for every four seats granted to members of the 'majority' clans – further limited the scope for the political participation of minorities in 2010. Although the exact size of the minority population in Somalia is unknown, population estimates are far greater than the proportion reflected in the 4.5

Right: Interior of a Bantu family home in Puntland, Somalia. *Petterik Wiggers/Panos.*

formula. And even with this system in place, the government is disproportionately dominated by members of 'majority' clans.

Having been postponed for two years, Somaliland's second presidential election took place on 26 June 2010, resulting in the victory of opposition candidate Ahmed Mohamud Silanyo. HRW reported that the election was 'reasonably free and fair' with the exception of one incident in the Sool region, where an individual was killed.

Large areas of both south-central Somalia and Puntland were affected by droughts in both early and late 2010. In March, the UN Security Council reported that over half of UN aid was not reaching civilians, due to it being diverted en route, although this was denied by the UN World Food Programme. According to news reports, al-Shabaab has banned more than 20 aid agencies from working in south-central Somalia. Taken in the context of Somalia's brutal and ongoing civil war, it is unsurprising that the UN Independent Expert on Somalia, Shamsul Bari, concluded from his visit that in 2010 that: 'Somalia continued to slide deeper and deeper into humanitarian crisis'.

South-central Somalia
South-central Somalia is populated by a number of different minority groups, who face considerable discrimination. These include Bantu, Benadiri and Bajuni fishing people. All these minority groups are diminishing in size, as thousands move to camps for internally displaced people's (IDPs) camps in Somaliland and Puntland and refugee camps in Kenya, where they face renewed discrimination.

Victims of multiple discrimination, minority women across south-central Somalia encounter barriers in every aspect of life, including access to education, health care and employment. One Bantu woman living in south-central Somalia told MRG:

'Ethnic minority women don't play a significant role on the social, [economic] and political platforms in mainstream communities. Most are illiterate and have no capability to improve their quality of livelihoods; most do household chores and other domestic errands mainly in the major clans' homes. Due to high poverty [levels] and discrimination against ethnic minority

women, they do not have access to quality health care as compared to women from major clans who usurp all relief or other medical facilities.'

Fighting between militant Islamist groups and the TFG's forces, the African Union Mission for Somalia (AMISOM), gave rise to gross human rights violations and discrimination in Mogadishu in 2010. The UN High Commissioner for Refugees (UNHCR) reported an average of at least 20 weapon-related casualties per day in Mogadishu, with intensified fighting during Ramadan, marking 2010 as the worst year for fighting in over a decade.

The version of Shari'a law that al-Shabaab enforces severely breaches international standards and includes a number of 'morality laws', such as dress codes for women, the systematic closure of cinemas, and bans on smoking, *khat*, music, television and sport. Both Amnesty International and HRW reported that girls in Mogadishu and other al-Shabaab-controlled regions, as well as in IDP camps and refugee camps in Kenya, were being forced to cook and clean for al-Shabaab soldiers, and were also forced to marry them in some instances. MRG and Al Arabiya also reported that al-Shabaab conscripted Bantu and Madhiban children into their militia.

Several minority groups, including Bantu, Benadiri and Christians, have been targeted by al-Shabaab for practising their own religions. MRG's 2010 report on Somalia revealed that Bantu women have been forced to wear the hijab, and that some have faced attacks from al-Shabaab members. In January, Compass Direct News (CDN) reported the murder of Christian community leader Mohammed Ahmed Ali, whose wife was subsequently forced to flee the country following death threats. CDN also reported the murder of 17-year-old Christian convert Nurta Farah in the Galgadud region. The teenager was shot dead after fleeing her family, who had beaten her and shackled her to a tree when they discovered she had converted from Islam to Christianity.

A 2010 HRW report also revealed severe restrictions placed upon women by al-Shabaab, including the continued obligation to wear the abaya, a garment supplied by al-Shabaab, which covers the entire body. Due to its expense, families can often only afford one per household, which in turn limits freedom of movement, as only one woman can leave the house at a time.

As in Somaliland and Puntland, minority women experience sexual violence in IDP camps in south-central Somalia. In one camp, three to five cases of rape were being reported every one to two weeks. However the actual number is likely to be higher, as many women do not report attacks due to stigma and fear.

Somaliland

Despite the relative success of the 2010 Somaliland election, tensions remain high in the Sool, Sanag and Cayn regions claimed by both Somaliland and Puntland administrations. June 2010 saw increasing tension between clans and competition over resources, leading to the displacement of thousands of civilians from these regions.

The maltreatment of minorities in Somaliland remains a significant problem. Somaliland's Gaboye minority held protests in Burao, Somaliland and London, UK in 2010, in order to 'raise awareness [of] the continual suffering of Somaliland, and the minority tribes in Somalia'. In particular, the protests focused on the unwarranted detention and abuse of two Gaboye men and a Gaboye woman in the Aynabo district of Somaliland. According to the protesters, Gaboye lack legal representation and access to justice, and also face violence in the Somaliland courts. Most notably, the Gaboye Minority Organization Europe highlighted an incident involving the abuse and kidnapping of two Gaboye women during a trial, in the presence of a judge and police officers.

In a July 2010 article published by the African Press International, Gaboye clan elder Ahmed Shide Jama identified some of the problems facing Gaboye, including discrimination in the labour market, and lack of political representation and access to healthcare. Moreover, he identified inter-marriage between clans as something treated as a problem, 'despite the fact that [Gaboye] are Somalis and Muslims' as well.

Puntland

According to the United Nations Development Programme (UNDP), Puntland is home to about 35,000 IDPs, many of whom belong to minorities from south-central Somalia, displaced by civil war. These minorities face further and renewed discrimination in IDP camps. A UN database cites '409 incidents of rape, attempted rape/sexual

Five years on: the Protocol on the Rights of Women in Africa

On 25 November 2010 it was five years since the Protocol to the African Charter on Human and Peoples' Rights on the Rights of Women in Africa (hereafter the Protocol) entered into force. The Protocol has been ratified by 29 out of 53 AU member states. Of the countries covered in this edition of *State of the World's Minorities and Indigenous Peoples*, only Democratic Republic of Congo, Kenya, Mauritania, Nigeria, Rwanda, South Africa, Uganda, and Zimbabwe have signed and ratified the Protocol.

Drawn up with the close involvement of women's rights activists from across the region, the Protocol essentially supplements the non-discrimination and equality clauses (Articles 2 and 18) of the principal human rights treaty in Africa – the African Charter on Human and Peoples' Rights – by elaborating norms and standards that are crucial for the protection and promotion of women's rights on the continent. The Protocol also seeks inspiration from international standards and instruments such as the International Covenant on Civil and Political Rights (ICCPR), the International Covenant on Economic Social and Cultural Rights (ICESCR), the Convention on the Elimination of All Forms of Discrimination Against Women (CEDAW) and UN Security Council Resolution 1325 (2000).

The Protocol codifies important international standards relating to the protection of women's rights, including but not limited to: non-discrimination; dignity; life, integrity and security of the person; elimination of harmful practices; marriage, divorce and inheritance; rights of widows; access to justice and equal protection before the law; right to peace; participation in political activity and decision making; economic and social welfare; health and reproductive rights; and sustainable development. Article 24 specifically refers to protection of women from 'marginalized population groups'.

In addition, Articles 2(2) and 5 prohibit harmful traditional cultural practices (such as female genital mutilation – FGM). Article 6 prescribes a minimum age for marriage (18 years). Given the prevalence of FGM and early marriage among some minority and indigenous communities in the region, the Protocol thus has the potential to function as a vital advocacy tool for minority and indigenous women (and men) wishing to challenge such practices within their communities.

The Protocol also seeks to give women a central role in the promotion and maintenance of peace and protection from armed conflicts (Articles 10 and 11). Again, given the prevalence of armed conflict in many of the areas where minority and indigenous groups live, these clauses also have the potential to enable minority and indigenous women to press for protection and a role in conflict resolution.

Another provision that is of significant importance to minority and indigenous women is Article 18(2)(c), which seeks to protect and enable the development of indigenous knowledge systems. In addition, the continued economic and social marginalization of minorities and indigenous peoples could be reversed and redressed in Africa if state parties complied with the Protocol to guarantee minority and indigenous women the right to education and training, socio-economic rights, health and reproductive rights, the right to food security, the right to adequate housing, the right to a healthy and sustainable environment, and the right to a sustainable development.

The Protocol thus provides a comprehensive framework for the protection of women's rights in Africa, but what difference has its coming into force made to the realization of these rights? This question is even more pertinent for women from minority and indigenous communities in Africa, who face even greater and almost insurmountable challenges – poverty, inadequate resources, illiteracy, and living in inaccessible and remote locations – in employing domestic legal standards and norms for their human rights protection, let alone regional and international standards.

First of all, states ratifying the Protocol are able to list reservations, some of which dilute the enjoyment of the rights enunciated in the Protocol. To date, none of the countries party to the Protocol included in *State of the World's Minorities and Indigenous Peoples 2011* has listed reservations, with the exception of South Africa (the reservations relate to South African law being *more* progressive than certain provisions in the Protocol relating to marriage, the death penalty and nationality).

Further, it is important to note that, without incorporation of the Protocol's clauses into national law, its application remains fraught with numerous challenges. Principal among these is that, at present, implementation of the Protocol effectively relies on the will of individual progressive and judicial activist judges (who may not always be easy to come by). This means that while some judges may choose to draw on the Protocol, overall there is inadequate and inconsistent interpretation and enforcement of the Protocol's standards at the national level. For instance, Zambia has yet to incorporate the Protocol, but it was invoked in a 2006 case by Judge Philip Musonda, with the effect of advancing domestic jurisprudence on eradicating sexual violence against women,

whether the violence takes place in public or private. The case involved the rape of a 13-year-old girl by her teacher in his house (*R.M. v. Edward Hakasenke, Attorney-General* (2006) HP 0327 (Zambia)). In his judgment, the High Court Judge invoked and cited at length the Protocol and found the state in breach of its duty to protect the girl, called on the state to arrest and prosecute the accused, and awarded damages to the girl. He also called on the Ministry of Education to put into place guidelines to protect girls from sexual abuse in schools.

In addition to its championing by individual judges, the Protocol has also been employed by women's rights activists across the continent to develop campaigns to lobby for legal reforms pertinent to the protection of women rights. In the Gambia, the Protocol was the key reference tool in the drafting of the Women's Act, as was the case in Mozambique during the drafting of the Domestic Violence Act. The Protocol has also been employed by activists to lobby against FGM in Tanzania, where it affects minority and indigenous women.

All in all, although five years is not a long time to measure the impact of an international instrument at national level, there is no doubt that, in the short period since its coming into force, the Protocol has stirred progress in Africa with respect to the protection of the rights of women. Of course, much remains to be done, especially for minority and indigenous women. Beyond a drive towards continent-wide ratification of the instrument by the remaining 24 states, what is most important is practical implementation of the Protocol to ensure that women in Africa, including those from minority and indigenous communities, truly realize and enjoy their fundamental rights. ■

assault, forced prostitution and domestic violence' between January and June 2010, with much of this sexual violence occurring in IDP settlements. The women who experience sexual violence in these camps 'are generally of minority clan origin, bereft of clan protection and often forced to engage in risky coping mechanisms', according to UN Independent Expert Bari. A Somali researcher who interviewed women in the Puntland camps for MRG reiterated the dangers facing minority women: '[M]inority women said they seemed to be more vulnerable because there will be no revenge for [sexual violence], or there will be no justice at the end.' Indeed, the researcher suggested that these women are seen as 'easy prey'. As a result, there is a demand for a more robust legal system 'that is accessible to women of all groups' and that recognizes the specific needs of minority women and girls. This is particularly important considering that most cases go undocumented, either because minority women's rights are often neglected by the legal system or because of the stigma associated with sexual violence.

Human trafficking remains a serious issue for IDPs in Somalia. The International Organization for Migration (IOM) emphasizes the susceptibility of IDPs and other vulnerable groups to trafficking, with the Middle East, Sudan and South Africa identified as some of the destinations for human trafficking.

Sudan

The indictment of President Omar al-Bashir in 2009 by the ICC continued to raise uproar among his political supporters, just as it garnered support from victims of his alleged crimes in Darfur. Many of these victims are members of minority groups, including women who have endured rape, sexual violence and displacement. Although a ceasefire held for much of 2010 between the rebels and the government forces in Darfur – while peace negotiations and discussions were ongoing in Doha and elsewhere – sporadic incidents of violence continued, leading to loss of lives and destruction of property.

The April 2010 general elections did not help much. These were won by the ruling National Congress Party (NCP) of Omar al-Bashir, but were boycotted by the main opposition parties and judged by international observers as falling short of international standards. One of the main

international election observers – the Carter Centre – observed that:

'the continuing state of emergency, repression of civil liberties, and ongoing conflict in Darfur did not permit an environment conducive to acceptable elections. Given the limited participation of internally displaced persons (IDPs) in Darfur in the census and voter registration, much of the population was left out of the process.'

Attention was also focused during the reporting period on the upcoming South Sudan referendum, one of the provisions in the 2005 Comprehensive Peace Agreement, which took place in January 2011. The CPA had also envisaged a separate but concurrent referendum for the residents of Abyei – an oil-rich special administrative region – to determine if its residents would elect to join the North or South in case of secession in the January referendum. However, unresolved border issues and residency criteria of who qualifies to vote in that particular referendum led to an indefinite postponement. The decision prompted attendant rising tensions and violent clashes among the residents that are still ongoing and have claimed lives. This includes disputes between Misseriya pastoralists, who are nomadic and seasonally cross into Abyei to graze their animals, and Ngok Dinka, who are the settled inhabitants of the region. It is feared that unless a comprehensive and amicable resolution of the outstanding issues is found, these clashes could escalate into a wider civil conflict. Experts suggest that to avoid this and address the Abyei question would entail granting full grazing rights for Misseriya herders if Abyei does join the South, an open and flexible approach to citizenship by both Khartoum and Juba, that allows for citizenship for Southerners who are established residents in the North (and vice versa), resources invested in citizen-led mediation mechanisms in case of tensions between Misseriya and Ngok Dinka, and a fair and transparent process for a referendum in Abyei, with international observers.

At the time of writing this report, the South had suspended post-referendum talks with Khartoum, accusing President Bashir of plotting to overthrow the new government ahead of the region's secession. According to Pagan Amum Okiech, the Secretary-General of the Sudan People's Liberation Movement, that decision followed reports alleging that 'the ruling National Congress Party (NCP) of Sudan was recruiting, arming, financing and deploying militias in South Sudan with the aim of destabilizing the South'. Reports in March 2011 indicated that the escalation of fighting between the Sudan People's Liberation Army and rebel groups had left more than 100 dead since the referendum, with Fangal, in Jonglei and Malakal, the capital of Sudan's Upper Nile state, all particularly badly affected.

The South Sudan referendum concluded peacefully in favour of secession, and heralded the 54th independent state in Africa (expected to be declared officially in July 2011). But there is concern that the tenfold surge in population in Juba (the capital of the South) in anticipation of better prospects that occurred over the course of 2010 is already stretching available resources to the limit. The long period of civil war in Sudan and the inequitable distribution of resources by the North to the South mean that infrastructure is inadequate for rapid economic development in the South, and the new state will have to start from scratch. The sudden increase in population is also impacting on levels of gender-based violence. A 2010 report by the Humanitarian Policy Group entitled *Gender, Violence and Survival in Juba, Southern Sudan* reveals that urbanization and people's experiences during the displacement have led to changed gender roles and challenges, leading to increased domestic and sexual violence. The UN news agency IRIN also observed that 'if there is one group that faces special challenges in Southern Sudan, it is women. Principal among them is gender-based violence, which is under-reported and spreading given the long history of conflict, certain traditional practices and weak judicial systems'.

Southern Africa

Rahnuma Hassan

Across Southern Africa, the indigenous peoples known as Khoisan, San, Basarwa or Bushmen continue to face discrimination. Driven to the margins of society, their struggle to retain their culture and use of their traditional land has had a huge negative impact on their well-being. In 2010, the most prominent of these struggles for land rights took place between the Botswana government and G/wi and G//ana communities living in the Central Kalahari Game Reserve (CKGR). In Namibia, Khwe people also expressed their concern over the establishment of a 10,000 hectare farm in the Bwabwata National Park. The proposed site covers a forested area which is home to many plants that are important for tribal livelihoods; any clearing of the area will have a negative impact on the community. Khwe consider the land to be theirs, but were not consulted when the decision to build the farm was made. Instead, permission to use the land was granted by the Hambukushu Chief, who technically represents the Khwe community, since the community's own traditional leaders are not recognized by Namibian law. This dispute highlights the need for Khwe people to have their traditional leaders recognized under the Traditional Authorities Act 25 of 2000. In May 2010, in protest against government actions, Khwe community members boycotted a meeting called by the Hambukushu Traditional Authority.

Although more research is required on the lives of women from San communities, a 2001 study entitled 'A Gender Perspective on the Status of the San in Southern Africa' provides some insight into how the lives of San women have been negatively affected by continuous marginalization. The study notes how the status of San women has changed over time, from being considered equals to being regarded as inferior to men. Suggested reasons for these changes include: 'sedentarization following wide-scale loss of land, the shift to pastoralism and waged labour', as well as the 'influence of male-dominated neighbouring communities'.

In Zimbabwe, political unrest has continued to affect civil society as violence becomes more commonplace and tensions still run high. There were also reports of tensions among minority religious groups.

Across the region, gender-based violence remained a pervasive problem, particularly for women from minority and other marginalized communities. In addition, both minority and majority women continue to be affected by the dual legal systems operating in many countries, whereby both civil/common law and customary law are recognized. Customary law in Southern Africa tends to reflect the patriarchal attitudes of society more explicitly than common law, and puts women at a socio-political and economic disadvantage. Codified customary law may also often reflect the customs of the dominant ethnic group, meaning that women belonging to minority groups are denied rights that they are entitled to under their group's customary laws.

Botswana

The year 2010 saw a continuation of the tensions between G/wi and G//ana communities of the Basarwa indigenous group and Botswana's government regarding G/wi and G//ana's rights to land inside the Central Kalahari Game Reserve (CKGR). Despite having been granted the right to occupy land within the CKGR as a result of a court ruling in 2006, the government has been slow to respond to the additional needs of the community.

Since their return to the CKGR, G/wi and G//ana community members have continued to suffer due to poor provision of social services within the reserve, including health services, with an adverse effect on women's access to reproductive health care. Due to the government's refusal to reopen the only borehole within the CKGR, the community has struggled to secure access to water sources. Community members have to leave the reserve and travel 300 km in order to fetch water for their homes. In addition to the dispute regarding the borehole, Survival International reported that wildlife scouts had told family members of the community that using donkeys to transport water into the park is not permitted. This increases the difficulty of bringing water into the reserve further, as the Basarwa community do not have access to vehicles and are dependent on donkeys for transport.

James Anaya, the United Nations (UN) Special Rapporteur on the situation of human rights and fundamental freedoms of indigenous people, expressed concern over the treatment of the Basarwa indigenous group by Botswana's government, in a report released in February 2010. The report stated that although the government, 'may or may not be following the order of the Court in the Sesana case in a technical sense', its behaviour was neither congruent 'with the spirit and underlying logic of the decision, nor with the relevant international human rights standards'.

At the beginning of June 2010, a court heard an appeal made by the G/wi and G//ana community regarding their access to the borehole in the CKGR. More than a month later, on 21 July 2010, the court announced that it had ruled against the appeal. Human rights activists around the globe decried the decisions made by the government and another appeal was submitted in September 2010. In January 2011, the appeal court overruled the previous judgment, finally allowing the G/wi and G//ana community access to the water borehole.

In regard to women's rights, Botswana has made progress in establishing gender equality over the past years with laws such as the 2004 Abolition of Marital Powers Act, which establishes 'equal control of marriage estates and equal custody of children, [removing] restrictive domicile rules, and [setting] the minimum marriage age at 18.' However, despite theoretical commitment to gender equality, some laws continue to discriminate against women (such as the failure to recognize rape within marriage), and social pressure prevents women from speaking out about gender-based violence, or leaving abusive partners.

In February 2010, in its Concluding Observations on Botswana, the UN Committee on the Elimination of Discrimination against Women (CEDAW committee) expressed concern over the continued violations of women's rights due to the coexistence of customary law and common law. While common law recognizes and protects the rights of women in regard to marriage and property rights, customary law is deeply patriarchal and women's rights are often forsaken for the rights of men. For instance, under customary law, women are considered to be minors. This has particular relevance to women from minority ethnic groups, because customary law as recognized in Botswana reflects the patriarchal practices of the majority ethnic group, the Tswana. Therefore, the specific cultural rights to which minority women are entitled are not expressed in either of Botswana's legal systems, leaving them unprotected from violations against their human rights. For instance, the practices of matrilineal minority groups such as the Wayeyi are not recognized. A case lodged in 2006 with the African Commission for Human and People's Rights (ACHPR) in relation to this issue is still pending.

In late 2010, it was reported that the Paramount

Chief of the Bakgatla (one of the eight major Tswana tribes in Botswana), Kgosi Kgolo Kgafela II, had mobilized Bakgatla against the government and was demanding constitutional reform. They claimed that the current Constitution, with its colonial roots, did not reflect the culture and values of the people and thus should be changed accordingly. It is unclear how this situation will develop, but if the Constitution is changed, it could have serious implications for the rights of non-Tswana groups as well as the rights of women.

In September 2010, it was announced that the government passed an amendment to its Employment Act that will make the dismissal of employees due to their sexual orientation or HIV status illegal. This is significant as homosexuality is criminalized, and 24.8 per cent of 15–49-year-olds are HIV positive in Botswana. The response from civil society organizations was positive yet muted, as many felt that an amendment was not enough to end discrimination in the workplace against those who are HIV positive.

South Africa

Although women's rights are enshrined in the South African Constitution, women continue to suffer from mistreatment as patriarchal attitudes prevail within the dominant culture. Women are more likely to experience unemployment than men, to have lower levels of education, and to experience violence. Women living in rural communities that follow customary law can be particularly vulnerable to discrimination, as some traditional practices undermine the rights women have under civil law.

A recent study by Community Agency for Social Enquiry (CASE) on women and their access to land ownership shows that even though women's rights are increasingly recognized, conservative attitudes continue to form a barrier to women in accessing land. Of the three areas studied, the municipality of Msinga in KwaZulu-Natal, reputedly a stronghold of Zulu culture and tradition, was found to have the most conservative attitudes towards women and land ownership. Zulu women in Msinga continue to have to rely on male members of their family to access land, as traditions dictate that women can only inherit land through their husbands or in-laws, or through the eldest male child. In the case of polygamous marriages, only the first wife has a right to inherit her deceased husband's land, unless he has

made specific arrangements indicating otherwise. To protect widows from potential landlessness, it is customary for men to marry their brother's widow. However, this often does not happen, and women can be chased away from their homes by their in-laws upon the death of their spouse.

In contrast to women who are affected by traditional customs, Muslim women face discrimination because Islamic marriages are not legally recognized in South Africa. The 2010 case of a Muslim woman in Cape Town, represented by the Women's Legal Centre (WLC), highlights the consequences of such discrimination. The client asked for and was awarded 50 per cent ownership of a property she had previously shared with her ex-husband, on the grounds that, at the time, she had not been allowed to purchase the property jointly because she was not married to her husband under civil law. As a result, the sole ownership rights were transferred to her spouse upon their divorce. Although the Cape Town Housing Policy has now been changed, those in living arrangements agreed upon before the change in policy are still vulnerable to its discriminatory effects.

In February 2010, the Muslim Marriage Bill came under discussion. The aim of the bill is to uphold and protect the constitutional rights of individuals, while respecting the religious significance of marrying under Islamic law for South African Muslims. If passed, the bill would address issues such as the lack of protection available to women married under Islamic law, who subsequently divorce or become widowed. At the beginning of 2011, the draft of the Muslim Marriage Bill was approved by the cabinet and put forward for discussion in parliament.

Gender-based violence is part of the reality for many South African women. For women who are marginalized by mainstream society, this is of particular concern, as violence towards them may be more easily accepted, making support less readily available. In the case of 'corrective' rape, lesbian women (or women assumed to be lesbian) are targeted by heterosexual men who rape them in an attempt to 'change their sexuality'. This practice received global attention in 2010 when members of the lesbian, gay, bisexual and transgender (LGBT) community in South Africa launched a worldwide petition demanding that 'corrective' rape be listed as a hate crime in South Africa, and that the harshest

Reed dances and virginity tests: balancing cultural rights and women's rights in South Africa

The traditional Zulu reed dance, uMkhosi WoMhlanga, drew international press coverage in 2010, when South African President Jacob Zuma attended the ceremony as a guest. The reed dance is the culmination of an annual ritual of virginity testing, where young Zulu women submit to an inspection of their virginity (usually undertaken by an older female member of the community). Once their virginity has been ascertained, they are permitted to participate in the reed dance, a ceremony where thousands of young women perform in front of the Zulu king and present him with reeds as a symbol of their chastity. The ceremony has gained popularity as a tourist attraction over recent years and concern has been expressed over the event being targeted by pornography syndicates, as the participating women perform semi-clothed. During the 2010 reed dance, King Goodwill Zwelithini also expressed dismay over problems regarding 'rogue' virginity testers and photos of virginity testing being published online.

The tradition of virginity testing has been condemned by human rights and gender activists as a practice that polices the sexuality of young girls and women, and stigmatizes those who fail to comply with traditional notions of femininity. Additionally, the practice has been associated with spreading the belief that having sex with a virgin can cure HIV, which puts proclaimed virgins at great risk. Although supporters of the practice claim that encouraging chastity through virginity testing helps to curb HIV infection rates, critics have rejected this notion, highlighting how ultimately, the practice merely delays sexual activity and thereby the chance to become infected.

The issue of virginity testing in the Zulu community highlights the difficult balance governments often have to strike between respecting the cultural traditions of minority groups, while also ensuring that the civil rights of women in those groups are not violated by discriminatory practices. In the case of the South African government, the conclusion was reached that the practice of virginity testing harmed women and so it was outlawed in 2005. However, supporters of the practice have largely ignored the ban and continue to perform virginity tests.

The Commission for Gender Equality in South Africa sums it up best by stating:

'Religious, cultural and traditional practices have every right of expression, but within a human rights framework and without minimizing any other values as expressed in the Constitution. Therefore, when these practices are patriarchal, misogynist and/ or discriminatory, this cannot be allowed with the State's consent.' ∎

sentences be made applicable for perpetrators. But during the same period, concerns regarding the humiliating and violent sexual assaults faced by migrants crossing the border from Zimbabwe into South Africa at the hands of armed men and women, known as *magumaguma*, were overshadowed by the FIFA World Cup, held in June and July of 2010.

Zimbabwe

Despite hopes that the formation of the 2009 coalition government would lead to political stability and constitutional reform, Zimbabwe continued to be affected by political turmoil throughout 2010.

In April 2010, Human Rights Watch (HRW) published a report detailing the 'illusion of reform' in Zimbabwe. The organization expressed concerns over the continued 'lack [of] both political freedom and accurate, non-partisan information about the state of the country and the activities of government'.

In the past, political affiliation was largely determined by ethnicity, as ZANU-PF, President Robert Mugabe's political party historically represented the interests of the Shona majority ethnic group. Due to the gross mistreatment of Ndebele in the past by Mugabe and the ZANU-

PF, the Ndebele minority group was represented by political parties like the now defunct ZAPU party. Although the relationship between political affiliation and ethnicity is no longer as overt, tensions between the two ethnic groups remain. It is difficult, though, to separate violence that occurs along ethnic lines from violence that occurs along political lines.

In the months leading up to the World Cup (that began in July 2010), civil society groups expressed outrage at the government's decision to let the Democratic People's Republic of Korea (North Korea) football team train in Zimbabwe. North Korea was involved in the training of the Fifth Brigade, a group responsible for killing over 20,000 Ndebele during the 1980s. The action showed a great insensitivity of the government towards Ndebele concerns; however, the tourism minister maintained that this was a sporting, not a political matter. In May 2010, it was announced that the North Korean team had cancelled their scheduled stay in Zimbabwe.

In December 2010, a new party was launched, the Mthwakazi Liberation Front. The party has been identified as an Ndebele nationalist party, and seeks to represent the region of Matabeleland, the Ndebele home region. It is unclear if they will be participating in the forthcoming elections announced for 2011.

A 2010 report on international religious freedom published by the US Department of State showed a continuation of violence against Anglicans. Anglicans were arrested, harassed and denied access to their church buildings throughout the year. In May 2010, more than 2,000 Anglicans were barred by the police from attending a special service for Pentecost in the main cathedral in Harare. The report also mentions rising tensions between African Independent/Initiated Churches (AIS) members and Anglicans, due to religious practices such as polygamy. The relationship between the AIS community and Anglicans became particularly strained in Chipinge, a community near the border with Mozambique, as the exacerbation of a measles outbreak was blamed on the AIS community for not vaccinating their children. A health official interviewed by the UN news agency IRIN confided that the government was working on regulations to make it an offence for parents to deny their children vaccinations against 'killer' diseases.

In 2010, a South African court ruled unlawful the violent land grabs that had occurred in Zimbabwe against white minority farmers. The papers to a house owned by the Zimbabwean government in Cape Town were given to the plaintiffs as compensation. Although any money received from the sale of the house will go towards legal fees, the ruling creates a precedent for farmers who lost property in Zimbabwe to file for compensation in South African courts.

Like Botswana, Zimbabwe has a dual legal system, supporting both common and customary law. Although common law protects the rights of women in some respects, gender equality is undermined by customary law. Forced and early marriages under customary law are common, women are considered to be minors, widows are not allowed to inherit property from their husbands, and daughters are only allowed to inherit property from their fathers if there are no sons. Additionally, the custom of the bride price, also known as *lobola* or *bogadi*, is protected by common law and continues to stigmatize women.

Political instability has had a negative impact on the well-being of women in Zimbabwe. Violence against women, particularly rape, is a common tool used to intimidate women who support political opposition groups. Women in rural areas are also particularly vulnerable. Violence is predicted to escalate in 2011 if the proposed elections go ahead; such political unrest will continue to put those who oppose Robert Mugabe's rule at risk. ■

Americas

Maurice Bryan

Stretching from Alaska in the north, through Central America and the Caribbean Basin, to Tierra del Fuego to the south, the immense and diverse Americas region contains countries with large, ethnically diverse populations, made up of immigrants from European, Asia-Pacific and Middle Eastern countries, as well as tens of millions of indigenous and African descendant people. In some Central and South American states, indigenous peoples and African descendant populations constitute more than 40 per cent of the national total.

Of these groups, African descendants and indigenous peoples remained the most marginalized and disadvantaged, and are particularly vulnerable to human rights abuses. In 2010, their main concerns continued to be daily societal and institutional discrimination, poverty, resource and land seizures, socio-economic exclusion, limited political participation, and inadequate access to social services such as health and education.

Many of these patterns of marginalization can be traced to social and economic structures established at the very beginning of the colonial era in the Americas. Their ongoing influence constrains current attempts to effect real and lasting social and economic change, including meeting the Millennium Development Goals (MDGs) by 2015. And as has been the case for more than 500 years, it is African descendant and indigenous women who face particular hardship, and limited opportunities for civic, economic and political participation, as a result of ethnicity and gender-based discrimination.

Economics
During 2010, the unstable state of the region's economies continued to have a direct and indirect impact on indigenous and African descendant populations, partly determined by the degree to which the respective groups were integrated into their countries' economic life.

In the United States (US), Native American-owned timber firms (which make up a third of all Native American-owned businesses) were amongst those hardest hit by the crisis in the housing market, and tribes with lucrative gaming casinos have also seen a decline in revenue. But elsewhere, indigenous First Nation-owned corporations in Canada reported increasing profits, and South American countries with large indigenous and African descendant populations have been managing to weather the economic downturn (although not necessarily to the benefit of already marginalized groups).

In Central and South America, remittances sent home from migrants in the industrialized economies of Europe and North America remained an important source of income for indigenous and African descendant communities. While still not regaining pre-economic crisis levels, these remittances did not slip any lower, and service sectors such as international tourism, which employ many indigenous women and those of African descent, began to show small gains. Nevertheless, rising food prices were an increasing concern in most of the region.

Social insecurity
Continuing economic uncertainty, limited opportunities and consistent lack of social investment helped to fuel increases in violence and crime, and the expansion of criminal youth gang activities in some Latin American countries. While this did not have an immediate impact on the majority of rural-dwelling indigenous peoples and African descendants, the ongoing social threat to their communities remained real, especially given the influence and speed of contemporary global communication. More directly, the continuing state of public insecurity has become one of the greatest impediments to achieving the MDGs for these groups, as the social and economic development concerns of indigenous peoples and African descendant populations now stand even less of a chance of becoming national priority issues. With citizen safety having become the main focus of daily public and official discourse, larger amounts of already scarce national resources continued to be diverted away from social investment, in order to strengthen police, army and other internal state security structures.

Central American gangs – whose in-country memberships alone run into the tens of thousands and include equally violent female participants – function largely with impunity, and are increasingly capable of effectively challenging state authority.

Along with youth gangs, other major sources of violence include powerful drug cartels and various forms of organized crime, as well as assassination squads made up of retired and active duty members of the police and military. According to Mexico's National Human Rights Commission, the problem of criminal gangs in Central America extends up to the northern border with the US. In addition to cross-border arms smuggling and drug trafficking, Central American Maras and Mexican Zetas kidnap, extort, rob, rape and even murder economic migrants on their way to the US. These include indigenous arrivals in transit from as far south as Bolivia and Ecuador.

In Central America, governments are battling to find ways to deal with the situation. A 2008 study found that zero tolerance laws and repressive tactics – such as those adopted unsuccessfully in El Salvador and Honduras – have actually served to fuel gang activities. With diminishing access to other income-earning opportunities, thousands of gang members now provide an abundant and lethal labour pool for drug trafficking mafias and other organized crime groups; for example, as collectors of 'protection' payments from local residents, shopkeepers and bus drivers. Elsewhere, the Central American Coalition for the Prevention of Youth Violence points out that these laws are ineffective because they do not address the root causes of the problem, namely: poverty, discrimination, and lack of employment opportunities, education and health care. Consequently, government actions such as raising incarceration rates are often merely politically motivated responses to growing pressure and criticism from an increasingly tense and fearful public.

Elsewhere in the region, gang violence and criminality has not developed – or been addressed – in the same way. In South American countries like Brazil and Venezuela, the local youth gangs have not turned into crime rings like their Central American counterparts. In Quito, the capital of Ecuador, young migrants from indigenous rural zones have formed urban subcultures that include indigenous gangs and an indigenous music scene. Indigenous community leaders have been attempting to counter instances of violent criminal activity among rural indigenous youth by imposing traditional measures of penance (discussed in greater detail below). In North America as well, tribal nation leaders continued to be concerned about high crime rates on US Native American reservations. During 2010, US President Barack Obama signed into effect a new Tribal Law and Order Act, intended to help Native American communities combat crime and violence and provide leaders with greater authority to prosecute and punish offenders in their areas.

The high numbers of indigenous youth who are sent to prison was one of the themes discussed at the 9th Session of the United Nations (UN) Permanent Forum on Indigenous Issues in 2010. According to a UN Habitat report, although First Nations make up only 5 per cent of the total youth population in Canada, in some provinces they account for 34 per cent of all male and 41 per cent of all female young offenders. As IPS news agency reported, Max Maciel, coordinator of Central Única das Favelas (a movement of young slum-dwellers) in Brasilia, has advised that instead of trying to quash gangs and criminalize young people, state authorities should find ways to develop the positive qualities of many of the young people, such as their leadership abilities, and develop initiatives which will allow ethno-cultural self expression and provide tools to enable them to enter the workforce.

Environment

In addition to social and economic challenges, the Americas region also had to deal with the effects of unprecedented weather patterns. Floods and droughts in Brazil, Colombia, Guatemala, Honduras and Venezuela brought destruction to rural and urban areas and often had a direct impact on indigenous and African descendant communities, which tend to be located in marginal areas.

Gender and ethnicity were major factors in determining who was badly affected by these natural disasters. Across the region, significant numbers of poor indigenous and African descendant women are self-employed in farming or informal sector food preparation and sales, and are primarily responsible for looking after children. Natural disasters that destroy food crops and homes thus have a disproportionate effect on women from these groups, which is compounded by national shortages leading to rises in food prices. In addition, indigenous and African descendant women faced discrimination during relief efforts, when their already marginalized communities were often the last to be served – if at all. For instance, following the 2010 Chilean earthquake, indigenous Mapuche resorted to using internet sites to complain about discrimination and the absence of aid and relief efforts in their communities from the Chilean government.

Above: Bolivian indigenous women attend the World People's Conference on Climate Change and the Rights of Mother Earth in Tiquipaya, on the outskirts of Cochabamba, April 2010. *David Mercado/Reuters.*

The overall reduction in subsistence agricultural productivity, crop losses, poor economic opportunities, destructive weather patterns and increasing strains on the social fabric, when coupled with the ongoing denial of rights, meant that during 2010 the overall picture for indigenous peoples and African descendant populations in the Americas remained essentially one of socio-economic stagnation.

Politics
The political arena, however, continued to see minor gains for African descendants and indigenous peoples, in regard to representation in parliaments and inclusion of their ethnic categories in more representative national census counts. At the end of 2010, Mexico was the only major country in Latin America that had still not taken steps to include an African descendant identifying category in its national census. However, region-wide efforts at greater inclusion did not translate into any significant new gains for indigenous and African descendant women, especially in formal politics. In addition, full-term and mid-term elections in a number of states in the

Americas during 2010 saw a resurgence of centre-right coalitions, which may bring a halt to moves that have been made to address indigenous and minority concerns in some countries.

International Year for People of African Descent
In March 2010, the UN designated 2011 as 'International Year for People of African Descent'. Activists hope that this will afford an opportunity to focus on the conditions of African descendants. In response to the UN designation, the Organization of American States (OAS) pointed out that people of African descent are among the most vulnerable social groups in the region. Both the OAS and the Summits of the Americas Process have repeatedly expressed their concern with regard to the exclusion and human rights violations confronting African descendant communities.

African descendant activists point out that African descendants constitute a third of the overall regional population. Moreover, they have a distinct history, as well as proprietary traditions, beliefs and cultural patterns, and were present in the Americas long before any nation-state formation. Therefore, they argue that there needs to be recognition of African descendants as a special type of constituency, as the UN already does for groups such as women and indigenous peoples. In addition, African

Electoral processes, political participation and indigenous women in Latin America

In the past decade there has been a groundbreaking trend across Latin America towards electing women to political office. This began with the election of Michelle Bachelet as President of Chile in 2006; Bachelet went on to be appointed head of UN Women, the new UN Entity for Gender Equality and the Empowerment of Women, in 2010. Other notables include the current President of Argentina, Cristina Fernandez de Kirchner, as well as Presidents Laura Chinchilla of Costa Rica and Dilma Rousseff of Brazil, both of whom took office in 2010.

In the main, however, women still face marked discrimination in regional political life, rooted in social, economic, cultural and historical factors of human and institutional development. And the situation is even worse for African descendant and indigenous women.

Accurate data on the situation of indigenous and African descendant women in the Americas is limited. In most Latin American and Caribbean countries, the gender-disaggregated data that does exist relates to very broad general categories and is not disaggregated further to determine factors such as age or educational

levels. There is an even greater lack of disaggregated data pertaining to indigenous women and those of African descent, especially with respect to income levels, employment opportunities and positions in government. But the available information shows that in 2010, very few African descendant and indigenous women held significant positions in politics or public administration. According to the Network of Afro-Caribbean and Afro-Latino Women, there are at least 75 million black women in Latin America and the Caribbean; however those who occupy high-level political or public administration posts number less than 70.

Despite considerable obstacles, a small number of African descendant women have indeed managed to enter political life in Brazil, Colombia, Costa Rica, Honduras, Nicaragua and Panama. But the same is not true for indigenous women. Some countries such as Bolivia, Ecuador, Peru and Venezuela that have significant indigenous populations have made some space in Congress for a few indigenous women, but on the whole the situation remains poor. In Mexico for example, in 2007–8, there were only four indigenous female office-holders in local legislature in the entire country: one in the Congress of the State of Veracruz; two in the Congress of Oaxaca; and one in Puebla State.

At a presentation to the International Parliamentary Conference in Chiapas, Mexico, during the autumn of 2010, female Mexican Senator Ludivina Menchaca explained that while women in general face a patriarchal male-dominated political structure, indigenous women must also confront a 'mono-ethnic' political environment that historically has excluded any diversity.

Nevertheless, there have been some advances. According to the UN Department of Economic and Social Affairs *Report on the World's Women 2010*, seven countries in Central America and ten in South America have taken steps towards ensuring the inclusion of more women in political processes, using a combination of official and voluntary mechanisms. These include reserved places on

electoral lists, reserved seats in the legislature
and voluntary political party quotas, aimed at
including a certain percentage of women as
party-sponsored election candidates.

There are also small quotas for the inclusion
of indigenous and African descendant
representatives in parliaments. For instance,
following pressure from social activists in the
1970s, Colombia introduced ethnic quotas,
whereby indigenous peoples are allocated two
representatives in the Senate and one in the
House of Representatives. But in Colombia and
elsewhere, no special measures have been taken
to specifically ensure the participation of female
indigenous or African descendant candidates.
And unlike the high-profile Afro-Colombian
senator Piedad Cordoba, thus far no indigenous
woman has ever been elected as a senator in
that country.

In Nicaragua, following the recognition
of the autonomous regions, some indigenous
women have made it to the parliament. In
Ecuador, the participation of independent
movements in the electoral process alongside
traditional political parties in 1996 enabled four
seats to go to indigenous candidates; however,
none was female. In Mexico, there have been
some constitutional changes with respect to
involving women and indigenous peoples.
Nevertheless, at the federal level indigenous
people have to participate in the electoral
process as members of one of the traditional
political parties. These groupings generally
do not favour the inclusion of the indigenous
community, much less indigenous women. It
should be noted that in the 2008 election cycle,
of the 23 women who represent 18 per cent of
the total number of federal senators, none self-
identified as indigenous.

The ongoing lack of indigenous women in
political life in the region should not come
as a surprise. To begin with, in order to

become candidates for public office, indigenous
women must first confront a political culture that
in most instances pointedly favours mainstream
male candidates. Despite the fact that some
electoral systems have established quotas for female
candidates at between 30 and 40 per cent, female
activists in Latin American political circles claim
that mainstream political parties tend to give their
more difficult districts to women to contest. This
serves to limit their chances of success. Should they
win these difficult seats, female representatives then
have to struggle within the parliamentary structure
to have their opinions count, and to participate in
the commissions and committees that deal with
public administration matters.

In addition to challenges facing all women
candidates, prospective indigenous women

Above: Dilma Rousseff, president of Brazil with Cristina Fernández de Kirchner, president of Argentina during an official state visit by Rousseff to Buenos Aires. *Roberto Stuckert Filho/PR.*

candidates must also cope with a number of constraints peculiar to their historically marginalized constituencies. These include their own lack of access to educational opportunities; an educationally deprived and inadequately informed predominantly rural electorate; negative perceptions of indigenous candidate intellectual competence, both as women and as minorities; pressure to reject traditional clothing and language styles and to speak and dress in accordance with mainstream cultural norms; and existing machismo cultural attitudes among both

men and women in their own communities that do not encourage women to assume leadership roles. This means that if there is to be any positive change in this regard, it is first necessary to implement concrete measures to overcome the multiple forms of discrimination that indigenous and minority women experience in the political arena.

Women's rights activists in Mexico and across the region have called on state and federal congresses to publish data on the number of indigenous women active as members and in leadership positions in the various national political parties at regional, municipal and indigenous community levels. Mexican activists also want this information to be disaggregated by ethnic group, and to include details on the commissions, initiatives and legislative achievements of indigenous women leaders. They also call for current gender quotas to be raised to 50 per cent parity in the federal and local electoral codes, and for the establishment of indigenous quotas within the female quota itself.

In practical terms, this means that political parties in Mexico and across the region, as well as other institutions, would have to begin allocating funding to the training, political promotion and empowerment of female candidates, so that they stop being regarded as inexperienced beginners. This would include funding being directed to female political hopefuls who come from areas with large indigenous populations. Among other measures, activists argue that it would also require instituting indigenous women's forums to analyse what training indigenous women need to be able to stand as candidates, and to facilitate the integration of indigenous women into electoral councils and human rights commissions, especially in those countries with large indigenous populations such as Bolivia, Ecuador, Guatemala and Mexico. ▪

descendants in the Americas are often overlooked by being broadly categorized along with other minorities and/or as 'the poor'. However, the fact that in 2010 African descendants remain marginalized and invisible in real terms, and that 92 per cent of all African descendants in Latin America remain below the poverty threshold, continues to be cause for concern and to justify calls for more focus on this group. Finally, it is argued that poverty, marginality and exclusion of African descendants in their respective countries are not just standard socio-economic manifestations, but have very deep historical roots underpinning an ongoing denial of justice.

Reflecting this reality, during 2010, activists in countries such as Colombia, Nicaragua and Peru continued to insist that development programmes identify African descendant communities as a specific target category in regional development projects. They also advocated engaging in greater consultation during decision-making and project design processes, since such an approach would help overcome firmly entrenched institutionalized discrimination and marginalization.

Argentina

Argentina is a federal republic with a population of approximately 40.1 million. For the first time since the late nineteenth century, the 2010 census (conducted in October 2010) included questions to compile information on the number of African descendants in Argentina. The last census to count the black population in Argentina occurred in 1895. Since then, Argentines of African descent have remained statistically invisible, which activists claim has fuelled a myth that a significant Afro-Argentine population no longer exists. It also means there is no data available on the actual number or socio-economic conditions of Afro-Argentine women.

Although many Afro-Argentines no longer have the more obvious physical attributes stereotypically associated with African descent, and although some may even be reluctant to claim African ancestry, in 2010 rights organizations, such as Diafar, estimated that there were about 2 million people of African descent in the country. Along with Afro-Argentine descendants from the colonial period and Afro-descendant migrants from neighbouring countries such as Brazil and Uruguay, the Argentine black population in 2010 included post-war migrants

from the Cape Verde islands, and an ever-increasing number of – mostly male – political exiles and economic migrants from West and Central Africa.

The 2010 inclusion of census questions regarding the black population can be seen as a small victory for the predominantly female-led Argentine ethnic rights organizations, such as MRG partner Casa de la Cultura Indo-Afro Americana. These have fought in a persistent and sustained manner for over a decade to increase the visibility of African descendants.

The census was not without controversy. Rights activists charge that a number of African descendants and indigenous people who were trained to be census-takers during pilot trials were not actually used, contrary to agreements between rights organizations and the government's National Institute of Statistics and Censuses (INDEC). It also emerged that two types of questionnaires were deployed in 2010, a long and a short form. Only the long version included questions on 'Black' or 'Afro-descendant' and indigenous origins as one of the identifying categories. As Afro-Argentine activists discovered, this longer form was only applied to one in every ten households, meaning that within Argentina's highly diverse urban neighbourhoods, there was a high probability that census-takers would miss homes inhabited by African descendants and indigenous people, and once again leave them undifferentiated.

Disappointment among the Afro-Argentine community prompted concerns regarding the bureaucratic challenges Afro-Argentineans would eventually face at national, regional and local levels, as a result of inaccurate data generated by the census, and the resulting lack of statistical data relating to their demographic and socio-economic situation. They are particularly concerned that the data gap will continue to make it difficult to develop and implement appropriate policies and programmes to address the specific needs of their marginalized communities. In response, at the end of 2010, African descendant rights groups in Argentina began strengthening their efforts to develop rights monitoring and data compilation bodies of their own.

Brazil

Brazil is a federal republic with a population of approximately 192 million. The law requires that 30 per cent of the candidates registered by each political party must be women. In 2010, voters elected Dilma Rousseff of the left-wing Workers' Party (PT) to a four-year term, making her the first woman to be elected president in Brazil's history. Indications at the end of 2010 were that the new Rousseff government would have a greater female presence. The new cabinet includes nine women out of a total of 37 members, who will hold key positions, such as planning, social development and the environment. None of these women, however, are from indigenous or African descendant backgrounds.

Of greatest potential significance to indigenous and African descendant communities is that the female-led Planning Ministry will now have direct control over large public works projects in Brazil (this was previously the responsibility of the President's Chief of Staff), including municipal-level infrastructure projects in areas that they inhabit.

Indigenous concerns

Government estimates are that half of Brazil's indigenous people continue to live in poverty in communities whose traditional ways of life are threatened on a variety of fronts. These include land development, agricultural expansion and urbanization. In a country report published in 2009, James Anaya, UN Special Rapporteur on the rights of indigenous peoples, noted the absence of an effective mechanism for consultation with Brazil's indigenous peoples on the planning of major development projects, such as large-scale mining, and highway and dam construction. There was also inadequate attention to indigenous people's health care and educational needs.

One particularly controversial project is the massive Belo Monte Amazon rainforest hydroelectric dam on the Xingu River, an Amazon tributary. The US $17 billion dam in the northern state of Pará will be the world's third-largest after those in China's Three Gorges and the Itaipu on the Brazil–Paraguay border. It will require excavation of earth and rocks in the ecologically highly sensitive Amazon region on a scale similar to that of building the Panama Canal. The government argues that the dam will be vital to economic growth; however, critics counter that flooding 500 sq. km of rainforest will permanently kill trees, damage fish stocks and wildlife, and force the displacement of indigenous peoples (such as the Xinguano).

The Belo Monte dam project was actually started in the 1990s but abandoned amid widespread local and international protests. Within Brazil, the project's resurgence has triggered a huge outcry from a united front made up of indigenous peoples, scientists and the Movement of People Affected by Dams, which claims to represent 1 million people displaced from their land. The Environment Ministry indicated that the land to be flooded would be a fraction of the 5,000 sq. km originally planned and would not cause the displacement of indigenous peoples. However, this does not apply to indigenous communities inhabiting lands that are not demarcated as tribal territory. Residents still stand to lose their homes and complain that they were not properly consulted over the project.

Environmental rights groups from around the world have pointed out that promoting energy efficiency could cut demand by 40 per cent over the next decade, which would be the energy equivalent of several Belo Monte dams. Biologists have also warned that diverting part of the river to run the turbine generators will dry out a curve of the waterway called Volta Grande, whose riverbanks are inhabited by indigenous peoples and thousands of small farmers, who will see a massive reduction in fish, river turtles and other staple foods.

Countering these objections, Brazil's Ministry of Mines and Energy has projected that the country's electricity consumption will rise by 5.9 per cent annually until 2019, and determined that economically competitive hydroelectric supply will be the main source of power in the country. With two-thirds of Brazil's hydroelectric potential located in the Amazon jungle region, all indications are that hydroelectric plants will continue to be built there and that indigenous groups in the Amazon region will continue to see large expanses of water submerge their ancestral lands.

Rights of indigenous women

Brazil appears to be taking steps to develop mechanisms that will promote and protect the rights of indigenous women and ensure their inclusion in decision-making processes. For instance, the government's National Indian Foundation (FUNAI), which is responsible for indigenous affairs, has created a special new internal structure which is led by indigenous women and has a specific budget and mandate to develop a gender action plan.

In November 2010, a National Meeting of Indigenous Women for the Protection and Promotion of their Rights was held in the province of Mato Grosso and attended by 80 delegates. This was the culmination of a round of seminars organized across Brazil during 2010 by the Secretary of Policies for Women and FUNAI. All together, 457 indigenous women from different indigenous communities attended the preliminary seminars. Among the proposals advanced at the national meeting was an amendment to Draft Law No. 2057/91, which is pending in Brazil's House of Representatives and which aims to modify and revise the country's so-called Indian Act (Law No. 6.001/73). The amendment would introduce a gender and generational dimension to all programmes and policies affecting indigenous peoples in Brazil. The proposal also calls upon the state to adopt appropriate measures, in consultation with indigenous peoples, to ensure that indigenous women, children and the elderly enjoy full protection and guarantees against all forms of violence and discrimination. This reflected acknowledgement that violence against women cannot necessarily be addressed within the traditions of indigenous communities, and may require support from mainstream laws and organizations.

The 80 indigenous women delegates suggested that FUNAI and key government departments, including the Ministries of Justice and Human Rights, the Secretariat for Policies for Women, and the Presidential National Commission on Indigenous Policy (CNPI), should all collaborate with the indigenous movement to ensure that Draft Law No. 2057/91 is included in the 2011 agenda of Brazil's House of Representatives.

Afro-Brazilians

There are approximately 90 million Afro-Brazilians, representing almost half the national population. During 2010, they continued to be significantly under-represented in government, professional positions, and the middle and upper classes. The majority of Afro-Brazilians continued to exist as a virtual 'lower caste', and during 2010 notably disrespectful attitudes and daily social pressures continued in conscious as well as unconscious efforts to maintain this caste relationship.

Consequently, during 2010 Afro-Brazilians – especially those with dark skin – continued to experience a higher rate of unemployment and lower wages that averaged approximately half those of people with pale skin. Afro-Brazilian women were doubly disadvantaged, since according to the Ministry of Labor and Employment (MTE), women in Brazil in general are often paid less than men, with women workers receiving on average 64 per cent of men's wages. Moreover, there is a sizeable education gap related to Afro-Brazilian ethnicity, which continues to fuel negative stereotypes regarding the capabilities of Afro-Brazilians as a group and to keep many in the ranks of the poor. According to Feminist Africa, only 6 per cent of employed Afro-Brazilian women had completed 12 or more years of schooling, compared to 23 per cent of employed Euro-Brazilian women.

In recent years, some of these issues have prompted Afro-descendant women in Brazil to become more politically active. Since 2001, Afro-Brazilian women's non-governmental organizations (NGOs) have formed at least one-third of the National Council of Women's Rights in Brazil, and have been able to achieve some success in lobbying the state to redress racial and gender inequities. This has included pressuring the government to implement affirmative action and other policies that are designed to increase Afro-Brazilian access to education and jobs, and to disaggregate race- and gender-based data on health, education and wages.

Afro-Brazilian women's NGOs have also effectively made the case for incorporating ethno-cultural factors in public health delivery and disease diagnosis. This reflects the prevalence of certain specific medical conditions within Afro-Brazilian populations, including type-2 diabetes, uterine tumours, hypertension and sickle-cell anaemia. In addition, maternal mortality rates are much higher among Afro-Brazilian women than among Euro-Brazilian women.

However, despite being very involved at the family and community levels, the activism of Afro-Brazilian women's NGOs has not translated into political power at the national level. Part of the problem – besides the existence of a discriminatory mainstream political structure – is that Afro-descendant women's NGOs have been unable to mobilize mass grassroots support and instead have focused more attention on lobbying for policy change.

In addition to infrastructure development, it should be noted that the Planning Ministry will also be responsible for the Growth Acceleration Programme (PAC), a programme of infrastructure and social investment, including cash transfers to poor families for child health and education. The programme enjoys great popularity among low-income groups, of which African descendants make up a sizeable majority. The programme has helped 30 million of Brazil's 198 million people to escape poverty (according to UN figures). Besides promoting a greater feeling of social inclusion, it helped to give the outgoing Lula administration an 80 per cent approval rating.

Chile

During 2010, a cultural and inequality gap persisted between the mainstream population and most of the indigenous peoples of Chile. These include the Aymara, Mapuche, Polynesian Rapanui of Easter Island and small groups of Tierra del Fuegian nations, such as the Qawasqar and Yamana.

Shortly before leaving office at the end of January 2010, outgoing President Michelle Bachelet apologized to the descendants of a group of Qawasqar whose ancestors were among 11 individuals captured by German explorers in 1881 and shipped to Europe to be exhibited as curiosities.

Below: A mother and son from the indigenous Wauras community of Brazil's Amazon rainforest. *Fernando Bizerra Jr/EPA.*

In a speech at the ceremony honouring the return of the remains of five of the group, the president acknowledged the historical mistreatment of Chile's indigenous peoples and linked it to racist attitudes towards 'our indigenous forefathers'.

Earlier in January, Chileans had elected as president billionaire businessman Sebastian Piñera Echenique of the center-right Coalition for Change. They also voted in members of Congress. Seventeen of the 120 members of the Chamber of Deputies and 5 of the 38 members of the Senate were women. None of the elected were known to self-identify as indigenous.

Among Piñera's early pronouncements was his intention to restructure public institutions devoted to indigenous affairs to make them more efficient. In addition, he indicated his government would pursue a land policy focused more on individual subsidies, rather than on recognizing collective rights.

Earthquake
Shortly after the new President took office, a 7.8-magnitude earthquake and related tsunamis battered south-central Chile on 27 February

2010. The earthquake caused widespread damage and distress, including to the region's indigenous Mapuche who were already marginalized long before the disaster struck.

Although Mapuche communities were close to the epicentre of the earthquake and were among the most severely affected, there was a notable absence of media coverage about their situation. Even more striking, there was a complete lack of government disaster relief support for their small communities, despite the fact that in addition to deaths and disappearances the disaster caused structural damage to Mapuche community houses and water supplies, and contamination of natural water sources. Mapuche activists viewed the lack of government response and apparent official lack of interest as another demonstration of the discrimination and exclusion of their indigenous communities. They accused the various government authorities of concentrating only on the north of the country and the big southern cities such as Concepción, while ignoring their rural indigenous communities, also located in the south.

With help still not arriving in their areas a week after the earthquake, Mapuche activists began using the internet to make online appeals for international assistance. The news agency MapuExpress published a statement by a group of organizations collectively called La Sociedad Civil (The Civil Society), which specified the measures the group would employ to ensure that affected Mapuche households received any foreign aid that was provided.

Reclaiming ancestral lands
The major concern for indigenous peoples in Chile during 2010 remained their ongoing struggle to regain ancestral lands. Closely linked to this were efforts to repeal the controversial anti-terrorist law that hampers their ability to protest and receive just treatment from state authorities. The anti-terror law, which dates back to the era of dictator General Pinochet, treats as acts of terrorism all illegal land occupations and attacks on the equipment or personnel of multinational companies. Those

charged are subjected to both civilian and military trials, and the law sanctions the use of 'anonymous' or unidentified prosecution witnesses. Those labelled as terrorists can be held in indefinite detention.

On 16 September 2010, as Chile celebrated the bicentennial anniversary of its independence from Spain and the attention of the nation, and the world, was simultaneously focused on this patriotic spectacle and on the drama-filled rescue of 33 Chilean miners trapped deep underground, some 34 Mapuche detainees were on a long-running hunger strike in six prisons across southern Chile. Among their demands were for their trials to be held in civil rather than military courts, and the withdrawal of charges under the anti-terror law. They noted that from its inception this law had been used exclusively against Mapuches, as a direct consequence of their activism. Media coverage of their protest was minimal.

As reported in previous editions of *State of the World's Minorities and Indigenous Peoples*, land invasions and clashes between Mapuche and the police have become increasingly violent in recent years. Chilean police responses have been notably firm-handed, including heavily armed community presences, helicopter overflights, house searches and even lethal force. This has led to even more protests, arrests, detentions and hunger strikes. In August 2010, Mapuche leaders and non-governmental organization (NGO) legal aid providers indicated that it was the continuing failure of the state to address Mapuche concerns that ultimately led to the 2010 hunger strike. They especially criticized the apparent lack of political will to engage in talks and recognize the existence of a conflict over Mapuche land and autonomy.

With the hunger strike in its tenth week, a group of 12 Chilean activists, including student leaders and members of the copper workers' union (CUT), began a 'massive solidarity fast' to support the imprisoned protesters. In an apparent effort to defuse the situation, the government authorized the release of two of the striking prisoners on bail. However, both indicated they would continue their protest. Moreover, a week later on 21 September

four Chilean opposition lawmakers also joined the hunger strike, which may have helped increase pressure on the government to begin talks to end the protest.

In the final weeks of September 2010, President Piñera proposed legislation that would forbid civilians and minors from being tried in military courts, and reduce sentences under the anti-terror statutes. He also announced a US $4 billion 'Plan Araucania', package of economic and social measures aimed at improving socio-economic opportunities and the quality of life for Mapuche in their home territory. Piñera's government also agreed to begin talks involving cabinet ministers, delegates from Mapuche communities and representatives of religious and social organizations, with the archbishop of Concepción serving as a mediator. The hunger strikers called off their protests and agreed to begin negotiations which they hoped would result in the government meeting some of the key Mapuche demands.

Nevertheless, despite promises of substantial investments in Mapuche home areas, at the end of 2010 the earthquake-affected Mapuche residents of southern Chile were still awaiting the arrival of government support and commenting on the lack of any significant reconstruction or infrastructure rehabilitation in their communities.

Afro-Chileans
During 2010, the small Afro-Chilean population registered a few modest but important gains in their efforts to achieve formal statistical inclusion and national recognition as one of the country's ethnic groups.

Chileans who identify as African descendants live mainly in the towns of Salamanca and Ovalle in the north-central region of Coquimbo, as well as in Arica and Parinacota, in the arid northernmost region near the border with Peru. At the end of 2009, the three organizations that comprise the Afro-Chilean Alliance – Lumbanga, Oro Negro (Black Gold) and Arica Negro (Black Arica) – carried out an independent survey of 500 families and came up with a preliminary estimate of more than 8,000 people of African descent in Arica and Parinacota. While no official statistics have ever been collected, Fabiana Del Popolo, an expert on population issues with the UN Economic Commission for Latin America and the

Caribbean (ECLAC), has observed that people of African descent in Chile have significant poverty levels and are excluded from public policies that target other vulnerable groups, such as indigenous peoples.

In June 2010, Chile's first community development office for Afro-Chileans opened in the city of Arica. It was regarded as a historic achievement after years of advocacy. In the same month, the Afro-Chilean Alliance met with officials of the National Institute of Statistics (INE), which is responsible for developing the 2012 census form. At the end of 2010, Afro-Chileans were waiting to hear if their advocacy efforts had been successful, and hoping that inclusion in the census form would help put an end to what rights groups regard as structural discrimination and invisibility at the national level.

Rapa Nui

Like the indigenous Mapuche on the South American mainland, indigenous Rapa Nui on Chile-controlled Easter Island in the Pacific are becoming increasingly vocal about control of ancestral lands.

In August 2010, Rapa Nui families – who are originally of Polynesian ancestry – began occupying contested areas on Easter Island after failing to obtain legal redress for their land claims. In early December 2010, Chilean police were flown 3,000 miles to the island to enforce a court decree ordering the removal of the Rapa Nui protesters. According to news reports, the Chilean police shot at protesters with rubber bullets and used batons, resulting in the wounding of 24 people, including the president of the autonomously created Rapa Nui Parliament.

In October 2010, in the hope of preventing further violence, the Washington, DC-based Indian Law Resource Center (ILRC) – which is representing the 28 Rapa Nui clans – filed a Request for Protection before the Inter-American Commission on Human Rights. As of February 2011, the Commission had granted precautionary measures in favour of the islanders, ordering the Chilean government to immediately stop the violent use of armed force against the Rapa Nui, to guarantee the safety and humane treatment of Rapa Nui, and to begin an investigation into recent events. Meanwhile, Rapa Nui vowed to continue their protests.

Colombia

Approximately 27 per cent of Colombia's nearly 45 million inhabitants self-identifies as Afro-Colombian, although NGOs put the number much higher. Indigenous peoples comprise 3.5 per cent of the population.

According to the Colombian relief agency, Acción Social, the long-running internal armed conflict has produced more than 4 million internally displaced people (IDPs), one of the largest populations of IDPs in the world. Many of those displaced are from indigenous or African descendant communities.

In February 2010, following her first official visit to the country, the UN Independent Expert on Minority Issues, Gay McDougall, called on the Colombian government to do more to improve the situation of Afro-Colombians. This was with special reference to key issues such as internal displacement, territorial dispossession, poverty, and violence against individuals and communities in both rural and urban areas. Colombia's legislative framework recognizes many Afro-Colombian rights. However, the UN Independent Expert pointed out that consultations with Afro-Colombian communities and organizations had revealed a pattern of sporadic implementation and limited observance of legal provisions, and a lack of follow-up and enforcement.

The top priority issue for many Afro-Colombians continued to be displacement from their lands despite – and sometimes because of – the prior granting of collective titles for some 90 per cent of Afro-Colombian ancestral territory. Prior to the visit of the Independent Expert, a UN Human Rights Council envoy had pointed out that large-scale economic operations, often involving national and multinational companies, had contributed significantly to the dispossession and displacement that deprives the Afro-Colombian population of access to their lands. In 2009, Colombia's Constitutional Court ordered the national government to implement a range of measures to protect Afro-Colombian communities from forced displacement; however, thus far there has been no observable compliance.

Afro-Colombian women and violence

Among the key issues highlighted by the report of the UN Independent Expert was the situation

Above: A mother and her daughter in a settlement for displaced families, Choco Department, Colombia. *Paul Smith/Panos.*

of Afro-Colombian women. An NGO survey of displaced women found that the majority of displaced Afro-Colombians are women and many are heads of households with children. Such women continued to face multiple forms of discrimination in 2010, placing them at a distinct disadvantage. Indeed, according to the UN High Commissioner for Refugees (UNHCR), only 5.3 per cent of displaced Afro-Colombian women earn a minimum salary.

Rights activists point out that all parties in the conflict zones, that is, the two guerrilla groups – the Revolutionary Armed Forces of Colombia (FARC) and the National Liberation Army (ELN) – as well as government forces are involved in human rights abuses, including violence against women. During their displacement, Afro-Colombian women have frequently reported traumatic acts of physical aggression and sexual violence. This has included economic exploitation, violence and rape. Few victims register complaints due to fear or ignorance of complaint channels.

In the case of African descendant women, rape – especially of young women – continued to result in many unwanted pregnancies and the birth of children of mixed ethnicity. Such children, as well as their mothers, are frequently ostracized within their communities, and therefore doubly victimized. Women also complained to the Independent Expert about Afro-Colombian children being coerced into joining armed groups, and about threats made to Afro-Colombian women leaders and members of women's organizations.

Afro-Colombian women reported a pattern of unequal treatment from government officials charged with their protection. They complained that threats against female leaders are not regarded with the same gravity as those against male leaders. They view this as an indication of the disrespect and lack of recognition of their leadership roles, and another example of ethnicity- and gender-linked discrimination by government agencies.

It should be noted that in 2008 the Colombian Congress adopted Law 1257 on 'Measures to raise awareness, prevent and punish all forms of violence and discrimination against women'. This law recognizes a wide range of public and private acts of violence and according to the government, the Presidential Office on Equality for Women, the Independent Ombudsman and the Office of the Attorney-General have set up a Monitoring Committee to promote its implementation. However, Afro-Colombian women's groups reported that during 2010 they saw no evidence of any implementation.

Aerial fumigation of coca crops

Minority women are also primarily affected by the aerial fumigation used to eradicate illicit coca plantations as part of the US-sponsored Plan Colombia programme. Spraying of the chemical Glysophate not only destroys illegal coca cultivations, but also kills food crops. Since Afro-descendant women are principally involved in growing staple food crops such as rice and bananas, not only do they lose their harvests but also suffer the side-effects of the chemical spray. These reportedly include skin irritations as well as an increased risk of damage to internal organs as well as miscarriages.

Indigenous women

Along with Afro-Colombians, hundreds of thousands of indigenous peoples have also been forced off their resource-rich lands as a result of intense military conflict. According to a 2008 report by UNHCR, almost the entirety of the indigenous population in Colombia has been a victim of forced displacement, meaning that indigenous women have also been disproportionately affected by physical and sexual violence as a result of the conflict and of displacement.

In light of this reality, Colombia's indigenous women are now seeking to participate more directly in decision-making processes, by becoming involved in local and national politics. They face considerable obstacles, including low levels of education in their communities and limited participation among the predominantly rural indigenous electorate. Reflecting this, it was only in 2007 that two indigenous women candidates were elected to

local government office for the first time, one to Colombia's Cauca Regional Indigenous Council, and the other to the Bogotá Municipal Council. But despite the challenges, obtaining positions of political leadership and supporting other women candidates has become an important priority for indigenous women leaders.

However, with just two seats in the 102-person Senate and one in the 166-person Representative Chamber reserved for indigenous candidates, efforts to change policy on key issues that affect indigenous people face considerable challenges, particularly as these issues include ending the armed conflict, legalization of indigenous lands, environmental protection, and an end to discrimination against minority women. In addition, among the 3.5 per cent of Colombia's 40 million inhabitants who are indigenous, there are some 84 different indigenous peoples who speak 75 languages, and who extend from the Andean highlands to the lowland rainforests. This complexity – and the fact that many indigenous people are more concerned with indigenous territorial governance than national-level issues – has caused some indigenous activists to query whether Congress is the best place to resolve the acute issues confronting the country's indigenous communities at the local level.

Reflecting this, during 2010 female indigenous activists from the Huitoto community in Amazonas developed a training plan to enable young women to learn about governance and land issues, and increase their participation in decision-making at the local level. With national laws already in place that allow Colombia's indigenous people to run their own communities, the move towards greater indigenous female political participation and empowerment at this level is likely to gather momentum.

Dominican Republic and Haiti

The Dominican Republic (DR) shares the island of Hispaniola with Haiti. The latter is the most economically deprived country in the region, and Haiti's large African descendant population has sometimes been described as a marginalized majority.

The majority of the population of the DR is of mixed African descent, and many Dominicans have Haitian ancestors and connections. Despite this, anti-Haitian feeling is rife. Haitians represent a substantial minority of up to 1 million people within the DR, and form a distinct cultural and linguistic group. Relations between Haiti and the DR have often been contentious, primarily as a result of treatment of the Haitian migrant population in the DR, many of whom are undocumented.

In January 2010, Haiti was hit with a massive magnitude 7.0 Mw earthquake, whose epicentre was approximately 25 km west of Port-au-Prince, Haiti's capital. Two months after the earthquake, the government's Directorate of Civil Protection stated that an estimated 222,517 people had died and another 310,928 were injured. According to the UN Office for the Coordination of Humanitarian Affairs (OCHA), there were 460 camps with a total population of 1,170,000 people in Port-au-Prince alone. The vast majority of the displaced population in camps were children.

The earthquake caused major damage in the capital. Almost 250,000 residences, 30,000 commercial buildings and more than 1,300 schools and 50 health care facilities were destroyed.

DR response

The DR was the first country to provide aid to Haiti, including water, mobile medical units, health personnel, communications technicians, food and heavy-lifting machinery to aid rescue efforts. Hospitals in the DR were made available, and the airport opened to receive aid destined for Haiti. Immediately following the disaster, towns in the eastern DR began preparing for tens of thousands of refugees. However, given the history of thorny relations between the two countries, the border was reinforced by Dominican soldiers, and officials indicated that all Haitians who entered for medical assistance would be allowed to stay only temporarily. By 16 January, hospitals close to the border had become filled to capacity, with some institutions running out of critical medical supplies. The DR won international praise for its commitment to helping Haiti recover, however the long history of intolerance and discrimination against its Haitian migrant minority continued to influence local responses to the disaster.

Every year, the DR repatriates thousands of undocumented Haitians. According to a report from the Universidad Centroamericana, between 2003 and 2008 Dominican authorities deported an average of 20,417 Haitians a year. At the end of 2010, the Dominican migration director, Sigfrido Pared Perez, estimated that the earthquake had resulted in a 15 per cent increase in the estimated 1 million Haitian migrant population.

The issue of trafficking of Haitian children – a cause for concern by rights activists even before the earthquake – came under special scrutiny after the disaster. On 5 February, ten DR-based Baptist missionaries from Idaho, USA, were charged with criminal association and kidnapping for trying to smuggle 33 children out of Haiti into the DR. The missionaries claimed they were rescuing orphaned children, but investigations revealed that more than 20 of the children had been taken from their parents after they were told their offspring would have a better life in America. The leader of the group was held in custody and the others deported.

At the official level at any rate, the earthquake offered an opportunity for some degree of reconciliation between the two countries. In July 2010, Dominican President Leonel Fernandez Fernandez met with Haitian President René Preval. They pledged to cooperate closely in several areas, such as agriculture, trade, education and health and to re-address traditionally contentious issues such as migration. The DR also promised ongoing assistance. What form this will actually take is hard to determine, given the state of rebuilding efforts.

Ongoing humanitarian crisis in Haiti

Following the January quake, some US $1.1 billion was collected for relief efforts by 23 major charities, however by July 2010 only 2 per cent of the money had actually been released. By October 2010, organizations such as Refugees International were characterizing aid agency efforts in Haiti as 'dysfunctional' and 'inexperienced'. By the end of 2010, almost no transitional housing had been built, and Haitians were still living in a state of emergency. There were 1.6 million displaced people still in tent camps, most of which had no electricity, running water or sewage disposal. There were also increasing reports of gang leaders and landowners intimidating the displaced. Women and young girls in the crowded camps were at particular risk of sexual violence and the UN force was accused of not doing enough to protect them. Additionally, by the end of the year, the Haiti Recovery Commission led by former US President

Bill Clinton and Haitian Prime Minister Jean-Max Bellerive to facilitate reconstruction projects had not begun any major reconstruction work. Some 98 per cent of the rubble from the quake – an estimated 20 million cubic metres – had still not been cleared. Critics also note that existing transitional housing and other rebuilding plans are aimed exclusively at neighbourhoods and homeowners, making no allowances for the estimated 200,000 'propertyless poor', who were living in rented property at the time the disaster struck.

The situation was compounded in October by the outbreak of a cholera epidemic, the first to hit the country in 200 years. With health officials speculating about the origin of the disease and suggesting it may have entered via a UN peacekeeper, numerous angry demonstrations erupted against the 'blue helmets' and foreign aid workers in general. Regardless of the source, continuing limited access to clean water and sanitation did much to aid the spread of the disease. By the end of 2010, the Haitian health ministry announced that more than 2,500 people had died.

The cholera outbreak once again tested cross-border relations and the general perception of Haitians in the DR. It prompted officials to close the border and introduce strict rules for entry, in order to prevent the spread of the disease. This had a direct effect on the many Haitians who regularly cross into the DR to trade. However, the cholera outbreak was just one more reminder of the lack of overall progress in recovery efforts, according to a report by Oxfam, raising the possibility of increased migration of Haitians into the DR.

In November 2010, the situation prompted Haitian-born Michaëlle Jean, who recently served as the Governor-General of Canada and was appointed United Nations Educational, Scientific and Cultural Organization (UNESCO) Special Envoy for Haiti, to co-author a public letter with UNESCO head Irina Bokova. It placed much of the blame for the slow recovery on the international development community and charged its members with abandoning their commitments. According to Jean, 'As time passes, what began as a natural disaster is becoming a disgraceful reflection on the international community.'

Observers note that the rebuilding phase has once again revealed the uncertain nature of long-term post-disaster assistance, and reinforced the importance of improving DR–Haiti relations, especially in regard to the issue of migration. For one thing, the lack of progress in post-earthquake rebuilding further stalls the growth of the Haitian economy, and especially the possibility of local employment in the construction sector. This is perhaps ironic since construction is one of the major sources of employment for Haitian migrants to the DR. At the end of 2010, therefore, it was clear that economic migration from Haiti to the DR would continue, at least in the short term. Despite the history of prejudice and discrimination, the island neighbours are well aware of the importance of migrant labour to the DR economy, as well as of the value of cooperation. The fact is that while international relief may have received significant media coverage, in the end much of the rescue effort was actually conducted by Haitians themselves, with the DR being the first country on the scene to lend a helping hand.

Ecuador

Ecuador has a population of 15 million (according to the 2001 census), of which more than 8 per cent self-identify as indigenous. If language use is factored in, the indigenous population reaches 14 per cent.

As elsewhere in the Americas, local authorities in Ecuador's indigenous areas are trying to deal with issues such as urbanization, rising youth violence and erosion of cultural traditions. In combating violent crime in the community, indigenous groups in 2010 increasingly turned to the use of communal justice, sparking debates regarding the role of and relationship between state legal norms and the practice of traditional indigenous customary law.

Neither corporal punishment nor the death penalty is included in Ecuador's legislation. However, in the country's 2008 Constitution, which sought to promote greater indigenous inclusion, allowances were made for indigenous communities to impart their own justice under their customary laws. This was in accordance with indigenous rights consecrated in International Labour Organization (ILO) Convention No. 169. At a time when growing numbers of young people are rejecting traditional communal structures and indigenous values in favour of a more globalized, urban-centred world view, community leaders are increasingly trying to address these challenges using

Femicide: gender-based violence against women

The connection between violence, insecurity, discrimination and the challenges to meeting the MDGs is partly exemplified by the issue of femicide. This is the name given to the murder of women, targeted and killed solely on the basis of their gender identity. While used to describe the targeted, gender-based killing of women all over the world, femicide has come to be associated particularly with the killing of young, low-status women (including those from indigenous and other minority communities) in parts of Central America and northern Mexico, and with state indifference to these crimes. As an extreme form of gender-based violence, femicide undermines the third MDG, that of achieving gender equality and empowering women. As such, it places communities ever further away from meeting the MDGs, as well as representing the ultimate violation of women's rights.

At the annual memorial march for Murdered and Missing Indigenous Women, held in 2010 in Montreal, Canada, a spokesperson for the rights group Missing Justice, indicated that indigenous women in Canada are about five times more likely than other women to die as a result of violence. According to Canada's CTV news network, a study found that 521 indigenous women have gone missing or been murdered in Canada over the past four decades. In what activists argue is a function of ethnic as well as gender discrimination, the family members of female indigenous victims in Canada – and elsewhere – have complained that

when they report missing women, the authorities fail to investigate and do not seem to give credence to the reports.

A similar situation has been reported in the Central American country of Guatemala. Violent crime has continued to increase over the last decade, mostly in urban areas, and so has the number of femicide victims. Indeed, in 2010, some women's rights organizations spoke of an 'epidemic' of gender-based murder in the country. According to official figures, in the last eight years, more than 4,500 women and girls (mostly from ages 13 to 36) have been killed in a remarkably brutal or violent manner. In the first seven months of 2010 alone, over 30 women died by firearms or knives as a result of 'machista' or sexist violence.

Femicides in Guatemala have gained attention due to their extreme nature. There are frequent instances of dismemberment, mutilations, torture and extreme sexual violence. In many cases the perpetrators are boyfriends, current or ex-husbands, relatives or men known to the victims.

Women in Guatemala are no strangers to physical and sexual violence used as instruments of control. During Guatemala's 1960–96 armed conflict, in which over 200,000 people died, the use of sexual violence was systematized and widely practised. The majority of the victims of this aggression were indigenous women. Sexual violence was used by the armed units and security forces to subdue women, to terrify them, and to sow fear throughout the whole population (as discussed in the article in this publication 'Minority women and armed conflict: from victims to activists').

Laws against femicide were introduced for the first time in Guatemala in 2008. This included a legal definition of the crime which recognized its gender-specific nature and a prison sentence for those who commit it. Nevertheless, full implementation depends on the existence of effectively functioning state mechanisms.

A diagnostic study by the Guatemalan Group for Women (GGW) found that only 26 per cent of

possible femicide cases were ever investigated, and that impunity is common. The perpetrators of these crimes against women enjoy widespread immunity, with only 1–2 per cent of crimes being successfully prosecuted. As in the case of Canada, the families of the victims also complain of a lack of credence on the part of officials who handle their missing person reports. The study also reveals that an autopsy was ordered in only 12 per cent of the female murder cases that occurred between 2006 and 2008. Activists argue that this reflects the scant importance prosecutors have placed so far on sexual assault committed prior to death.

During 2010, the issue of gender-related violence in Guatemala gained increased international attention. Peruvian lawyer Gladys Acosta, Latin American and Caribbean director for the United Nations Development Fund for Women (UNIFEM), has called on the international community to mobilize and act against what she has called 'Guatemala's epidemic of gender-motivated murders'.

Elsewhere, in a case brought at the Inter-American Court of Human Rights (IACtHR) against Mexico, the duty of the state to take measures to protect women from gender-related violence has now been recognized by international law. There is therefore now a legal precedent that holds states responsible for preventing gender-related killings.

In a landmark ruling handed down in November 2009, the IACtHR held the Mexican state responsible for the absence of measures to protect female murder victims and for the lack of prevention of these crimes. Furthermore, it argued that official neglect prevailed in spite of full awareness of the existence of a pattern of gender-related violence that had resulted in the deaths of hundreds of women in the Mexican Ciudad Juárez, a sprawling industrial city on the border with the US.

With its high murder rate and regular shoot-outs between heavily armed criminal gangs and security forces, Ciudad Juárez has the reputation of being one of the most violent cities on earth. According to

an Amnesty International report, between 1993 and 2004 more than 370 women and girls were killed in Ciudad Juárez; however, local residents and rights groups put the number higher.

In the Campo Algodonero ('the cotton field') case, the Court found the Mexican state guilty of denial of justice to three specific victims: Claudia González (20), Esmeralda Herrera (15) and Berenice Ramos (17). Their bodies were found along with the corpses of five other women on a piece of waste ground on the outskirts of the city in November 2001. The verdict cited the lack of official response to the initial disappearance of the women and the lack of due diligence in the investigation of the murders, as well as the denial of justice and the lack of adequate compensation to the families.

The Mexican government was ordered to pay amounts of over US $130,000 to each of the victim's families for reparations and legal costs. In addition, the Court instructed the authorities to undertake a number of special measures, including expanding gender-

sensitivity and human rights training for police, holding a public ceremony to apologize for the killings, and building a monument to the three young women in Ciudad Juárez. Furthermore, the Mexican authorities were ordered to create a website with information about women and girls killed in Ciudad Juárez since 1993, increase efforts to find women who have gone missing and investigate gender-related murders seriously.

This precedent-setting ruling cannot be appealed, and it represents the first time anywhere in the world that a state has been found responsible in cases of gender-based murders. The IACtHR gave Mexico one year to comply. Nevertheless, by the end of 2010, remarkably little had been done. According to IPS news agency, of the 16 specific Court orders, the only action carried out so far by the government was the publication of the Court's ruling in the official government record, and in one nationally distributed daily newspaper.

In case of failure to comply, the IACtHR can turn to the OAS General Assembly. If that happens, Mexico could be declared in breach of international human rights law. However, experience in the Americas has shown that full compliance with IACtHR rulings continues to be a challenge, with states doing only just enough to avoid outright reprimand. To this end, the female head of the state National Commission to Prevent and Eradicate Violence against Women has indicated that, along with developing a protocol to be followed when women go missing, a number of Casas de Justicia, (Houses of Justice) will be created that will include shelters for victims of gender-based violence. The first one is to be built in Ciudad Juárez. ▪

decidedly traditional measures.

In May 2010, a 22-year-old man was publicly castigated and subjected to corporal punishment by community members after he had confessed on video to the murder of a young indigenous resident of La Cocha village, in the rural highland Pujilí district. Following the public castigation, the young man was taken back to his home area by his mother and community leaders. There a local assembly ordered him to perform community service for five years, and restricted him from leaving the area during all that time. He was also required to pay US $1,750 to the victim's mother.

The corporal punishment was widely covered by the local and regional media, and caused a national outcry. Editorial writers in Ecuador called upon the government to limit the practice of indigenous communal justice, which they argued has the potential to produce social chaos. Similarly, members of the Constituent Assembly, who had prepared the new Constitution, indicated that some cases of indigenous justice demonstrated the need for written standards and clear procedures, to ensure that indigenous justice was applied in accordance with international human rights standards.

In contrast, some researchers, such as sociologist Luciano Martínez, Professor at the Latin American School of Social Sciences (FLACSO), argued that indigenous forms of communal justice, such as a one-time public flogging or cold water dousing, are more effective than sending a young man away for a four-year prison sentence that is devoid of social context and lacks rehabilitation measures. Supporters also point out that Western-influenced mainstream law does not take into account indigenous community processes that aim at victim compensation and the reinsertion of offenders back into responsible community life. Indigenous rights advocates especially point to the fact that notions of communal solidarity and traditional reciprocity in indigenous communities are increasingly facing serious new challenges. This includes an increase in suicide rates among indigenous youth, who are unable to find their place either in their indigenous communities or in the individualistic culture of the mainstream urban world.

Meanwhile, in May 2010, President Rafael Correa threatened the use of armed intervention in cases where the state feels indigenous justice is going 'too far'.

Guatemala

The population of the Central American state of Guatemala is estimated at 14 million. According to official statistics, 40 per cent of Guatemala's inhabitants are indigenous, and include Garífuna, Maya and Xinca peoples. During 2010, indigenous spokespeople continued to challenge these figures, claiming that in fact more than 60 per cent of Guatemalans are indigenous.

According to Eduardo Sacayón, director of the Interethnic Studies Institute at Guatemala's University of San Carlos, the situation of Guatemala's indigenous communities continues to deteriorate. Poverty has increased, the quality of education remains very poor, and there continues to be no intercultural perspective in the provision of health services. This latter particularly affects indigenous women in the areas of reproductive and maternal health.

Indigenous women predominantly inhabit rural areas, and may have to walk several hours to get to a health centre. Once there, there is no guarantee they will get the attention they need. A joint USAID/Guatemala Ministry of Health report revealed that the racist attitudes of health workers toward the Mayan population pose a significant problem. Doctors often doubt the ability of indigenous women to understand instructions, and only 65 per cent of health centres have bilingual staff.

The 2009–10 *Human Development Report* for Guatemala, published by the United Nations Development Programme (UNDP), indicates that in the area of education, indigenous peoples continue to be at a distinct disadvantage, constituting just 13.2 per cent of the post-secondary student population.

According to the third report presented by the government in December 2010 on progress towards meeting the MDGs, 80 per cent of indigenous Guatemalans are living in poverty, compared to 40 per cent of the non-indigenous population. Also, according to the government report, while nationwide poverty in Guatemala over the past six years fell nearly 5.2 per cent, extreme poverty, which primarily affects indigenous peoples, declined just half a percentage point (15.7 to 15.2 per cent). During 2010, the prevalence of chronic malnutrition among indigenous children aged five and under continued to be twice that of non-indigenous children (30.6 per cent), which translates into some 69.5 per cent of indigenous children who suffer chronic malnutrition.

These conditions were not aided during 2010 by the recurrence of extreme weather patterns, including droughts and Tropical Storm Agatha, which damaged road communications, infrastructure and threatened indigenous peoples' food security. A World Food Programme (WFP) study indicated that 235,000 people – most of whom are indigenous people – will need emergency food aid, and a further 95,000 who are engaged in subsistence agriculture will require supplementary food up to early 2011, just to be able to survive in areas that have been swept by torrential rains, floods, deadly landslides and a volcanic eruption.

Critics point out that, despite earlier political promises, no government policies have been developed for indigenous peoples, nor is there compliance with ILO Convention No. 169 on Indigenous and Tribal Peoples.

Mining

Transnational and mining interests continued to prevail in areas where indigenous communities are located. With mining royalties increasing by as much as 10 per cent a year, the Ministry of Energy and Mining (MEM) proposed the creation of a Collective Mining Fund specifically devoted to overseeing the use of mining royalties for rural development. The MEM proposes splitting the profits from activities like gold sales between the company and the state, with 75 per cent of the government's revenue going to the Collective Mining Fund, to be passed on to communities in the form of development projects. This was partly to offset widespread rejection of mines by nearby indigenous communities.

There are valid reasons for their rejection. A research team from the Pastoral Commission for Peace and Ecology (COPAE) that tested local water supplies in the municipality of San Miguel Ixtahuacan found toxic levels of arsenic as high as 0.70 mg/L or 70 ppb (parts per billion) in a river downstream from one mine. Engineer Fausto Valiente from COPAE pointed out that, in comparison, the maximum standard limit established by the World Bank, is 0.1 mg/L (10 ppb), while the US Environmental Protection Agency sets an even lower limit level of 0.01 mg/L. The country's indigenous populations have continued to oppose mining concessions at public hearings held in accordance with Convention No. 169. They cite the environmental degradation and health risks. Nevertheless, the projects continue.

At an International Parliamentary Conference in Chiapas, Mexico in October–November 2010, Otilia Lux, an indigenous Mayan Guatemalan lawmaker on the congressional Indigenous Affairs Committee explained that although important bills benefiting indigenous peoples have been presented to Congress, these have still not been passed. They include a proposed rural development law to improve access to land and housing, and a law to make indigenous hearings binding with respect to transnational mining company operations. Moreover, the Fund for Guatemalan Indigenous Development, created in 1994, and the 2002 Presidential Commission Against Discrimination and Racism continue to lack the necessary capacity for effective action.

Guyana

The Co-operative Republic of Guyana has a population of approximately 760,000 people. The majority of its inhabitants are concentrated along the coast, and are of African and East Indian descent, with Indo-Guyanese being the dominant group in government and business. According to the 2002 census, Guyana's indigenous people (locally termed Amerindians) constituted 9 per cent of the population, with 90 per cent of their communities located in the vast and remote savannah, riverain and heavily rain-forested interior. Amerindians share many national cultural traits with Afro- and Indo-Guyanese; however, the traditional Amerindian communal hinterland lifestyle and the use of ancestral idioms (as opposed to English) as their first language serve to set Amerindians apart from the more urban mainstream coastal population.

In 2010, the standard of living of indigenous peoples in Guyana remained lower than most of the non-indigenous population. Indigenous peoples continued to receive poor social services, inadequate education and lower incomes, and have limited opportunities to participate in decisions affecting their lands, cultures, traditions and allocation of natural resources.

Two Amerindian women hold positions in the government, as heads of the Ministry of Amerindian Affairs and the high-profile Ministry of Foreign

Affairs. Nevertheless, a long history of discrimination, marginalization and poverty has ensured that in 2010, the majority of Amerindians in Guyana still risk being viewed as second-class citizens by some of their fellow Guyanese on the coast.

Guyana Reduced Emissions from Deforestation and Forest Degradation project

In November 2009, the Norwegian government agreed to pay Guyana US $250 million over a five-year period. This money, allocated under the international Reduced Emissions for Deforestation and Degradation (REDD+) initiative, would allow the country to protect and manage its rainforest, via the Guyana Reduced Emissions from Deforestation and Forest Degradation (GRIFF) project. Three years earlier, in late 2007, Guyana's President Bharrat Jagdeo had offered up the country's large tracts of standing forest as a giant carbon offsetting zone to counter climate change. At the time, he explained that the main aim was national revenue generation for the cash-strapped government, and not environmental altruism.

Since 2006, almost 13 per cent of the country's land has been recognized as indigenous property. As a large part of this is within the densely tree-covered rainforest zone, Amerindian participation in the GRIFF project is important to its implementation. As a result, the scheme was formally introduced to Amerindian leaders (*toshaos*) at a November 2010 conference of the National Toshaos Council (NTC) (a body of indigenous leaders established under the 2006 Guyana Amerindian Act), where the president announced that US $8 million of the Norway Fund would be allocated to various projects to benefit Amerindian villages under a Low Carbon Development Strategy (LCDS). This included US $1.5 million for solar panels for all Amerindian houses, US $2.5 million to finance development activities, and US $4 million for demarcating community boundaries.

Of the 171 Amerindian representatives present at the meeting, 166 signed the LCDS resolution. But there was very strong criticism from those leaders who withheld their signatures, some of whom charged that the LCDS resolution was drafted without their knowledge and first presented to them just minutes before their signatures were required. They also claimed that neither the organization's executives nor many of the leaders who actually

signed had any prior knowledge of the contents, and that Guyana's Amerindians should have been consulted during the drafting process, in accordance with their right to free, prior and informed consent. In addition, the dissenting leaders contended that many communities do not understand the conditions of the agreement between Guyana and the government of Norway with respect to REDD+ and the LCDS, and needed more details in order to assess fully the likely impact on their own way of life. They also objected to clauses that could mean the complete exclusion of any role for NGOs, such as indigenous rights defenders and environmental protection advocates.

From the outset, some of the the country's indigenous groups and others have viewed the President's LCDS as another government effort to appropriate densely forested timber-rich indigenous lands and the sub-surface resources. The dissenting leaders charged that the conference was another example of a pattern of flawed consultation by the Guyana government, which they say is characterized by the one-way dissemination of information and no real dialogue.

As it turns out, the indigenous peoples of Guyana may have good reasons to query government motives and actions. According to the local daily *Stabroek News*, it was revealed in 2010 that the much proclaimed landmark Amerindian Act of 2006 – around which all Amerindian policies revolve – had never actually been signed into law.

The revelation came as a particular surprise to the indigenous population. The 2006 Amerindian Act mandated an annual transfer of 20 per cent of the royalties from mining activities to a fund designated by the Minister of Amerindian Affairs, to be used for the benefit of the Amerindian villages. Since 2006, the money accruing to Amerindian communities from the Guyana Geology and Mines Commission (GGMC) would have amounted to many millions. As it turns out, during this period the GGMC did transfer some US $9 million to a government-owned investment company. However, indigenous leaders appeared unaware of the existence of these funds, which total more than the amount allocated to Amerindian communities under the Norway programme.

Following the revelation, the government was hurriedly forced to table a bill to commence

implementation of the Amerindian Act of 2006
and backdate a large number of related decisions.
As of the end of the year, however, there was no
indication of what had become of the millions of
dollars in royalties owed to Guyana's Amerindian
communities.

Amerindian women

Income generation has become increasingly
important to continued Amerindian community
survival. The traditional Amerindian subsistence
living is based on fishing, hunting and agriculture,
but the demands of the contemporary economic
structure necessitates a source of cash income,
in order to supplement diets, pay for children's
education, clothing, transportation and specialized
medical treatment.

In 2010, income-earning opportunities in

Above: An Amerindian woman and her young
daughter return to their village in Guyana after
fetching water from the well. *Grete Howard.*

Amerindian communities remained limited. Low
levels of education constrict the range of options,
and commercial outlets for traditional handicrafts
(usually produced by women) and agricultural
produce are minimal, as both depend on access
to coastal markets. Some government-sponsored
economic pilot projects do exist and some –
mostly male – Amerindians have gone into mining
in the gold-bearing region. But in the main, there
are few income-earning options in Amerindian
home areas.

This drives Amerindian women in particular to
seek work along the coast, often in cheap restaurants

Amerindian domestic worker faces exploitation and abuse

The exploitation of indigenous women working as live-in domestic workers on the Guyana coast does not receive much local media coverage. But during 2010 the case of a 22-year-old Amerindian woman, who was held as a virtual prisoner by her employers, received considerable media attention, as *Maurice Bryan* recounts.

The woman had answered a newspaper advertisement for a live-in domestic worker at the home of a business couple in the capital city. However, after just three months of employment she found herself a virtual prisoner in the home of her employers, and had to be removed by the police and officials from the Ministry of Labour and the Ministry of Amerindian Affairs, who responded to a call from a neighbour to investigate the situation.

According to one local daily, the *Stabroek News*, the woman complained that she was made to work extremely long hours, seven days a week, without ever receiving overtime pay, and was allowed only two days and one night off a month. Her personal mobile phone was confiscated by her employers and replaced by another.

The confiscation was specifically intended to deny the woman the right to use her native language. The employers indicated they had become uneasy after she was heard speaking to her mother in her indigenous idiom, which the employers did not understand. But without her personal mobile phone, the woman was unable to communicate with her mother and family members back home, where she had left her six-month-old child.

Six weeks prior to her rescue, the woman had expressed dissatisfaction with her working conditions and indicated she wished to leave. However, her employers informed her that she could not go until a replacement was found, and then proceeded to withhold her pay.

In her account, the Amerindian woman revealed that her employers subjected her to belittling verbal abuse, including derogatory racial terms. According to the news story, the woman also alleged that shortly before she left her employers, there were instances of inappropriate behaviour and requests from the husband that could be regarded as sexual harassment.

Matters came to a head after the distraught young woman began to confide in a neighbour and smuggle her clothes out of the employer's house in preparation for a quick escape. The neighbour then called the authorities, who quickly intervened. According to media reports, one police officer who participated in the removal of the young woman revealed that the couple was already known for hiring Amerindian persons from the interior and having them work under difficult conditions.

At the end of the year the matter was still under investigation and no charges had been brought against the former employers. According to the Ministry of Labour website, the government's Ministry of Human Services will now pay for the young woman to obtain vocational training in a chosen field and cover her expenses during the period. However, there were no indications as to whether the authorities intend to develop any comprehensive measures to educate and empower the country's Amerindian women in general, and make it less likely for them to be abused and exploited in the future. ∎

and bars, or as domestic servants, making them particularly vulnerable to exploitation and abuse, both as indigenous people and as women. Amerindian women brought from the Guyana interior to work as domestics far from home are particularly exposed to the risk of mistreatment at the hands of their employers, especially if they are hired as live-in domestic workers.

Mexico

Mexico is a federal republic composed of 31 states and a federal district, with a population of approximately 108 million.

Afro-Mexicans and the 2010 Census

In May 2010, Mexico conducted a national census, gathering information on age, gender, education, religion and birthplace from about 25 million households in 2,456 municipalities. Disappointingly, despite efforts on the part of organizations like the Alliance for the Empowerment of Indigenous Regions and Afro-Mexican Communities, this census failed to include questions on Afro-Mexican identity, ignoring their presence as an identifiable group. The census carried ethnic references related only to language and self-identification of people of indigenous origin, and, further, defined municipalities as indigenous only if the local population preserved native languages, traditions, beliefs and cultures. Officials of the National Institute of Statistics and Geography (INEGI) cited limited time and resources as reasons for being unable to modify the document to include questions relevant to Afro-Mexicans.

The official government stance as promoted by agencies such as the National Council on Population is that the majority of Mexicans are *mestizo* (of mixed Spanish European and indigenous ancestry), with no acknowledgement of any historical or contemporary African presence. However, according to US anthropologist Bobby Vaughn, blacks far outnumbered the Spanish in early colonial times. The black population was three times that of the Spanish in 1570 and 2.5 times in 1646; not until the early nineteenth century did the Spanish outnumber the African heritage population. Mexico is quite likely the last country in the Americas to continue excluding the African descendant category in its census, thereby implicitly ignoring the historical and contemporary

significance of people of African descent within its overall population.

With marginalized Afro-Mexicans languishing at the bottom of the socio-economic scale, inclusive and fully disaggregated census data is particularly important in terms of meeting MDG targets for them. This is because census data is used to create a demographic and socio-economic profile of each area of the country, including information necessary to develop suitable public policies and infrastructure that would benefit the poorest populations.

Poverty among Mexico's indigenous peoples

According to indigenous organizations, at least a third of Mexico's 108 million people are of native descent; however, there are only about 14 million Mexicans who are classified by the census as indigenous and as belonging to one of the country's 62 native groups. The majority of indigenous people live in the southern states of Guerrero, Oaxaca and Chiapas, which are the poorest in the country. It should also be noted that the insecurity and violence so prevalent today in many parts of Mexico is particularly notable in states with significant numbers of indigenous peoples and/or African descendant populations. These include Sinaloa and Chihuahua in the north, Tamaulipas in the east, Michoacán in the west, and Guerrero in the south. In these areas during 2010, large drug trafficking enterprises battled with impunity over control of distribution routes to the US market. Corruption is rife, and uncooperative functionaries are regular targets of assassination. This seriously compromises the effectiveness of municipal and state structures and their ability to meet MDG targets, especially for the indigenous and African descendant populations.

The relationship between violence, poverty and lack of development of Mexico's indigenous peoples. is very evident in a report issued in October 2010 by the UNDP human development research office in Mexico City. It indicated that Mexico continued be a long way from meeting MDG goals for the country's indigenous population. For the first time, the UN study compares the living conditions in Mexico's 156 indigenous municipalities, 393 non-indigenous municipalities and 1,905 municipalities inhabited by people of mixed-race descent. It indicates that although overall poverty in Mexico has been reduced, inequality persists. The National Commission for the Development of Indigenous

Peoples in 2010 also admitted that social spending in indigenous areas was lower than in non-indigenous zones.

Of particular concern with respect to women's rights is that the least progress has been made in the area of cutting maternal mortality among indigenous women. In the indigenous areas of Mexico – places where the local population retains indigenous languages, traditions, beliefs and cultures – the maternal mortality rate stands at 300 per 100,000 live births. This is among the highest in the world and is in stark contrast to the national average of 60 maternal deaths per 100,000 live births. And according to the government's National Population Council (CONAPO), during 2010 the infant mortality rate among indigenous people of 22.8 per 1,000 live births was also significantly higher than the 14.2 per 1,000 for the population at large

Issues like poverty, nutrition, health and education, as well as marginalization lie behind these figures. According to the UN report, 38 per cent of Mexico's indigenous people live in poverty, and Ministry of Social Development data indicates that 3.3 million indigenous people are unable to satisfy their basic nutritional needs.

In the area of education, 50 per cent of indigenous women have not completed primary school, versus 42 per cent of indigenous men. Indigenous girls tend to marry between the ages of 13 and 16 in arrangements that sometimes involve the exchange of cash. Also, from childhood indigenous girls are expected to help their mothers: their 'normal' workday can last 18 hours leaving little time for education, which in many cases is unaffordable.

Chiapas

There is one state in Mexico that has taken steps to address indigenous population issues. The state of Chiapas, located near the border with Guatemala, is very likely the only state in the world where the MDGs have been written in to the State Constitution. This translates into a legal mandate to comply with the MDGs, especially as they relate to indigenous peoples.

Nevertheless, in the 2010 UNDP report the Human Development Index (HDI) value for indigenous people of Chiapas was rated at 0.61, compared to 0.76 for Mexico's non-indigenous population. This is the worst HDI figure of

any of Mexico's 31 states or federal district; however, it represents a significant improvement compared to previous years, in a state that was long characterized by little social investment, and violent confrontations between the indigenous Zapatista Army of National Liberation (EZLN) and government forces.

During an International Parliamentary Conference hosted by the State of Chiapas in October–November 2010, the Chiapas State Governor explained how the publication of an earlier UNDP *Human Development Report* on Mexico had served to motivate a change in approach. This had prompted the Chiapas government to address the needs of the state's indigenous communities directly, and to implement the MDGs with a particular focus on indigenous peoples. A third of the Chiapas state budget is now allocated to the 28 municipalities with the lowest indices, all of which are indigenous. So although CONAPO reported that the infant mortality rate for 2010 in Chiapas stood at 24.2 per 1,000 live births – one of the highest in Mexico – in fact this represents the result of three years of sustained reduction at the fastest rate in the country.

Of significant importance was the orientation of state policies and structures towards greater indigenous inclusion. This allowed the local indigenous representatives at the Inter-Parliamentary Union conference – including some high-level female municipal officials – to state that indigenous voices were increasingly being heard. Consultation in both formal and informal settings has become official state practice at many different levels, and this has resulted in more opportunities to address problems and adapt solutions based on the needs and aspirations of the large indigenous population.

United States

Compared to the rest of the US population, Native Americans during 2010 continued to experience higher rates of illness and mortality from diseases such as diabetes, pneumonia and tuberculosis. In the area of education, Native Americans were also far more likely to drop out of high school and far less likely to go to college. On the other hand, those who attend tribal colleges were much more likely to complete their degree programmes, with the vast majority undertaking careers that serve their indigenous nations and preserve language and culture. Activists argue that much of this is the result of a history of marginalization and territorial dispossession.

United Nations Declaration on the Rights of Indigenous Peoples

On 16 December 2010, the US finally agreed to officially endorse the United Nations Declaration on the Rights of Indigenous Peoples (UNDRIP). The change in stance comes three years after the UN adopted the measure, despite opposition from the US, as well as Australia, Canada and New Zealand (who all subsequently endorsed the declaration). Although some UN member states remain in abstention, by reversing its decision, the US has ensured that no country now remains opposed. Moreover, as a state with significant influence, it has now joined the international community in recognizing that indigenous peoples have rights to non-discrimination, self-determination, land, natural resources and culture. UNDRIP promotes their effective participation in all matters that concern them and ensures their right to remain distinct.

Though not legally binding, UNDRIP is recognized as having moral and political weight; consequently, for over a year, indigenous rights advocates in the US had been urging President Barack Obama to reassess the US stance on the declaration. Following a promise to comply, the US administration undertook a series of consultations with indigenous leaders and NGOs from April to October, which culminated in the official endorsement at the opening of the second annual White House Tribal Nations Conference. Along with the declaration, the president outlined other initiatives, such as providing funding for improved indigenous health care, community school construction, helping tribes combat violence and crime, and resolving long-standing disputes over discrimination and resource rights. Tribal leaders are hoping that the willingness to engage in dialogue shown by the Obama administration will help end the historical marginalization of Alaskan and Native American nations within the US, and help improve the relationship between their autonomous governments and councils, and that of the US.

The US endorsement of the UNDRIP was especially symbolic given that activists in the US Native American community were involved in the original proposal as well as the initial work of drafting it some 30 years ago. These activists, including Tim Coulter, now executive director of the Washington, DC-based Indian Law Resource Center, resorted to the international legal system in an effort to improve US national laws and practices, and gain a place for indigenous peoples in the international community. They are therefore hoping that UNDRIP can be used as a basis for ensuring that the US federal government fulfils its responsibilities to indigenous peoples, and carries out its obligation to promote and respect the human rights of Native American nations and tribes.

Violations of migrant rights in Arizona

On 13 April 2010, the State of Arizona passed the strongest anti-illegal immigrant bill in the US. The 'Support Our Law Enforcement and Safe Neighborhoods Act', introduced as Arizona Senate Bill 1070 (SB 1070), authorizes police to check the legal status of anyone they suspect of being an undocumented migrant, and to arrest all who lack proper identification.

According to US federal law, all foreign nationals over 14 years old who are in the country for longer than 30 days are required to register with the US government, and to have the related documents in their possession at all times. SB1070 makes it a crime for a foreign national to be without these documents or others that verify a legal presence in the US, and also prosecutes anyone sheltering, hiring and transporting illegal aliens. This especially targets undocumented migrant day-labourers by making it a crime to look for work on the street, and fines anyone who harbours or transports them including family members.

According to Associated Press, prior to the law Arizona had been hosting an estimated 460,000 mostly Hispanic undocumented migrants, partly as a result of being the main illegal border crossing point between Mexico and the US. Traversing the harsh Arizona Desert on foot is one method used by thousands of Mexicans and Central Americans seeking to enter the US illegally. By the 1990s, the largest number of arrests by the United States Border Patrol was occurring in Arizona. There was also concern that lethal drug-trafficking and human-smuggling related violence in Mexico would spill across the border into the state, particularly given that over the past five years, the state capital

Phoenix had been averaging one kidnapping per day – the highest number of any city in the US.

However, what began as a local discussion over state control of undocumented migrants quickly became a heated national debate. The passage of the bill sparked protests, rallies and calls to Republican Governor Jan Brewer to veto the legislation. Fears were expressed that the Arizona bill would fuel the anger of people frustrated with the lack of progress on federal US immigration reform, and inspire other states to follow suit with similar controversial measures.

Critics charged that the law infringed a number of key human rights by subjecting minorities to police scrutiny, detentions and arrests based on their race or origin. It also violated freedom of speech by exposing speakers to scrutiny based on their language or accent; and eliminated the right to freedom of movement without being stopped,

questioned or detained. Opponents also argued that the bill would subject police departments to civil rights lawsuits for engaging in racial profiling or for not enforcing the law. In a press statement, the Arizona Association of Chiefs of Police warned that the legislation would increase community distrust of local police and deter immigrants from reporting crimes – including domestic violence – and from cooperating in other investigations.

Human rights groups travelled to Arizona to denounce the legislation, and tens of thousands of people demonstrated in over 70 US cities. State governments in California, Minnesota and Colorado banned employee visits, and passed resolutions limiting business transactions with Arizona-based companies. There were also protests from the Mexican Senate, and according to the *Washington Post*, Mexican President Felipe Calderón condemned the bill and called it a 'violation of human rights'.

According to a poll conducted by the Arizona State University, researchers found – not surprisingly – that 81 per cent of registered Latino voters in Arizona opposed SB 1070. Supporters such as the sponsor and co-author of the bill, State Senator Russell Pearce, argued that the absence of federal immigration enforcement had left the state little choice but to take its own measures. It should also be noted that, despite the vocal public protests, the Arizona law seemed to enjoy strong backing across most of the US.

The Act was signed into law by Governor Jan Brewer on 23 April 2010, and amended two days later to prevent it from being applied in a discriminatory fashion. However its constitutionality and compliance with civil rights law was immediately challenged in the courts by the National Coalition of Latino Clergy and Christian Leaders, the American Civil Liberties Union (ACLU), the Anti-Defamation League and the Mexican government. Moreover, on 6 July 2010, the US Department of Justice filed a lawsuit against the state of Arizona asking that the law be declared invalid, and requested the federal courts to issue an injunction to halt enforcement before it went into effect. A preliminary injunction was granted that blocked the law's most controversial provisions.

Nevertheless, supporters could argue that the law is already making a difference. A study released in November 2010 stated that there were already 100,000 fewer Hispanics in Arizona than before the debate about the law began. It also suggested that Arizona's poor economic climate could be a contributing factor in the decline. According to Associated Press, the government of Mexico reported that between June and September 2010 over 23,000 of its citizens had returned to the country from Arizona. Migrants who have remained in Arizona have modified their behaviour to avoid detection. According to local television station news reports, domestic violence shelters have noted that some women with questionable immigration status have been avoiding domestic abuse hotlines and shelters for fear of deportation.

In other parts of the country, bills similar to SB 1070 were introduced in Michigan, Minnesota, Pennsylvania, Rhode Island and South Carolina. Politicians in nearly 20 states were proposing to introduce similar legislation during their 2011 legislative calendars. By the end of 2010, none of the bills had gone to final vote.

In the end, the ethnic make-up of a state may have a role to play in whatever decisions are taken regarding the issue of illegal immigration. For example, according to MSNBC News, states along the Mexican border – California, New Mexico and Texas – that have large and influential Hispanic communities and cultural ties to Mexico have shown little interest in following Arizona's lead, indicating that they do not see illegal immigration to be such a serious problem. ∎

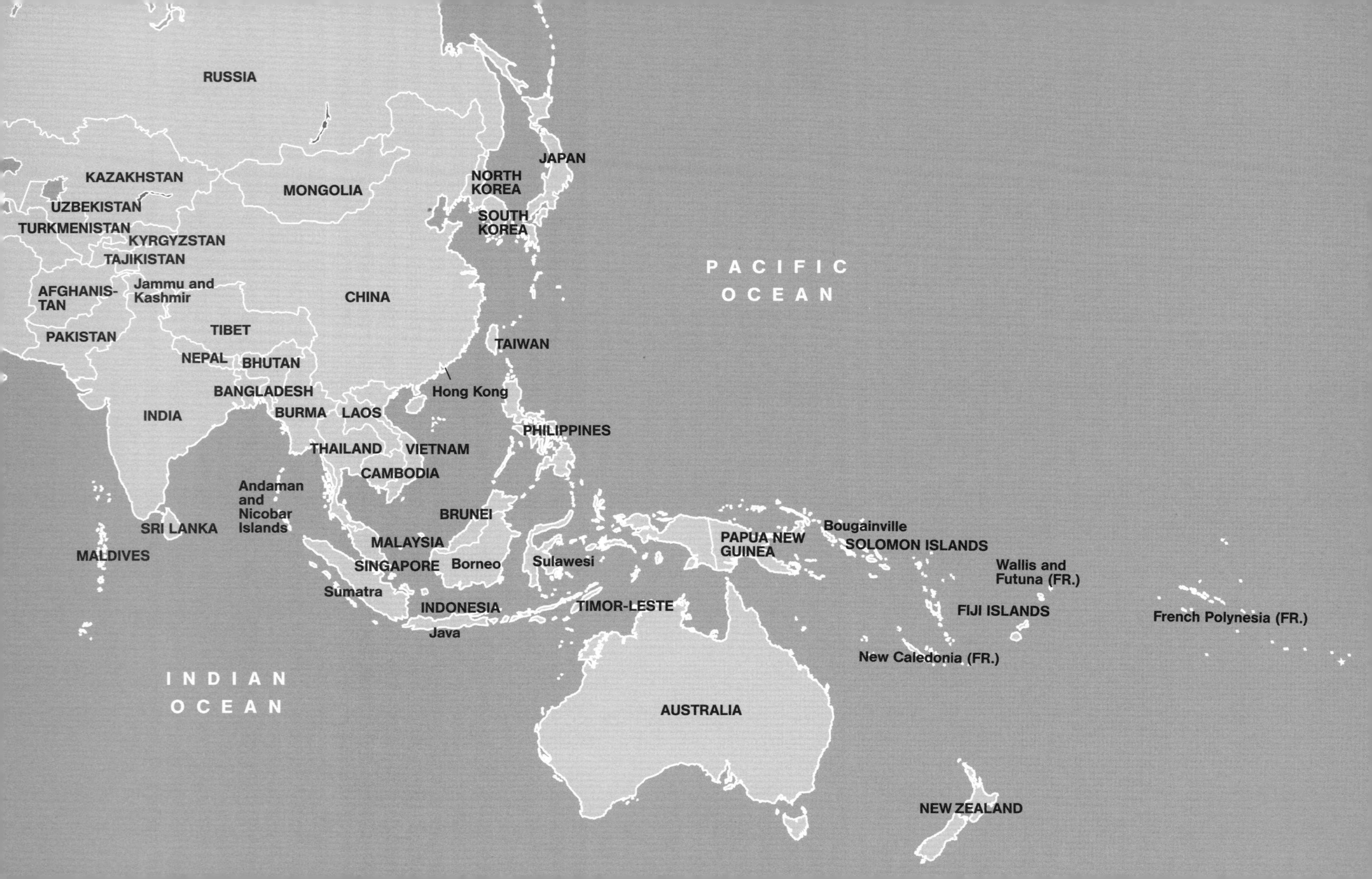

French Polynesia (FR.)

Wallis and
Futuna (FR.)

FIJI ISLANDS

New Caledonia (FR.)

NEW ZEALAND

Bougainville

SOLOMON ISLANDS

PAPUA NEW
GUINEA

PACIFIC
OCEAN

AUSTRALIA

TIMOR-LESTE

Sulawesi

JAPAN

NORTH
KOREA

SOUTH
KOREA

TAIWAN

PHILIPPINES

Hong Kong

BRUNEI

Borneo

RUSSIA

MONGOLIA

CHINA

VIETNAM

THAILAND

CAMBODIA

MALAYSIA

SINGAPORE

INDONESIA

Java

Sumatra

KAZAKHSTAN

UZBEKISTAN

TURKMENISTAN

KYRGYZSTAN

TAJIKISTAN

Jammu and
Kashmir

AFGHANIS-
TAN

PAKISTAN

TIBET

NEPAL

BHUTAN

BANGLADESH

BURMA

LAOS

INDIA

Andaman
and
Nicobar
Islands

SRI LANKA

MALDIVES

INDIAN
OCEAN

Asia and Oceania

Joshua Castellino, Irwin Loy,
Matthew Naumann, Marusca Perazzi
and Jacqui Zalcberg

Central Asia

Matthew Naumann

The key event for minorities in Central Asia in 2010 was the violent unrest that occurred between ethnic Uzbeks and Kyrgyz in southern Kyrgyzstan in June. The riots focused on the southern city of Osh. At least 418 people died, with some estimating a total of more than 2,000 fatalities. In the aftermath of the conflict, ethnic Uzbeks in southern Kyrgyzstan, who were collectively accused by many Kyrgyz of instigating the violence, reported intensified discrimination and persecution. Approximately 400,000 people fled the violence in early June, of whom 100,000 crossed the border into Uzbekistan. While most returned within three weeks, Uzbeks have continued to leave Kyrgyzstan since then.

Kyrgyzstan also saw parliamentary elections in October 2010. The resulting coalition consists of parties that appealed to both ethnic nationalism and inter-ethnic unity during the campaign. It remains to be seen how the coalition will approach the urgent need for reconciliation in the south of the country.

The Osh tragedy has had a particular impact on women. There have been repeated accounts of ethnicity- and gender-based violence against women, both during and after June. In December, human rights activists accused the security forces of not doing enough to investigate and prevent a spate of kidnappings of Uzbek women, who were allegedly submitted to repeated rape and then released after several days. Security concerns among the Uzbek population have led to cases of women dropping out of education, girls being married early (in the hope that others would be able to provide better protection), and women not daring to go to health care facilities. Meanwhile, many Uzbek women have also lost their jobs with state health care and educational institutions, or been forced by Kyrgyz colleagues to abandon market stalls.

The violence in Kyrgyzstan led to some anti-Kyrgyz sentiment among the population of Uzbekistan. Uzbekistan's security forces were deployed to prevent vigilante attacks on the country's ethnic Kyrgyz communities. Throughout the crisis, the Uzbekistan government emphasized that inter-ethnic unity was essential. Separately, media reports indicate an upsurge in anti-Uzbek sentiment in the Karakalpak autonomous republic where ethnic Kazakhs and Karakalpaks between them make up the majority of the population.

Kazakhstan's President Nazarbaev has also stressed inter-ethnic unity in response to the June events. However, the government policies to promote use of the Kazakh language are continuing to raise concerns among ethnic minorities, as well as ethnic Kazakhs who do not speak the language. Meanwhile, an ethnic Russian politician who plans to stand for president in 2012 was pelted with eggs by Kazakh nationalists at a press conference in October.

In Tajikistan, a media blackout obscured information about a military campaign against alleged armed Islamist groups in Rasht Valley in the autumn. However, it is likely that extensive damage has been inflicted on the local Gharmi population, and that ethnic Kyrgyz citizens of Tajikistan from the Jergetal area to the north of the valley were also caught up in the violence. The country has seen a spate of security incidents believed to have been carried out by militants. Meanwhile, there has also been growth in forms of Sunni and Shi'a Islam that are not officially sanctioned. The Tajik government has responded with a campaign to crack down on citizens studying Islam abroad, and against Muslim missionaries coming to Tajikistan from other countries.

In Turkmenistan, a *de facto* liberalization of the policy on dual nationality in recent years was reversed in July, when the government made an official statement that dual citizenship was unconstitutional, after several holders of Russian passports were not allowed to leave the country. A *rapprochement* between the presidents of Turkmenistan and Uzbekistan has not led to an improvement in the lives of border residents; ethnic Uzbeks are still subjected to a Turkmenization policy in education and state bodies. In addition, marriages of women from across the border to citizens of Turkmenistan are not officially recognized without a substantial payment to the government, in contravention of the country's

Sexual and gender-based violence in southern Kyrgyzstan

The Uzbek and Kyrgyz communities in southern Kyrgyzstan are both predominantly Sunni Muslim and traditionally are more conservative than people living in other areas of Kyrgyzstan. As a result, both communities collectively react to sexual and gender-based violence with particular anger, while victims of such attacks often feel intense shame and may experience stigma from within their own communities. In this context, during the violence that occurred in southern Kyrgyzstan in June, corroborated cases of sexual assault, (as well as rumours that such attacks had taken place subsequently discovered to be unfounded), provoked violent responses on both sides, and were used as justification for revenge attacks. Sexual assaults continued to be reported by human rights activists into December, primarily involving Kyrgyz men assaulting Uzbek women.

Soon after the conflict erupted on the night of 11 June, rumours began to spread among ethnic Kyrgyz that an Uzbek mob in central Osh had raped and killed female Kyrgyz students in a university dormitory. These allegations were subsequently investigated by human rights activists and found to be untrue. However, the rumours spread quickly around the girls' home villages in southern Kyrgyzstan, and led to thousands of Kyrgyz men descending on the city from these villages to free the hostages and take revenge.

At the peak of the ethnic violence in Osh on 11–14 June, both sides reported sexual assault being used as an instrument of the conflict by the other ethnic group. Websites were quickly set up by supporters of both sides which documented some cases of sexual and gender-based violence in gruesome detail.

There were many reports of sexual assaults that took place during the destruction of ethnic Uzbek areas. An Uzbek human rights activist reported meeting at least 50 victims of sexual assault in a refugee camp in Uzbekistan after the June events. But overall, it is impossible – for several reasons – to quantify the scale of gender-based violence during the conflict. Cultural and social norms make it very difficult for women to report attacks as to do so entails bringing shame and dishonour on their families. In addition, there have been reports of anonymous warnings to victims to prevent them from reporting incidents. Finally, many victims were sent abroad to Russia or Uzbekistan to escape from the violence, or were killed after the assaults.

A gender-based violence assessment report produced by UNIFEM in August 2010 indicates that while both communities generally felt insecure after the violence, there were particular concerns among Uzbek women survivors. They were afraid of repeated sexual or physical violence against themselves or their children, and thus severely limited their own movements in the city. In addition, access for victims to almost all services has been very limited, including psychosocial counselling, legal advice and education. Some ethnic Uzbek service providers have been sacked from their jobs, while others have left the country. Therefore, many ethnic Uzbek victims have relied on support from international organizations and non-governmental organizations (NGOs). Even in women's crisis centres which are sympathetic to Uzbek victims, some sources have reported that hostility among ethnic Kyrgyz clients can make residential support for ethnic Uzbeks impossible.

Sexual and gender-based violence against Uzbek

women has reportedly continued in southern Kyrgyzstan throughout the year. In December, local human rights groups registered with the authorities seven instances of kidnap and rape between October and December. Women were reportedly tortured, made to drink a medicine, beaten and held in captivity for several days, before being left near their houses. The cases continue to make many female Uzbek school students scared to leave their homes because of fear of assault. There has also been a rise in early marriage among Uzbek girls since June, including some girls younger than 16. Their parents are looking for others to take responsibility for their daughters' security.

The justice system has so far proved ineffective at prosecuting the perpetrators of gender-based violence against Uzbek women. However, on 8 December, six ethnic Uzbeks were jailed for the rape and murder of a Kyrgyz woman on 12 June. While both Uzbeks and Kyrgyz were implicated in the June violence, Human Rights Watch (HRW) and Amnesty International have raised concerns about the disproportionate targeting of suspected Uzbeks for arrest and prosecution. ■

commitments under international human rights law. Meanwhile, local and regional elections this year reportedly saw no minority ethnic candidates elected.

In the religious sphere, those following Islamic religious practices not sanctioned by the state have faced restrictions across the region. This has had particular repercussions for Muslim women choosing to wear the *hijab* (a headscarf that encircles the face, covering the neck and shoulders rather than tied at the back of the neck, as is common across Central Asia and the Caucasus) or the *niqab* (which covers the whole face). Cases of girls and women being turned away from educational institutions because of Islamic dress have been recorded in all countries in the region. The crackdowns are particularly severely imposed in areas that the authorities regard as of concern in terms of security, such as Turkmenistan's border regions with Iran, and Uzbekistan's portion of the Fergana Valley, an area that has traditionally been more conservative and religious than other parts of the country.

Kazakhstan

Kazakhstan's President Nursultan Nazarbaev responded to the June events in Kyrgyzstan by highlighting his commitment to inter-ethnic unity. However, there are indications that Kazakhstan is planning to strengthen the role of the Kazakh language in the country, at the expense of Russian, the other official language. The government is developing a plan to ensure that 95 per cent of the population are able to speak Kazakh by 2020. In particular, it is intended that there will be a shift to the use of Kazakh in government offices. This will build on existing education and media policies promoting use of the language.

According to the 2009 census, however, only 64 per cent believe they have command of the Kazakh language. After Kazakhs (63 per cent of the population), Russians are the largest ethnic group (24 per cent). Only 6 per cent of ethnic Russians can read and write Kazakh, and a quarter understand spoken Kazakh. Meanwhile, 94 per cent of the population understand Russian, with 85 per cent able to read and write it. There are concerns that promotion of Kazakh may lead to discrimination against non-speakers, including Kazakhs who are not fluent in the language. Official

Above: A Tatar woman in front of her house near Burabay, Kazakhstan. *Eric Lafforgue.*

usage of Russian in some areas is decreasing: a journalist in South Kazakhstan province states that many public employees do not speak Russian and find it difficult to communicate with ethnic Russians who do not speak Kazakh.

Because of state policy to promote the Kazakh language, several ethnic groups have reportedly been unable to officially register mosques where sermons are read in non-official languages, including Tartar, Kyrgyz and Azerbaijani. In addition, ethnic Kazakhs have been appointed imams in several Uighur mosques. The policy is particularly problematic for Azerbaijanis, many of whom are Shi'ite Muslims, unlike the majority Sunni population. Azerbaijanis are only entitled to build prayer houses, which cannot host Friday prayers or resemble mosques.

Women from minority religious groups face particular problems in Kazakhstan. Kazakh society is largely secular and most women do not wear head coverings. There is growing official resistance to the practice of wearing the *hijab*. A ban was introduced on 26 October 2009, and criticized by a group of parliamentarians in December that year. It is likely that the rule will be tested in the Constitutional

Court against Kazakhstan's international human rights obligations. In August, the Minister of Education reiterated that the ministry is against the wearing of the *hijab* in academic institutions because of the precedent it would set. In November this year, a group of female students were reportedly banned from attending classes at Atyrau State University for refusing to remove their headscarves. Meanwhile, in February, a Baptist woman was fined for holding morning worship in her home with local women and children. The authorities deemed it an 'illegally functioning religious community'.

On 27 October, ethnic Russian opposition politician Vladimir Kozlov announced that he would run for president in 2012. To meet requirements, he has pledged to be fluent in Kazakh by 2012. However, his announcement caused nationalists attending the press conference to throw eggs at him, characterizing the bid as an 'insult'. One protester was fined, with another receiving a seven-day prison sentence. Analysts suggest that the reaction to the bid highlighted an undertone of chauvinistic nationalism in Kazakhstan.

The 2010 report on the United Nations (UN) Independent Expert on Minority Issues' mission to Kazakhstan stated that women are generally under-represented in Kazakh politics, and that 'minority women stressed that this is particularly the case for women from smaller ethnic groups'. Minority women are also concerned that minority girls are at a disadvantage in the education system, as parents often give priority to boys, particularly in more conservative communities.

On 1 January 2010 a new law came into force that stated that the country's migration authorities would no longer accept UN High Commissioner for Refugees (UNHCR) determination of the status of asylum-seekers and would make refugee status decisions itself. This led to several ethnic Uzbeks being returned to Uzbekistan from a group of 30, of whom 17 had previously received certificates from UNHCR that they were asylum-seekers. Since April, Kazakhstan has deported hundreds of labour migrants from Kyrgyzstan, Tajikistan and Uzbekistan. The campaign intensified in October.

The 2010 Report on the Millennium Development Goals (MDGs) in Kazakhstan highlighted the disadvantaged position of migrant women in Kazakhstan, pointing out that 'labour migrants are vulnerable to poverty, especially female labour migrants', due to 'poor awareness of the existence of organizations dealing with protection of the rights of migrant workers, non-observance of occupational safety rules and rights in employer–employee relations, irregular salaries and access to public health care services, which is not fully guaranteed'.

Kyrgyzstan

In 2009, ethnic Kyrgyz constituted 68 per cent of the population in the southern provinces of Batken, Jalalabad and Osh, with Uzbeks the largest minority, at 26 per cent. Uzbeks form a much higher percentage of the population in the densely populated fertile agricultural and urban areas of Jalalabad and Osh provinces, and are a majority in some of these areas, while mountainous areas have remained predominantly ethnic Kyrgyz.

Meanwhile, after large-scale emigration to Russia and Europe since the end of the Soviet Union, the north of the country has smaller non-Kyrgyz communities, often concentrated in cities or discrete villages in Chuy Valley. The instability that followed the overthrow of President Kurmanbek Bakiev in April saw a rise in inter-ethnic tension in Chuy province. On 8–9 April, anti-government protests in the city of Tokmok escalated into targeted riots against ethnic Uighur and Dungan businesses. On 17 April, six people died when ethnic Kyrgyz squatters attempted to seize land and property from Meskhetian Turkish residents of Maevka village on the outskirts of the capital Bishkek and met armed resistance from homeowners. A Dungan village was also targeted by land-grabbers on 22 April, but the police intervened to prevent escalation. Meanwhile, the Russian Federation also protested about incidents affecting ethnic Russians in April.

The interim government that took power in April committed itself to introducing parliamentary democracy. The approach was initially welcomed by ethnic Uzbek leaders in the south, who mobilized support for the interim government, and called for more Uzbek participation in the country's political life, and enhanced status for Uzbek language. However, a chain of events led to increased tensions and then inter-ethnic violence in Jalalabad in May.

The clashes intensified during the following month. At least 418 people died in southern Kyrgyzstan in June during violence largely between ethnic Kyrgyz and Uzbeks. Some reports say the true casualty figure could be more than 2,000. Most of the victims identified so far have been ethnic Uzbeks, although there were also many Kyrgyz victims. Destruction of property overwhelmingly, though not exclusively, targeted ethnic Uzbek areas and Uzbek-owned establishments. A National Commission of Enquiry published findings in January 2011 blaming Uzbek community leaders for provoking the violence, in alliance with other provocateurs; the report has been criticized for being poorly researched and overly political. Meanwhile, an International Commission of Enquiry into the events is due to release its findings in early 2011.

Security concerns among the ethnic Uzbek population, including fear of gender-based violence, have become much more prominent since the June events. In August, residents of Uzbek neighbourhoods told HRW that they were leaving their homes as little as possible, fearing attack, arrest, harassment or extortion by the security forces or other authorities. In December, a group of Uzbek community leaders met the mayor of

Osh, Melis Myrzakmatov, to discuss their security situation, including ongoing reports of kidnappings. The mayor assured the Uzbek leaders that the Osh authorities would do everything they could to provide security. This meeting was significant, as the role of Myrzakmatov in regard to the ethnic turmoil has been a prominent feature of discussions, given his previous declarations that he is a (Kyrgyz) 'nationalist', and his refusal to step down following the violence, when requested to do so by the interim government.

There are nevertheless concerns that Uzbeks are being disproportionately targeted in efforts to find the instigators of the violence. In the weeks and months following the violence, a series of sweep operations took place in predominantly Uzbek areas in and around Osh. These were accompanied by human rights violations including arbitrary arrest, illegal detention, torture and ill-treatment of detainees during arrest and in custody. There were also reports of looting and confiscation of property. With regard to judicial processes, as of early November, the overwhelming majority of those tried had been ethnic Uzbeks. According to Amnesty International, the trials have been 'seriously flawed with lawyers being harassed outside the courtrooms, and judges refusing to call defence witnesses or recognize that "confessions" may have been extracted under torture'. Relatives and lawyers of the defendants, as well as the defendants themselves, have been attacked on several occasions both inside and outside courtrooms.

There is also a culture of impunity for low-level attacks and crimes against ethnic Uzbeks in the post-conflict period. Verbal harassment, physical assault and theft are reported to be common in Osh. There are concerns that corrupt officials are taking advantage of the situation to demand more and higher bribes from ethnic Uzbeks for public services or to be released from police custody. In addition, ethnic Kyrgyz human rights activists and lawyers who have revealed abuses against ethnic Uzbeks have been harassed. In July, prominent activist Tolekan Ismailova left the country for several months alleging that death threats had been made against her.

Other ethnic groups were also affected by the June instability. A number of ethnic Tajiks from Batken province reportedly fled briefly with Uzbeks to Uzbekistan. There were also reports in June that hundreds of ethnic Uighurs had fled to Kazakhstan from northern Kyrgyzstan after receiving threats that they would be the next target of violence. However, despite several scares, no large-scale violence broke out in the north of the country.

Despite the June violence, the interim government pushed ahead with constitutional reforms. The draft Constitution, which was put to referendum on 27 June, gave the parliament greater authority. Earlier requests by Uzbek community leaders for state recognition of their language nationally or in majority-Uzbek areas were not reflected in the new Constitution, in which Kyrgyz remains the state language and Russian the official language.

Elections were held under the new Constitution on 10 October, with 29 parties participating and five winning seats. A narrow plurality was won by the then opposition party Ata Jurt, which is strongest among southern Kyrgyz. The party made several coded anti-diversity messages during the campaign. Meanwhile, the parties that came second and third in the election (the Social Democratic Party and Ar Namys) had consciously courted Uzbek votes in the south, and both saw prominent ethnic Uzbeks being elected as parliamentarians. Ar Namys was also popular among ethnic Russians and other minorities in the north.

A coalition government was formed in mid December. The new government's approach to inter-ethnic relations is unpredictable, as it includes both Ata Jurt and the Social Democrats, as well as fourth-placed Respublika, which had several minority ethnic candidates but then became the only party with no minority representation in parliament after two ethnic Russians withdrew from the party list after the election. In total, six Russians, three Uzbeks, one Korean and the first ever ethnic Tajik parliamentarian in Kyrgyzstan took up seats after the elections.

Tajikistan

Tajiks comprise the largest ethnic group in the country, accounting for 79.9 per cent of the population. Other groups include Uzbeks (15.3 per cent), Russians (1.1 per cent) and Kyrgyz (1.1 per cent). The Tajik population includes Pamiris in the east, who speak eastern Iranian languages, are primarily Ismaili Shi'ites, and were in early Soviet times considered a separate ethnic group.

'I feel there is no future here for our kids'

The violence in southern Kyrgyzstan and its aftermath have seen a sharp deterioration in the situation of the ethnic Uzbek population, with many losing employment, decreased opportunities to take part in education and public life, and *de facto* restrictions on freedom of movement. In October 2010, *Matthew Naumann* spoke to a human rights activist in Osh about the situation there.

Even before the violence, ethnic Uzbeks were under-represented in national politics, local government, the security forces, the civil service and the judicial system. Uzbek men were more likely to work in the private sector, while women would typically work in markets, health or education. After the conflict, economic opportunities have contracted further for ethnic Uzbeks: as of late November many formerly Uzbek-owned shops, cafes and other small businesses in Osh remained burned out, while many ethnic Uzbek traders in local markets had been replaced by ethnic Kyrgyz. Many workers in the social sector in areas such as health and education have also lost their jobs.

'Since the violence I've been staying with relatives in a village, for personal safety. I don't send my daughter to kindergarten, because it is mainly Kyrgyz, and I'm afraid for her safety. So for the moment she sits at home with relatives. Many children are afraid to go to school. In mixed classes, Uzbek boys and girls have been beaten.

'The [Osh] Mayor's Office has put on transport for schools, but only for city schools. There is no transport to nearby Uzbek-language schools in areas which are technically not part of the city. In four schools, the Uzbek-language classes have been closed. Because of the winter, the students from Tolstoy Uzbek-language school, which is being rebuilt, have been sent from their tent school to another Uzbek-language school in the centre of the city, and to other neighbouring schools with Kyrgyz children. But they are afraid and they don't go. The number attending school has fallen sharply, as people leave for Russia or Kazakhstan, or to stay with their relatives in Uzbekistan.

'The Kyrgyz-Uzbek University in the city has been transformed into Osh Social University. The ethnic Uzbek rector has been sacked. The previous Uzbek language and literature faculty, which had its own building, has been replaced by an Uzbek language and literature chair within the Kyrgyz language and literature faculty. About 40 lecturers have been sacked, reportedly because so few students are registered now.

'Many women have stopped studying – some were forbidden by their parents. Many just sit at home, praying for peace. Students at Osh State University pay 20,000 som a year for their studies. I even know a [final]-year student who was told that she would not receive a diploma because she is Uzbek – they asked for a bribe to allow her to graduate.

'There is open discrimination on public transport. Ethnically-based based fights or arguments often break out. Kyrgyz passengers often refuse to pay Uzbek drivers for their journeys. There are few buses travelling to Uzbek neighbourhoods after 5 p.m., so people have to leave work early.

'Fifty-six ethnic Uzbek workers in Osh city hospital

were sacked after not going to work because of concerns over security. Kyrgyz who did not go to work kept their jobs. Meanwhile, a private Uzbek-owned hospital in the city was burned down. They had modern equipment, and both Kyrgyz and Uzbek patients received good medical treatment there. Now, many Uzbeks are afraid to attend local hospitals, fearing that the doctors may try to harm them. Women are afraid to go to maternity hospitals. This has led to an increase in home births.

'The most difficult issue is the possibility of people wanting to take revenge. This could happen at any time.

'There are indications that there has been an increase in support among the Uzbek community for radical Islamist groups since the events. The leaders were prominent in Nookat, Aravan and Kara Suu districts during the events. Now lots of men and boys who lost their homes and possessions have joined up....

'I feel there is no future here for our kids, especially since all the textbooks published in Uzbekistan were taken from Uzbek schools at the end of December by the national security service, and no books were given to replace them, not even in Kyrgyz. There is bias everywhere against Uzbeks, from the education system to public services.

'Everybody is leaving. After the international organizations leave in the summer there will be no more work. The mahalla *[neighbourhood] is empty. My daughter used to play with lots of children in the* mahalla *but now she is alone. I am also thinking of leaving for Russia, to join my relatives there, because the situation here is not improving. It will take many years to restore confidence and trust between Uzbeks and Kyrgyz in the south.'* ∎

Meanwhile, the majority of Tajiks in Tajikistan speak a south-western Iranian language (closer to Farsi). Most Tajiks (excluding Pamiris) are Sunni Muslims, although there are reports of a large increase in adherence to twelver Shi'a Islam under the influence of Iranian missionaries, both in the Pamir area and in Khatlon and Soghd provinces in the south and north of western Tajikistan. This is reportedly due partly to a crackdown on radical Sunni missionary activity by the authorities, and partly to attempts by the government to build links with Iran.

The Tajik community is also subdivided by place of origin. The president continues to uphold a tight power-sharing structure made up of his family and others from his home-town of Dangara and province of Khatlon. This political elite has a disproportionate influence in government affairs and better access to political power than other ethnic and regional groups. One particularly disadvantaged ethnic group are the Gharmi people, who are originally from the Rasht Valley in north-central Tajikistan, though many were forcibly relocated to the west of the country in Soviet times. Gharmi people tend to be more religiously conservative, and the province is the heartland of the (predominantly Sunni) Islamic Renaissance Party, the only legally registered religious party in Central Asia. Many Gharmis and Pamiris joined the opposition during Tajikistan's civil war in the 1990s, and in the 1997 peace agreement, several opposition field commanders were given administrative positions in the Rasht Valley.

This year saw several security incidents connected to armed Islamist groups, including the country's first recorded suicide bombing, a mass jail-break in August, and an ambush that led to the deaths of 25 soldiers in the Rasht Valley on 19 September. A two-month military operation against Islamist groups in Rasht Valley was followed by reports that the Defence Ministry plans to open permanent military training bases in the area. The effect of the military operation on the local Gharmi population is unclear, because independent journalists have not been granted access to the area, and telephone connections have been cut. Some reports suggest that ethnic Kyrgyz citizens of Tajikistan, most of whom live in the Jergetal area to the north of the Rasht Valley, may also have died in the violence.

Government concerns about the rise of non-state-controlled forms of Sunni and Shi'a Islam have led to actions against those who practise unauthorized forms of Islam. Students from Tajikistan studying abroad at Islamic universities and *madrasas* have been pressured by officials to return home. Officially, as of November, around 1,400 Tajik students were known to be studying abroad at Islamic universities and *madrasas*. However, some estimates put the number of Tajiks studying in Pakistan alone at 4,000. In the autumn, the authorities stopped dozens of students and scholars from boarding a Tehran-bound flight at the airport of the capital, Dushanbe. The government said it was responding to a lack of information about the purpose of the trip. Meanwhile, in October, authorities shut down 20 unregistered religious schools in Khatlon province alone. Also in October, Tajikistan's only 'Women's Mosque' burned down the day after officials from the central Religious Affairs Committee came to the mosque and ordered that the mosque should stop being used for prayers. The Islamic Renaissance Party (IRP) implied in a statement that they suspected arson.

Women and men who follow what are sometimes referred to as Arab (rather than Tajik) Islamic dress codes continue to come under pressure in Tajikistan. Since 2007, there has been a ban on the *hijab* in state institutions, some public places and shops. In August, a group of women from Khatlon province were told that they would lose their stalls at a local market if they continued to wear the *hijab*. In spite of these restrictions, there has reportedly been a sharp rise in women wearing the *niqab*. In October it was also reported that men with long beards were being detained for identification on suspicion of being followers of the radical Salafi school of Sunni Islam.

Parliamentary elections held in February saw the ruling People's Democratic Party return with a majority. The party that came second in the popular vote, the Islamic Renaissance Party (IRP), only won two seats. The Organization for Security and Co-operation in Europe (OSCE) stated that the elections failed to meet democratic standards. In the elections, the OSCE reports that the number of candidates from minority groups was marginal and that minority issues were not raised during the campaign. Political parties, however, distributed campaign materials in minority languages, such as Russian and Uzbek, in the northern Sughd region and in the capital Dushanbe. In areas with

significant minority populations, ballots were printed in minority languages. No specific cases of discrimination on ethnic grounds related to the election process were observed or reported by OSCE observers.

Cross-border marriages between Tajiks and Uzbeks are common in border regions. However, strict and complex marital registration rules make it increasingly difficult for couples to register their marriages in Uzbekistan. Furthermore, immigration authorities only grant visas for up to five days, which makes movement between the two countries extremely difficult, as most citizens cannot afford the cost of applying for a longer, twelve-month visa.

Turkmenistan

It remains difficult to access information about minority issues in Turkmenistan, because of the lack of press freedom and restrictions on civil society. However, it is clear that minority groups continue to be sidelined from many educational, employment and political opportunities in Turkmenistan as a result of discriminatory government policies. Observers state that in the local and regional elections held on 5 December only ethnic Turkmen stood as candidates. Although three ethnic Russians reportedly have significant informal political roles, official government positions are dominated by ethnic Turkmen with a disproportionate number of government positions held by Turkmen belonging to President Gurbanguly Berdymuhammedov's Akhal Tekke clan. It has been reported that some Turkmen from outside Ashgabat speak Russian in the capital in order to hide their regional accents and avoid discrimination.

While the primarily Orthodox Russian-speaking community continues to enjoy more educational, cultural and religious opportunities than in the last years of former President Saparmurat Niyazov, there are indications that Turkmenistan's diversification from dependence on Russia for its gas exports means it feels less need to accommodate dual Russian–Turkmen nationals. Human rights activists estimate that about 100,000 Turkmen nationals – of Russian as well as Turkmen ethnicity – also hold Russian passports. On 7 July, the government issued a statement saying that the Constitution made no provision for dual citizenship. This followed several reports that Turkmen nationals who also held

Russian citizenship were not being allowed to leave the country, and were being told they must give up one of the two passports.

Despite a groundbreaking meeting between the presidents of Turkmenistan and Uzbekistan in October, ethnic Uzbeks in Turkmenistan are unhappy at the continuing policy of 'Turkmenization', which requires their children to learn Turkmen and wear Turkmen costumes at school. The regions of Dashoguz and Lebap in north-eastern Turkmenistan have significant ethnic Uzbek populations. Human rights organizations in Uzbekistan state that self-identification as ethnic Uzbek is decreasing in Turkmenistan, because of the difficulties this causes. There have also been violations of the right to family life: in June, a group of 30 women from Uzbekistan in Lebap province who had married Turkmen nationals and given birth to children eligible for Turkmen citizenship were summarily deported, simply because their marriages as foreigners were not recognized. Reports of fees as high of US$ 50,000 to validate such marriages have been received by the Turkmen Initiative for Human Rights. Mosques in Dashoguz continue to be led by ethnic Turkmen imams, with some local Muslims stating that they believe this is direct discrimination.

There are also reports that restrictions on crossing the border between Turkmenistan and Uzbekistan have become tighter this year, despite the thaw in government relations. In October it was reported that Dashoguz residents who had already been forcibly resettled were removed even further away from the Turkmen–Uzbek border by the Turkmen military. The Turkmen Initiative for Human Rights says that residents were given only a few days notice to leave before their homes were bulldozed.

All religious activity remains under strict control. The Muftiate (Muslim Board) is controlled through state appointments of the chief mufti and other imams. Although the government allows Sunni Islam to operate (within tightly controlled limits), this is not the case for Shi'a Islam, which is mainly professed by the ethnic Azeri and Iranian minorities in the west of the country. In certain areas, such as near the border with Iran, it is reported that beards and the *hijab* are not allowed.

Other religious minorities in the country also suffer discrimination. While Ashghabad's Catholic community finally gained legal status in March 2010 after 13 years of negotiation, some Shi'a Muslim communities, the Armenian Apostolic Church, a number of Protestant communities and Jehovah's Witnesses have been unable to register. Many religious communities have reportedly stopped applying for registration, and have decided to operate quietly without legal status. The lack of legal provision for conscientious objection or alternative service meant that eight Jehovah's Witnesses were in jail in November 2010 after refusing to perform military service, with a further three serving suspended sentences.

Uzbekistan

In response to the violence in Kyrgyzstan, Uzbekistan's President Karimov repeatedly stated that the conflict was not inter-ethnic, and stressed the importance of inter-ethnic unity. State television followed suit, carrying many programmes emphasizing inter-ethnic harmony in the country. However, local observers state that this campaign does not address structural discrimination, especially the issue of Uzbek nationalism and the exclusion of ethnic minorities from public life.

Uzbekistan allowed up to 100,000 refugees from Kyrgyzstan, the vast majority women and children, into the country in mid-June. Large refugee camps were established by the authorities, who requested international support. However, within two weeks, at the request of Kyrgyzstan's interim government, almost all were returned. Reports indicate that some were forced to return, in clear violation of the widely held international legal principle of *non-refoulement*, namely that no one should be returned to situations where their life or freedom is threatened. There were reports in December that several thousand ethnic Uzbeks from Kyrgyzstan remained illegally in Uzbekistan in December, but that many of them were seeking to leave for Russia or Western Europe for fear of deportation and lack of financial means.

Uzbekistan's ethnic Kyrgyz minority, which is primarily concentrated in Andijan, Fergana and Namangan provinces, remained fearful of potential reprisal attacks. There has reportedly been a sharp rise in hostility towards Kyrgyz in Uzbekistan, partially reflected by a prominent singer recording a song entitled 'To the Kyrgyz' about the inter-ethnic violence. Since the June events, there has been an increased security presence around Kyrgyz villages, ostensibly to protect villagers from potential attacks by Uzbek vigilantes.

The autonomous republic of Karakalpakstan makes up a third of the area of Uzbekistan (in the east), and has large reserves of oil, gas, titanium and gold. It surrounds the remnants of the Aral Sea, devastated by decades of overproduction of cotton in Central Asia. Sixty per cent of its population are ethnic Karakalpaks and Kazakhs, and there is apparently a separatist movement that would like the republic either to become part of Kazakhstan or secure full independence. Reportedly, tens of thousands of people have left Karakalpakstan for Kazakhstan in recent years, despite government measures to prevent this, including a ban on the sale of housing. This is partly connected to Kazakhstan's continued promotion of immigration of ethnic Kazakhs to the country. Recently, there have been reports of a rise in anger at perceived injustice against the people of Karakalpakstan. In November, the sale of equipment from an animal feed-producing plant in the town of Chimbay in Karakalpakstan to neighbouring Khorezm province by Uzbekistan's State Property Commission led to an angry anti-Uzbek demonstration in the town, which was broken up by riot police.

After a visit by the OSCE's High Commissioner for National Minorities in early April, Uzbekistan's government showed its defiance by cracking down on minority representation. In April, the Kazakh Cultural Centre in Nukus, Karakalpakstan's capital, was given one month to address alleged legal violations or face closure. Meanwhile, the head of the Jewish Cultural Centre in Tashkent was refused an extension to his accreditation in April after legal violations were also allegedly found there.

Uzbekistan has continued to tighten its borders with neighbouring countries, and this has affected local residents in border areas who are often from minority ethnic groups. In July, it was reported that 42 houses were to be demolished in a primarily ethnic Kazakh border village in Tashkent province. No government order was shared with residents, and it was unclear if compensation was to be paid. In September, the disputed village of Chek on the border with Kyrgyzstan was formally annexed by Uzbekistan. Twenty-four families who wanted to remain citizens of Kyrgyzstan (of whom 20 were ethnic Uzbeks and four Kyrgyz) had to relocate to another village inside Kyrgyzstan.

Tajiks, who are prevalent in and around the cities of Bukhara and Samarkand, have reported discriminatory government policies. There are reports that Bukhara city authorities recently closed Tajik-language schools. And the city administration in Samarkand is reported to have sacked Tajiks from the bureaucracy in 2009. Simmering Uzbek–Tajik tensions reportedly fuelled small-scale incidents in Risthan, a small town in the Ferghana Valley, as well as in Samarkand and Bukhara, according to local observers. The authorities reportedly suppressed media coverage of these episodes. Meanwhile, Samarkand has been undergoing renovation. According to an opposition website, approximately 100 private residences and 30 businesses were demolished between October 2009 and May 2010, despite protests by their owners. Citing residents, the report claimed that officials gave residents only three days to vacate their properties. Many of those who lost their homes are now reportedly staying with relatives, or living in rental housing. Government promises of compensation have not been kept.

Discrimination against religious minorities is also common in Uzbekistan. Forum 18 reported that in 2010 short-term sentences were reinstated for members of religious minorities for organizing or taking part in unauthorized religious meetings or otherwise expressing their religious beliefs. Some Protestants and Jehovah's Witnesses were sentenced to 10- and 15-day prison terms, while a Baptist who had been sentenced to ten years' imprisonment lost his appeal. In April, three Muslim women were sentenced to between six and a half and seven years in a labour camp for leading and taking part in illegal religious meetings. Furthermore, female members of these religious groups have reportedly been threatened with sexual violence and torture by the police while in detention for practising their religion.

South Asia

Joshua Castellino

South Asia remained high on the international agenda in 2010. The ongoing operation in Afghanistan appeared no closer to a longer-term, sustainable resolution, despite a US and UK troop surge. The accompanying declaration by President Barack Obama, which has since been cast into doubt, of beginning the withdrawal of US forces in July 2011 added to uncertainty in the state and the region.

The difficulties faced by Pakistan were exacerbated in 2009 by events in the Swat Valley and South Waziristan, bordering Afghanistan. Local imposition of Sharia law was at the expense of minorities as well as women's and girls' rights to freedom of movement and access to education (as discussed in last year's edition of *State of the World's Minorities and Indigenous Peoples*). While 2010 saw an uneasy peace return to these regions, the semblance of stability masked the ongoing failure of the Pakistani government to adequately support the reconstruction needs of the Pashtun community and other minority groups who have returned to the areas, helping to create a political base for the Taliban to regroup and plan its strategy for Afghanistan in the years to come. The general culture of violence and intimidation has had a disproportionate effect on minorities in the region.

Newspaper headlines in Pakistan were dominated during the latter months of the year by the case of Aasia Bibi, a Christian woman, who was sentenced to death in November under the country's blasphemy laws. The laws, actually several sections of the Penal Code, have a disproportionate impact on religious minorities, including Christians and Ahmadiyya. There were moves in parliament to repeal or at least amend the provisions. The year ended with Pakistan in political turmoil. Punjab province's Governor Salman Taseer was assassinated by a bodyguard on 4 January 2011, after he spoke out in favour of repeal. Taseer had visited Bibi in prison.

Violence and intimidation was also prominent in parts of India, as a result of the ongoing conflict between government forces and the Naxalites, a Maoist movement that has a presence in a third of all Indian districts. This movement has appealed directly to marginalized communities, including Dalits and indigenous peoples (Adivasis), as well as landless labourers, arguing that they have been excluded from the wealth being generated in the country. Despite the country's strong economic performance in the midst of a global crisis, new indicators contained in the Oxford Poverty and Human Development Initiative's Multidimensional Poverty Index demonstrate that inequality is growing, with minority communities like the Dalits and Adivasis falling further behind the national average in terms of socio-economic attainments. In India, discussion around minority rights issues has often been synonymous in the past with suspicions concerning the loyalty of the Muslim community. The year 2010 marks a shift in thinking as the Naxalites have been identified as the single biggest threat to Indian stability.

The failure on the part of the Sri Lankan government to accept accountability for violations of international humanitarian law has brought it under pressure, with the government responding by clamping down on the independence of the media, civil society organizations, and in some cases on public institutions. To repair its image abroad the government of Sri Lanka has hired a leading public relations firm to shore up its credentials, while at home the prospect of reconciliation between minorities and the majority Sinhalese population appears increasingly distant.

Afghanistan

Following elections in September, President Karzai consolidated his hold on the Afghan premiership, and played the role of a statesman in numerous international conferences on the future of Afghanistan. With the exception of the 20 per cent participation of women at the Peace Consultative Jirga in June 2010, very few women took part in any of these conferences. In terms of political representation, the parliamentary elections saw 406 women stand for election, running for the 64 seats reserved for women. In addition, the Hazara minority won about 25 per cent of seats in the parliamentary elections held in 2010, although, according to a report by National Public Radio, this was in part because voters in some Pashtun-dominant areas were unable to vote, due to ongoing violence.

Contrary to the successes announced by US President Obama concerning the NATO-led coalition's efforts in Afghanistan, the United Nations Assistance Mission to Afghanistan (UNAMA) security assessments showed an escalating pattern of violence throughout 2010. The ongoing lack of stability in the country provides the backdrop for significant human rights concerns,

Above: An ethnic Hazara woman washes dishes in the village of Bamyan, Afghanistan. *Fakhria Ibrahimi.*

particularly among representatives of minority communities and women's rights groups, who are anxious about the role of the opposition Taliban in any future peace settlement.

In 2010, armed opposition groups appeared to be able to strike right in the heart of Kabul. According to the UK Foreign Office, between summer 2009 and summer 2010, there were 14 suicide bombings in the city, with at least five further suicide attacks known to have been stopped. Of these 14 attacks, the majority were aimed at the International Security Assistance Force (ISAF). A large-scale attack against various ministries occurred in January. While the rate of attacks eased during the second half of the year, the ability of armed opposition groups to act against highly defended targets in the capital city was troubling.

The Afghan national security forces (the Afghan National Army, ANA, and the Afghan National Police, ANP) have been unable to curb mounting civilian casualties, attributed to armed opposition groups. Questions remain as to the ethnic and tribal composition of this security infrastructure, its continued lack of adequate training, and the extent to which it can operate effectively in an increasingly fragmented Afghanistan.

In 2010 women and children bore an ever greater burden of the cost of war, according to figures included in a report entitled *Nowhere to Turn: The Failure to Protect Civilians in Afghanistan* (November 2010). There was an increase of 31 per cent in civilian deaths for the first half of 2010 over the figure for a similar period the previous year, including a 6 per cent increase in women casualties and a 55 per cent rise in that of children. The sharp rise in assassinations and executions by armed opposition groups points to an atmosphere of intimidation and the continued break-down in the rule of law. The report, compiled by 29 highly respected international and national non-governmental organizations (NGOs), including two prominent national women's NGOs, highlighted the worsening security situation for civilians. They predict increased violence in 2011 leading to greater civilian casualties, increased displacement, reduction in access to basic services and limitations on the ability of aid agencies to reach the vulnerable. The

Ongoing rights violations against women and girls in Afghanistan

With the prospect of NATO troop withdrawal being likely to take place sooner rather than later, focus has returned to the extent to which Afghanistan will be able to sustain itself in the future. NATO troops have had limited success in maintaining peace and security: despite the recent surge, reports indicate that a third of Afghanistan remains under the effective control of the Taliban and other armed opposition groups. A series of conferences has been held to underline the importance of including the Taliban and other hardline groups such as Hezb-i-Islami (Gulbuddin) in any negotiated post-occupation strategy, in the face of concern voiced by minority and women's rights activists with regard to the impact this could have on the limited progress made under President Hamid Karzai in regard to their rights.

According to the United Nations Development Programme (UNDP)'s Human Development Index (HDI), Afghanistan saw a marked improvement in 2010, meriting a rise from a ranking of 181 to 155 (although the rise was partly due to a change in UNDP's methodology). The HDI figures were backed by poll results indicating that nearly half the population was content with the direction of public policy. However, outside government-controlled areas, the scenario is starkly different. In areas under the effective control of the Taliban, the intimidation of women in the public sphere, their abuse and the general violence perpetrated against them are forceful reminders of the ethos that drives the opposition.

During 2010, violence against women attributed to or alleged to be perpetrated directly or indirectly by the Taliban continued, affecting women at every stratum in society and from all ethnic and religious groups. Two separate phenomena that became commonplace in 2010 are worth highlighting. The first concerns a resurgence in the use of 'night letters' to intimidate women who operate in any role in the public sphere. These 'night letters' are written threats delivered at night to a home or mosque, addressed to individuals. 'Night letters' have a historical significance in the Afghan context, in part due to the fact that they were used by armed *mujahideen* groups against women who were perceived to be 'Western' in dress or attitudes, during the conflict in the 1980s and 1990s. They are followed up with real violence, and in some cases murder. As a result many women have been forced to give up jobs or risk undermining their family's safety. There have been direct attacks on women in politics, including on parliamentarian Fawzia Kufi and provincial councillor Neda Pyani, who was seriously injured in a drive-by shooting in Pul-e Khumri, the capital of Baghlan province, in the first quarter of 2010. The government's lack of action in identifying and prosecuting the killers of several prominent women in public life, including Sitara Achakzai, Malalai Kakar, Zakia Zaki and Safia Amajan, undermines any confidence in the government's commitment to ensuring accountability for crimes committed. The lack of such efforts is part of a context of regular abuse, insults and physical violence and intimidation that women in public life bear when performing their duties.

A second phenomenon that underscores the Taliban threat is episodes of suspected poisoning in girls' schools. In April 2010, more than 100 girls and women teachers fell ill in Kunduz province, in northern Afghanistan. Similar attacks were reported in other parts of the country, including on 4 May 2010, when 17 girls fell ill at Durkhani High School in Kabul and were taken to hospital. Forty-six students and nine teachers were treated in hospital after a suspected poison attack against another Kabul girls' school in August. There appears to be evidence that the illnesses are linked to poisoning, and the actions themselves are attributed to the Taliban, though whether concrete evidence for the claims exists remains unproven. Whatever the cause of these incidents, they reflect an atmosphere of intimidation with the result that families are afraid to send their daughters to school. In addition, badly needed schools and clinics built in insecure areas rapidly turn into targets for the insurgents.

While these attacks appear to target women and girls in the public sphere, irrespective of their ethnicity, they do of course affect those who belong to minorities. Unless women's rights can be included as a non-negotiable element of any future settlement, it is difficult to see how a new Afghanistan can emerge that is more promising for minority women and girls than that of the last two decades. The European Union has made a commitment to this in its involvement in the peace talks, but it is time the issue was given higher prominence. ∎

report highlights that armed opposition groups currently control more territory than at any other time since 2001.

A fundamental concern from the perspective of minority and women's rights leaders remains the role that the Taliban are likely to have in the peace settlement, especially after the withdrawal of NATO troops. The indeterminate results of the 2010 elections saw the Pashtun community's share of seats drop by 20 seats, leading President Karzai to label the election results as a 'threat to national unity', on the basis that any meaningful settlement in Afghanistan has to include Pashtuns for it to be sustainable. Pashtuns represent the largest ethnic group in the country; the Taliban primarily draw their support from among this group. The inclusion of representatives of the different communities in Afghanistan while excluding the Taliban poses a challenge.

Representatives of Afghanistan's Hazara, Tajik and Uzbek communities (together roughly constituting half the population) remain gravely concerned about the involvement of the Taliban in the peace process. The Hazara minority in particular suffered considerable discrimination and violence during the Taliban period, and, following parliamentary elections, members of the Hazara minority interviewed for a report by National Public Radio expressed concern as to what would happen were the Taliban to regain control over the country. Elsewhere, Rehman Oghly, an Uzbek Member of Parliament and former member of an anti-Taliban militia warned in a *New York Times* article that these communities are likely to resist with force inclusion of the Taliban, which may signal a return to civil war and the spectre of dismemberment of the state.

A similar concern has been expressed by a number of prominent women's rights activists. Human Rights Watch's (HRW 2010) report *The 'Ten-Dollar Talib' and Women's Rights* highlights the damage to women from all ethnic groups in the conflict, and the threat lurking to women's rights in any political compromise that involves dampening down the positive developments regarding issues such as girls' access to education. Thus, while the future of Afghanistan depends on whether a peace deal can be struck with the Taliban and groups such as Hezb-i-Islami (Gulbuddin), the price of such involvement would be high. Hezb-i-Islami (Gulbuddin) has clearly stated repressive views on women's participation in public life and any compromise with this group could undermine progress. The Taliban's attempt to eliminate women – including those from minority groups – from the public sphere has also resulted in new strategies, including the use of night letters and poisonings at girls' schools (see Special Report, p. 139).

The ongoing instability and violence disproportionately affects minorities, with the beheading of 11 Hazaras in June 2010 in Uruzgan province, attributed by police to the Taliban, standing as a stark reminder of the challenge in re-building Afghanistan. There has also been a growth in tension between communities, typified by an incident in May in Behsud, where Hazaras and Kuchis clashed over land issues. Kuchis are ethnic Pashtun nomads. The government has been unable to bring perpetrators of such violence to account. On 5 August 2010, ten members of an International Assistance Mission eye team were killed in Badakhshan. Observers feared that this incident, along with an increase in killings of civilians in the region, could signal an expansion of the conflict into northern areas of Afghanistan. The population of Badakhshan is mainly Tajik, but also includes a sizeable Ismaili religious community.

When asked for a clarification of the impact on women and minorities of the reintegration of pro-Taliban forces in national politics, Mohammad Masoom Stanekzai, who is in charge of government reintegration programmes, reiterated that any resulting policy changes will not infringe on the promises of Article 22 of the Afghan Constitution. This article, promising equality, provides shallow protection to minorities and women and could easily be subverted by a stricter reading of Article 3, which guarantees the primacy of Sharia law, raising deeper questions about the commitment of the government to values of equality.

Bangladesh

The year 2010 promised much for minorities in Bangladesh, in light of a landmark decision by a Division Bench of the High Court Division of the Supreme Court on 6 May 2010, in a case concerning the forcible eviction of a Hindu community from their land at Mothbariya Pirojpur. In directing that religious communities be rehabilitated and accommodated on the lands from which they had previously been displaced,

the judges appeared to be tackling one of the fundamental issues affecting religious minorities and indigenous communities in Bangladesh. Another positive development was the high-profile inclusion of minorities in government, including three non-Muslim men among 38 ministerial positions.

However, aside from these promising signs, minorities continued to face violations of their human rights. The most significant example was the killing of indigenous Jumma in the Chittagong Hill Tracts on 20 February. The killings took place during a strike called by the United People's Democratic Front, a political party representing indigenous Jumma. Amnesty International reported at least two people killed, although it noted that locals spoke of six further deaths. The peaceful protest was called in reaction to the burning of at least 40 houses by majority settlers in the Baghaichhari area of Rangamati district during the night of 19 February. When the protesters refused to move, army personnel opened fire with live ammunition; at least 25 people were injured, Amnesty stated. Afterwards, settlers reportedly burned down at least 160 more houses. Houses were destroyed in 11 villages in Rangamati district; a Buddhist temple was also burned down. Following the incident, security personnel prevented journalists from accessing the site, and vital medical treatment and information was restricted to residents of the villages.

In its annual report, the NGO Odhikar reported 384 incidents of injuries sustained by religious and ethnic minorities, eight deaths, 12 incidents of property seizures ('land-grabbing'), as well as 23 attacks against temples and a further 20 against property owned by minorities. The report also documents 10 cases of rape, one of which occurred on 19 March 2010, when a young Hindu girl was gang-raped in the Patuakhali district. Odhikar also reported at least two Ahmadi communities being attacked by mobs. In Chantara village, a 10-year-old Ahmadi girl was reportedly abducted and sexually assaulted. In February, Bangladesh Minority Watch reported that a Dalit Hindu woman was sexually assaulted by a police officer. The officer in question was suspended from duty, although the report also alleged that the woman was pressured against pursuing the case. This kind of attack appears to be relatively rare, as much of the violence against minorities has been perpetrated by citizens rather than state officials. But the lack of accountability for

India in a state of turmoil

In the context of the ongoing struggle between government and the Maoist movement known as the Naxalites, some Indian state governments, notably Chhattisgarh, have engaged in a concerted campaign of intimidation, drawing in significant sections of civil society. In Chhattisgarh, the government has equated humanitarian actions such as the provision of legal and medical services as signalling complicity with the Maoists. On 24 December 2010, the local police re-arrested Dr Binayak Sen, a medical doctor and prominent grassroots human rights activist, on charges of complicity. The fact that the Maoists appear to advocate a wider agenda of social inclusion (diluted by their use of violence), including (forced) land redistribution and women's equal rights, has made the conflict probably the most central question relevant to minorities in India today. This is compounded by their control of territory in remote areas that are often home to Adivasis and Dalits.

Rather than a stray moment of misjudgement, the arrest of Dr Sen is part of a concerted strategy aimed to silence governmental critics. On 6 May, the Home Ministry issued a statement referring to 'intellectual support' that had been given to Maoists. The Home Ministry warned that the Unlawful Activities (Prevention) Act, 1967, with a penalty of 10 years' imprisonment, could be used against those 'in contact' with Maoists. Since then there have been many instances of harassment of human rights defenders through surveillance, arbitrary arrests, detentions, travel restrictions and slander. The culture of intimidation has led to self-censorship on the part of journalists, and unequal reporting of the conflict raging in several districts across the country.

Neither the security forces nor the Maoists are likely to win either the conflict or the legitimacy each craves. Support for the Naxalites wanes with every cost imposed on civilians, while the government's ill thought-out strategy for their defeat is one of the only factors that ensures continued recruitment.

The attention devoted to the Maoist uprising in 2010 drew the focus away from the conflict in Kashmir, which remained in a state of impasse. The Kashmir Valley saw significant violence in 2010, most tragically with the killing by security forces of at least 20 people during often violent protests following the announcement by a pastor in the United States that he intended to set fire to a copy of the Qur'an in September (the threat was temporarily withdrawn). The culture of violence in the Valley by state and non-state actors continues to be a source of worry for all, and in this series of protests, government buildings, police stations and a Christian school were attacked and destroyed. The tension had already been heightened in April after the extra-judicial killing of three villagers by security forces, and the killing of a teenager in June. The situation resulted in the declaration of curfews across the Valley, but was also accompanied by violence against security personnel, which in turn resulted in a response which included excessive force, and the use of live and rubber bullets and tear gas. Once again the action and response locked militants, security personnel and the local population in a cycle of violence, with significant casualties on every side.

The sense of siege felt by the government and security forces has resulted in a tightening of legislation. Three pieces of legislation merit

....

....

closer attention. First, the impact of the amendments made to the Unlawful Activities (Prevention) Act, enacted in the aftermath of the attacks in Mumbai in 2008, was experienced in 2010. These amendments allow authorities to include a range of peaceful opposition activities within the definition of 'terrorist' activities. They provide security forces with the mandate to conduct searches and make arrests on the basis of 'personal knowledge' of the officer. The new amendments were used by security forces in many parts of the country, and resulted in abuses of terror suspects and the erosion of rights of due process. Second, the much-contested Armed Forces Special Powers Act provided security forces with *carte blanche* in what are euphemistically described 'disturbed areas', resulting in a pervasive culture of impunity. It has to be noted that previous iterations of such legislation, the Terrorist and Disruptive Activities (Prevention) Act (TADA) of 1985 and the Prevention of Terrorism Act (POTA) of 2002, had both been discontinued due to the arbitrary detention, enforced disappearance and extra-judicial killings of many members of minorities including Dalits, Muslims, Sikhs and others in the north-eastern states. A third piece of legislation, the National Investigation Agency Act (NIAA), creating a new specialized federal police agency, is also of concern. Its mandate includes the investigation of terrorism and national security crimes, providing for the creation of special courts and in-camera trials. ∎

these crimes and the authorities' reluctance to bring perpetrators to justice highlights a failure on the part of the state in its duty to protect minority groups.

Several attacks on minority religious buildings or property belonging to religious minorities took place over the course of the year. On 21 March 2010, an armed gang attacked, desecrated and destroyed a Hindu temple, destroyed Hindu homes and assaulted their inhabitants in Chandpur district. Bangla-language newspaper *Amar Desh* reported the land-grabbing of Hindu cremation grounds at Zia Nagar in Perojpur District on 21 May. The paper's critique of government policies and its reporting of some of these incidents led to the revocation of its licence, seizure of its property and the arrest of its editor Mahmudur Rahman on 2 June 2010. In contrast, some reports from NGOs suggested that violence against Ahmadiyya diminished during 2010, due to improved police protection for the community.

Several issues continue to pose a challenge to the well-being of minorities in Bangladesh. The first pertains to the extent to which the authorities can guarantee minorities' physical security. A failure to react to the rise in attacks against communities and their property will engender a culture of impunity in the state. Many commentators claim that this has already become ingrained through the activities of the Rapid Action Battalion (RAB), a paramilitary unit composed of some 4,500 military and police personnel formed in 2004 to combat widespread lawlessness. The second issue is the secular nature of the state, something the Supreme Court has sought to achieve in its judgments, and that the legislature has sought to instil through increased participation of minorities and greater freedoms in education. However, the impact of these measures is limited without society-wide consensus in regard to such polices. Finally, it is 13 years since the signing of the Chittagong Hill Tracts Accord, but the failure to implement its provisions means that tensions continue in the region. The failure to pay adequate attention to the situation of the economic and social rights of indigenous women, highlighted at a high-profile conference held in Dhaka on 23 November, means that indigenous communities are victim to continued discrimination and deprivation.

India

Recently, India has assumed new prominence in the international arena, demonstrated by the country's ambition to gain a seat on the United Nations (UN) Security Council (which received the backing of the United States in 2010). But a number of serious issues remain that must be addressed if the envisaged economic growth is to continue and if this growth is to benefit all segments of the country's vast population.

The biggest human rights issue in India during 2010 was the spread of the Maoist movement (known as the Naxalites) and the security forces' response. The Maoists claim to be giving voice to the frustrations of India's marginalized communities, among them landless labourers, tribal groups and Dalits, and appear to advocate that the only way in which the current pattern of exploitation can be terminated is through the use of armed force. While, according to statements made, this force is aimed at the state (leading to fatalities among security forces), the movement has been implicated in serious abuses of the population, including the destruction of schools and hospitals, accompanied by extortion, torture and killings of civilians.

The government has identified the Maoist threat as the number one priority for its security forces. With the conflict now rampant in 200 of India's 600 plus districts, a nation-wide strategy has been launched (Operation Green Hunt) to curb its impact. The government has admitted that support to the Maoists has grown due to the failure of development to benefit the most marginalized, and has launched a two-pronged strategy of 'security and development' in response. However, through its provision of federal paramilitary assistance to state governments, it is clear that the 'security' aspect is most prominent. One of the most noted events in 2010 was an incident involving the vigilante Salwa Judum, evicting villagers from their homes in Chhattisgarh and into government camps, accompanied by a campaign of killing, rape and arson.

The Indian government runs the risk of undermining its own legal and moral stance if it violates human rights in its attempt to defeat the Maoists. At the same time, it risks acting as a recruitment tool for them. The population in affected areas are among the most marginalized in Indian society, and are now caught in an additional layer of danger: they are intimidated by Maoists demanding food and shelter at gunpoint, and penalized by security forces for associating with the Maoists. Adivasis, Dalits and landless labourers face

regular pressure from militants, and often succumb to it: not necessarily as an expression of genuine support, but as a result of the grave physical threat against them if they do not.

Beyond the response to the Maoist uprising, there are other indications that the human rights situation in India is deteriorating, while the poor socio-economic situation of minorities – and minority women in particular – shows little signs of improvement. The year began with the launch of the 'Leadership Development of Minority Women' programme, a government scheme aimed at increasing minority women's awareness of their rights in regard to education, employment, health, hygiene, immunization and family planning, as well as improving access to microcredit. But it ended with the suppression of a protest organized by minority women calling for those very rights. The events that took place at Barwari, in Madhya Pradesh on 28 December 2010 illustrate the extent to which freedom of speech and association has been curbed in recent years. The protest, called by a grassroots organization of Dalits and tribal communities, consisted of about 1,000 tribal women. They were protesting against the poor quality of health care that had resulted in nine deaths at a maternal hospital the previous month. Overall, there were 25 maternal deaths at this hospital between April and November 2010. In breaking up the protest, police used colonial-era sedition laws to arrest the organizers and others, at the same time as the Indian government was celebrating membership of the UN Commission on Information and Accountability for Women's and Children's Health. It may be recalled that, according to a 2007 UN Children's Fund (UNICEF) report, nearly 60 per cent of maternal deaths in six northern states occurred in what could be classed Dalit or tribal communities. Elsewhere, minority women's rights activists called for a 'quota within a quota' for Dalit women and women from religious minorities to be included in the Women's Reservation Bill (still under discussion at the end of the year). Without this, they argued, the right to political representation of Dalit women and women from religious minorities would not be protected by the proposed 'women's quota'.

Elsewhere, medical practitioner and human rights activist Dr Binayak Sen was arrested under the sedition legislation, and an attempt was made

'Etch it upon your hearts, this is what I am.' Life at an intersection: caste, gender and sexuality

In a landmark decision of 2 July 2009, the Indian High Court in Delhi decriminalized consensual same-sex sexual relations between adults in private. The decision emphasizes inclusiveness as an underlying theme of the Indian Constitution and diversity as a matter of constitutional morality. No doubt a milestone for the rights of lesbian, gay, bisexual and transgender (LGBT) persons in India, the decision is an important step forward for LGBT persons belonging to ethnic, religious or linguistic minorities. At a wider level then, it will have an impact on members of all minority groups: religious, ethnic, national, linguistic or sexual. As it awaits appellate scrutiny in the Supreme Court of India, a gay Dalit in New Delhi tells *Sumit Baudh* about his life at an intersection – of caste, gender and sexuality.

I think in my case, no one can tell.

They say to me, 'You don't look gay. You can get married.'

I tell them, 'If I find a man, I will get married.'
They say, 'But you look okay ...'
'Others look okay too.'

'Nahi, vo hilte zyaada hai [No, they are effeminate].'
'So what? If I act like that, will that be wrong?'

In my village, neighbourhoods are [divided] on caste lines. If boys of a certain caste hang out in another caste neighbourhood, there can be trouble.

I have an impressive personality. I consider myself good looking. But sometimes it happens to me too. I tell you an incident from last year. I was talking to this boy in front of his house. He thinks well of me. Behind him, a man from his lane yelled:
'Hey you, what are you doing here?'
'I am talking to this [boy] here, can you not see?' I retorted.
'I can see very well you are a Chamaar, aren't you?' he made a casteist slur.

I said to him, 'Yes, I am a Chamaar, so? So what? [The person] I'm talking to, does he not know I am Chamaar?'

The man glared at me and hissed, 'Get lost from here.'

What more could I have said to someone of that mentality?

I felt very bad.

When I was in school, the Principal was himself a Dalit. Even he once addressed me like that: 'Get up, you Chamaar.' I never got a bigger shock in my life.

I used to think I was the only one. I wasn't interested in girls. All my friends were attracted to girls. They'd go on about it. I used to wonder why I don't feel the same way. I used to worry. Some people would tell me it's a disease. I had so many questions, I didn't have any answers. I had no one to share my loneliness. I couldn't have told my family, I didn't know myself – who or what am I?

Some of my early relationships were consensual, some weren't. There were those with whom I couldn't even bear to sit – they were by force. It was terrible. I had to fight, I had to cajole. What else could I do?

This is common. They consider this their man-power [masculinity]. If somebody is below them they feel happy. Maybe they consider it an honour, that 'I have fucked him, now he will be subservient to me all his life, he will not lift his eyes in front of me.'

I think when this is revealed about a boy,

everyone wants to use him. They think, 'He is a soft target, he will not tell anyone. And if he does, it will only bring him shame. He will be beaten up. His family will think he is to blame.'

With me this went on from the age of 13 to 25.

I used to prefer staying home, not going out. I used to feel scared making new friends. If there'd be a new friendship building, I used to wonder if I should get into it. Will I end up with the tag Gaandoo *[bugger]?*

My friends would say, 'People say this and that about you. If you learn self-defence, it will be good for you.' So I started learning martial arts; my body became strong.

It was an era of struggle for me. I knew I had to win against these people, and to win it is necessary to have power. Physical power is necessary in a village. The kind of mentality people have – is not for people like us. They speak another language, they have to be tackled in that language.

They would say, 'We can't get our hands on him these days, wonder what he is up to. After all that we have done to him, how dare he stand up to us! Even now he is seeing someone. The day he gets caught, we will do it to him again.' They used to make many more jibes. Slowly and gradually I overcame all that.

I was wary not to get the tag Gaandoo *again. I used to [enter] relationships after a lot of thought and consideration. I'd be willing to have a relationship if I found the man worthy. If not, I'd say to him, 'Don't mess with me. If you try to grab me, your hands will be chopped off.'*

At this stage of my life, I don't care what my neighbours think. Some of my family members support me, some don't. I can only tell them I am gay. I can only say, 'Yes, my relationships will be with men, not women. Open your eyes and look at this, open your minds and understand this. Etch it upon your hearts, this is what I am.'

Edited extracts from an interview, translated from Hindi, with inputs from Jaya Sharma. ∎

to prosecute award-winning author and public commentator Arundhati Roy. The allegations against Roy and others are based on speeches they are purported to have made on 21 October 2010 in New Delhi, supposedly in support of Kashmiri secession. The original attempt to use sedition laws was stymied by the Home Ministry, who admitted that such a course of action would be inappropriate since no violence was incited.

Nepal

With various deadlocks in the process of transition to democracy, Nepal witnessed another year of political uncertainty in 2010. While the 2006 peace agreement ending the conflict between the Maoists and the government continued to hold, Prime Minister Madav Kumar Nepal of the Unified Marxist-Leninist party resigned on 30 June. The Maoists had been pressuring him to form a government with themselves at its helm. Parliament failed to form another government during the rest of the year. Attention continued to focus on the contents of the interim Constitution as well as what the process of drafting the next Constitution can offer Nepal's multi-ethnic population. The Constituent Assembly missed its deadline of 28 May and had its mandate extended for another year. The disarming of Maoist forces was one of the key issues in the mandate of the UN Mission in Nepal, which ended in January 2011 with a last-minute agreement to continue the decommissioning of weapons, auguring well for the future of peace in the country. Meanwhile, discrimination on the basis of caste, gender and ethnicity continued, characterized by a lack of access to justice and accentuated by geography, despite some efforts on the part of the government to address this.

The political agenda during 2010 was dominated by the issue of federalism, which, despite the slipping of the deadline for constitutional progress on the issue, continues to be seen as positive by many of Nepal's numerous ethnic minorities. This was a cause espoused by the Maoists, who continue to support its inclusion in the new Constitution which will hopefully be finalized during 2011. Federalism could guarantee an agenda of inclusion, paving the way for proportional representation and the redefinition of the state structure in order to better recognize ethnic and cultural diversity. However, there is concern over the citizenship provision in the draft Constitution, which makes the granting of Nepali citizenship to a child conditional on both parents being Nepali citizens – which as the UN High Commissioner for Refugees (UNHCR) highlights, runs the risk of engendering statelessness.

The government appears to be striving to erode age-old practices of caste-based discrimination, and there is acceptance of the need for the introduction of reservations for the Dalit community in order to realize equality. Draft legislation vetted by a high-level panel and released in December 2010 contained provisions to guarantee equality and provide measures through which to realize language rights and proportional representation. In addition, there were two progressive judgments on these issues in January and March 2010 (handed down by the District Court in Baitadi in the west of the country), both of which upheld Dalit rights. The first sentenced a man to two years' imprisonment for an attack on Dalits whom he believed were not following discriminatory temple rituals, while the second convicted a man for physical assault on the father of the groom at a Dalit wedding, where the perpetrator believed rituals practised were reserved for 'high-caste communities'.

These decisions indicate some official appetite for combating caste-based discrimination, though inevitably tackling societal perceptions is a significant challenge. Indeed, discrimination on the basis of caste identity appears to continue to be widespread in Nepal, affecting the estimated 13–20 per cent of the population who are Dalit. For instance, according to the Asian Human Rights Commission (AHRC), Dalits are often refused entry to tea shops, restaurants and hotels, and to Hindu temples, denying their right to practise their religion. Those who speak out against such discrimination face hostility. In October, the AHRC reported that a non-Dalit teacher who had spoken out against discriminatory practices against Dalit students at her school in Kailali District (including separate facilities for Dalit students and banning Dalit students from attending certain classes) remained suspended. In addition, she had been blocked by the local school board from applying for other teaching posts in the district.

In a similar vein, although the government declared 2010 to be the year to focus on gender-based violence, ingrained attitudes have meant that women, especially from marginalized communities, continue to face violence, due to their lower status and financial dependence on their spouses. Women from marginalized communities such as Haliya, or bonded labourers in the mid- and far western regions of Nepal continue to face difficulties that are accentuated by poverty and the lack of employment opportunities, in accessing food, clothing, shelter, health care and education, despite the abolition of bonded labour nearly three years ago. For instance, the AHRC alleges that Dalit women and girls are at particular risk of sexual violence at the hands of higher-caste men, and that such cases are rarely brought to justice due to complicity between the police and the perpetrators. The year 2010 also saw the murder of two Dalit women and a girl in Bardiya National Park by army personnel. The soldiers involved alleged that they had killed the women and child – who were collecting firewood along with others from their village – instantly, and in self-defence. But other members of the party reportedly stated that they had been shot at while they were sleeping, and that the women and the girl were abducted, sexually assaulted, and later killed.

Attacks against journalists have also continued. There were three high-profile murders during the year: the first, of reporter Uma Singh in January, was followed in February by that of Jamin Shah in Kathmandu and of Arun Singhaniya in Janakpur on 1 March.

Ethnic tensions between various Nepali communities continued in 2010 in the Terai region. disproportionately affecting the Dalit population who were affected by virtue of being the biggest group among the landless labourers. These tensions subsequently extended to the Madhesi communities in the south of the region, who have been agitating for greater autonomy and inclusion in the administrative machinery of government. The UN expressed concern regarding extortion of teachers, local officials and businesspeople by armed groups. Human rights organizations report that the government's special security policy has actually led to an increase in violations. The UN Office of the High Commissioner for Human Rights (OHCHR) reported 57 deaths caused by the unlawful use of lethal force by government security forces in the Terai region between January 2008 and June 2010. HRW reported the forced recruitment by armed groups of children as messengers for extortion and ransom notes as well enforcers of strikes (*bandhs*).

Nepal's Tibetan community faced some official pressure during 2010, with reports of police intimidation and high-handed presence at religious ceremonies. In one incident on 3 October, Nepalese police seized ballot boxes at Tibetan government-in-exile polling stations in Kathmandu. The pressure on the community emanates from closer ties between Nepal and China, as evidenced in the forced deportation to China of three Tibetan new arrivals (including one Buddhist monk) by the Nepali government in June 2010. At year's end, HRW reported that two are believed to be in detention in China. The deportations represent a violation of the *non-refoulement* principle in international law, whereby no person should be returned to a country where that person's life or freedom is in serious danger.

While overall 2010 saw relatively peaceful coexistence between the majority Hindu community and Buddhist, Muslim and Christian communities, there have been incidents of intimidation reported, largely attributed to Pashupati Sena, Shiv Sena Nepal and Nepal Shivsena (affiliated to the Indian Shiv Sena – a Hindu fundamentalist party). These groups are unhappy with the former Hindu kingdom's move towards secularism and greater inclusion of other faiths, as guaranteed in the 2007 interim Constitution. Two incidents that were reported included the 23 May attack on a Christian church in Dhobighat, in which three people were killed, and the beating of two Christians for refusing to offer donations for a Hindu *puja* in Kapilvastu on 25 May.

Pakistan

In 2010, ongoing hostilities in Afghanistan had a direct impact on Pakistan, which has also borne the biggest burden from the attendant refugee flows. This, coupled with the inevitable pressures from militants, has made the maintenance of law and order a close to impossible task. In addition, the country was devastated by the worst floods in its history in June, affecting nearly 20 million people, with a death toll estimated in excess of 2,000, and nearly US $10 billion worth of damage. These events contributed to further displacement of populations, accompanied by ethnic and religious tension.

According to a statement made by the Potohar Organization for Development Advocacy (PODA) at the 2010 UN Forum on Minority Issues, women in general were particularly affected by the floods,

given that they were more likely to have been at home when the flooding struck, were less likely to have been able to swim, and would have felt a responsibility to try to rescue children and animals. The statement also mentioned that women from minority groups in particular often do not have a national identity card, meaning that those who survived would not have been able to claim relief and compensation in the period following the flooding.

As is perhaps inevitable in these conditions, the situation for minorities worsened during the year, leading Ibn Abdur Rehman, Secretary-General of the Human Rights Commission of Pakistan, to declare that the organization had recorded an increase in hatred of minorities by extremists. In addition, minorities in Pakistan continue to face day-to-day societal discrimination and marginalization, impacting on development outcomes. For women from minority groups, this is compounded by the discrimination that they experience as women, and may also be compounded by caste-based discrimination. A recent survey reported by the AHRC found that primary school enrolment rates for girls belonging to scheduled Hindu castes in Pakistan were just 10.2 per cent; the national female primary enrolment rate was given as 48 per cent. Overall, 87 per cent of women from scheduled Hindu castes were illiterate, compared to 58 per cent of women nationally. This indicates a huge discrepancy in regard to access to education between this minority group and the Muslim majority. The AHRC also reports that religious minority women have limited employment options, and are most often found in low-status work, such as manual scavenging or cleaning in urban areas, or subsistence or bonded agricultural labour in rural areas. Gender discrimination and patriarchal norms within their own communities mean that few women within minority communities are able to retain control over income that they bring into the family. Violence against women also remains a considerable problem. At the end of the year, the country's Domestic Violence (Prevention and Protection) Bill remained in 'legislative limbo', having been passed by the National Assembly in August 2009, but then allowed to lapse by the Senate.

Under such circumstances it was perhaps inevitable that the tension between religious communities grew, with widespread discrimination and persistent violence perpetrated by armed groups and individuals. Tensions were heightened in multi-ethnic cities such as Karachi with regular attacks against residents. There was a sharp rise in kidnappings, with Pakistan's Hindu community particularly affected. One report suggested that in Lyari district of Karachi alone there were 10–15 such kidnappings a month, with similar estimates in Balochistan. According to the AHRC, this has included the kidnapping and forced marriage of young Hindu girls. In one case documented by the AHRC in March 2010, a 17-year-old Hindu girl was kidnapped by three Muslim brothers, raped by one of them, and pressured into marrying her rapist and converting to Islam. Allegedly, local police took no action.

The continued non-recognition of Ahmadiyya, seen as violating Pakistan's notorious blasphemy laws by declaring themselves believers in Islam, means that this community of around 600,000 continues to face serious discrimination in all areas of life. The requirement of religious affiliation on

national identity cards excludes them from being registered as Muslim, meaning that they are unable to vote in elections. In 2010, there were regular reports of violence against Ahmadiyya, including attacks on two mosques in Lahore on 28 May which resulted in 94 casualties and injured over 100 more. Three days later, gunmen attacked victims who were still recuperating in the city's Jinnah Hospital.

Sikhs too have come under pressure. According to last year's edition of *State of the World's Minorities and Indigenous Peoples*, Sikhs in the Federally Administered Tribal Areas (FATA) controlled by the Taliban were being made to pay a tax, *jizya*. Pressure on the community has since increased. A group of Sikhs were kidnapped in the Khyber and Orakzai regions in early 2010. The BBC reported that one of the men was later discovered beheaded, although other news agencies reported that two were killed. In April, 72 hectares of *gurdwara* (i.e. the Sikh place of worship) property was transferred without due process to the Defense Housing Association.

A very worrying trend has been the increased vulnerability of followers of Sufism, a moderate strain of Islam practised by many Pakistanis. The prominent Data Darbar shrine, the burial site of a famous Sufi saint in Lahore, was attacked by three suicide bombers on 1 July, which resulted in 42 deaths and nearly 200 wounded.

An incident that reveals the seriousness of the situation facing minorities was the sentencing to death of Aasia Bibi. Bibi, a Christian, and mother of five, was attacked by others and prevented from drawing water from a communal well on the grounds that she was 'impure'. In the course of the altercation, she reportedly accused the others of following religious laws that were antiquated. Based on hearsay evidence that she had blasphemed the Prophet Muhammad, which she denies, Bibi was subsequently sentenced to death under Pakistan's controversial blasphemy laws. Although no one has actually been executed under their provisions, according to the BBC, some 30 accused have been killed by lynch mobs. There were moves in parliament to repeal or at least amend the provisions. When President Asif Zardari sought to pardon Bibi, the Sheikhpura District Court passed an order on 29 November preventing this, indicating that it would violate religious laws. On 31 December, a 24-hour strike was held in the country's major cities to protest against any changes to the legislation. The Governor of Punjab, Salman Taseer, visited Bibi in order to show his support and called for the abolition of laws that treat individuals in this manner. His statements ultimately proved fatal, as in January 2011 he was killed by his bodyguard, who was subsequently celebrated as a hero by certain segments of Pakistani society.

Developments in Balochistan demonstrate the complex nature of the kinds of pressures minorities face in Pakistan. Baloch activists have been pressing for greater regional control, not least due to the fact that the region suffers from severe under-development at the same time as the country in general gains from having access to the rich natural gas reserves that are found in the province. While the Pakistani parliament passed reforms in 2010 aimed at increasing local autonomy and addressing grievances of the Baloch minority, the civilian authorities struggled to implement these changes in a highly polarized environment. Some more extreme groups view the presence of other minorities as a threat to their aspirations. As a result, there have been numerous attacks against religious establishments and harassment of other minority communities. The attacks against educational

establishments have been particularly disruptive of the social fabric in the province, as highlighted in an HRW report entitled *Their Future is at Stake*, which reports that attacks have particularly targeted girls' schools and schools where boys and girls are taught together. It also appears that some extremist groups in Balochistan may be coercing women into following strict Islamic dress codes, infringing the rights of religious minority women, as well as those of Muslim women who choose not to cover their faces. A statement from the extremist Baloch Ghaeratmand Group included in a news report by the ACHR stated that acid would be thrown at the faces of any women or girls appearing in public with their faces uncovered. In addition, the HRW report mentioned above details examples of extreme acts of gender-based violence against women that have been sanctioned by local legislators on the basis of 'tribal custom', denying women's and girls' access to justice and protection from the state.

Meanwhile, the Pakistani security forces appeared to continue with its practice of forced disappearances, as the bodies of suspected Baloch militants who had disappeared were regularly uncovered.

The violence has taken on a sectarian tone as tensions have mounted between the Shi'a and Sunni communities in Balochistan and other parts of Pakistan. According to one estimate, nearly 400 people died in 2010 in such sectarian clashes across the country.

Some areas of Pakistan's north-west, especially those bordering Afghanistan, remain under the influence of the Taliban, and the general lawlessness in these parts has led to attacks against tribal communities. There were two such notable attacks in 2010. The first, in April, resulting in 42 deaths, took place in the Kacha Pukha camp near Kohat for internally displaced who had fled fighting in Orakzai Agency. The dead belonged to the Mani Khel and Baramad Khel tribes. The second occurred on 25 December when a suicide bomber killed over 40 and injured over 100 members of the Salarzai tribe in the Bajaur Agency. The attack occurred at a World Food Programme (WFP) distribution point. The Tehrik-e-Taliban Pakistan (TTP) claimed responsibility for the attack. These Pashtun tribes have sought to organize their own militias (*lashkars*) for their self-protection which have evoked further wrath from extremists.

In the midst of this, the government has paid

lip service to the need to protect minorities. The authorities have sought to regulate *madrasas*, especially those preaching extremism. However, the number and severity of high-profile cases of violations of minority rights have increased, with security forces and government agencies apparently unwilling and unable to act against the discrimination and exclusion facing minorities. The Ministry of Minority Affairs has been mandated to increase protection for minorities, but a severe lack of resources means that such efforts inevitably flounder. In addition, the failure to recognize civil or common law marriages disproportionately affects Sikhs and Hindus, especially Dalits, with women from these communities subsequently faced with insurmountable obstacles in accessing property rights, health or administrative services.

Sri Lanka

The government came under severe pressure throughout 2010 to begin the promised process of seeking accountability for the violations of humanitarian law that occurred on both sides, in their bid to end the 29-year conflict with the Liberation Tigers for Tamil Eelam (LTTE) in 2009. There were allegations of grave atrocities committed in the final months of fighting in 2009, including filmed evidence of the arbitrary killing of captives by the 53rd Division of the Sri Lankan army that took place in May 2009. With pressure mounting for an independent inquiry, the UN Secretary-General Ban Ki-moon announced the creation of a three-member investigative panel. In response, the Sri Lankan government, which has resisted international scrutiny, announced the establishment of the Lessons Learnt and Reconciliation Commission (LLRC) in May 2010. The international community and human rights organizations reacted sharply to the creation of this commission, since it is headed by a former Attorney-General, raising questions about its independence. In fact, international NGOs such as HRW, Amnesty International and the International Crisis Group (ICG) decided not to provide testimony to the commission in view of its composition and mandate (which goes back to 2002 but without specific coverage of the events of 2009). The issues received heightened attention with the screening of a detailed video clip of the May 2009 killings by the UK's *Channel Four News* on 30 November 2010.

Without a genuine process that examines the atrocities committed during the war, any reconciliation between the minority Tamil population and the majority Sinhalese is likely to be superficial. Throughout 2010, the issue of the large number of internally displaced people (IDPs) remained high on the agenda and led to continuing humanitarian challenges. Concern was heightened by the government's pressure on the International Committee of the Red Cross (ICRC) to shut down operations, in view of the end of the conflict. The danger of the process derailing was highlighted on 30 December in the Boosa IDP camp, where security forces are alleged to have tortured and committed extra-judicial killings of LTTE prisoners. The International Commission of Jurists stressed that the continued arbitrary detention of nearly 8,000 prisoners alleged to be linked with the LTTE violates international legal principles and is akin to collective punishment against a community. Interviews with women IDPs undertaken for a recent MRG report indicated that a large number of IDP households are headed by women, who face considerable material deprivation as a result of limited or absent income-generation opportunities. Women interviewed for MRG's report *No War, No Peace: The Denial of Minority Rights and Justice in Sri Lanka* also reported cases of sexual harassment and assault in resettled areas.

The IDP issue is not exclusively a Tamil question since there remains a sizeable Muslim population (estimated at between 65,000 and 150,000) among those displaced by the fighting. These Muslims were expelled from the north by the LTTE in 1990, and their reintegration back into the towns and villages from where they were displaced is already proving to be a sensitive process. Muslims displaced by the conflict have long felt marginalized and neglected by both the government and international relief agencies working in Sri Lanka. In addition, Tamil and Muslim communities are having to learn to live side by side once again, after 20 years of separation. Overall, tension has grown between Tamil and Muslim populations, as described in an ICG report of April 2010.

Ethnic and religious tensions have continued to mount between communities. Tensions remain between Buddhists and Christians, with sporadic attacks on churches by Buddhist extremists, sometimes led by monks who are angry at what they see as proselytization by Christians. This has manifested itself in several acts by vigilantes and state authorities, as highlighted by two incidents, one on 6 March and another on 25 June. In the first incident, a mob led by monks linked to a political party disrupted services at a Christian church in the Kalutara District; in the second, police were dispatched to a Christian church in Rajagiriya, assaulted the pastor and attempted to demolish the place of worship on the grounds that it was an unauthorized structure. State authorities also acted directly in the arrest in April of Sarah Malanie Perera, a Sri Lankan resident in Bahrain for 19 years. Perera was apprehended under the Prevention of Terrorism Act for her book *From Darkness to Light*, which narrates the experience of her conversion from Buddhism to Islam, and which was deemed subversive by the authorities.

According to the AHRC, women and girls from minority groups are at particular risk of sexual violence, and are likely to face ostracism and even punishment from within their communities in the event that they report what has happened to them. Minority women who have experienced violence within their own communities may also have their right to justice violated. In a 2010 case, the AHRC reported that a young Muslim woman was subjected to corporal punishment by the village mosque committee after she became pregnant outside of marriage. When she and her husband went to the police station to complain, police were reluctant to pursue the case, and did not take any formal statement from the woman.

The outlook for minorities in Sri Lanka is worrying. The re-election of President Mahinda Rajapaksa was achieved on the back of the 'success' of eliminating the LTTE. He has sought to consolidate his power by eliminating the opposition, including through the detention of former army chief Sarath Fonseka on charges of engaging in politics while in active military service. In September, Rajapaksa pushed through significant constitutional amendments eliminating presidential terms, and providing himself with sweeping powers of appointment of individuals onto governmental bodies, undermining their independence. He has also appointed three of his brothers as Secretaries of Defence and Economic Development, and Speaker of Parliament, and has clamped down on any criticism of his policies.

South East Asia

Irwin Loy

Political change was the theme in parts of Asia during 2010. During the year, Burma, the Philippines and Laos all experienced varying degrees of change, while Vietnam and Thailand prepared for their own leadership decisions in 2011. The policies enacted by the countries' political leaders will continue to impact on minorities and indigenous peoples throughout the year.

There was perhaps least change in Burma. All eyes were trained on the military-controlled state throughout 2010 as observers awaited Burma's first elections in two decades. But the regime made it clear it had no intention of staging free and fair elections, banning many of the main opposition party's key figures from participating and promoting former military officers loyal to the junta as candidates. As the year unfolded, it became clear that many of Burma's already beleaguered minority groups would face increased hardship. Some ethnic-based armed groups, even those that had previously signed ceasefires with the regime, rebelled over the insistence of Burma's rulers that they be included in a joint border force. Violence erupted in eastern Burma as the election got under way and has continued in the poll's aftermath. Though opposition figure Aung San Suu Kyi was a free woman by the end of the year, observers fear that 2011 will only hold more violence for Burma's ethnic and religious minorities. In particular, it is marginalized women who are facing increasing levels of rights abuses as they take on more prominent roles in their communities.

In the Philippines national elections saw Benigno Aquino III elected president. Reconciliation in parts of the Mindanao island region, where Islamist groups have engaged in conflict with the national government, was at the top of his agenda by the end of the year.

Single-party states Laos and Vietnam, too, experienced political developments at the top. In Laos, Prime Minister Bouasone Bouphavanh announced his surprise resignation in late December 2010, months before his term was supposed to end. In the case of Vietnam, the ruling Communist Party's congress was not until early 2011. Nevertheless, the Vietnamese government cracked down on dissent in the run-up to the congress, including against campaigners on minority issues and members of unauthorized religious groups.

Migration continued to be a key issue, as rights groups highlighted problems across the region in policies towards migrants, including in Thailand – a nation still reeling from the Red Shirt political protests that shook the country. Asylum-seekers also continued to face challenges throughout South East Asia, from Malaysia to Cambodia, where a group of Montagnard refugees faced a deportation deadline in early 2011.

From Laos to Cambodia and Malaysia to Indonesia, the communal land of indigenous communities is rich in natural resources. The quest for hydropower, valuable extractives and agriculture cash crops can only put a further squeeze on the region's indigenous peoples as 2011 unfolds.

Burma

The state of human rights in Burma remained dire in 2010. The major story centred on the country's first general elections in two decades and the eventual release of opposition figure Aung San Suu Kyi from long-term house arrest. Few observers expected the election would be a catalyst for immediate change and, in its aftermath, there was little difference in behaviour from Burma's military regime. Instead, renewed fighting between the Burmese Army and armed groups from the country's numerous ethnic communities put hopes of peace in doubt.

Burma is an ethnically diverse country with at least 135 ethnic groups and seven ethnic minority states. Armed factions from the various groups have waged decades-long warfare against the repressive regime, and the conflict has resulted in large-scale displacement. It is estimated that at least half a million people have been displaced within Burma as a result of the fighting in eastern states; a further 140,000 refugees live in refugee camps along the border in Thailand.

Military abuses against civilians in conflict areas are believed to be 'widespread and systematic', according to Human Rights Watch (HRW). These abuses include extra-judicial killings, forced labour, torture and confiscation of land. In what constitutes a clear pattern of repression, women from ethnic minorities are singled out for particularly egregious treatment, including sexual violence, forced labour and being used as human shields. In testimony before the International Tribunal on Crimes against Women of Burma held in Tokyo in June, Kanae Doi, HRW's Japan director and David Mathieson, a Burma researcher, said:

'Women and girls living in Shan and Kachin states in eastern Burma, and in parts of Chin and Arakan [now Rakhine] states in western Burma, are frequent targets of rape and other ill-treatment. Impunity for such abuses is widespread and Burmese government soldiers are rarely brought to justice for sexual violence.'

K'nyaw Paw, education programme coordinator for the Karen Women Organization (KWO), said in an interview:

'The Burmese military arrest women and force them to be porters … they worry and are frightened for themselves that they will be raped, tortured and killed.'

In western Burma's Christian-dominated Chin state, researchers acting on behalf of the group Physicians for Human Rights (PHR) documented evidence to suggest that civilians have suffered a high rate of abuse at the hands of the military. Researchers found that 92 per cent of people interviewed for the study reported at least one instance in the past year where a member of the household was forced into hard labour. Other abuses, PHR said when it released its report in January 2011, may well constitute crimes against humanity and should be investigated.

Burma continued to view minority religions with suspicion, as ethnic identity among several of the minority communities is closely intertwined with religious identity. The ruling junta claims that Buddhists represent almost 90 per cent of the population, though minority religious groups are almost certainly undercounted. Religious minorities, including Muslim Rohingya, and Chin, Kachin and Karen communities that identify as Christian, continued to face rights abuses.

Rohingya, in particular, are subject to very severe forms of discrimination. The regime continued to deny citizenship to Rohingya or grant them Foreigner Registration Cards. This deprives them of access to secondary education in state-run schools.

Before the election, human rights advocates warned that a renewed campaign by the regime to bring ethnic-based armed groups under the umbrella of a joint border guard force could send the country spiralling into conflict. The regime had demanded that the various armed groups that had signed ceasefire agreements should disarm and join the border force. Instead, observers say the move has fuelled a new level of unrest. While Burma's rulers say 17 armed groups have signed on to 'arms for peace' deals over the last two decades, HRW and others say only five militias had agreed to join the border force by the end of the year.

The warnings of increased violence due to the regime's border guard plan seemed to be becoming reality at year's end. The Democratic Karen Buddhist Army (DKBA) had employed a ceasefire with the Burmese regime following its split from the Karen National Liberation Army (KNLA) in the mid 1990s. However, on 7 November, election day, a DKBA faction occupied the town of Myawaddy. The fighters were unhappy with the regime's demands that they be incorporated into the border guard. A counter-attack from the Burmese Army caused thousands of civilians to flee into neighbouring Thailand. The television network Al Jazeera reported in late November that the DKBA faction and the KNLA had agreed to cooperate against the Burmese Army. In the meantime, reports from media and rights groups say the fighting is ongoing in Karen state, with civilians continuing to be affected. Rights groups have criticized Thailand for repeatedly forcing fleeing refugees to return to their homes before their safety can be guaranteed.

The November election was widely viewed as illegitimate, with the regime doing everything in its power to ensure victory. As the Burma Campaign UK noted, the number of political prisoners doubled in the years leading up to the poll, all media outlets continued to be censored, international media and election observers were barred and voting was cancelled in several regions where ethnic minorities predominate. The main opposition, Aung San Suu Kyi's National League for Democracy (NLD), did not register for the election in protest at its strict rules, and was later disbanded. In the end, the Union Solidarity and Development Party (USDP), the

newly formed political entity headed by incumbent Prime Minister Thein Sein, took almost 80 per cent of the elected seats in the national parliament. Thein Sein was later named president. Political analyst Richard Horsey noted that parties from six of the states where ethnic minorities dominate fared relatively well. While the USDP and the military together occupy enough seats in the national legislature to allow them to amend the Constitution or to impeach, they do not enjoy such dominance in all ethnic minority state legislatures. In Chin, Kachin, Kayin, Mon, Rakhine and Shan states, the USDP is the leading party but lacks a majority on its own. Horsey said this development 'at least gives ethnic parties some influence over their affairs'.

A week after the election, Aung San Suu Kyi was released from house arrest. While the move was welcomed, there were no indications her release would be accompanied by additional freedoms for Burma's citizens. As one supporter told *The Irrawaddy* newspaper, 'The moment they feel Daw Suu is getting too powerful again, I am sure they will just place restrictions on her and lock up her supporters.'

Cambodia

Evictions and land-grabbing continued to dominate headlines in Cambodia during 2010. Rights workers say the loss of land is one of the most pressing issues in the country, trapping the nation's marginalized in a cycle of poverty. This has particularly affected many of the country's indigenous communities, whose communal land ownership traditions have been at odds with a government push toward land privatization. The majority of the country's population lacks basic land titles, a legacy of the Khmer Rouge regime.

The government has instituted a policy of granting 'economic land concessions', ostensibly part of a bid to stimulate development. Officially, authorities have distributed more than 950,000 hectares of land to 85 companies. However, as a World Bank report released in September 2010 noted, the government has failed to update its statistics since 2006. The *Phnom Penh Post* newspaper quoted a forestry official in September as saying that land concessions totalled more than 1.3 million hectares. Critics say such concessions continue to spark disputes between companies and affected villagers, leading to sometimes-violent evictions.

In its State of Human Rights country report for 2010, the Asian Human Rights Commission (AHRC) noted that 133,000 people in Phnom Penh alone have been evicted since 1990. The report stated that cases of land-grabbing have reached 'epidemic dimensions, with a clear pattern of rich and powerful individuals or private companies depriving the poor and marginalized of the land they inhabit or farm'. A public opinion survey conducted in July and August by the International Republican Institute (IRI), found that 7 per cent of respondents who owned farmland reported that someone had 'attempted to take some or all of their land in the previous three years; 5 per cent said they eventually lost the territory in question. (See Box: 'Land rush threatens indigenous communities in South East Asia'.)

Pung Chhiv Kek, president of local rights group Licadho, said women often find themselves heading their families in cases of urban evictions; whereas women take their children to resettlement sites on the edge of Phnom Penh, men remain in town to find work. 'Families are split; the man finds a new partner, while the situation of his wife and children becomes catastrophic,' she said in an interview. Minorities and indigenous people have often been particularly at risk. People from these communities, 'may not understand legal problems and are generally poor with no political connections, which makes them more vulnerable'.

The highest-profile case in 2010 continued to be the secretive real estate project around Phnom Penh's Boeung Kak Lake, which is being developed by a company linked to a ruling party senator and rumoured to be funded by Chinese backers. Roughly 4,000 residents, including a community of Cham Muslims, have been denied land titles and told they must move to make way for a sprawling 133-hectare complex of office towers and apartment blocks. Tensions simmered toward the end of the year after dozens of homes were buried under sludge and sand meant to fill in the lake. The resulting protests have at times turned violent.

Though land evictions affect the general population, indigenous peoples face particular challenges, as their ancestral lands are often located in areas rich in natural resources. In north-eastern Ratanakkiri province, for example, the majority of the population is comprised of indigenous communities. Various groups have continued to complain they have lost land due to the government's controversial land concession policy.

Members of one of Cambodia's minority groups, the Khmer Krom, continued to experience difficulties in 2010. They are the same ethnicity as Cambodia's Khmer majority, but hail from what is now southern Vietnam. Rights groups say they are a persecuted minority in Vietnam, yet not entirely accepted in Cambodia either. Their situation was highlighted in the past year after a group of Khmer Krom entered Cambodia in late 2009 after being deported from Thailand. Though authorities acknowledged the group had full rights to live in Cambodia, they nonetheless refused throughout 2010 to provide them with basic identification cards necessary to obtain employment, or access education or health care in the country. Thach N Thach, president of the US-based advocacy group Khmer Kampuchea-Krom Federation, said, 'Khmer Krom arriving in Cambodia from Vietnam live in legal limbo for significant stretches of time as they are neither treated as citizens nor as refugees.'

In July, the United Nations (UN) backed war crimes tribunal prosecuting the atrocities of the Khmer Rouge period handed down its first verdict against the regime's chief jailer. Kaing Guek Eav, also known as Duch, was sentenced to 35 years in prison for his role as head of the notorious torture centre S-21. However, some Cambodians reacted with disbelief after the court reduced his sentence by 16 years for time already served and illegal detention.

In September, the tribunal officially indicted four former leaders of the regime. Nuon Chea, Ieng Sary, Ieng Thirith and Khieu Samphan would be the first and only senior Khmer Rouge leaders to answer for the regime's rule. Their trials are expected to start some time in 2011. Controversy arose though when the co-investigating judges in the case confirmed that the four senior leaders would face genocide charges in connection with the Khmer Rouge's treatment of ethnic Vietnamese as well as Cham Muslims, but not the Khmer Krom.

UN Secretary-General Ban Ki-moon staged an official visit to Cambodia in late October. Prime Minister Hun Sen, who has frequently lashed out at international officials who criticize the government, subsequently threatened to shut down the Phnom Penh Office of the High Commissioner for Human Rights (OHCHR) and accused its country representative of siding with the main political opposition party.

In December, the government announced it would close a UN-run centre which was home to 76 Montagnard asylum-seekers, including 62 who had already been granted refugee status. Rights groups raised concerns that the group, part of a largely Christian minority from Vietnam's Central Highlands, might be deported back to their homeland, where they would face repression because of their ethnicity and the fact that many Montagnards sided with the US during the Vietnam War. Cambodian authorities later set a mid-February 2011 deadline for the UN High Commissioner for Refugees (UNHCR) to resolve their cases. Otherwise, the group would face deportation. Critics drew a parallel between the Montagnard situation and the late 2009 deportation of 20 Uighurs back to China. That controversial move came days before China and Cambodia signed aid agreements totalling US $1.2 billion. Similarly, as noted by the Cambodian Centre for Human Rights, news that the government planned to shut the Montagnard facility came one month after a state visit from a senior Vietnamese delegation.

Indonesia
Additional material by Jacqui Zalcberg
Questions around religious freedoms and persecution continued to surface throughout 2010 in Muslim-dominated Indonesia. Repeated cases of threats and violence against religious minorities – as well as the apparent inability of local authorities to respond to such issues – caused some observers to lament conditions for the country's religious minorities, including Hindus and Christians.

In its annual report for Indonesia, the AHRC said:

'The political influence of mainstream religious groups has increased, as have the fundamentalist views among them. Neither the government nor local officials and the police have taken a strong stance concerning the protection of religious minorities.'

Various reported incidents of violence or threats illustrated the situation throughout the year. In August, for example, the *Jakarta Globe* reported that 300 Islamic hardliners 'intimidated, bullied and assaulted' a priest and 20 Christians who were praying in a field in West Java. In December, 100 members of the Batak Christian Protestant Church (HKBP) fled houses in which they were

Land rush threatens indigenous communities in South East Asia

In the highlands of north-eastern Cambodia, ubiquitous cash crop plantations are pushing indigenous peoples off their ancestral lands. Up the winding Mekong River, 2,000 villagers in northern Laos have started pondering what their future holds as plans develop for a large-scale hydropower dam. And across the South China Sea, a global demand for edible oils is fuelling wide-scale destruction of indigenous lands in Malaysia and Indonesia.

Each case is linked by a common thread that bound together indigenous peoples in South East Asia in 2010: the quest for the region's rich natural resources, which is exerting greater pressures throughout the region. The global economic crisis and the impact of climate change have sparked a rush for land, with the futures of many indigenous peoples hanging in the balance, advocates say. 'The remaining natural resources are now in indigenous lands,' said Joan Carling, Secretary-General of the Asia Indigenous Peoples Pact (AIPP), which advocates on behalf of the region's indigenous communities. 'There's a rush to acquire these resources, not only by states, but by corporations.'

In Cambodia, for example, evictions across the country displaced roughly 27,000 people in 2009, according to the UN Special Rapporteur for human rights to Cambodia. Nationwide,

one's identity. Losing land is more than just an economic burden; it is life-altering. Joan Carling says:

'All indigenous communities regard land as their life. It's their source of existence and survival collectively. So the culture and ways of life are very much tied up to their land. So any threat to their land is like a threat to their life.'

In the Mekong region, environmentalists have taken aim at wide-scale plans for massive hydropower along the mighty river and its tributaries. But it is the human cost of such projects that has rights groups alarmed. In 1996, Vietnam completed construction of the Yali Falls Dam, the country's second largest. But 80 km downstream along the Sesan River in Cambodia's north-eastern Ratanakkiri province, indigenous communities say the dam has irrevocably altered the natural flow of the water. They can no longer count on the once abundant fish and plant life along the riverbanks to fulfil their needs. Instead, they search further afield for food, or move to larger urban centres in search of menial jobs. And often it is women who are the hardest hit by such changes. 'Women face the burden of having to work harder to meet their families' needs,' said Ame Trandem, the Mekong campaigner with the advocacy group International Rivers.

Critics say the situation is replicated throughout the region, where governments across South East Asia are contemplating large-scale dam projects to meet regional energy needs. Twelve projects are planned for the main branch of the Lower Mekong, and many more have already been built along its tributaries. In Malaysia, campaigners are raising concerns over a series of a dozen dams planned in Sarawak state.

On land, a voracious appetite for agricultural

the government says it has distributed more than 950,000 hectares of land to 85 companies, though rights groups say the actual figures are even higher. Frequently, such 'economic land concessions' ignite into disputes between the companies and impoverished villagers.

It is these communities – many of which include indigenous peoples – that are often the least equipped to defend their rights. Though villagers may have lived on their land for years, they often lack basic land titles to establish claims to it. Already marginalized from the mainstream, they do not enjoy equal access to justice that is necessary to fight for their rights. And for indigenous peoples, land is inextricably tied to

cash crops is threatening many indigenous communities' ways of life. Indonesia and Malaysia have come to dominate global production of palm oil. In Sarawak state, government plans have set a target of between 60,000 and 100,000 hectares a year for new oil palm plantations on indigenous land, according to a January 2011 report released by the non-governmental organization (NGO) Forest Peoples Programme (FPP) and the International Land Coalition (ILC). Similarly, in Indonesia, estimates suggest land for oil palm is being cleared at a rate of 600,000 hectares every year. The report stated that the situation has produced land conflicts and widespread human rights abuses.

Back in Cambodia's Ratanakkiri province, Dam Chanthy says she sees no signs of a slow-down in the rubber, soy bean and cassava plantations that are sprouting up in her region. An ethnic Tampuan, she started a local advocacy group a decade ago after she lost part of her land to a businessman. These days, she said, available land in the lowland areas has become scarce, putting greater pressure on forest lands local indigenous communities view as sacred. With little free space, many men have left their villages to find work as migrant labourers, leaving even greater responsibilities on the remaining women. Chanthy said:

'When the government gives away the forest land, the water dries up so they have to go far away to fetch water. Sometimes, it's even hard to grow rice.'

She also said many local villagers want development to come to their homelands – they just want to be included in the discussions. For now, that is not happening, 'The land is vital to our lives. The land is our life. Without the land, we will die', she concluded. ∎

worshipping following angry protests from Muslims demonstrating outside. The Christians said they held the services in their homes because local authorities had refused to approve permits to build a church. Agence France-Presse quoted a local police official as saying law enforcement officers were powerless to stop the protests because the Christians were worshiping illegally. Similarly, some Muslims reported difficulties in opening mosques in areas where they form a religious minority, including the provinces of North Sulawesi and Papua.

Many local faith-based NGOs reported that incidents of religious intolerance appeared to rise during 2010. The Moderate Muslim Society (MMS), for example, reported 81 such cases during the year, compared with 59 the year before. The Jakarta-based Wahid Institute, meanwhile, reported 64 'violations of religious freedoms', a figure nearly double the previous year's tally. These included cases in which people or congregations were prohibited from attending houses of worship or forcing worshipers to denounce their beliefs. Police or local government officials reportedly committed almost three-quarters of the violations. Similarly, the Wahid Institute also noted 135 cases of 'intolerance' compared with 93 the year before. These included threats of violence or physical attacks, with individuals or religious societies responsible for the majority of such cases. 'The data clearly indicates deterioration in the guarantee of religious freedom and increasingly low levels of tolerance in society,' its report concluded.

A public opinion survey also suggested an increase in intolerance among the country's Muslim majority. The poll, conducted by the Centre for the Study of Islam and Society, declared 'a worrying increase' in intolerance among Muslims during the year compared with 2001, with a greater percentage of respondents indicating that they opposed the construction of churches or would be unhappy to allow non-Muslims to teach their children.

Rights groups expressed serious concerns over the treatment of the Ahmadiyya community after the Religious Affairs Minister reportedly stated that he planned to institute an official ban on the Islamic sect, which is considered to be heretical by some orthodox Muslims. HRW also reported several incidences of violence against Ahmadis, including one case in which a mob attacked an Ahmadiyya community south of Jakarta and burned down a mosque.

In April, the country's Constitutional Court upheld Indonesia's so-called 'blasphemy law' following a challenge from a group of petitioners. Rights groups called the decision a setback for religious freedoms.

Meanwhile, authorities in Aceh province continued their controversial implementation of Islamic Sharia law. Aceh is the only province in the country authorized to adopt Islamic laws. In a December report, HRW criticized two specific laws for infringing on the rights of women, children and the poor to make decisions about their lives. HRW reported that a 'seclusion' law in effect in Aceh, which is meant to punish adultery, has been used to criminalize even casual associations between unmarried individuals of the opposite sex. HRW also criticized the implementation of an Islamic dress law, calling it discriminatory because it places 'far more stringent restrictions on women than it does on men'. Women interviewed by HRW suggested law enforcement agencies use the law disproportionately to target the poor, as Sharia police were rarely seen reprimanding people with obvious signs of wealth.

Tensions in areas of the country where separatist movements are active continued to draw concern from rights groups. Indonesia granted the Province of Papua special autonomy status in 2001. However, many Papuans claim that the central government has failed to decentralize the full range of responsibility to the region, and there has been little improvement in the delivery of basic services and rights as promised. Moreover, the splitting of the province into two sections in 2003, has further frustrated the Melanesian indigenous population. The Indonesian government has announced that in 2011 it will conduct a comprehensive evaluation of the implementation of Papua's special autonomy. Many West Papuans continue to demand full independence from Indonesia, as well as international action on gross human rights violations reported in their community. The Vanuatu parliament passed a bill in June for the government to sponsor a move to grant Observer Status to West Papua at the regional organization, the Pacific Islands Forum.

In October, the AHRC released a graphic video from West Papua that showed members of the Indonesian military torturing indigenous people suspected of links to separatist groups. The group said the video showed authorities were quick to fall back on 'excessive force'. In January 2011, three soldiers accused of disobedience eventually faced court martial for the incident in a trial international observers saw as a 'test case' for the government. However, critics said the sentences handed down, each amounting to fewer than 10 months, did not fit the severity of the crimes.

In September, Amnesty International called on the government to investigate the in-custody death of Yusuf Sapakoly, a political activist from the Maluku Islands who died from kidney failure after prison authorities allegedly refused him adequate medical access. The 52-year-old had been imprisoned in 2007 after unfurling a symbolic flag advocating independence in front of the president.

Meanwhile, environmental issues continued to cause concern for the future of Indonesia's indigenous peoples, who are conservatively estimated to number between 30 and 40 million. An FPP report analysing the country's rapid redevelopment of indigenous customary land into oil palm plantations noted that women were increasingly suffering problems due to unequal development. Women responsible for household duties now face greater hardships accessing clean water or cooking supplies, as well as food and income, the report stated. Changes in traditional gender roles have reportedly resulted in an increase in domestic violence against women and children.

Laos

Rights groups, UN officials and diplomats spent the beginning of 2010 dealing with the aftermath of Thailand's sudden deportation of more than 4,000 Hmong asylum-seekers back to Laos in late December 2009. Critics warned that the Hmong would face persecution once returned to Laos. Historically, the Hmong supported the United States in its operations against the Pathet Laos, which took command of the country in the mid 1970s. Since 2005, the forced return of Hmong minorities from Thailand has resulted in 'enforced disappearances, torture and arbitrary detention', according to Amnesty International.

After initially denying journalists and UN officials access to the Hmong returnees, in March the government allowed a heavily stage-managed visit of foreign dignitaries and media to a relocation camp in Phonkham village, a newly built settlement in

the Bolikhamsay province of central Laos. Some resettled Hmong interviewed by journalists during the visit expressed fear over their situations, with one woman telling a reporter with Radio Free Asia (RFA), 'I feel scared and do not want to stay in Laos'. While reports suggested there was no immediate evidence the resettled Hmong had been abused, the event was also clearly tightly controlled. Indeed, reports suggested that Lao authorities cut the meeting short when the resettled Hmong approached diplomats and journalists.

One US-based group, the Hmong International Human Rights Watch, suggested that Lao officials had warned the Hmong returnees before the meeting to say 'good things about the Lao government and how well they were being treated'.

The group also warned that the resettled Hmong faced resistance from a group of ethnic Khmu already living in the resettlement area. Group co-founder Joe Davy said in a statement, 'The Khmu feel that this is their land and are very upset with the central government's decision to resettle so many Hmong here, especially when there's not enough resources available.'

Also in March, RFA reported that Lao authorities had deported seven Muslim Uighurs, all members of the same family, back to China, from where the group had fled in 2009. Gulbahar Sadiq told RFA that she, husband Mernet Eli Rozi and the couple's five children were arrested and deported in March. She said she and her children spent 32 days in captivity following their arrival back in China, before they were freed and returned to her hometown. However, her husband remained in captivity in western Kashgar as of December. Gulbahar Sadiq told RFA that her husband had been one of 22 Uighurs who originally sought asylum in neighbouring Cambodia. But he had fled to Laos as the Cambodian government expelled 20 of the asylum-seekers to China in late 2009.

The Lao government recognizes Buddhism, Christianity, Islam and Bahá'í as official religions, though tolerance of religion appeared to vary by region, according to the US State Department's annual human rights report on Laos released in 2010. The report noted that Lao authorities have begun to step in when local governments are seen to have mistreated religious practitioners and have also become 'more proactive' in training local officials in the rights of believers.

That said, religious persecution continued to be an issue in Laos throughout 2010. The group Human Rights Watch for Lao Religious Freedom claimed that authorities in Savannakhet province refused to allow 10 children, whose parents are Christian, to attend school. The group also reported that leaders of a village in Saravan province had evicted seven Christian families at gunpoint after the families refused to renounce their faiths. They join another 11 families who had previously been ejected from the village. And in January 2011, the group reported that 11 Christians, including a church pastor, were arrested while eating a meal. They were accused of staging a meeting in secret without official approval.

In September, Laos officially announced its intention to build a 1,260-megawatt hydropower dam along the Mekong River in Xayaboury province. This would be the first project to dam the main branch of the vital Lower Mekong River. The proposal has caused much controversy among environmentalists and other observers, who are concerned by the dam's possible effects on regional fisheries and livelihoods. More than 2,000 people in 10 villages – comprising a variety of ethnicities, including communities from the indigenous Lao Teung – around the dam site would be resettled as part of the project's construction, according to the advocacy group International Rivers.

Critics say previous examples have shown that dams can threaten the livelihoods of communities living around such sites, particularly for women, who are often put in the position of having to work harder to meet their families' needs when confronted with food shortages or drops in income. The Nam Theun 2 Dam, built on a tributary of the Mekong, began operations in March. The project saw 6,200 indigenous people living in the area resettled; these communities still lack the means to earn a living, according to International Rivers. In addition, a further 110,000 people downstream have experienced the negative impacts of poor water quality and diminished fisheries, the group claims. Overall, the Lao government has at least 55 dam projects in the pipeline as part of its plan to turn the nation into 'the battery of Southeast Asia'.

Malaysia

Malaysia faced continuing challenges in uniting its multi-ethnic society. The year began with heightened tensions following a 31 December 2009 court ruling that overturned the government's ban on the use of the word 'Allah' in Malay-language Christian publications. That decision angered some in the Muslim community and led to a series of attacks on Christian churches around the country. Days later, Malaysia's High Court issued a stay on enforcement of its ruling after the government argued it could cause 'racial conflict'. The attacks were not restricted to churches. In late January, severed pigs' heads were discovered at two mosques. In response, the Council of Churches of Malaysia (CCM) issued a statement condemning 'people trying to inflame religious emotions in the country'.

Questions continued to be raised about the country's Islamic Syariah (Sharia) courts, which run parallel to Malaysia's judicial system. The courts do not have direct jurisdiction over non-Muslims, however there have been cases in which religious minorities have been affected by Syariah court rulings. In March, a civil court found in favour of a Hindu woman after a Syariah court had earlier awarded custody of her children to her husband, a Muslim convert. The case was seen as a potential landmark in defining the legal rights of religious minorities in the majority Muslim nation.

In February, three women were caned under

Islamic law after they were convicted of committing adultery. It was believed to be the first ever case in which such punishment had been handed down to women, as the country's civil law prohibits caning sentences against women. The news raised questions in the media over the balance between the secular and the religious in Malaysia's dual-track legal system.

Local NGO Sisters in Islam (SIS) has called cases of caning ordered against women an example of how female Muslims face discrimination in Malaysia. The organization has reportedly faced retaliation from conservative Islamic groups over its promotion of gender equality. For example, a member of parliament urged the National Fatwa Council to investigate the group. In March, after SIS issued a press release questioning the caning of the three women convicted of adultery, police took statements from employees of the NGO. According to the US State Department, the questioning was part of an investigation into 'alleged violation of the penal code for causing disharmony, disunity, feelings of enmity, hatred, or ill-will, or prejudicing the maintenance of harmony or unity, on grounds of religion'. Malaysia also appointed its first female judges in Islamic courts in August, a move critics said was 'long overdue'.

Amnesty International last year called for a moratorium on canings. A report released late in the year estimated that 10,000 people are caned each year, including many marginalized foreign migrants. These include asylum-seekers caned for 'immigration violations'.

In August, a report by TV network Al Jazeera claimed that indigenous peoples in Pahang state were being offered development aid only in exchange for converting to Islam. Yusri Bin Ahon, an indigenous rights campaigner, told Al Jazeera, 'Government officials visited my people and tried to convert us. They said, "If you want facilities and easy access into the village, you have to be a Muslim."' The government rejected all allegations of pressured conversion.

While the Malaysian Constitution permits freedom of religion, Shi'a Islam is among a number of religious sects considered 'deviant'. In December, Shi'a Muslims urged the government to let them worship legally. Earlier in the month, authorities had detained more than 200 Shi'ites at a prayer meeting in what media reports described as one of the largest mass arrests of its kind.

Malaysia continued to face questions over the treatment of foreign domestic workers, most of whom are female. It is common for Malaysians to hire live-in maids from neighbouring countries like Indonesia, the Philippines and Cambodia, and it is estimated that there are at least 300,000 migrant domestic workers in the in the country. Critics say they lack crucial protections afforded to Malaysian citizens. Migrant live-in domestic workers, for example, are excluded from basic labour protection covering maximum work hours, days off and sick leave. Rights groups have documented numerous cases in which foreign workers claim to have been abused by their employers, leading some critics to dub the worst examples as cases of 'modern-day slavery'.

Indigenous peoples in Malaysia continued to be affected by the government's push toward large-scale hydropower projects. The controversial Bakun Dam in Sarawak state was completed during 2010 and is expected to start supplying power in mid-2011. Thousands of indigenous villagers were relocated to make way for the project. Critics have warned that a series of new hydropower projects planned for the Borneo states of Sarawak and Sabah will further threaten indigenous communities. Sixteen dams have reportedly been planned for Sabah along with another 23 for Sarawak.

The Philippines

Debate continued in 2010 over reproductive health legislation. A proposed bill, which would provide women universal access to birth control methods, has caused great political and religious controversy in the Philippines, where the Catholic Church is influential. The church has reportedly threatened to excommunicate politicians who support the bill.

The Philippines is one of the only countries in the world that explicitly criminalizes abortion with no exceptions, according to a report released last year by the US-based Center for Reproductive Rights. Faced with the ban, pregnant women often turn to unsafe illegal abortion methods. In 2008, roughly 560,000 induced abortions took place throughout the country, the report noted. Arguably, the criminalization of abortion and denial of access to methods for birth control represents a particular violation of the rights of the country's non-Catholic minority, who may not believe in the church's opposition to abortion or contraception. Indeed, as the report notes, not only was abortion legal in pre-colonial times, it was widely practised by indigenous groups.

Several religious-based attacks were reported during the year, including bombings of places of worship. In January, a grenade exploded near a cathedral in Sulu province where Christians form a minority. In May, two people died and a dozen people were injured after a hand grenade exploded inside a mosque in Cotabato. Also in Sulu, a bomb exploded on Christmas Day inside a chapel, wounding 11 people including a priest

In February, the government passed a law creating the National Commission on Muslim Filipinos, a cabinet-level body tasked with promoting the rights of Muslims. The agency was formed with the stated aim of ensuring Filipino Muslims are 'active participants in nation-building'. By law, at least one of the seven members of the commission must be a woman.

In May, Benigno Aquino III was elected president following national elections. Aquino has in part prioritized reconciliation, promising in December to work toward establishing stability in the Mindanao region, which is home to a significant population of Muslims and which has seen a long-running anti-government insurgency in some areas. Aquino has pledged to push forward with the on-going peace process with the Moro Islamic Liberation Front (MILF), a major armed Islamic group. MILF fighters have for years staged guerrilla warfare against authorities, though a ceasefire was signed in July 2009.

The number of internally displaced persons (IDPs) fleeing conflict in Mindanao peaked at around 750,000 by spring 2009. By the end of 2010, that figure had fallen to between 100,000 and 123,000 civilians, according to the Internal Displacement Monitoring Centre. At the end of 2010, the UN IRIN news agency quoted a government official as saying authorities hoped to resettle all IDPs within one year.

The quest for energy continued to cause concern for indigenous communities. In Mindanao, critics of a proposed 300-megawatt hydropower project, dubbed Pulangi 5, say the plan could flood huge swathes of land claimed by indigenous people. Proponents of the project have argued the plan is necessary to counter a 'power crisis' in Mindanao.

Thailand

In March, April and May 2010, Thailand was rocked by mass protests from the opposition-aligned United Front for Democracy Against Dictatorship (commonly referred to as the Red Shirts). While peaceful at first, the situation became violent when Thai security forces confronted the protesters; at least 91 people were killed, most of them civilians. Many Red Shirt supporters are disaffected members of ethnic minorities who come from Thailand's rural north and north-east. The Red Shirts had demanded that Prime Minister Abhisit dissolve parliament and hold elections. The Thai leader refused, instead later pledging to hold elections sometime in 2011. Amid the protests, the government enacted emergency powers throughout parts of the country, which critics said violated basic human rights.

Meanwhile, in the country's Muslim-dominated south, tensions continued to simmer between the government and separatist groups. Frequently, it has been civilians that have suffered. In April, six Buddhist villagers in Narathiwat were shot dead by suspected Islamic insurgents. In a bid to restore order to the region in late December, the Thai cabinet lifted a state of emergency in one district in Pattani province. Officials described the move as a 'test case' in the region. But in the same week, a Buddhist man was gunned down while riding his motorcycle to work, while two Muslim men were also shot dead. The deaths added to a toll that has seen more than 4,400 people killed in the region since early 2004. In a September report, HRW warned that the separatist attacks combined with the government's use of schools as military bases are 'greatly harming the education of children'. Bede Sheppard, HRW's senior researcher for children's rights, said, 'Being a teacher in southern Thailand sadly means putting yourself on the front lines of conflict.'

The insurgency and the resulting government crackdowns have thrust added responsibilities onto Muslim women, according to researcher Angkhana Neelapaijit. In environments where it can be unsafe for men to leave the home, women find themselves in the new role of breadwinners and leaders of their families, tasked with advocating for their rights when their husbands cannot or do not.

The year 2010 saw Thailand take a harsh stance against undocumented migrant workers, drawing concern and criticism from rights groups and international observers. Estimates suggest there could be between 1.8 and 3 million migrant workers and accompanying family members in Thailand, mainly from neighbouring Burma, Cambodia and Laos.

Above: A Karenni woman makes sticky rice wine in a small factory in Ban Huay Tor village, near Mae Hong Son, Thailand. *Eric Lafforgue.*

Early in the year, the government set a February deadline for some 1.3 million migrants, both legal and undocumented workers, to register under a 'nationality verification process' to remain in the country for two years. Those who did not do so could be deported. Jorge Bustamante, the UN Special Rapporteur on the human rights of migrants, warned that the system would place many migrants at risk of suffering human rights violations. Bustamante also warned that there could be some among the potential deportees who qualified for 'international protection'. The statement came less than two months after Thailand controversially deported some 4,000 Hmong refugees to Laos, including 158 who had already been granted refugee status.

Though the mass deportations did not materialize during 2010, authorities nonetheless executed a series of raids that resulted in arrests. Over a ten-day period in June, authorities detained at least 2,200 undocumented migrant workers throughout the country, according to the Human Rights and Development Foundation (HRDF). December raids

led to the arrests of more than 1,500 workers.

Amid the arrests, Thai authorities pressed on with further measures to crack down on migrants. In October, according to HRDF, the government announced a plan to set up a 'migrant worker deportation fund', into which migrant workers themselves would be required to pay a portion of their salaries. In early January 2011, the government postponed enforcement of the measure until 2012. Later in October, Prime Minister Abhisit Vejjajiva invoked legislation to set up a 'Centre to Suppress, Arrest and Prosecute Alien Workers Working Underground and Human Trafficking Processes'. The centre would be charged with 'drawing up a plan of action for resolving the problem of alien workers working underground in a systematic manner', according to a translated copy of the order.

The government's 2010 measures may be indicative of the contradictory attitude towards migrants among people with power in Thailand, including the military, the police and the media, whereby migrants are recognized as an economic necessity but also as a threat to national security and a drain on essential services. Other critics say Thai migration policy has been a 'failure'.

A scathing report released by HRW in February

'The situation has forced women to take up leadership'

K'nyaw Paw is a woman from the ethnic Karen minority of eastern Burma. Now an education programme coordinator for the Karen Women Organization, based in Thailand, her parents fled to Thailand in 1978, and she grew up in refugee camps along the Thailand–Burma border. She talks to *Irwin Loy* about how Karen women in Burma are increasingly being thrust into the role of village chief, and how this dramatic change is putting women at even greater risk of abuse.

Karen village chiefs serve important roles as leaders of their communities: they settle internal disputes; they arbitrate on key issues; and, crucially, they are the main point of contact with the outside world. Men have traditionally dominated the position. But in the 1980s, with male chiefs facing increasing violence, torture and forced labour, women began taking on the job instead.

'The situation has forced women to take up leadership. This is a common resolution in conflict areas where it is very dangerous, where men are afraid to take up a leadership role. Women will be asked, or sometimes forced, to take up leadership.'

But female village chiefs now face horrific violence as the military regime continues its rule over the country. In interviews, the KWO has documented cases of crucifixion, women being burned alive, gang rape, beheadings and torture.

'This struggle shows how gender equality is only represented on the outside but in practice this is not representing gender equality. Women are called on and expected to deal with situations [that are] dangerous and complex. It is not because men are always kind, understanding, and recognize women's abilities and agree with gender equality.

'The situation forces women to take up important positions because they do not want to see the abuse of their people. They want to protect them. No one is protecting and assisting the community, so women have to take dangerous risks.'

The situation has been exacerbated by the uncertainty that surrounded the November national elections, which were widely derided as a sham. Thousands fled after violence erupted between the Burmese military and a faction of the Democratic Karen Buddhist Army in the weeks following the poll.

'They are afraid they will be killed or raped. Women worry about their children, that they will be taken by the military, that they do not have enough food to feed themselves and their children. They are also worried and frightened about when they will be attacked by the Burmese military.

'... There is an endless sense of worry and fear for women. A woman's heart is like fire. They are always living in fear.' ∎

suggested that migrants face abuse, extortion and rights violations through every aspect of the labour process. Migrants interviewed by HRW researchers claimed to have witnessed beatings of workers in detention, sexual harassment and extortion. Women can face particular hardships. One police informant told HRW he had spoken with several women who had been raped at a particular law enforcement outpost. After a Thai general publicly suggested that migrants found to be pregnant should be deported, migrant women have become less willing to seek medical assistance, HRW noted. 'Migrants suffer silently and rarely complain because they fear retribution, are not proficient enough in the Thai language to protest, or lack faith in Thai institutions that too often turn a blind eye to their plight', the report concluded. Days after the report's release, three children were killed when Thai soldiers opened fire on a pick-up truck carrying undocumented workers from Burma.

In early November, following the Burmese national elections, fighting between Burmese government forces and a faction of the Democratic Karen Buddhist Army (DKBA) in the town of Myawaddy sent an estimated 20,000 refugees flooding into Thailand. While most of the refugees returned within days, the situation highlighted the long-standing situation along the Thai–Burmese border, where an estimated 140,000 Burmese refugees and asylum-seekers still live in government-run camps with only basic services, according to the UN refugee agency UNHCR. On 25 December, Thai authorities returned 166 Burmese nationals who had been seeking protection. Shortly after, the UNHCR issued a statement criticizing the government for what it called the 'hasty manner' in which these and other returns had taken place over the preceding weeks.

In December, Thai authorities arrested a group of 85 Pakistani asylum-seekers belonging to the Ahmadiyya sect of Islam. Regional rights groups warned that the group could be in danger of deportation back to Pakistan in 2011, where they could face persecution.

Vietnam

Religious and ethnic minorities in Vietnam continued to experience restrictions on freedoms during 2010, a year in which authorities harassed and jailed activists and critics.

The Vietnamese government holds significant control over the activities of organized religions, and instances of harassment were reported throughout the year. Half the population is estimated to be Buddhist. Catholics make up the largest religious minority at 7 per cent, according to the US Department of State, which also noted that Vietnam had made slight improvements on the issues of religious freedom and practice. For example, the government has helped to build new churches, prayer houses and pagodas and facilitated the education of clergy. The year also saw the state officially sanction a new religious group and two Protestant denominations, according to the department's annual Religious Freedom Report, released in November.

Despite this progress, various religious groups reported facing harassment at the hands of local authorities. In the first half of the year, two Protestant churches in Hue reported incidents in which local police shut down services. There were various other reports throughout the country of local police interrupting religious services, with parishioners being accused of 'gathering illegally'. In May, police clashed with Catholic parishioners who were trying to bury the body of an elderly woman, according to RFA. Witnesses reported that 66 people were beaten. Tensions also flared in January, when police demolished a cross near a Catholic cemetery south of Hanoi. The Catholic website, AsiaNews.it, reported that police then shot tear gas at parishioners.

Ethnic minorities and indigenous people, who together comprise an estimated 14 per cent of Vietnam's population, continued to face difficulty throughout the year and activists from minority communities continued to be jailed. HRW estimated those currently in prison for their religious or political beliefs include 300 Montagnard Christians, Hoa Hao Buddhists and members of the Cao Dai religion. In January, two Montagnards – members of Vietnam's persecuted highland minority – were imprisoned on charges of 'violating the country's unity policy', according to HRW. In March, an activist from the Khmer Krom minority was sentenced on charges of 'abusing democratic rights'. Thach N Thach, president of the US-based advocacy group Khmer Kampuchea-Krom Federation, claimed Khmer Krom Buddhist monks are forced to learn communist ideology in state-sanctioned temples. The government must also approve all religious teachings beforehand, he said.

Statistics continued to show that ethnic minorities are disproportionately represented among Vietnam's poor. The government has pegged the poverty rate in ethnic minority communities at around 50 per cent – a drop of 36 percentage points since 1993, but still more than triple the national rate. Women from ethnic minority groups also have some of the country's highest maternal mortality rates.

After a visit to Vietnam, the UN's Independent Expert on Minority Issues, Gay McDougall, offered praise to the government for what she said was an 'evident political will to address the sizeable socio-economic gap' between ethnic minorities and the majority Kinh. But she also said there were too few opportunities for ethnic minority students to be taught in their own language, and she highlighted instances that may constitute denial of religious freedoms and 'serious violations of civil rights'.

As elsewhere in South East Asia, hydropower dams continued to have significant negative effects on minorities. The first turbine for the massive Son La hydropower plant in north-western Vietnam was turned on in December. The project is expected to be South East Asia's largest power station when it becomes fully operational in 2012. But it has also been the cause of Vietnam's largest resettlement in history. An estimated 91,000 people, mostly from ethnic minorities in the region, were moved to make way for the project, according to the advocacy group International Rivers. Relocated villagers have already reported difficulty growing enough food to feed their families.

East Asia

Irwin Loy

China
Marusca Perazzi
According to figures from the Chinese Ministry of Foreign Affairs released in 2006, China's ethnic minority population is almost 124 million. This makes it the largest ethnic minority population in the world, and is evidence of the country's great diversity and cultural wealth. Minorities are found in every province, region and county, in border areas (Bai, Yi and Zhuang in the south, Mongolians and Uighars in the north) or spread throughout the country (Hui and Manchus). Even the majority Han population is culturally and ethnically diverse, and its members have begun to reassert their different identities, histories and cultures. However, shortcomings in the implementation of fundamental rights in autonomous and other areas inhabited by ethnic groups continued to deprive minorities of the full enjoyment of their cultural, religious and linguistic rights. In November 2010, China initiated its sixth population census which will record the demographic changes that have occurred over the last decade.

Civil and political rights
China's human rights record worsened during 2010, and the government responded more aggressively than in the past to international scrutiny and criticism. This was most evident in the Chinese government's reaction to the nomination and

subsequent selection of democracy activist Liu Xiaobo for the Nobel Peace Prize, which included a campaign to dissuade foreign dignitaries from attending the award ceremony in Oslo, Norway. Liu is currently serving an 11-year sentence for allegedly 'subverting the country and authority'. On 10 December, the UN High Commissioner for Human Rights, Navi Pillay, called for Liu to be released from prison, stating that 'Liu Xiaobo illustrates the dangers and abuse to which human rights defenders around the world are subjected.' In addition, three UN Experts voiced concerns over China's crackdown on rights defenders after receiving numerous reports of arbitrary arrests and detentions, travel restrictions, forced relocations, intimidation, harassment and punishment of activists.

In his report to the 13th Session of the UN Human Rights Council (following a fact-finding mission to China), UN Special Rapporteur on Torture Manfred Nowak wrote:

'China maintains the most institutionalized method of opposing political dissidents that I have encountered. Political dissidents and human rights defenders, ethnic groups that are often suspected of separation (particularly Tibetans and Uyghurs), as well as spiritual groups such as Falun Gong are often accused of political crimes such as endangering national security through undermining the unity of the country, subversion or unlawfully supplying State secrets to individuals outside the country. Such individuals are not only at a high risk of torture when arrested, but the Re-education Through Labor (RTL) Regime that is often used as a sentence for political crimes employs measures of coercion, humiliation and punishment aimed at altering the personality of detainees up to the point of breaking their will.'

Education and linguistic rights
As reported by the Xinhua news agency in September, a White Paper published by the government entitled Progress in China's Human Rights in 2009 referred to 38 publishers producing material in 26 different minority languages, and stated that 'over 60 per cent of the population of China's 55 minority groups, or approximately 60 million people regularly speak their own language, [and] about 30 million of them regularly use their own script'. According to the document, government support to socio-economic development

in areas primarily inhabited by ethnic minorities has increased, bringing about a gradual improvement in living conditions among minorities, as demonstrated by the increased levels of education and use of public health care systems among these groups. The paper also stated that:

'The ethnic minorities' rights to study, use and develop their own languages are protected [and] at present, over 10,000 schools with a total of 6 million students use 29 languages of 21 ethnic groups in classroom teaching.'

Previous to this, in June an official notice from China's State Ethnic Affairs Commission (SEAC) urged the teaching and official use of minority languages in ethnic minority areas. The notice advised local ethnic affairs authorities to pursue 'bilingual' education, train more teachers, and increase the publishing of textbooks for minorities in compliance with national legislation. The notice also called for identity cards in autonomous minority areas to be written in each respective minority language, as well as Mandarin Chinese. Finally, the notice called for the use of minority languages in publishing, broadcasting and online in an attempt to preserve ethnic minority languages on the verge of extinction.

However, China's rhetoric on compliance with international human rights standards clashed with well-documented cases of violations of national and international norms. In October, the Associated Press reported that Tibetan students marched in Tongren (Qinghai province) and Beijing protesting against a plan to establish Mandarin Chinese as the main language of instruction in Tibetan schools in the region. Such a plan would contravene the Chinese Constitution, the 2002 'Regulations on the Study, Use and Development of the Tibetan Language' (in accordance with the Regional National autonomy law), and international standards. In response, the European Parliament passed a resolution on Tibet – Plans to Institute Chinese as Main Language of Instruction in November. It noted that in all areas of the Tibetan Autonomous Region (TAR):

'Tibetan language is gradually being replaced by Chinese in schools at different levels [...] with official documents usually unavailable in Tibetan and textbooks and subjects made available only in

Chinese [...]. Despite the claim by Chinese officials that a bilingual teaching system has been adopted in the education sector of Tibet, with priority given to teaching in Tibetan, the Tibetan language is given either 50 per cent weight or no weight at all in university exams.'

In November, RFA reported the dismissal of 518 Uighur teachers in Toksun County (out of a total of 2,000) over the sensitive issue of 'bilingual education' in the Xinjiang Uighur Autonomous Region (XUAR). Bilingual education policies have in fact meant that the use of Mandarin Chinese has been prioritized over the minority language as the main language of instruction in schools and universities across the region, according to a XUAR October directive. Reports and testimonies to MRG also indicated that the situation with regard to linguistic rights has deteriorated in the XUAR, with instances of the forced closure of local publishing houses specialized in the printing of textbooks in Uighur during the reporting period.

Meanwhile, in other regions, UN agencies are supporting the Chinese government in designing and implementing policies aimed at promoting and protecting the rights of smaller ethnic minorities in regions such as Yunnan, Guizhou and Qinghai. Some cultural preservation programmes aimed at smaller communities have apparently been carried out successfully, while others, for instance the UN–China joint programmes aimed at preserving ethnic cultural resources in south-west China, have met with mixed results, according to an evaluation by UN Development Programme (UNDP). The China Culture and Development Partnership Framework (CDPF), a three-year programme begun in 2009 and funded by the Millennium Development Goals (MDG) Achievement Fund, as reported by the Director and Representative of UNESCO Beijing Office and Co-Chair of the CDPF, has so far reached:

'More than 5,000 members of ethnic minorities in remote and inaccessible counties in South-West China who directly benefited from the programme [...] that promoted inclusive governance and culturally sensitive basic education; improved the quality and uptake of maternal and child health services; introduced community-based cultural tourism initiatives; strengthened local crafts sectors; and contributed to the understanding and protection of tangible and intangible cultural heritage'.

Religious freedom
In 2010, the government strengthened state control over religious practices, continuing to exclude minority religious communities from the minimal room to manoeuvre that is afforded to state-sanctioned religious groups. Relations between the Vatican and China were seriously damaged in the past year, with a series of accusations and heavy criticism from both sides that affected religious freedom for Christians across the country. The Chinese authorities continued to maintain oppressive control over some ethnic groups' religious activities. For example, according to RFA, 'the campaigns include restrictions on the wearing of traditional headscarves and beards' in the XUAR.

In March, the UN Special Rapporteurs on freedom of religion and belief, on torture, and on the status of human rights defenders presented their reports and concluding observations, based on their fact-finding investigations in China at the 13th Session of the UN Human Rights Council. The reports detailed on-going human rights violations against Falun Gong practitioners, including cases of beatings, harassment, torture and deaths while in police custody. Instances of lawyers defending Falun Gong practitioners being jailed were also documented. The Chinese government ignored the reports or denied the validity of their findings.

Minorities in Inner Mongolia, Tibet and Xinjiang
In the White Paper, Progress in China's Human Rights in 2009, the Chinese government publicized what it considered to be the successful achievements of the First National Human Rights Plan, and reaffirmed that 'citizens of all ethnic groups in China enjoy equal rights and special rights' and that 'the state guarantees by law ethnic minorities' equal rights in participation in the administration of state and regional affairs'. However, during the year the government continued to implement restrictive measures to limit civil society engagement and action on minority rights issues, particularly in the three autonomous regions of Inner Mongolia (IMAR), the TAR and the XUAR. In these regions, Chinese majority and minority journalists, editors and activists advocating or reporting on minority rights faced intimidation, harassment and

punishment by the authorities, and continued to be denied their fundamental rights of freedom of speech and expression over the course of the year. In part, this was through the use of vaguely worded criminal laws furthering the mechanism of 'prior restraints' to curb or deny groups or individuals the right to freedom of assembly and expression. Punishments included, for example, confiscation of books, educational or religious materials, as well as imprisonment of minority individuals including webmasters, editors and activists for alleged crimes against the state.

Local authorities' arbitrary interpretation and application of laws in minorities' autonomous areas heavily circumscribed the rights of minorities in many other spheres of life. In fostering economic development policies in autonomous areas such as the IMAR, the TAR and the XUAR, persecution, harassment, punishment and forced assimilation is steadily wiping out minorities' hopes for meaningful expression of their identity and genuine public participation. In a poignant testimony to MRG, an ethnic minority source from the XUAR stated:

'the Chinese authorities harden state policies and adopted measures that control, interfere and deliberately manipulate minority communities' life. Local authorities abuse their power to police and dictate the day-to-day existence of our communities. It is an impossible way of living that is gradually erasing our culture and tradition. China is staging a silent cultural genocide in the XUAR that no one seems willing to halt.'

Other reports from human rights activists and civil society groups pointed to the on-going forced removal of girls and younger women from the XUAR by the authorities, as reported in previous editions of the *State of the World's Minorities*. This process of forced assimilation is destroying the fragile social fabric of Uighur families that during the year endured abuse, mistreatment, punishment and violations of their individual and collective rights. Elsewhere, local governments continue to be unofficially instructed to target migrant workers and ethno-linguistic and religious minorities through population planning policies that interfere and control the reproductive lives of women using forced sterilization and abortion, arbitrary detention and forced disappearances, including of Mongol activists and their families.

In April, the National People's Congress (NPC) Standing Committee adopted a revision to the Law on Guarding State Secrets by narrowing the definition of 'state secrets', boosting transparency and ensuring the people's right to know. However, in August, Human Rights House reported that, in a series of closed trials, Urumqi Intermediate People's Court sentenced three ethnic Uighur webmasters to life in jail for alleged separatist offences and for 'endangering state security'.

There were indications that some of the economic and social issues underlying the 2009 violent unrest in the XUAR and discontent among minority groups more generally were being addressed, although many others remained ignored. In the XUAR, communication channels that had remained shut down for months after the riots were re-established, and in March, unpopular Party Secretary Wang Lequan was suddenly removed. Secretary Wang had been in place since 1995, and had overseen harsh policies in the region, resented by both Han and ethnic minorities alike. Some commentators take the view, looking back over 2010, that the very promising genuine concern and dialogue being built between Uighurs and a growing number of Han Chinese holds the potential for a meaningful solution to Uighur issues. However, news in December of the deportation of seven Uighur asylum-seekers from Laos, who fled there after the July 2009 incidents, raised serious concerns over the situation of Uighur people who have been forcibly returned to China, where they face possible persecution.

Gender equality and minority women's rights
The promotion of equality between men and women is a basic objective in China's social development. According to official Chinese statistics, women's economic, social and cultural rights are being more effectively guaranteed with women accounting for 38 per cent of the workforce. However, no updated government statistics regarding ethno-linguistic minority women in employment are available. Historically, unemployment rates among ethnic minority women and girls have been higher than among Han women; outdated estimates indicate figures of less than 10 million ethnic minority women in employment at that time.

In May 2001, the Chinese government promulgated the Program for the Development of

Chinese Women (2001–10) (PDCW), with the goal of fostering women's development, including by promoting women's employment and enhancing their participation in administration, management and decision-making regarding social affairs. After the Law on the Protection of Women's Rights and Interests was revised and enacted in December 2005, legislative bodies at the provincial, autonomous region and municipal levels, including the XUAR, Hunan and Jiangxi provinces, revised implementation measures significantly, taking into account local conditions and characteristics. According to the Legal Department of the All China Women's Federation (ACWF), the measures have helped to secure some breakthroughs, in terms of stipulating the percentage of women candidates for local people's congresses, reinforcing the functions of local working committees on women and children, fighting domestic violence, defining and outlining punishment for sexual harassment, signing collective contracts with women workers, and ensuring specific funding for efforts aimed at protecting women's rights.

Despite China's commitment to women's equality and empowerment, women's political representation remains state-supported; that is, there is token representation where state policies are used to increase the numbers of women in leadership positions rather than promoting them into roles with real influence. In part to address this, in 2010 the ACWF received US $2.4 million from the UN Fund for Gender Equality towards implementing a programme to increase women's political profiles and their participation in institutions of governance at national and local levels by 2013. It is unclear whether the programme will also include and benefit minority women representatives.

Democratic People's Republic of Korea

The Democratic People's Republic of Korea, or North Korea, continued to be a state shrouded in secrecy throughout 2010. Nevertheless, reports from NGOs and international observers suggest that North Korea has done little to improve its deplorable human rights record.

The country is considered racially and ethnically homogeneous and there are no official minorities. However, there is reportedly a small Chinese community numbering around 50,000, as well as fewer than 2,000 ethnic Japanese women married to Korean men who returned to the North from Japan between 1959 and 1962.

North Korea's Constitution allows for freedom of religious belief, but this is limited to state-controlled places of worship. Government estimates in 2002, supplied to the UN High Commissioner for Human Rights, reported that there were roughly 12,000 Protestants, 10,000 Buddhists and 800 Catholics, though outside groups suggest the numbers are much higher.

Some foreigners living in the capital, Pyongyang, who attended sanctioned Christian churches reported that the services 'appeared staged and contained political content supportive of the government, in addition to religious themes'. It is believed that the government persecutes those who participate in 'unauthorized' religious gatherings. In August, Asianews.it, a Catholic news site, reported that authorities arrested 23 'underground Christians' who had congregated at a house in Pyongan province. Three people were tried and executed, the website reported, citing unnamed sources. 'Such sentences are meant to scare people', the source was quoted as saying.

In its annual report released in May, the United States Commission on International Religious Freedom stated that imprisoning religious believers is a common practice in North Korea. Estimates suggest there are 40,000 religious prisoners currently being held throughout the country.

In March, the UN Human Rights Council adopted a strongly worded resolution that expressed 'serious concern at on-going grave, widespread and systematic human rights violations in the Democratic People's Republic of Korea'. Five members voted against the resolution, including China and Russia. North Korea's delegate, in turn, reportedly criticized the resolution, saying that it was 'full of distortions and fabrications based on political bias'.

Japan

Japan continues to have no civil or criminal law against racial discrimination, a key issue for minorities. Such an absence has the effect of enabling discriminatory practices, according to a February report prepared by the Solidarity Network with Migrants Japan (SNMJ) and submitted to the UN Committee on the Elimination of Racial

Discrimination (CERD). The report even noted instances in which stores and restaurants were seen to have signs explicitly stating 'Japanese Only'.

The Japanese government's position on the matter is that such a law is unnecessary because the country's Constitution already forbids 'discrimination on the basis of race, creed, sex, social status and family origin', according to a February statement released by CERD following discussions with a senior delegation from the government. However, observers say minorities in Japan still face barriers. In March, following a nine-day visit, Jorge Bustamante, the UN's expert on migrants' rights, urged Japan to step up its protection of migrants, and noted that, 'Racism and discrimination based on nationality are still too common in Japan, including in the workplace, in schools, in health care establishments and housing.'

Migrant women in Japan were seen as particularly vulnerable to discrimination and violence. The SNMJ report highlighted the issue of discrimination and domestic violence against women, including many from Asia and Latin America. Non-Japanese nationals were reported to be six times more likely to be abused than Japanese women in domestic situations, according to the report. Japan has a law against domestic violence, yet undocumented migrant women enjoy only minimal protection, the report notes. For example, undocumented women are permitted to stay in government-run shelters for only two weeks and cannot access crucial support services. Faced with a lack of support and the threat of being deported, 'a significant number of undocumented migrant women and children choose to bear abuses, or if they are already in a shelter, to return to their violent partners or become homeless,' the report notes.

Japan also excludes undocumented migrant workers from its public health system – a position the group Human Rights Watch (HRW) says may be a violation of basic rights to access health services, including anti-retroviral therapy.

Children of minorities also face difficulties in the education system, particularly those of Nikkei-Brazilian, Nikkei-Peruvian (who have Japanese ancestry but whose families emigrated to South America during the last century) and Filipino ancestry. Roughly 20 per cent of children from these groups are believed not to attend school at all, according to local government surveys. And since

the high school entrance exam system makes little allowance for students who do not speak Japanese as a native language, the number of children from minority groups who move on to high school drops precipitously. Less than 30 per cent of the children of migrants and migrant workers go on to high school, according to estimates. For Japanese nationals, that figure is 97 per cent, according to the SNMJ report. The national government has yet to compile a wide-reaching nationwide survey on the children of non-Japanese nationals or ethnic minorities.

Schools catering to the children of Brazilian- and Peruvian-Japanese are also underfunded, with most of the costs coming from tuition fees paid by parents. Following the global economic crisis in 2008, when 60 per cent of Brazilian migrant workers lost their jobs, 16 schools catering to their children shut down. The SNMJ report notes that half of the affected students returned to Brazil; however, 22 per cent 'still remain completely out of school in Japan'.

The SNMJ report also notes that naturalized citizens faced pressure to alter their names to Japanese names. In one January case, a Thai woman who went to a legal office to apply for Japanese nationality claimed she was told to 'come back with a Japanese name in mind for when you acquire Japanese nationality'.

Minority groups in Japan also continued to experience discrimination, according to reports. For example, the 3 million Burakumin, who are ethnically Japanese but the descendants of feudal-era outcasts, 'frequently were victims of entrenched societal discrimination, including restricted access to housing, education and employment opportunities', according to the US State Department's Human Rights country report for Japan, released in March.

While the government has been lauded for its 2008 decision to officially recognize Ainu as an indigenous people, it has been slow to acknowledge other groups. The Japanese government has not yet acknowledged Ryukyuan people as indigenous even though, as noted by CERD, the group appeared 'to have a distinct language, culture and history' that would lead other countries to recognize them as such.

The year 2010 also marked the 65th anniversary of the end of the Second World War. But Japan has yet to accept legal responsibility for the so-called 'comfort women' system implemented by the Japanese Imperial Army starting in 1932, whereby women from Asian countries colonized by Japan were forced into sexual slavery. The remaining survivors are elderly and many have died without seeing redress. In August, the rights group Amnesty International reiterated calls for the Japanese government to 'accept full responsibility, including legal responsibility, in a way that publicly acknowledges the harm these women have suffered'.

Mongolia
Marusca Perazzi

In August 2010, the government of Mongolia strongly reaffirmed its commitment to obligations under the Universal Declaration of Human Rights (UDHR), further stating that 'protecting the rights of national minorities stand[s] as a priority'. Yet, in the past year, the Legatum Prosperity Index ranked Mongolia in the lower half of the list on the variable of welcoming ethnic minorities. For despite Mongolia's commitment to democratic principles and constitutional guarantees of equality and non-discrimination on the basis of ethnicity, in the absence of a designated institution to enforce anti-discrimination legal provisions, ethnic and linguistic minorities continue to be penalized by discriminatory policies. This means that in 2010, minorities were unable to realize their rights in accessing information, education and effective participation in public life.

Minorities make up 18.2 per cent of the population and include Barga, Bayad, Buryat, Chantuu, Durbet, Kazakhs and Tsaatan mainly concentrated in the *aimags* of Bayan-Ölgii, Dornod, Hentiy, Khovd and Uvsnd. In 2010, Mongolia's ethnic minority groups faced a number of challenges, as did the majority ethnic group, Khalks. Structural inequalities, environmental crisis, poverty and development divides between urban and rural areas tested the capacity and willingness of a government already struggling to address the needs of the third of the population that lives in poverty. Mongolian herders, mostly minorities and indigenous peoples, were confronted with severe drought and a harsh winter, forcing thousands of them to abandon their nomadic life. Meanwhile, an Asian Development Bank (ADB) programme implemented policy measures in the social welfare, health and education sectors to ensure the provision of essential basic services to the poorest and most vulnerable. This included provision of early childhood education to nomadic and ethnic minority children.

Civil society groups continued to play an important role in tackling social issues and helping to strengthen political institutions. In April, protests in the capital Ulaan Baator called for the dissolution of the parliament and a fairer distribution of the country's natural wealth. In December the Mongolian parliament reportedly agreed to discuss the new Constitution Amendment Procedures of the 1992 Constitution of Mongolia. It is unclear whether any public consultative process will take place in regard to the constitutional amendments, and if so, to what extent minorities will be encouraged to participate.

Mongolia's women's rights activists played a key role in advocating for human rights, public participation, fostering social change and a more gender-balanced society through increased efforts in tackling domestic violence and child trafficking, and promoting minority rights protection. Mongolia's Women Fund (MONES), for example, concentrated its policy work on national mechanisms to strengthen the voices of ethnic minorities and herder women, and on raising public awareness of the need for a more comprehensive legal framework and a stronger protection regime for minorities and other vulnerable groups in society.

In the effort to strengthen women's rights and reduce violence against women, the Law on Fighting against Domestic Violence (2004) and the National Programme on Fighting against Domestic Violence (effective as of 2008) represent a considerable achievement. Yet domestic violence remains a critical but taboo issue in Mongolia, in the absence of laws prohibiting marital rape. Facilities are limited for victims of sexual and gender-based violence in remote areas, where most minority groups reside. In spite of the government's efforts, poor implementation of existing legislation still reflects the lack of political will to tackle these issues, while women continue to face social, economic and procedural barriers in accessing state protection, according to the Common Country Assessment conducted by the UN in Mongolia in 2010. This is even more the case for minority women. Young women from rural areas (where most minority communities live) remained most vulnerable to trafficking and abduction for commercial sexual exploitation.

Concerns over shortcomings in the implementation of existing human rights legislation and failure to incorporate Mongolia's international human rights obligations into national legislation have surfaced during the year. In an official submission to the ninth round of the Universal Periodic Review (UPR), a national working group argued that ethnic Kazakhs and Dukha (or Tsaatan) face 'widespread societal and institutional discrimination within Mongolian society'. The document reported lack of basic freedoms, on-going systematic discriminatory practices and attitudes, and human rights violations. It exposed a lack of institutional and legislative measures coupled with the absence or inaccessibility of redress mechanisms. The working group recommended that, 'Mongolia enact an anti-hate crime law to protect minorities from hate crimes, ensure privacy and confidentiality of information, emphasize education and conciliation, and provide for speedy and effective criminal, administrative and civil remedies'.

The draft report of the 9th Session of the UPR Working Group of the UN Human Rights Council on Mongolia reported concerns about discrimination against women and girls, and stressed the need for women's greater participation at the highest levels of decision-making. In the reporting year, women and ethnic minorities remained under-represented in political decision-making at all levels, or 'in the case of the Dukha, were entirely absent from the policy-making sphere' (according to local NGOs). In 2010, out of 76 seats in parliament there were only three women MPs (3.9 per cent), as well as two female vice-ministers in a cabinet of 15. Of these, none are believed to be from ethnic minorities, although there are three male ethnic Kazakh MPs.

In a positive sign, a female MP interviewed by the website News English Mongolia stated that, by year's end, the government had submitted a draft law on gender, which includes a 30 per cent quota for women in parliament. In 2010, the National Human Rights Commission of Mongolia (NHRCM) encouraged the government of Mongolia to promote greater representation of women and national minorities in decision-making by setting quotas for minority groups as well as women, including in local legislatures. This proposal

was also made in the draft UPR report. However, women and members of minority groups find entering the political realm particularly difficult, since party politics is deeply influenced by money and corruption, making it difficult for those without connections to gain a foothold.

The draft UPR report also raised concerns regarding the continued difficulties faced by minority religious groups in officially registering and building places of worship. The report stated that these problems could be eradicated by establishing clear national guidelines to allow all faith groups equal access to registration.

Finally, the UPR process also recorded that ethnic minority children do not fully enjoy their right to education, noting that '[the] Kazakh minority province of Bayan-Ölgii registered the highest rate of education dropouts and the lowest pre-school participation rate in the country with illiteracy rates of 6.8 per cent (compared to the national average of 4.6 per cent)'. In northern Mongolia, Tuva minority children's access to any level of education also remained limited. During the year, the Committee on the Rights of the Child (CRC) expressed concern about lack of awareness among herder families in the western regions of the importance of birth registration. Almost 10 per cent of births in remote areas remained unregistered.

Oceania

Jacqui Zalcberg

The Oceania region is ethnically diverse. It is characterized by a high proportion of indigenous peoples, who form majority populations in many of the Pacific Island region, as well as numerous minority groups, resettled peoples and internal migrants from different islands in the region.

In 2010, indigenous peoples in Oceania began to assert their voice on the international stage. The United Nations (UN) Special Rapporteur on the rights of indigenous peoples, Professor James Anaya, visited New Caledonia in February 2011, and New Zealand in July 2010. During these visits, he assessed the human rights situation of the indigenous Kanak and the Māori peoples respectively. These were the first visits of the mandate to the Pacific region.

In 2010, three Oceanic countries were also considered by the UN Committee on the Elimination of Discrimination Against Women (CEDAW committee): Australia, Fiji and Papua New Guinea. In its observations on Fiji, the CEDAW committee noted high levels of violence against women in all its forms, in both the private and public spheres. It also noted the impact of cultural stereotypes which perpetuate discrimination against women and girls, and the impact of the practice of reconciliation and forgiveness ceremonies such as *bulubulu*. Victims of gender-based violence may be forced to participate in such ceremonies, after which they have little choice but to remain in abusive and violent relationships.

According to Amnesty International, overall levels of violence against women in the Pacific are amongst the highest in the world, with the United Nations Development Fund for Women (UNIFEM) estimating prevalence as high as 85 per cent in some countries. This has a devastating impact not only on individual women but also on communities and the Pacific region as a whole. Sexual violence is common and severe and is most often committed by men against their intimate partners.

The situation in Fiji continues to be a major issue for the region. The current regime, which overthrew the Laisenia Qarase-led government in a coup in December 2006, claims to protect the rights of the Indo-Fijian minority against the indigenous majority. The regime continues to be charged with human rights violations, and in particular has been criticized for its restrictions on freedom of expression, and for silencing dissidents and critics of the government.

The environmental impacts of climate change continue to pose a major threat to the Pacific island-states, many of which are low-lying and are at particular risk of disappearing due to rising tides. According to a 2010 policy paper by the International Organization for Migration (IOM), there could be 200 million climate-displaced persons and refugees by 2050, a large number of whom will be coming from the Pacific Island region. Papua New Guineans from the Carteret Islands have already become the world's first climate displaced persons, with Tuvalu expected to become uninhabitable over the coming decades due to rising sea levels. The Papua New Guinea government pledged financial assistance to the residents of the Carteret atolls to help the population shift to the main island of Bougainville, but affected persons have yet to receive this support.

The Australian Labor Party's recent report on the issue, *Our Drowning Neighbours*, identifies the potential security impacts of changing climate patterns, and recommends that Australia play a key role in helping establish an international coalition to address the issue. The New Zealand government has recently established a 'Pacific Access Category' to enable Pacific Islanders from Kiribati, Tuvalu and Tonga to migrate to New Zealand. However, numbers are extremely limited, and eligibility is based on age and language criteria, which limits the effectiveness of the programme to address the needs of those experiencing the impacts of climate change in the region.

The issue of new migrant populations is also of growing importance in the region. While a large proportion consists of migrants from Asia to Australia and New Zealand, there is also significant movement and settlement of Pacific Islander populations to those countries. Both New Zealand and Australia have introduced pilot programmes inviting seasonal workers from Pacific Island countries, with the aim of providing temporary employment for Pacific Islanders and providing Australian and New Zealand agricultural farmers with labour. The Australian programme, which promised 2,500 visas to workers from Kiribati, Papua New Guinea, Tonga and Vanuatu over three years, has been criticized for its ineffectiveness. Halfway through the scheme, only 137 islanders had been brought to Australia, amounting to around 10 per cent of what might have been expected. The New Zealand scheme has had far greater success, with approximately 5,000 Pacific Islanders benefiting from the scheme every year since its launch.

Australia

The 2010 federal elections in Australia resulted in a hung parliament, with the incumbent Labor Party forming a minority government with the support of an Australian Greens' MP and three independent MPs. The treatment of asylum seekers was once again a major issue in the national election.

Aboriginal Australians

Following former Prime Minister Kevin Rudd's

apology in 2008 to indigenous Australians for the Stolen Generation (children of Aboriginal or Torres Strait islander descent who were systematically removed from their families by federal or state officials, in a policy that was in place until the 1960s), in 2010 current Prime Minister Julia Gillard announced the government's intention to hold a referendum to recognize Aboriginal and Torres Strait Islander People in the Australian Constitution. The government has established an expert panel to lead a national discussion and broad consultation which will take place in 2011. A key issue will be whether this recognition will be in the form of a new provision inserted into the text of the Constitution, or a reference in the preamble.

In all social indicators, Aboriginal and Torres Strait Islander peoples continue to rank as the most disadvantaged peoples in Australia, for example in indices of education, employment, health, standard of living, life expectancy and incidence of domestic violence. They are also grossly over-represented in the child protection and criminal justice systems.

In June 2010, Australia was considered by the CEDAW committee. While congratulating Australia on a range of indicators regarding the status of women, the CEDAW committee noted that indigenous women and girls face the highest levels of violence of any ethnic group in the country, especially at home, where indigenous women are 35 times as likely to be hospitalized as a result of family violence-related assaults as non-indigenous females. The CEDAW committee also observed that indigenous women have fewer opportunities, are less likely to participate in public life, and have more restricted access to justice, and to quality education, health care and legal aid services.

The Australian government's response to the levels of disadvantage faced by Aboriginal and Torres Strait Islander peoples has been the 'Closing the Gap' campaign. This campaign has been criticized by the UN Special Rapporteur on the rights of indigenous peoples for insufficiently consulting and collaborating with indigenous communities regarding its design and implementation, and accordingly failing to achieve meaningful change in indigenous peoples' lives.

Asylum seekers

The issue of refugees and asylum seekers continues to capture the nation's attention, and national

debate continues around asylum seekers arriving or attempting to arrive on Australian shores by boat. A policy of mandatory indefinite detention remains in place for all asylum seekers. This policy has been applied indiscriminately, including to children, and as of mid-January 2011 there were 1,065 children living in immigration detention facilities around Australia. In October 2010, the government announced plans to release the majority of unaccompanied children and families into the community by June 2011.

On 15 December 2010, a wooden boat carrying up to 100 Iranian, Iraqi and Kurdish asylum seekers smashed onto the cliffs of Christmas Island. There were 42 survivors but at least 30 people lost their lives. Three children were orphaned by the tragedy. Those who survived were immediately detained on Christmas Island, where they await processing.

The Australian government recently announced that it is considering further offshore processing of asylum seekers in Timor Leste. Responsibility for legal processing, resettlement and processes for failed asylum seekers would fall to the Timorese government, which is a signatory to the 1951 Convention relating to the Status of Refugees.

Migrant communities

Since 1945, 7 million immigrants have come to Australia; 44 per cent of Australians were either born outside the country or have at least one parent who was.

Despite the large numbers of migrants in Australia, targeted discrimination against minority communities continues to be a serious issue in Australian society. African communities experience particularly high levels of discrimination. This is especially the case for the Sudanese community, which is one of the fastest growing ethnic minority communities in Australia. Sudanese Australians often suffer discrimination, racial vilification and negative stereotyping, which has been perpetuated by the media and the government by focusing the discourse on the community's alleged levels of criminality. This discrimination often extends to a range of economic and social rights, including finding or maintaining employment, accessing housing and public spaces, and discriminatory policing.

Muslim women in Australia are also particularly vulnerable, and report experiencing discrimination, and feeling unsafe and unwelcome. This affects their freedom of movement, and their sense of safety and control and agency over their own lives. The feeling of vulnerability is heightened for those women wearing the *hijab*, who are easily identifiable targets for discrimination. Migrant women overall also experience low levels of participation in the labour market, and are often engaged in low-paying jobs. There is a lack of linguistic and culturally appropriate services, limiting migrant women's access to public services, including health care.

In recognition of the discrimination and racism experienced by migrants, the Labor government announced a new policy on multiculturalism in February 2011. A new entity, the Australian Multicultural Council (AMC), will be established, which will operate as an independent and permanent body and advise the government on policies that pertain to multiculturalism. Its mandate will be broader than that held by the current advisory council, and the AMC will have a formal role in devising multicultural policy, as well as an advisory role.

New Zealand

Māori are the original inhabitants of New Zealand (Aotearoa), who today comprise approximately 15 per cent (575,000) of New Zealand's population of 4.25 million.

The government of New Zealand has made significant strides in advancing the rights of Māori people in comparison to the experiences of other indigenous peoples around the world, according to the UN Special Rapporteur on the rights of indigenous peoples (who visited the country in 2010). However, the Special Rapporteur also noted that Māori peoples continue to experience extreme disadvantage in a range of social and economic areas in comparison to the rest of New Zealand society.

Across a range of indicators, Māori women experience poorer economic, health and social outcomes than other New Zealand women. Almost

20 per cent of Māori women reported being assaulted or threatened by an intimate partner, three times the national average. Māori women also make up nearly 60 per cent of the female prison population.

The New Zealand government announced in December 2010 that it will conduct a wide-ranging review of New Zealand's constitutional arrangements. The review, expected to last three years, will cover a range of issues. Importantly, among these it will consider the role of the Treaty of Waitangi, the country's core founding instrument that established the partnership between Māori and the New Zealand government, in New Zealand's constitutional framework.

The Marine and Coastal Area (Takutai Moana) Bill was introduced into the House of Representatives in late 2010, to replace the Foreshore and Seabed Act (2004), which controversially extinguished any Māori customary title over coastal and marine areas. The new bill is expected to be passed into law in early 2011, and will restore the customary interests extinguished by the Foreshore and Seabed Act, subject to proof of Māori use and occupation of the area according to custom (*tikanga*), without substantial interruption from 1840 to the present day.

In April 2010, at the Permanent Forum on Indigenous Issues, New Zealand declared its endorsement of the United Nations Declaration on the Rights of Indigenous Peoples (UNDRIP).

Other minority groups
Over the last 10 years, net migration has accounted for around a third of New Zealand's population growth. By 2021, it is projected that minority groups, including those who identify as Māori, Asian or Pacific Islander, will make up a large proportion of the New Zealand population. Across these ethnic groups is a consistent pattern of a slightly higher percentage of females than males.

In recent decades in particular, there has been significant migration from the Pacific Islands (primarily from Polynesia) to New Zealand. The seven largest Pacific ethnic groups in New Zealand are Samoan, Cook Islands Māori, Tongan, Niuean, Fijian, Tokelauan and Tuvaluan. According to the Ministry of Pacific Island Affairs, by 2026, it is projected that Pacific people will be 10 per cent of the population, compared to 6.5 per cent in 2001. The largest urban concentration of Pacific Islanders

living outside their own countries is in Auckland, sometimes referred to as the 'Polynesian capital of the world'.

Pacific Islanders, who today constitute up to 7 per cent of the population, experienced societal discrimination in 2010. Recognizing this, the Ministries of Justice and Pacific Island Affairs have developed a programme to identify gaps in delivery of government services to Pacific Islanders.

Asians, who make up 10 per cent of the population, also reported discrimination. The government has appointed a Race Relations Commissioner and has developed a Diversity Action Programme aimed at the Asian, Māori and Pacific Island communities. The programme includes an annual Diversity Forum to challenge race-based discrimination.

Papua New Guinea
With around 840 distinct living languages, Papua New Guinea is the most ethnically diverse state in the world. There is no precise data regarding the total number of ethnic groups in Papua New Guinea, but estimates are in the region of 5,000–7,000 separate groups, in a total population of just over 5 million.

Papua New Guinea was considered for the first time by the CEDAW committee in July 2010. The CEDAW committee noted the severe disadvantages faced by women in a range of areas, including in education, participation in public life and decision-making, and in the persistence of violence against women. The CEDAW committee further expressed its serious concern regarding the persistence of harmful practices relating to the roles, responsibilities and identities of women and men in all spheres of life. These include polygamy, bride price (*baim meri*), and the custom of including women as part of compensation payment.

HIV and AIDS
Papua New Guinea accounted for more than 99 per cent of reported HIV cases in the Oceania region as of 2007, according to the World Health Organization (WHO) Aids Factsheet. Out of Papua New Guinea's population of 6.5 million people, 1.5 per cent have

largest gold producer. The mine accounts for 12 per cent of Papua New Guinea's export earnings. Human Rights Watch (HRW) documented five alleged incidents of gang rape by mine security personnel in 2009 and 2010, and a sixth in 2008, in an extensive report on the matter published in early 2011. While Barrick was traditionally very hostile to any criticism by human rights groups about their operations in Papua New Guinea, more recently the company has shown signs of a tangible shift toward more serious engagement with human rights concerns. In particular, the company has attempted to incorporate the Voluntary Principles on Security and Human Rights (a set of non-binding principles for companies, developed in 2000 with the input of national governments, non-governmental organizations (NGOs) and multinational companies) into the operations of the mine. However, HRW stated that Barrick's efforts have fallen short of what is required by the Voluntary Principles.

Environment

Environmental concerns also continue to plague the peoples of Papua New Guinea. A satellite analysis conducted by scientists at the University of Papua New Guinea and Australian National University shows that the country has been losing about 1,400 square miles of rain forest, or about 1.4 per cent of its total forest cover, each year, with estimates indicating that 83 per cent of the country's accessible forest – and 53 per cent of its total forested area – will be gone or severely damaged by 2021. Deforestation affects local communities in myriad ways, among them their abilities to maintain their traditional ways of life, including hunter-gathering practices and cultural activities.

Further concern has been voiced regarding the world's first deep-sea mineral mine in Papua New Guinea waters. Indigenous peoples and scientists fear it will damage local marine life. The project, entitled Solwara 1, is located at 1,600 metres depth in the Bismarck Sea, Papua New Guinea, and will be run by Canadian company Nautilus Minerals, which was granted its environmental permit in January 2011. An independent scientific review of the environmental impact assessment of the proposed project concluded, however, that the assessment was inadequate, and that the mining will result in severe and prolonged environmental damage. ■

been infected with the virus, leading to warnings of an epidemic. The CEDAW committee noted that women and girls are disproportionately affected by HIV, accounting for 60 per cent of the people living with HIV. Girls and women are infected at a younger age than boys and men, with twice as many women as men infected between the ages of 15 and 29 years. Girls between 15 and 19 years of age have the highest rate of HIV infection in the country, four times that of boys in the same age bracket. Gender-based violence is also one of the leading factors in the increased rates of HIV infection among women, the CEDAW committee noted. Violence against women and girls increases their vulnerability to HIV, and women who disclose are often then subject to further violence due to their status.

Barrick Gold

Private security personnel employed at a gold mine in Papua New Guinea have been implicated in alleged gang rapes and other violent assaults against Papua New Guinean women. The Porgera mine is operated and 95 per cent owned by Barrick Gold, a Canadian company that is the world's

ICELAND
ATLANTIC
OCEAN
NORWAY
SWEDEN
FINLAND
RUSSIA
ESTONIA
LATVIA
LITHUANIA
IRELAND
UNITED
KINGDOM
DENMARK
Kaliningrad
(Rus.)
BELARUS
NETHERLANDS
GERMANY
POLAND
BELGIUM
LUXEMBOURG
CZECH REP.
UKRAINE
SLOVAKIA
FRANCE
SWITZERLAND
LIECH.
AUSTRIA
HUNGARY
MOLDOVA
SLOVENIA
CROATIA
ROMANIA
PORTUGAL
ANDORRA
MONACO
SAN MARINO
BOSNIA
AND HERZE.
SERBIA
MONTENEGRO
BLACK SEA
GEORGIA
AZERBAIJAN
SPAIN
KOSOVO
BULGARIA
ARMENIA
MACEDONIA
ITALY
ALBANIA
AZER.
TURKEY
GREECE

Europe

Katalin Halász and
Nurçan Kaya

I n 2010, the international financial crisis exposed existing human rights violations and increased the hardships faced by the most vulnerable minority groups in Europe. In many countries, the far right made its presence felt, with xenophobic and racist rhetoric pervading mainstream politics, media and public dialogue more widely. Conversely, Europe has developed beyond a mere economic partnership to a region whose governance is based on fundamental rights. Every European country has ratified the International Convention on the Elimination of All Forms of Racial Discrimination (ICERD); the Charter of Fundamental Rights is given effect within the European Union (EU) by the Treaty of Lisbon entering into force at the end of 2009; and the EU is moving to ratify the European Convention on Human Rights (ECHR).

The emerging human rights framework
The successful passage of the Lisbon Treaty means that, ten years after its formulation, the Charter of Fundamental Rights has finally acquired legally binding status, and as such sets out a Bill of Rights for citizens and residents of the EU. The Charter draws on rights already enshrined in existing EU law (e.g. the right of free movement in Article 45), the ECHR and the case law of the European Court of Justice. Its legal effect means that individuals are now able to claim Charter rights against member states and EU institutions when they are implementing EU law. In terms of minority rights protection, the new Treaty and the Charter establish that the rights of persons belonging to minorities should be respected and that the EU should respect cultural, religious and linguistic diversity, with Article 21 of the Charter significantly extending the list of protected grounds. Furthermore, third-country nationals have acquired a set of rights through the Charter, which extends the scope of rights holders beyond citizens of EU member states. In October, the European Commission launched a strategy to ensure the effective implementation of the Charter. According to the strategy, the European Commission should provide information for individuals on when it can intervene in fundamental rights issues, and it should verify that all EU laws are compatible with the Charter.

Official talks on the EU's accession to the ECHR started on 7 July 2010 marking another historic

moment in furthering human rights protection within the EU. Thorbjørn Jagland, the Secretary-General of the Council of Europe stated that:

'The European Convention on Human Rights is the essential reference for human rights protection for all of Europe. By accepting to submit the work of its institutions to the same human rights rules and the same scrutiny which applies to all European democracies, the European Union is sending a very powerful message.'

With the accession of the EU to the ECHR, the European Court of Human Rights (ECtHR) will have jurisdiction over alleged fundamental rights breaches by the EU and over breaches of EU law committed by member states.

Despite these positive developments, negotiations have reached a standstill on the proposal for a new anti-discrimination directive to prohibit discrimination on the grounds of religion or belief, age, disability and sexual orientation outside employment. Amnesty International collected 50,000 signatures in favour of the draft directive to hand over to representatives of Germany, which has been against the adoption of the draft directive since it was proposed by the European Commission in 2008. The new anti-discrimination directive is also blocked by the difficulties some member states still face in transposing the Race Equality and Employment Equality Directives adopted in 2000 into national law. In 2010, the European Commission closed legal proceedings against Germany and the Czech Republic on the two directives, after both countries presented evidence of complying with EU requirements. The Commission also referred Poland to the European Court of Justice for failing to implement the Race Equality Directive correctly in its national law.

The evolution of a stronger human rights framework that provides additional means to hold nation-states to account is a significant development in terms of furthering minority protection. The economic reality may, however, endanger the full implementation of these rights. European countries have been through a major economic upheaval, the social consequences of which are only starting to come to light. In June 2010, the EU adopted the

'Europe 2020' strategy to prepare the EU economy for the battle for growth and jobs. Two of the strategy's five targets relate to employment and poverty: 75 per cent of the population aged 20–64 should be employed, and 20 million fewer people should be at risk of poverty by 2020. The strategy was heavily criticized by analysts for its reliance on the political will of member states, and by human rights non-governmental organizations (NGOs) for the lack of emphasis on the human dimension and fundamental rights. On 19 November, a coalition of NGOs initiated a human ring around the European parliament to call for a more equitable response to the crisis, one that puts human rights and equality between men and women and ending all forms of discrimination at its centre.

Rise of the far right

The legal framework and fine declarations are at odds with the rhetoric of intolerance witnessed across the continent, and with the lived experience of minority communities in every European country. The rise of the far right across Europe has been a significant concern for some time. Racist rhetoric

has gained ground as the anti-terrorism agenda of many governments has led to the targeting and demonization of minority communities. The economic crisis has given an added dimension to this, as extremist groups target minorities as scapegoats (for example Roma in Hungary and the Czech Republic). The recruiting grounds for the far right have become those communities which, at a very local level, are often untouched by, or distrusting of, European discussions. A poll conducted by the Vienna-based research agency Karmasin showed that although the majority of respondents agreed with adhering to human rights, only 18 per cent of Austrians think ethnic minorities are in need of protection and only 20 per cent think the same about asylum seekers and migrants.

With campaign advertisements that were blatantly racist, xenophobic and reminiscent of Nazi slogans, such as *'Mehr Mut für Wiener Blut'* ('More courage for Viennese blood'), Austria's right-wing Freedom Party's (FPÖ) gained considerable ground in local elections in Vienna in October, winning more than double the number of seats it had previously had in the regional parliament. Elsewhere, Jean-Marie Le

Pen's National Front in France, the Geert Wilders-led Freedom Party in the Netherlands, Jimmie Åkesson's far-right Sweden Democrats and the Hungarian far-right party Jobbik also scored election victories in 2010. The British National Party did not, however, manage to secure any seats in the 2010 United Kingdom parliamentary elections.

Exploiting the mood of victimhood created by the financial crisis and using formerly left-wing terminology such as solidarity and community, the far right has successfully played on a fear of the 'other' and defined Muslims in Europe as the new common enemy. Belgium's Flemish separatists of the Vlaams Belang joined the Danish People's Party, Austria's Freedom Party, Italy's anti-immigrant Northern League, the Slovak National Party and the Sweden Democrats for a meeting in Vienna in October to discuss immigration and Islam in Europe, and the possibility of a pan-European referendum on Turkey's accession to the EU.

The EU Framework Decision on combating certain forms and expressions of racism and xenophobia by means of criminal law would set standards to fight racism and xenophobia in all member states of the EU. Despite the fact that 28 November was the deadline for transposing the decision into national law, several governments had not fulfilled their obligations so far. These include Cyprus, where racist attacks were staged by far-right groups at an anti-racist 'Rainbow Festival', organized by the migrant support group KISA on 5 November. The far right is also gaining visibility in Germany, which has seen clashes between neo-Nazis and anti-Nazi campaigners. The anti-fascist group, Dresden without Nazis, called on city residents to block a planned right-wing extremist march to commemorate the city being firebombed during the Second World War. Neo-Nazis confronted 1,000 anti-Nazi demonstrators in Bad Nenndorf near Hannover as well, where the local population staged their own event under the motto 'Bad Nenndorf is colourful'.

While rarely being explicit, many mainstream European political parties and media outlets have also adopted racist and anti-immigration rhetoric. Debates on national identity, that could have been an opportunity to encourage integration while celebrating diversity, deteriorated into 'them and us' debates of conflict rather than inclusion. After a strongly worded speech making a link between immigration and crime, French President Nicolas Sarkozy was accused of using the language of the far right in order to regain popularity.

Migration and asylum

According to the 2010 *World Migration Report* issued by the International Organization for Migration (IOM), almost a third of the world's 214 million migrants head for Europe. After the USA, six of the top ten countries with the largest foreign-born populations are in Europe: Russia, Germany, France, Spain, Ukraine and the United Kingdom. The mistreatment of persons seeking asylum or migrating within and to Europe is a serious concern, and was denounced by the Council of Europe and the United Nations (UN) on several occasions in 2010. On 19 October, UN Secretary-General Ban Ki-moon addressed the European parliament in Strasbourg, France, and pointed to a 'new politics of polarization' in Europe, and to a growing intolerance of and discrimination against migrants, whether from Europe or beyond, and against Muslim immigrants in particular.

The 2010 *International Migration Outlook*, published by the Organization for Economic Co-operation and Development (OECD), analyses recent developments in migration movements, highlighting the fact that international migration has fallen during the economic crisis. The report emphasized that, in order to fill labour and skills shortages, migrants will be the key to long-term economic growth. However, the lack of recognition of the contribution that is made by immigrant communities to Europe's economy, society and culture, and the denial of their human rights has been a key feature of the European migration debate. While states and the EU are moving towards a more restrictive security approach, human rights NGOs are urging governments to end violations of economic, social and cultural rights of many migrants, including asylum seekers, undocumented migrants and others.

On the 20th anniversary of the adoption of the UN Migrants Workers Convention (ICRMW), not a single EU member state had signed or ratified the instrument, which provides a comprehensive normative framework for the protection of the rights of all migrant workers and members of their families. The Commissioner for Human Rights of the Council of Europe, Thomas Hammarberg, stated:

'I find it worrying that democratic countries governed by the rule of law, with significant numbers of migrants living in their societies, are hesitant to become a party to this core UN human rights treaty, and commit themselves to guaranteeing migrant workers their fundamental rights.'

Hammarberg also raised his voice against the trend to criminalize the irregular entry and presence of migrants in Europe. He visited Calais in northern France and the surrounding area in May, after the police closed down a makeshift shelter that was used by Afghan migrants and run by a local campaign group. French Immigration Minister Eric Besson had termed the camp 'a new jungle'. In a letter issued after the visit, the Commissioner called for detention and return practices to be reformed. The French parliament instead adopted stricter immigration provisions in October, including the extension of the French nationality removal provision that was previously only applicable in cases of terrorist acts. It will now apply to French citizens who have been naturalized for less than ten years and who have been convicted of murder of a police or fire brigade officer.

The Stockholm Programme, the EU's strategy for 2010–14 covering migration and asylum, has been criticized for its strong focus on controlling 'illegal' migration to the detriment of developing an adequate framework for legal migration, and for slow progress in establishing a common asylum system (set to be in place by 2012). The consideration of the status and protection of undocumented migrants is strikingly absent from the programme.

Spain's move to join 12 other European countries – the Czech Republic, Denmark, Finland, France, Iceland, Ireland, the Netherlands, Norway, Portugal, Romania, Sweden and the UK – to establish an annual resettlement programme was welcomed by the UN High Commissioner for Refugees (UNHCR). Meanwhile, other countries, including Belgium, are struggling to provide basic care for asylum seekers. The government promised to provide housing for an additional 2,000 asylum seekers only after Belgian refugee organization Vluchtelingenwerk Vlaanderen warned that the upcoming winter could result in a humanitarian crisis.

Europe's record in providing asylum seekers and refugees with safe and adequate protection is relatively poor. Frontex, the EU's external borders agency, has no protection mandate. Nonetheless, UNHCR called on the agency to carry out its activities in accordance with fundamental rights, and to incorporate operational safeguards into its procedures in order to guarantee that persons seeking international protection are identified and given access to EU territory, as well as to fair and effective asylum procedures and adequate support.

The growing participation of women in global migratory movements has been a striking phenomenon of the last decade. According to IOM figures, the share of female migrants had grown to 50.1 per cent in 2010. The need to integrate a gender perspective and to address the discrimination faced by immigrant women as well as their specific circumstances is now accepted, but how these commitments will be translated into practice remains to be seen.

The year 2010 also marked the 15th anniversary of the Beijing Platform for Action, formulated at the fourth UN World Conference on Women, in which states made commitments to addressing inequality between women and men. The European Women's Lobby published a report on implementation across the twelve critical areas of concern identified in the platform at national and European level. It found recurrent shortcomings in relation to data collection, lack of targeted financial resources and coordination between the national and EU levels, as well as neglected policy areas, such as media policies, the environment, education, health and the girl-child. Invisibility of migrant women still remains an issue as regards other related policy and legislative initiatives. The 2000 Equality Directives, for example, recognize that women can be victims of multiple discrimination but effective gender mainstreaming mechanisms are lacking, and issues related to gender and ethnicity are not addressed as part of an integrated approach.

Political rights

National and ethnic minority groups and migrants continue to face a range of barriers when accessing

the political sphere. In most EU member states, only nationals and EU citizens are eligible to stand for elections and to vote, with the exception of the Netherlands and Sweden, which grant voting rights at municipal elections after five years of residence. In Denmark, Finland and Ireland, third-country nationals are also allowed to vote at administrative elections. In Latvia, members of the Russian minority must pass a strict language test in order to acquire Latvian citizenship. Otherwise, they are classed as 'resident-aliens' – even if born in Latvia – and as such are seen as non-citizens who are denied access to voting rights.

In the current 2007–12 French legislature, four out of 555 deputies are from an ethnic minority background. The reshuffling of the French government in November left Rama Yade and Fadela Amara, respectively ex-Secretary of State for Sports and ex-Secretary of State for Urban Policy, without ministerial posts. Together with Rachida Data, now a member of the European parliament, they were the three members of the French government who entered office in 2007 who had an African background. Sworn in as Lower Saxony's social affairs minister in April, Ayguel Oezkan became Germany's first female Muslim minister. She caused controversy and reportedly received death threats after she suggested the removal of religious symbols, including crucifixes, from state schools. Slovenia also saw its first African-born mayor in 2010, when Peter Bossman (originally from Ghana) was elected mayor by the inhabitants of Piran.

After the October elections in Bosnia and Herzegovina, issues concerning the Constitution remained unaddressed. This was despite the successful challenge mounted at the ECtHR by Jakob Finci and Dervo Sejdić to Bosnia's discriminatory constitutional and electoral provisions that deny the right to public participation on the basis of ethnicity (this case and its implications are discussed in detail in *State of the World's Minorities and Indigenous Peoples 2010*). The year 2010 also marked the 15th anniversary of the massacre in the Bosnian town of Srebrenica. During the 1992–5 Bosnian conflict, some 8,000 Muslim men and boys were executed after Serbian forces overran the UN-protected town.

Religious intolerance

In March, some hundred people protested against the planned building of a mosque in Warsaw, only a couple of days after the UN Human Rights Council condemned Switzerland's ban on building minarets (which is still pending before the ECtHR), and other recent discriminatory measures as 'manifestations of Islamophobia that stand in sharp contradiction to international human rights obligations concerning freedoms of religions'.

Increasing intolerance towards the Jewish community and blatant incidents of anti-Semitism across Europe have also been grave concerns discussed at several UN meetings during 2010. At an International Conference on Anti-Semitism and Holocaust Denial in Ireland, the UN urged delegates to fight religious extremism and to dispel myths associated with anti-Semitism and Holocaust denial. A study published in April by the Stephen Roth Institute for the Study of Contemporary Anti-Semitism and Racism at Tel Aviv University in Israel analysed the upswing in anti-Semitic attacks in Europe. According to the report, there was a considerable increase in violent incidents against Jewish

sites and individuals after Israel's assault on Gaza in early 2009. Looking at the number of violent incidents in absolute terms, the UK and France led the EU league table, followed by Germany, Belgium and Austria. Relatively high numbers are also seen in the Czech Republic, Denmark, Hungary, Italy, Lithuania, the Netherlands, Poland and Sweden.

The movement to outlaw the wearing of full-face veils (*niqab* and *burqa*) in public moved into the mainstream in 2010. First, the Belgian lower house voted to ban the wearing of full-face veils, imposing a fine of between €15 and €20, and up to a week in jail for wearing the veil. The Chamber of Deputies will consider the bill in 2011. France followed suit with a law which enters into force in spring 2011, setting out a fine of €150 or a compulsory citizenship course. The Northern League, part of Italy's ruling right-wing coalition, also proposed a bill suggesting that full-face veils be banned in Italy. Spain became the latest to propose legislation to ban the *burqa* and the *niqab* with Austria, the Netherlands and Switzerland also considering laws.

Human rights organizations, including MRG, Human Rights Watch (HRW) and Amnesty

International strongly condemned bans on the wearing of the full-face veil, arguing that these violate the right to freedom of expression and religion. The Parliamentary Assembly of the Council of Europe (PACE) unanimously opposed a general ban on wearing the full-face veil in a resolution adopted on 23 June. PACE stated that veiling is often perceived as 'a symbol of the subjugation of women to men' but a general ban would deny women 'who genuinely and freely desire to do so' their right to cover their face. It also added that legal restrictions may be justified 'for security purposes, or where the public or professional functions of individuals require their religious neutrality, or that their face can be seen'. On 8 March, International Women's Day, Commissioner Hammarberg stated that. 'Prohibition of the *burqa* and the *niqab* would not liberate oppressed women, but might instead lead to their further alienation in European societies.'

Roma
'This is a situation I had thought Europe would not have to witness again after the Second World War.'
Viviane Reding, Vice-President of the European Commission responsible for Justice, Fundamental Rights and Citizenship, September 2010

This unprecedentedly strong remark from one of the EU's highest officials came after several rounds of discussions between the EU and the French and Romanian governments on an anti-crime initiative launched by French President Nicolas Sarkozy on 28 July, specifically targeting the Roma community. The initiative included the expulsion from France of all Roma with Romanian and Bulgarian citizenship who had committed public offences, and the closure of unauthorized camps. The daily *EU Observer* reported that 200 Roma were deported to Romania the same day that Ms Reding spoke out, and some 230 people, including children, the day before. In what France was calling 'voluntary deportations' nearly 1,000 Romanian and Bulgarian citizens were expelled and 440 Roma camps were reportedly dismantled over a couple of weeks. In February, Bulgarian Roma were offered €300 per adult and €100 per child to return home from Bordeaux. The financial initiative, which was taken up by 200 Roma, was condemned by the human rights organization Romeurope as 'costly and unnecessary', as most will probably return.

The Roma controversy in France triggered strong reactions from all sides. Pierre Lellouche, the French Secretary of State for European Affairs was reported by the news agency Euractive to have warned Romania 'not to interpret freedom of movement in the EU as a right to get rid of its Roma at the expense of other countries', while Romanian Foreign Minister Teodor Baconschi spoke out against labelling any ethnic group as criminals. Ms Reding's statement was rejected by France's minister for EU affairs who said that the 'unseemly' remark in effect compared France to the Nazi regime. 'This is not how you speak to a major power like France, which is the mother of human rights', he said, according to Radio France.

The move by the EU Justice Commissioner to investigate France for violating EU law, in the event that the measures taken by the French authorities in applying the Free Movement Directive had targeted a certain group on the basis of nationality, race or ethnic origin, was supported by the EU College of Commissioners. In addition, László Andor, Commissioner in charge of social affairs, came to the defence of Ms Reding's strongly worded comment. According to the *EU Observer*, he spoke of how 'O Baro Porrajmos' ('Great Devouring') or the Roma Holocaust is part of the collective memory of Roma, and that the historical context cannot be ignored when the destruction of the camps has strong echoes within the community of the round-ups that took place across Europe 70 years ago. The European parliament also showed strong support and adopted a resolution requiring France and other EU member states to 'suspend all expulsions of Roma'.

After announcing that it would start infringement procedures against France for the discriminatory application of the Free Movement Directive and for lack of transposition of the procedural and substantive guarantees under it into national law, the European Commission gave Paris until mid-October to prove that its policies complied with EU laws guaranteeing the free circulation of people. At the same time, infringement procedures were launched against other EU countries for failing to transpose the directive into national law, ensuring that France was not singled out. The Commission finally dropped the charges against France on 19 October, once the French government had presented plans to bring the country's legislation in line with EU law. As expressed by Commissioner Reding, 'France has responded positively, constructively and in time to the Commission's request. […] This is proof of the good functioning of the European Union as a Community governed by the rule of law.' Human rights groups, however, were less satisfied with the outcome of the case. The European Roma Policy Coalition argued that the Commission's acceptance of France's pledge to adapt its immigration rules in the future meant that those who had already suffered discrimination and lost their homes were denied justice.

The violations of the rights of Roma in France underlined the need for a coordinated European response to the widespread discrimination and marginalization of Roma. The Second European Roma Summit had previously ended on 8 April with relatively limited commitments. In the so-called 'Cordoba Declaration', the EU trio presidencies of Spain, Belgium and Hungary pledged to ensure that the EU's financial instruments are made accessible to Roma in order to contribute to their social inclusion and improve living conditions. The summer's events demonstrated the urgent need for greater cooperation on Roma rights issues. On 20 October, the Council of Europe organized a meeting where 47 member states agreed to joint efforts and subscribed to the 'Strasbourg Declaration' that sets out common guidelines and training programmes for Roma. Developing and adopting a European Roma Policy on the basis of common economic and social conditions rather than on ethnicity is among the priorities of the Hungarian EU presidency, which took over on 1 January 2011.

Sadly, the forced sterilization of Roma women is still an unresolved issue in some countries, as are the issues of compensation for the victims, prosecution of perpetrators, and the urgent need for state medical reforms in the area of patients' rights. Following a call from the European Roma Rights Centre (ERRC) to the UN on the ongoing refusal of the Czech Republic to accord compensation to Roma women (who were subjected to coercive sterilization under the communist regime and up until 2007), the UN Committee on the Elimination of Discrimination against Women (CEDAW committee) urged the Czech government to ensure that victims of this gruesome practice can access justice. Despite an apology from the government, the pos-

sibility of compensation for the victims remained remote. Elena Gorolova from the Group of Women Harmed by Sterilization explained:

'The Czech government said it will not compensate us, but never discussed why. Since we know other countries have compensated women who were sterilized without their consent, why won't the Czech Republic compensate us? The government gave no explanation, just a very clear "no" to the idea of compensation.'

The ECtHR delivered some key judgments in cases relating to abuse by police forces and on segregated education in 2010. On 7 January, in the case *Sashov v. Bulgaria*, the Court found that Bulgarian police had engaged in inhuman and degrading treatment of three Bulgarian nationals of Roma origin during their arrest and detention in police custody, and that the use of force by the police against the applicants had been extensive and disproportionate. The applicants complained of police brutality, of verbal and physical abuse during their arrest in 2001 on suspicion of stealing metal, and of the failure of the state authorities to institute an effective criminal investigation into their allegations of ill-treatment. The applicants were awarded financial compensation by the Court.

In the case *Oršuš and Others v. Croatia*, the Court ruled on 16 March that the segregation of Roma children in separate classes based on language was unlawful discrimination. The case involved 14 primary school children who were placed in segregated Roma-only classes due to alleged language difficulties. The applicants argued that placement in these Roma-only classes stemmed from blatant discrimination based on ethnicity, reinforced by the local majority population's anti-Roma sentiments. Marking the three-year anniversary of the case *D.H. and Others v. the Czech Republic*, which first declared school segregation illegal, the Open Society Justice Initiative, the ERRC and the Greek Helsinki Monitor filed a complaint with the Committee of Ministers of Strasbourg, which is charged with overseeing implementation of ECtHR rulings. The human rights organizations argued that the Czech Republic had failed to implement the judgment and integrate Roma children into mainstream schools to date. The ERRC also filed a case with the European Committee on Social Rights against Portugal concerning the substandard housing situation of Roma in the country on 23 April.

Georgia

Following the conflict between Georgia and Russia in August 2008, which broke out in the break-away republic of South Ossetia/Tskhinvali region and quickly spread to parts of the break-away republic of Abkhazia, both republics declared full independence. This move was only backed by Russia, and the two regions have had a Russian military presence ever since. The conflict, which lasted only a couple of days, has had long-lasting consequences for the civilian population in South Ossetia. As reported by MRG, the active hostilities caused a significant displacement of civilians, forcing a high number of people to flee their homes, including members of minority groups such as ethnic Armenians and Svans, a Georgian ethnic sub-group with their own distinct language, as well as ethnic Georgians.

According to the UNHCR Global Appeal 2011 update on the country, there are some 355,000 people in need of protection by the UN body, of whom 247,000 are internally displaced persons (IDPs). The situation of those who returned to Abakhazia and South Ossetia as well as to other parts of Georgia, following earlier civil conflict, is described as precarious, with many going as long as 16 years without adequate shelter. In a 2010 submission to the Organization for Security and Co-operation in Europe (OSCE), the Georgian government identified 131,169 IDPs and victims of ethnic cleansing after the 2008 conflict, many of whom are in the process of returning, but who are facing problems in accessing adequate housing and employment. There are also some 900 refugees from the Chechen Republic and the Russian Federation, and 1,700 stateless people in the country. The UNHCR appeal refers to the lack of a strong asylum system (that would ensure the international legal principle of non-refoulement, namely that no person should be returned to a situation where her or his life or freedom is at serious risk) as a serious problem, as well as the fact that the country is neither a state party to the UN conventions on statelessness, nor to the European Convention on Nationality. Widespread gender-based and sexual violence, and a lack of effective protection for IDP women have also been reported.

The European Commission against Racism and Intolerance (ECRI) published its third report on the country in June 2010. ECRI's Chair, Nils Muiznieks, identified positive initiatives in fight-

ing discrimination on the grounds of nationality or national or ethnic origin, race, colour, language and religion. Key positive developments concern the work of the Georgian Ombudsman, who is setting up various regional branches such as the Tolerance Centre, the Council of Ethnic Minorities and the Council of Religion, in order to reach persons in need of protection. The report also notes the adoption of the National Strategy for Tolerance and Civil Integration, which aims to preserve ethnic minorities' culture and identity, and promote equal opportunities and the effective participation of ethnic minorities in all fields. The report stipulates that, when implemented, the strategy could help to make the majority population aware of the problems faced by minorities. At the same time, contacts between the majority population and ethnic minorities are limited due to language barriers and infrastructure problems that contribute to the isolation of Armenians, Azerbaijanis and others in the south and south-east of Georgia. According to the report, the Roma minority, as well as Jehovah's Witnesses and Muslims still face widespread prejudice, harassment and violations, and are not appropriately protected by the police.

The ECRI report highlights the particular situation of the Meskhetian Turks, a minority group deported in the 1940s by the Soviet authorities from the region of Meskhetia (now known as Samtskhe-Javakheti). National legislation in Georgia does not use the term Meskhetian Turks, as some of the persons concerned do not identify themselves as such. The law 'On forcefully deported persons from Georgia by the former USSR in the 1940s of the 20th century' in respect of the entire group was adopted in 2007, and ECRI refers to the recommendations of the 2009 Opinion of the Advisory Committee on the Framework Convention for the Protection of National Minorities (FCNM) on easing administrative burdens related to the repatriation process for formerly deported persons who would like to return.

The Swedish Kvinna till Kvinna Foundation has supported women's organizations in Armenia, Azerbaijan and Georgia since 2002 and advocates

on behalf of the rights of women in the South Caucasus. According to their findings, the difficult period that followed independence from the Soviet Union has had a particularly detrimental impact on women's access to their social and economic rights, as well as to basic medical care and health services. Denial of sexual and reproductive rights has led to a high abortion rate and high rates of sexually transmitted diseases, as well as high rates of child mortality and miscarriages. Bride kidnapping also occurs in certain rural communities in the region, and violence against women is widespread. In an interview for a regional information portal Leila Suleimanova, the director of the NGO Association of Azeri Women in Georgia, which has been active in speaking for the rights of Azeri and ethnic Georgian women in Kvemo Kartli, listed some of the many problems ethnic minority women face in Georgia, including early marriages, lack of education and violence in the family. 'We think that the stereotype, banning involvement of women and limiting our rights, which is considered to be cited from Koran and Islam, actually is not and things are not like that', she added.

Greece

The situation of minorities and asylum seekers featured prominently in the public debate in Greece, which still hasn't ratified the FCNM or signed the European Charter for Minority Languages. The Council of Europe Commissioner for Human Rights, Thomas Hammarberg, visited Greece in February to hold discussions with the authorities about issues relating to the human rights of asylum seekers and minorities.

The recognition of the right to freedom of association and expression of persons belonging to the ethnic Macedonian community (who live in the administrative region of Macedonia), and of members of the Turkish community (who, along with Pomaks and Roma, comprise a Muslim minority in Western Thrace) has been a long-standing concern that remains unresolved. Regarding ethnic Macedonians, the 1998 ECtHR judgment of *Sidiropoulos and Others v. Greece* found Greece in violation of Article 11 on its refusal to allow the registration of the organization 'Home of the Macedonian Culture'. The Greek courts refused the application on the basis that the use of the term 'Macedonian' questioned the Greek identity of Macedonia and undermined territorial integrity. Implementation of the 1998 judgment is still pending, and the organization has not yet been registered. In 2007 and 2008, the ECtHR rendered three judgements against Greece for violating Article 11 (freedom of assembly and association) of the ECHR regarding members of the Turkish community (in the cases *Bekir-Ousta and Others; Emin and Others; Tourkiki Enosi Xanthis and Others*).

In a letter to the Greek government, Commissioner Hammarberg raised concerns that ethnic Turkish and other minority associations that have recently tried to secure registration have been unable to do so. These cases strike at the heart of the right to self-identification for members of minorities in Greece, where ethnic Macedonians are not granted minority status, and the right to collective minority identity is denied to the Turkish minority, who are only counted as part of a larger Muslim minority. During his visit, the Commissioner recommended ratification of the FCNM, which Greece signed in 1999, and the implementation of the ECtHR judgments. He stressed that the Greek authorities need 'to show greater receptiveness to diversity in their society and to take further measures that would allow minority groups to express their identity on the basis of self-identification'.

The treatment of asylum seekers, refugees and migrants in Greece became a particular focus of international attention during 2010. In March, Amnesty International published a report highlighting the failure of the Greek asylum system to provide a fair asylum determination procedure and the right to an effective appeal. Amnesty urged state parties to the EU Dublin Regulation to stop transferring asylum seekers to Greece, where they face multiple violations of human rights, including the risk of being forcibly returned to a country where they are in danger of persecution. The Dublin Regulation is an EU law that determines which member state is responsible for examining an asylum application lodged within the EU, and usually requires that asylum seekers be returned to the first country they entered upon arriving in the territory of the EU. In September, in his first-ever oral intervention as a third party in an ECtHR case concerning the return of an Afghan asylum seeker from Belgium to Greece, Commissioner Hammarberg

expressed his particular concern regarding Greek asylum law and practice. Issues include the risk of refoulement, non-compliance with human rights safeguards, and asylum seekers' reception and detention conditions. He also added that 'under the "Dublin Regulation" certain countries face the challenge of dealing with numbers of asylum applications beyond their capacities' and called for a halt to transfers. The UNHCR echoed these concerns and recommended that EU member states not send asylum seekers back to Greece, where the 'continued absence of a functioning asylum system' was described as a 'humanitarian crisis', with many asylum seekers, including women and children, receiving no basic assistance and living on the streets.

The poor asylum detention practices of Greece, and in particular the detention of unaccompanied minors was examined by Médecins Sans Frontières in a report published in June 2010, which presented data from psychological counselling sessions as well as individual testimonies. The report demonstrates that detention can exacerbate existing problems and contribute to new traumas and psychological distress. Amnesty International also voiced its dismay concerning the substandard conditions in which unaccompanied minors are held.

Realizing the seriousness of the issue, Rapid Border Interventions Teams from the EU's border agency, Frontex, were sent to Greece on 24 October. The news agency Euractive quoted the European Commission as describing the vast inflow of refugees and undocumented migrants into the country from neighbouring Turkey as 'increasingly dramatic' and reported on the EU's call to its member states to assist Greece in dealing with the humanitarian situation. Athens has turned to the EU requesting assistance in administering the Turkey–Greece border, which has seen an increase in the number of undocumented migrants, since other EU member states tightened border controls in the Mediterranean Sea. In reaction to the deployment of Frontex border officials to Greece, UNHCR warned that the rights of asylum seekers must be protected.

The influx of immigrants also stirred up heated emotions within the borders of the economically distressed country. Violent incidents occurred as tensions grew over undocumented immigration at the busiest transit point for human trafficking in the EU. On 16 November, during the Muslim holiday

Eid-al-Adha, local residents and members of the far-right Chrysi Avgi, a group widely linked to a growing number of violent attacks against migrants, clashed with police at a prayer site. Chrysi Avgi also won its first ever seat on the Athens City Council in local elections in 2010.

Hungary

Parliamentary elections were held in Hungary in April 2010 and were won by the right-wing Fidesz party. Both the radical nationalist and openly anti-Roma and anti-Semitic Jobbik or 'Movement for a Better Hungary' party and the left-liberal LMP or 'Politics Can Be Different' also won seats for the first time. While 5 out of 16 of LMP's representatives are women, the 2010 European Gender Equality Law Review noted with concern that none of the parties addressed issues related to gender equality in their programmes. As a result, gender issues have effectively disappeared as an area of concern in Hungarian politics. The Third Opinion of the FCNM Advisory Committee adopted in 2010 also points out that 'although the Hungarian Constitution and the 1993 Law on the Rights of National and Ethnic Minorities guarantee in general terms the possibility for minorities to be represented in parliament, a specific mechanism for the representation of minorities in parliament is still lacking'. The Opinion also recommends that the institutional framework is adjusted rapidly to ensure adequate minority representation.

One of the new government's first moves was an amendment to the Hungarian citizenship law, passed almost unanimously in May 2010. The measure that came into effect on 1 January 2011 allows ethnic Hungarians living abroad to apply for dual citizenship, and will primarily affect ethnic Hungarian minorities living in neighbouring countries. Of these neighbouring countries, only Slovakia (home to 500,000 Hungarians) has objected to the new law. Robert Fico, Prime Minister of Slovakia at the time, called the move a 'security threat' and introduced counter-measures withdrawing Slovak citizenship for people who apply for Hungarian citizenship. In contrast, Romania raised no objections to members of its Hungarian minority obtaining dual citizenship.

Jobbik's election campaign had centred on addressing what it classed as 'Hungary's biggest domestic problem', namely 'the coexistence' of Roma and Hungarians. Once elected, in September Jobbik proposed the creation of 'public order zones' in Roma-inhabited areas of the north-eastern city of Miskolc. The proposal, which was condemned by governing party Fidesz as an 'outrageous proposition', amounted to the establishment of cordoned-off areas where public order offenders would be sealed off and kept under surveillance by local gendarmerie. Jobbik leader Gabor Vona also proposed schooling Roma children in segregated boarding schools.

Jobbik's racist proposals hit a nerve in the country, which saw a series of killings of Roma in 2008 and 2009. A delegation from the OSCE Office for Democratic Institutions and Human Rights (ODIHR) visited some 12 locations where fatal incidents had taken place, and published its report in June 2010. The resulting report identified challenges including:

'The relative frequency of extremist anti-Roma statements in the media and public/political discourse and the weakness of legal or political mechanisms to restrict or counter such extremist rhetoric'.

and

'The weakness of legislation specifically addressing hate crimes and limited capacity to investigate or prosecute such crimes.'

Hungary will come before the UN Human Rights Council in 2011, as part of the Universal Periodic Review (UPR), in order for its compliance with international human rights obligations to be assessed. In a joint submission to the Human Rights Council made in November 2010, MRG and other human rights organizations urged the Council to act firmly 'against flagrant human rights abuses of Roma'. The joint submission gives a detailed account of the ongoing discrimination that Roma suffer in the areas of employment, education, health care and housing. It raises grave concerns regarding the lack of adequate legal protection against the exploitation of Roma women in human trafficking, gender-based and domestic violence, and the over-representation of Roma children in the Hungarian child protection system. According to research conducted by the ERRC, gender-based violence is an acute problem for Roma women, who are reluctant to report incidents of violence for fear of experiencing further victimization and discrimination from the police. The submission points out that there is no specific law on domestic violence against women, and existing measures do not provide adequate protection.

The 2010 European Gender Equality Law Review reports of a case lodged before the Equal Treatment Authority (ETA) by a member of the Roma minority self-government against the mayor of Edelény, a town with a large Roma population. The mayor had alleged that some pregnant Roma women had intentionally harmed their foetuses, damaging their mental or physical health in order to receive higher child benefits. As the Review states:

'the ETA found that this statement – which was then widely spread across the media by its opposition – violated the dignity of pregnant Roma women and Roma women in general and created a hostile and degrading environment for them, thus constituting discrimination in the form of harassment. The ETA ordered the cessation of the violation and, after the Court of the Capital City had turned down the appeal against the decision it acquired final and binding force.'

Fidesz, the mayor's political party withdrew his candidacy, but he ran in the elections and won a seat as the only independent representative in the new parliament.

Hungary took over the Presidency of the EU on 1 January 2011, with the ambitious objective of pushing through the adoption of the Framework Strategy on Roma Integration at the 2011 June meeting of the European Council. The Framework Strategy is supported by the European Roma Policy Coalition (a coalition of human rights NGOs) and has been under discussion at the European Commission and the European parliament since 2008. As stated on Hungary's official EU Presidency website, 'the Framework Strategy would be the cornerstone of a unified European Roma Policy, on the basis of which Member states would in the future develop their own Roma integration reform programs'. It remains to be seen whether the adoption of such a Roma strategy is realistic at the EU level, and whether Hungary, itself facing major problems in protecting the human rights of its Roma population, will succeed in negotiating and seeing through the adoption of the Framework Strategy at the European Council.

Italy

Responses to trafficking in women in Europe: the emergence of a rights-based framework?

Human trafficking is an issue that has attracted increasing attention in recent decades. Although international conventions from 1926 and 1949 on slavery and trafficking demonstrate that trafficking has long been an international policy concern, more recent efforts by global and transnational actors such as the UN, the Council of Europe, the EU, and the OSCE, as well as numerous NGOs have combined to bring about the near-universal recognition that human trafficking constitutes an international crisis requiring coordinated legislative, political and social responses.

The 2000 UN Convention against Transnational Organized Crime and the annexed protocols on human trafficking and human smuggling define what constitutes trafficking in modern times. According to Article 3 (a) of the Protocol to Prevent, Suppress and Punish Trafficking in Persons, especially Women and Children (referred commonly to as the Trafficking Protocol):

'[T]rafficking in persons shall mean the recruitment, transportation, transfer, harbouring or receipt of persons, by means of the threat or use of

victim of trafficking in persons to the intended exploitation set forth in subparagraph (a) of this article shall be irrelevant where any of the means set forth in subparagraph (a) have been used.'

According to the most recent UN Global Report on Trafficking in Persons (2009), recent years have seen international pressure exerted on individual states to enact legislation and define policies on the issue. In particular, the 2003 UN Trafficking Protocol prompted a wave of amendments to criminal codes to introduce specific offences on trafficking in persons. Today, virtually every country in Europe and Central Asia outlaws trafficking in persons as a criminal offence, with Turkmenistan being the only exception. Data from the *UN Global Report* demonstrates that sexual exploitation is the most common form of human trafficking worldwide (79 per cent). Victims of sexual exploitation are predominantly women and girls, and almost 20 per cent of all trafficking victims are children. Where available, data also show that women play a key role among traffickers.

Due to its clandestine nature, differing national definitions, victims' unwillingness to report their experiences and lack of harmonized data –to name just a few basic problems obstructing quantification – the true extent of trafficking remains hidden. The *UN Global Report* recognizes the methodological weaknesses in gathering data and sticks to prosecuted and convicted cases of trafficking. Regarding labour exploitation, which is recognized by international law as the second most common form of trafficking, the report advises for example that its finding of forced labour constituting 18 per cent of the total cases 'may be a misinterpretation because forced labour is less frequently detected and reported than trafficking for sexual exploitation'. This goes to the

force or other forms of coercion, abduction, fraud, deception, abuse of power or position of vulnerability, giving or receiving payments or benefits to achieve consent of a person, having control of another, for the purpose of, exploitation. Exploitation shall include at a minimum, the exploitation of the prostitution of others, or other forms of sexual exploitation, forced labour or services, slavery or practices similar to slavery, servitude, or the removal of organs.'

Subparagraph (b) states that 'the consent of the

heart of the many debates on women's rights and trafficking, as it is argued that the narrow focus on exploitation in the sex industry masks the abuse of women and men who are trafficked into other industries, as well as the root causes of trafficking. As a result, other forms of exploitation remain under-reported, including 'forced or bonded labour; domestic servitude and forced marriage; organ removal; and the exploitation of children in begging, the sex trade and warfare'.

The definition of trafficking included in the UN Trafficking Protocol was used in the majority of instances by states party to the protocol as a model when drawing up national anti-trafficking legislation. The tripartite definition of trafficking as involving deceptive/coercive recruitment, transportation and exploitation of a person without their consent has sparked debate, as it is difficult to prove all three parts of the claim. Coercion and deception are complex issues. Studies have found that deception occurs not only when victims are told half-truths of the nature of the work, but also when they know they will be working in the sex industry but are unaware of the extent of exploitation and control. In many cases, victims are physically restrained and constantly controlled, but coercion can also be psychological. According to Anti-Slavery International, coercion occurs in 'any situation in which the person involved has no real and acceptable alternative but to submit to the abuse involved'. Trafficking then can be described as ownership of persons: the individual effectively becomes the possession of the trafficker, a commodity that one can buy and sell. Further, some commentators, like Antonio Maria Costa, Executive Director of the UN Office on Drugs and Crime, whose foreword introduces the *UN Global Report*, claim that too much emphasis is placed on the process, rather than 'on the transaction aspects of a crime that is more accurately described as

enslavement'. Indeed, the difference between people smuggling and trafficking – both involving a process of movement – may be apparent at the point of destination. A smuggled person is normally free when they arrive, whereas trafficked persons are denied personal autonomy.

The Human Trafficking Indicators produced by the UN Office on Drugs and Crime give some indication of when human trafficking is taking place, and when the presence of any of the indicators can lead to investigation. These include general indicators, as well as indicators specific to: trafficking in children; domestic servitude, sexual and labour exploitation; and begging and petty crime. Having tattoos or other marks indicating 'ownership' by exploiters, the inability to show an identity document, knowing only sex-related words in the local language and (in the case of children) lack of smiling are some of the indicators that may be exhibited by children and adults trafficked for sexual exploitation.

Discrimination and exploitation suffered by women in their home countries is one of the root causes of trafficking. In much of its project work, Anti-Slavery International has clearly established the link between discrimination and slavery. According to its findings, victims of slavery practices, including trafficking and forced labour, are 'frequently from minority or marginalized groups who face institutionalized discrimination and live on the margins of society where they are vulnerable to slavery practices'. This includes those facing caste-based discrimination – Dalits in India for example – or members of indigenous and other minority groups, including religious minorities.

The unstable political, social and economic situation in countries of origin, resulting in high unemployment, abject poverty, internal conflicts and grave violations of human rights, are push factors that drive many women to Europe. The political and economic crises in the former communist states of Central and Eastern Europe and in Russia have fuelled migration predominantly to the western part of Europe. The move towards increasingly restrictive migration policies closes routes of legal migration to the EU, however, and leaves many women prey to traffickers. Trafficking in women occurs within the borders of the EU too. A conference on Trafficking in Romani Communities held on International Human Rights Day, 10 December 2010, discussed research conducted recently by the ERRC in Central and Eastern European countries. The ERRC found that Roma are highly vulnerable to trafficking. According to the research findings:

'Roma are perceived to represent 50–80 per cent of trafficking victims in Bulgaria, 40–80 per cent in Hungary, 70 per cent in Slovakia, up to 50 per cent in parts of Romania and up to 70 per cent in parts of the Czech Republic. At the same time, very few Roma were reported to access victim prevention and protection services in the target countries and general social protection systems are failing to reduce the extreme vulnerability of Roma to trafficking.'

A 2010 publication on the character, causes and consequences of human trafficking in Europe includes analysis on trafficking of women and girls from Russian and Ukraine. On the controversial question of coercion and consent, the study argues that:

'[M]any women live in coercive contexts underpinned by poverty, gender inequality and demand for sexual services which make the concept of choice meaningless. As expressed by one woman who was sold by a criminal group but managed to escape and return to Ukraine: "I understood everything and had a foreboding, but I never imagined that it would be so horrible. But I had no other way of feeding my child".'

Protection of victims, acknowledgement of their

human rights, and preventative measures must be put at the core of policies to address trafficking. At the launch of a global action plan to combat human trafficking on 31 August, UN representatives underlined the importance of prevention, which has recently moved up the UN policy agenda. The action plan calls for the establishment of a UN voluntary trust fund for victims of trafficking (especially women and children), and stresses the need for more research, data and analysis.

A human rights-based approach that puts protecting the victim at the centre is slowly developing. This is a departure from initial policies and legislation that were developed within the framework of criminal justice and law-enforcement against organized crime, and on the basis of the UN Trafficking Protocol, that itself grew out of the UN Convention Against Transnational Organized Crime. EU responses, like the 2002 Council Framework Decision 'On Combating Trafficking in Human Beings' and the 2004 Council Directive 'On the Residence Permit Issued to Third-country Nationals Who Are Victims of Trafficking', were also bound up with defining the crime of human trafficking and with irregular migration, leaving little room for protection or prevention. An increasing concern with the exploitation of people, and with addressing global injustice and pull factors at the demand side, is slowly being brought to centre stage. While retaining criminal provisions, the draft Council Framework on Preventing and Combating Trafficking includes enforceable rights for the victims and measures on the demand for sexual services. OSCE and Council of Europe initiatives are also beginning to employ a human rights-based approach; the Council of Europe Convention on Action Against Trafficking in Human Beings represents a notable step in this direction. ■

The poor treatment accorded to Roma and migrants by the Italian authorities prompted the UN High Commissioner for Human Rights Navi Pillay to undertake her first ever country visit in 2010. On 11 March, the same day the UN human rights chief visited Italy, Amnesty International published a report examining the 'Nomad Plan', a scheme developed under the 2008 'Nomad Emergency' presidential decree which allows forced evictions of Roma and resettlement to camps on the outskirts of Rome. Amnesty found the plan discriminatory and in violation of the housing rights of Roma, who were not consulted before evictions started in July 2009. According to the report, under the plan an estimated 6,000 Roma are to be resettled into just 13 camps, and over 100 settlements are to be dismantled. The major demolition of Roma camps could leave as many as 1,000 Roma homeless.

In January, Italian police began evicting Roma from one of the largest and oldest camps in Europe. The Castilio 900 camp in Rome has been in existence for over 40 years and is home to 600 people. While some welcomed the prospect of better housing conditions, many did not want to leave. Voice of America quoted a Roma woman who had lived in Castilio 900 for 35 years and who said, 'My

Left: A Roma family stand by their belongings during the evacuation of the Casilino 900 camp in Rome, Italy, January 2010.
Andrew Medichini/AP Photo.

'[T]he situation is the result of years of neglect, inadequate policies and discrimination by successive administrations. [The] plan is incomplete and risks making the situation for many other Roma even worse. It is the wrong answer.'

The UN High Commissioner raised her concern regarding 'the excessive resort to repressive measures such as police surveillance and forced evictions', but such practices continued throughout the year. In Milan alone, at least 61 forced evictions took place, rendering many Sinti and Roma homeless. Italian Interior Minister Roberto Maroni was also active in lobbying the EU for permission to expel Roma and announced in August that he would push for endorsement to expel citizens of other EU countries who 'are a burden on the social welfare system hosting them'. When opposition parties accused him of racism and discrimination, Maroni commented that the policy would apply to all non-Italian citizens.

During September and October, further camps were dismantled in Rome and Milan. As with neighbouring France, rising rates of crime was the rationale for the bulldozing of hundreds of small, impromptu camps inhabited by new immigrants, and the eviction of Triboniano, Milan's largest authorized Roma camp. A landmark decision in the case *COHRE v. Italy* delivered by the Council of Europe's European Committee of Social Rights may call a halt to forced evictions. On 3 November, the Committee found Italy in violation of the prohibition on discrimination, and in violation of the rights of Roma people to adequate housing; social, legal and economic protection; protection against poverty and social exclusion; and the right of migrant Roma families to protection and assistance. The destruction of camps was condemned, as were the illegal evictions that had been enforced without notice, and without offering alternative housing.

grandchildren live here as well and what they are doing is not right. It's not right that they are creating problems among us.' During her visit, the UN High Commissioner visited authorized Roma camps on the outskirts of Rome and commented with dismay, 'I am profoundly shocked by the conditions of the camps. [...] For a moment I thought I was in one of the poorest developing countries and not in one of the richest nations in the world', she said. Improving the living conditions of many Roma would be welcomed, given that many have been living without running water and basic hygiene. But as the Italy expert at Amnesty International stated,

In the city of Rosarno, some 320 African migrants were taken to an emergency centre in the aftermath of two days of rioting after injuries were inflicted on two immigrants by a group of local youth using air rifles. Human rights groups and the opposition criticized Italy's migration policies, raising their concerns that the violence revealed the consequences of long-term xenophobic and anti-immigrant discourse that had fuelled prejudice and tensions between migrants and the local population. Jorge Bustamante and Githu Muigai, respectively the UN Special Rapporteurs on the human rights of migrants and on contemporary forms of racism, issued a joint statement on the unrest stating, 'Violence, be it perpetrated by Italians or migrant workers, must be addressed in the most vigorous manner through the rule of law and human rights should always be protected, regardless of immigration laws.' Just a month later, racial violence broke out again, this time in Milan after the stabbing of a young Egyptian man, allegedly by a South American. The anti-immigrant Northern League responded with xenophobic comments and steadily increased its popularity, gaining important seats in the 2010 local and regional elections.

Russia

The extent of radical nationalism and a steady rise in ethnicity-based violence continued to be a cause of concern throughout 2010. According to data from the Moscow-based SOVA Centre for Information and Analysis, 37 people were killed and 368 injured in racially motivated attacks in 2010. The capital Moscow and the surrounding *oblast* saw the most violence, but incidents occurred in other cities across Russia, including St Petersburg and the surrounding Leningrad *oblast*, in Krasnodar, Nizhny Novgorod and in Rostov-on-Don.

An ultra-nationalist rampage in Moscow in the last month of the year caused an upsurge in xenophobic violence, resulting in the deaths of two people, and a further 68 sustaining injuries, according to SOVA. On 11 December, a group of ultra-right extremists gathered at Manezh Square in Moscow to commemorate the death of a football fan, Egor Sviridov, who allegedly had been killed by people from the North Caucasus a few days earlier. The demonstration, where '*Sieg Heil*' salutes were exchanged and xenophobic slogans like 'Russia for Russians', 'Moscow for Muscovites' and 'Kill, Kill' were chanted, ended in violent clashes with the police. Violence continued in the following days, targeting people from the North Caucasus. According to the *Moscow Times*, President Dmitry Medvedev described the rioting and violence as 'pogroms' and called for the prosecution of those responsible. According to a poll quoted by the media outlet, nationalism has gained a strong foothold amongst ethnic Russians, 56 per cent of whom support the ideology of a 'Russia for Russians'. Nonetheless, a counter-demonstration, 'Moscow for All', was organized after the rampage, and was attended by up to 2,500 people.

Another event that attracted headlines in the country was the murder of Federal Judge Eduard Chuvashov, who was shot dead in front of his home on 12 April. Chuvashov had received death threats on a number of occasions, as a result of his strict judgments against ultra-nationalists. Chuvashov conducted a number of trials on racially motivated crimes. This included one in February involving 9 people from the neo-Nazi group 'White Wolves', who were found guilty of murdering 11 people from Kyrgyzstan and Uzbekistan. A week before his death, Chuvashov had ruled in a case against Artur Ryno and Pavel Skachevsky (both minors), and Roman Kuzin, who received 10 years (the maximum penalty permitted for minors) and 22 years in prison respectively for committing 20 murders and attempting 12 murders of people of non-Slavic appearance. The group frequently uploaded video-footage of their activities onto the internet. An investigation into Chuvashov's death is ongoing.

Although comprehensive figures on hate crimes and violent attacks with xenophobic or racist motives are hard to establish, according to SOVA, 82 convictions were made and 283 people were sentenced in 2010 in cases involving violence with ethnic hatred as a motive. Fifty-two trials were conducted against 62 people on charges of incitement to hatred, and 4 charges were issued for the distribution of xenophobic propaganda. SOVA also published a report on the inappropriate enforcement of anti-extremist legislation during 2010. Incidents of racial violence are officially identified as 'extremist crimes' that threaten the security of the country. A Federal List of Extremist Materials and a separate one for extremist organizations are maintained and updated every year. In 2010, the list of extremist materials grew from 467 to 748, and the list of extremist organizations, which are banned from carrying out any activity, included 18 organizations by year's end. SOVA notes that anti-extremist legislation continues to be misused, including the 'criminal and administrative prosecution of Muslims and followers of new religious groups including Scientologists, Jehovah's Witnesses, and followers of

Said Nursi'.

In January, Russia ratified Protocol 14 to the ECHR, which paves the way to improve the efficiency of the Court. The Council of Europe welcomed the decision of the Russian parliament, the Duma; Russia was the last of the 47 member states to vote for the ratification of Protocol 14. Russia's Constitutional Court remained critical, however, of its Strasbourg counterpart, and issued statements about withdrawing from the jurisdiction of the ECtHR and introducing mechanisms to allow national authorities not to implement its judgments. The ECtHR has found Russia in violation of human rights in a series of cases in recent years. In November 2010, the PACE Committee on Legal Affairs and Human Rights issued its report on the implementation of judgements of the ECtHR and found that 'extremely worrying delays in implementation have arisen' in Russia. Key concerns relate to 'chronic non-enforcement of domestic judicial decisions' and 'death and ill-treatment by law enforcement officials, and a lack of effective investigations thereof', as well as 'repetitive grave human rights violations' in the Chechen Republic.

Chechnya is a semi-autonomous republic within the Russian Federation, governed by Chechen President Ramzan Kadyrov, who is directly appointed by the Kremlin. Although freedom of dress is guaranteed to all women in the Russian Federation, including those in Chechnya, and is enshrined in Russian law as part of the constitutional right to freedom of conscience, recent years have seen increasing harassment and discrimination against those who do not follow the publicly enforced dress code in Chechnya. Women and girls who choose not to wear a headscarf are banned from working in the public sector and from attending schools and universities. In June, a young woman was hospitalized following a paintball attack on the street, which occurred because she had not been wearing a headscarf. HRW quoted an interview with Kadyrov with the television station Grozny on 3 July, in which he expressed his 'unambiguous approval of this lawless practice by professing his readiness to "award commendation" to the men engaged in these activities'. Kadyrov went on to say that 'the targeted women's behaviour deserved this treatment and that they should be ashamed to the point of "disappearing from the face of the earth".'

Stressing ethnic minority women's particular vulnerability, and especially Chechens, Roma and women of African origin, the CEDAW committee called on Russia to adopt comprehensive anti-discrimination legislation, paying special attention to the needs of ethnic minority women. Multiple forms of discrimination experienced by 'certain groups of women and girls, including female domestic workers, asylum-seeking women, refugee women, internally displaced women, and girls living in the street', as well as violence, police harassment and discrimination against lesbian, bisexual and transgender women, were highlighted as particular concerns. In their alternative reports to the CEDAW committee, Amnesty International, the Russian Lesbian, Gay, Bisexual and Transgender (LGBT) Network and the ANNA National Centre for the Prevention of Violence voiced their dismay at Russia's non-compliance with its obligations under the Convention on the Elimination of All Forms of Discrimination against Women (CEDAW). The ANNA Centre drew attention to the continued practices of bride kidnapping and so-called 'honour' killings in some regions of the country, particularly the North Caucasus. Due to the lack of any official statistics on these crimes, the 2010 ANNA Centre submission to the CEDAW committee refers to NGO figures from 2008 that estimated the numbers of bride kidnappings in Dagestan at 180, but such crimes are committed in other parts of Russia and figures could reach several thousand every year. 'Honour' killings were also identified in Dagestan and Chechnya, although, again, the prevalence of this crime is very difficult to establish. The submission refers to dozens of women a year being victims of 'honour' killings in the whole country, and warns that perpetrators are often exempt from punishment as these crimes are most commonly covered up or reported as accidents.

Russia's Third State Report on the Implementation of the FCNM, submitted on 9 April 2010 states that, as regards anti-discrimination measures, which was a key concern raised by the CEDAW committee, no specific laws have been enacted. Instead, the report refers to legislation in the fields of education, labour, health care, judicial procedures, social protection and culture, including measures to protect human rights. In the field of extremist crimes, the report refers to the country's Constitution, which guarantees the rights of national and ethnic minorities and indigenous peoples,

and to the Criminal Code, which rules out terrorism and extremist activities. It states that 'investigation and proper classification of extremist crimes has
been gained, including hate crimes'.

Russia signed the European Charter for Regional
and Minority Languages on 10 May 2001; however,
the process of ratification is proving to be complex
and drawn out. In September 2010, the Council of
Europe reported on a series of events due to start
in October 2010, working towards the Charter
implementation in the 'Minorities in Russia' Joint
Programme. This includes awareness-raising activities with the participation of local and regional
officers, NGOs, and federal judicial authorities,
with a view to working towards ratification.

Turkey
Nurçan Kaya

2010 saw few changes in the situation of minorities
in Turkey. This was despite hopes raised in 2009
by the 'democracy opening' programme launched
by the government, with the aim of ensuring equality to all citizens and bringing a peaceful solution
to the Kurdish question. Promises made by the
government in 2009 to adopt a comprehensive anti-
discrimination law and set up an equality body, a
national human rights body and an independent
complaints mechanism against police forces also
came to nothing. In addition, the 10 per cent electoral threshold which prevents many parties, including the pro-Kurdish party from winning seats in the
parliament is still in place, despite suggestions from
an opposition party to lower the threshold.

In September 2010, a referendum was passed
by 58 per cent to amend some provisions of the
Constitution. The amendment strengthened provisions for positive measures to ensure equality
between women and men, and for the prosecution
of members of the military before civil courts for
crimes not related to their duties and/or committed against civilians. The 'No' campaign was run
by the main, Kemalist opposition party and many
left-wing groups, in the belief that the government
was aiming to establish control over the judiciary in
order to pursue an Islamist agenda and weaken the
secularity of the state. Nationalist conservative parties also ran a 'No' campaign, while the pro-Kurdish
party chose to boycott the referendum, arguing that
the proposed constitutional changes did not include
anything new for Kurds.

Following the referendum, many provisions in
the Constitution that affect minority groups have
remained in place, such as Article 42 that bans the
teaching of any languages other than Turkish as
a mother tongue, and Article 24 on compulsory
religious culture and ethics classes. Nevertheless,
civil society and minority activists see the approved
changes as an indication that more than half of
the population may be prepared to accept further
changes. The governing Justice and Development
Party has itself acknowledged that the changes were
not adequate, and promised that an entirely new
Constitution would be drawn up in 2011, although
only once national elections have taken place
(scheduled for June 2011). A new Constitution
would present an important opportunity to bring an
end to the state policy that has sought to assimilate
minorities and create one type of Turkish citizen,
who is secular Sunni Muslim, speaks Turkish and
is nationalist. Such a change would enable Turkey
to recognize the rights of minorities and effectively
guarantee equality to all its citizens, regardless of
their ethnic, religious or linguistic origins.

Turkey continues to accept only three non-
Muslim groups as minorities: Armenians, Greeks
and Jews. This means that other non-Muslim
groups and ethnic minorities, such as Alevis,
Assyrians, Circassians, Kurds, Laz and Roma, are
not officially recognized, limiting the exercise of
some political and cultural rights by these groups.
Even minorities with official recognition cannot
exercise their rights fully, as Turkey limits their
rights to those guaranteed in the Lausanne Peace
Treaty (signed in 1923 between Turkey and the
Allied forces following the First World War).

One positive development in 2010 was the
continuation of dialogue between the government
and some minority groups. But these dialogue
meetings did not lead to any concrete changes. For
example, during discussions, representatives of the
Alevi minority called for children from the group
to be exempted from attending obligatory religious
culture and ethics classes (which remain centred on
Sunni Islamic teachings, despite some revisions), but
this request was denied. Exempting Alevi children
from these classes would have given them the same
rights as Jewish and Christian children, who do not
have to attend, and would have reflected the judgments of the Court of Cassation and the ECtHR
(*Hasan and Eylem Zengin v. Turkey*, Application

no.1448/04, Judgment of 9 October 2007) given in favour of their exemption from this class. In addition, the Halki (Heybeliada) Rum Orthodox theological college remains closed (as it has been since 1971, when it was closed for refusing to align with a public university, which would have compromised its independence).

The Ministry of Education printed Armenian textbooks for Armenian minority schools for the first time, although these schools continued to receive no financial support from the state and remain subject to heavy financial and bureaucratic burdens. Only Armenian children who have Turkish citizenship can study at these schools, meaning that children who are Armenian citizens living in Turkey are excluded. More positively, the first Armenian language and literature department in the country was opened at Erciyes University.

Clashes between the Kurdish Workers' Party (PKK) and security forces diminished in the latter part of 2010, following the PKK's declaration of a ceasefire in August 2010. The armed conflict is ongoing, however; 152 Kurdish politicians and civil society activists (104 of whom are in prison) face charges of belonging to the Kurdish Communities Union (KCK), which is alleged to be the urban branch of the PKK. The trial is ongoing. The suspects' request to defend themselves in Kurdish has been rejected by the Court.

Education in Kurdish has been at the top of the agenda of the pro-Kurdish Peace and Democracy Party (BDP), and of many NGOs and academics. But this and demands for the use of Kurdish in public life have been rejected strongly by the government. Despite this, municipalities where the BDP are in charge have started to use bilingual signs and doorplates. Mardin Artuklu University applied to the High Board of Education for approval to set up a Kurdish language and literature department and a Kurdology Institute. Their application was rejected, and instead the Board decided to set up the Institute for Living Languages, without referring to Kurdish language in its name, but enabling the university to open an MA programme in Kurdish language within this Institute. There has also been greater public discussion of demands by Kurdish groups for the establishment of truth commissions and for the acknowledgment of gross human rights violations by the state.

The reported number of racist or hate crimes rose in 2010. Many of the perpetrators of these attacks have been arrested and convicted, including a 39-month prison sentence handed down to someone who threatened the staff of *AGOS*, an Armenian weekly newspaper based in Istanbul. But as the Penal Code contains no provisions relating to hate crimes, perpetrators are charged under ordinary criminal law. Roma homes and vehicles were attacked in Manisa/Selendi in January 2010, and 21 Roma families had to leave the town as they did not feel safe there. The displaced Roma families received some short-term support from the state, but have since then been living in very difficult conditions. Kurds were subject to racist attacks in Hatay/Dörtyol and Bursa/İnegöl in July. In Hatay/Dörtyol, the BDP building and some Kurdish offices were set on fire, and in Erzurum a BDP convoy was stoned. In Hatay/Iskenderun, Catholic Bishop Luigi Padovese was murdered. The trial of those suspected of murdering Armenian journalist and editor Hrant Dink in 2007 entered its fourth year, with as yet no prosecution of police and intelligence officers who failed to protect Dink. The Malatya case, brought against perpetrators of the brutal murder of Christian staff at the Zirve Publishing House, is still pending.

Data disaggregated by ethnicity is not collected in Turkey, meaning that there are no official figures to illustrate discrimination against minority women. However, the results of some surveys disclose disparities between access to education by girls and women in Turkey in general and those in east and south-east Turkey, regions mostly populated by Kurds. According to data provided by the United Nations Development Programme (UNDP) in 2008, the literacy rate of women is 60.3 per cent in south-east and 63.6 per cent in east Turkey, compared with 79.6 per cent nationally. School graduation rates also differ between east and west Turkey. A report published by MRG, *Forgotten or Assimilated? Minorities in the Education System of Turkey*, revealed problems in accessing education for minority children in general, and minority girls in particular. Poverty emerges as one of the most important factors, particularly for Roma, displaced Kurds and children of seasonal workers, who are mostly Kurds. Roma NGOs report that nowadays most Roma families enrol their children at school, but then withdraw them after a couple of years, as parents cannot

afford the expense and children are needed to work in order to contribute to the family budget. Girls are usually withdrawn before boys. Another factor cited was the lack of role models for Roma children, and early marriages are also reported to play a role in drop-out rates. In addition, urbanization projects carried out in some provinces of Turkey caused displacement of many Roma and affected many Roma children negatively, again impacting on education. National governmental programmes to address girls' access to education are being implemented and are seen as a positive development, although these programmes do not target minority girls specifically.

Women who have been displaced are among those most affected by the armed conflict in Turkey. It is estimated that over a million people, most of whom were Kurds, were displaced from east and south-east Turkey, in particular in the early 1990s. Some fled to Europe, but most moved to large cities in Turkey. Reports issued by some NGOs show that most of these people have not received any state support to enable them to integrate in their new places of residence, and that they form one of the poorest sections of society. Women and children are particularly affected. Many of the displaced women

Left: A Liberal Democrat representative tries to entice a passerby to vote at a polling station in London's East End, England, 2010. *Andrew Testa/Panos.*

age and trauma that cannot be compensated by cash payments.

UK

Passed on 8 April, the Equality Act was one of the last measures of the outgoing Labour government, which lost office in May 2010. The Act, which covers England, Wales and Scotland (Great Britain) but not Northern Ireland, reflects the pan-equalities (i.e. cross-cutting) approach towards addressing discrimination that gained pace under New Labour. The 2010 act was preceded by the 2006 Single Equality Act, which set up an independent single equality watchdog, the Equality and Human Rights Commission (EHRC). The integrated approach to equality law enforced by a single Commission is reflected in the new act that covers discrimination on grounds of race, religion, gender, disability, age and sexual orientation, as well as socio-economic status, pregnancy and gender reassignment. The pivotal aim of the 2010 act was to achieve simplification and harmonization of existing equality law – it replaces previous laws on all protected strands – and to harmonize protection for different grounds.

A notable feature of the act is the prohibition of multiple discrimination, although a provision that would have allowed for the combination of two grounds of discrimination was removed by the Conservative–Liberal Democrat coalition government in early 2011. The new legislation, which entered into force on 1 October 2010 and will be brought into operation in stages, could assist in closing some of the equality gaps that still exist in British society. A report entitled *How Fair Is Britain?* by the EHRC draws a picture of a country increasingly at ease with its diversity, but also where – for some minority groups – encountering negative stereotypes and gross violations of their human rights is an everyday experience. This is particularly the case for migrants and Gypsies, Roma and Travellers, but also for some settled minority ethnic groups. In its Fourth Report on the UK published in March, the Council of Europe's ECRI noted with concern that 'racist incidents had become more frequent, police powers were exercised in a manner

do not speak Turkish well and this prevents them from accessing public services, in particular health services. Literacy rates and integration in economic life are very low, and the state has not developed any specific programme to address the economic, social and cultural needs of these people. A law adopted to provide compensation to those displaced by or suffering other losses as a result of 'terrorism' provided monetary compensation to many people, although the application system and the amount of compensation awarded were strongly criticized by some NGOs. In addition, no rehabilitation programme has been developed to deal with the dam-

that disproportionately affected minority groups, Gypsies and Travellers still faced serious discrimination and asylum-seekers remained in a vulnerable position'. ECRI also pointed to severe levels of hostility and prejudice towards these groups, as well as towards Muslims, and to negative media and public discourse with racist and xenophobic overtones.

On the day the African-American activist Reverend Jesse Jackson arrived in the UK to launch a campaign against the discriminatory and disproportionate use of police stop and search powers against black and Asian people, the *Guardian* newspaper revealed shocking findings of recent research into the issue. According to analysis by the London School of Economics and Political Science (LSE) and the Open Society Justice Initiative, black people are 26.6 times more likely and Asians are 6.3 times more likely to be stopped and searched than white people, and there are 60 searches for every 1,000 blacks compared with 1.6 for whites. The analysis of government data on stop and search powers under section 60 of the Public Order Act, where a police officer does not require reasonable suspicion to undertake a search, demonstrated obvious racial profiling, according to the study. Revd Jackson said:

'We've gone through this process in our country of ethnic and religious targeting. [...] It resulted in disastrous consequences. Wherever it happens it undermines the moral authority of the democracy. It damages the image of Britain, because Britain is held in high esteem.'

He rejected police claims that race has nothing to do with the practice. 'It is racial profiling. It's as fundamental as that. It is based on sight, suspicion and fear. It's a systematic pattern.'

The excessive use of police force was confirmed by a 2010 ruling of the ECtHR. In the case *Gillan and Quinton v. the United Kingdom*, the Court investigated sections 44–47 of the Terrorism Act 2000 allowing the police to stop and search individuals without reasonable suspicion of wrongdoing. It found that the right to respect for the private and family life of the claimants was violated, that the stop and search powers were 'not sufficiently circumscribed' and there were no 'adequate legal safeguards against abuse'. It also concluded that 'the risks of the discriminatory use of the powers' were 'a very real consideration'.

Evidence of the discrimination and human rights abuses suffered by migrants increased considerably during the year. An EHRC inquiry in the meat and poultry processing sector uncovered widespread mistreatment and exploitation of migrant workers, including physical and verbal abuse and a lack of proper health and safety protection. The treatment of pregnant workers was highlighted as a particular concern. The report notes that many migrant workers had little knowledge of their rights. the *Guardian* newspaper quoted a community advocate of the London-based charity Kalayaan that advises migrant domestic workers, who stated:

'Two-thirds of the domestic workers we see report being psychologically abused. That means they've been threatened and humiliated, shouted at constantly and called dog, donkey, stupid, illiterate.'

Drawing from an investigation undertaken by the *Dispatches* documentary programme for Channel 4, the *Guardian* reported that 20 per cent of the 15,000 migrant workers who come to the UK every year hoping for better living standards and supporting families left behind are physically abused or assaulted. Examples of abuse included being burnt with irons, threatened with knives and having boiling water thrown at them. Conditions amounting to modern-day slavery were successfully challenged in a case in April. The employment tribunal found a farmer, who treated his workers 'like dogs', guilty of race discrimination, unlawfully docking wages and unfair dismissal.

Concerning Gypsy, Roma and Traveller communities, the Europe-wide trend towards forced evictions is evident in the UK as well. In a report analysing recent policy changes introduced by the new government, the Institute for Race Relations (IRR) points out that 'the scale of the Gypsy "problem" is remarkably modest.' The report's authors judge that in the whole of England there are probably only 3,729 caravans on unauthorized sites, and 13,708 on private or council sites, and that according to an EHRC report, 'the entire Gypsy and Traveller population could be legally accommodated if as little as one square mile of land were allocated for sites in England'. The new coalition government, however, has withdrawn the £30 million already offered to local authorities to develop Gypsy, Roma and Traveller sites, and on the whole abandoned Labour's more progressive policies to meet the needs of travelling communities. Eric Pickles, the new state secretary for communities said back in 2008, 'It's not fair that hard-working families have to save up to get on the housing ladder while Travellers get special treatment at taxpayers' expense.' Pickles is driving the new 'Travellers policy', including proposals to increase police powers to evict and arrest people for trespassing on private land by turning trespassing from a civil into a criminal offence; making it more difficult to obtain permission to put caravans on private land; abolishing regional planning bodies in charge of provision of registered sites; and revising the allocation of pitches within local authorities.

Human rights campaigners have condemned the prospect of families being evicted from plots of land many of them own and forced to move back onto illegal sites or wasteland camping. In one case, the UN Committee on the Elimination of Racial Discrimination requested clarification of plans to demolish the homes of 90 families erected on land they own at Dale Farm, on the outskirts of Basildon, Essex. As a woman living on the farm commented to the BBC:

'It used to be a dirty scrapyard, but we cleaned it up. Each family has their own deeds.[...] The government at the time said let Gypsies and Travellers provide for themselves and so we did.'

In April 2010, the UN Special Rapporteur on adequate housing, Raquel Rodnik, also wrote to the British Ambassador to the UN about the proposed mass eviction from Dale Farm. As reported by the IRR, the UK government's response given by the communities and local government minister with responsibility for Gypsies and Travellers has been condemned as inadequate and misleading by the Liberal peer Eric Avebury, for ignoring 'the endemic shortage of sites for Gypsies and Travellers in England' and for not addressing 'acute medical and educational needs of residents, and the combination of local authority cuts and endemic prejudice which has eroded provision of specialist education and welfare services for Gypsy and Traveller children'. ■

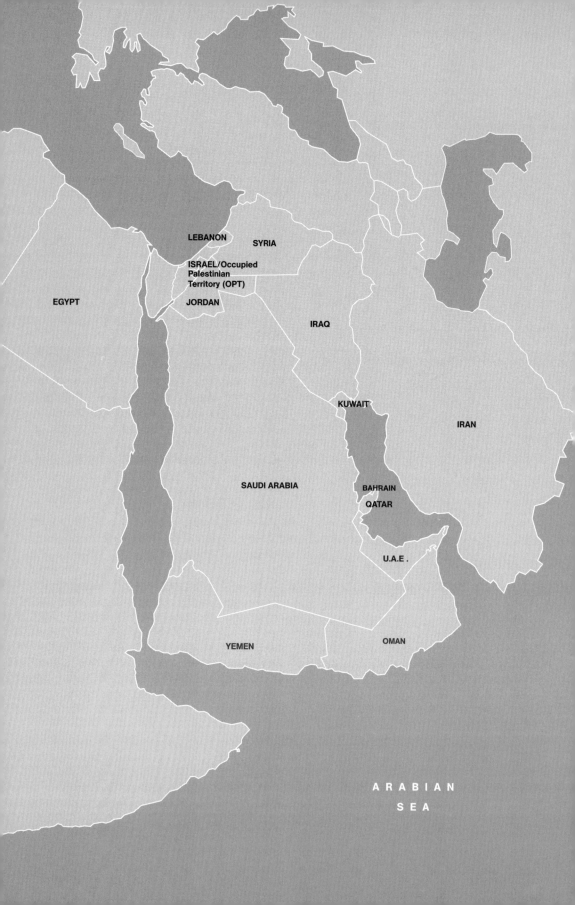

LEBANON

SYRIA

ISRAEL/Occupied
Palestinian
Territory (OPT)

EGYPT

JORDAN

IRAQ

KUWAIT

IRAN

SAUDI ARABIA

BAHRAIN

QATAR

U.A.E .

YEMEN

OMAN

ARABIAN
SEA

Middle East and North Africa

Preti Taneja

I n 2010, religious and ethnic minorities across the Middle East and North Africa remained disproportionately affected by ongoing conflict, political turmoil and state-sanctioned repression of their rights.

Though Iraqi parliamentary elections were held in March 2010, the government was not formed until November. In this political vacuum, which also saw the end of US combat operations in the country, violence against minority groups escalated. In February, attacks in Mosul over ten days left eight Christians dead, according to Human Rights Watch (HRW). In October, militants laid siege to Our Lady of Salvation Syriac Catholic Church in Baghdad, taking over 100 people hostage. Numbers of reported casualties vary. Amnesty International reported over 40 people killed while the BBC reported more than 50 fatalities in the ensuing violence.

The politically motivated violence contributed to the flight of traumatized minorities and others from Iraq, and this exodus continues to affect the whole region. The United Nations (UN) refugee agency, the UN High Commissioner for Refugees (UNHCR) placed the number of Iraqi refugees, most of whom are in neighbouring countries, at 1.8 million in a 2010 report. Of these, a large proportion is from religious and ethnic minority communities, who are increasingly targeted in Iraq for various reasons that are rooted in their minority status. In December 2010, UNHCR country offices in Jordan, Lebanon and Syria reported that following the October church siege, increasing numbers of Iraqi Christians were arriving and registering for assistance. Some had fled before and had been forcibly returned to Iraq by third countries in Europe, only to flee again.

The threat of civil unrest in Lebanon was also a matter of regional and international concern in 2010. Tensions over the as yet unreleased findings of a UN investigation into the 2005 assassination of Prime Minister Rafik Hariri – which is expected to implicate leaders of the country's Hezbollah party – led eventually to the resignation of Hezbollah members of the coalition cabinet in January 2011. At the time of writing, Lebanon remained without a government, and there were fears that tension between the two sides could erupt into violence that would affect the whole region.

Political controversy also rocked Jordan, a

country widely regarded as one of the most stable in the region. In November 2009, King Abdullah II dissolved a parliament that had only served two years of its four-year term. Elections were due to follow swiftly, but were postponed for the drafting of a new electoral law, and the country reverted to direct royal rule for a year-long period. Despite protests that the new electoral law further marginalizes the country's Palestinian population, elections were finally held in November 2010, but were boycotted by the country's main Islamist opposition group.

In addition to ongoing marginalization and discrimination, Palestinian Arabs in Israel bore the brunt of controversial new legislation considered by many to be discriminatory, as it requires all new non-Jewish citizens to pledge allegiance to Israel as a 'Jewish and democratic State'. Israeli Prime Minister Binyamin Netanyahu later announced that the proposal would apply to all new citizens; however, the disproportionate impact on Palestinians remained the same. Meanwhile, one year after the Israeli military's Operation Cast Lead claimed the lives of countless Palestinian civilians in Gaza, both Hamas and the Israeli government issued rebuttals of the 2009 UN investigation headed by Justice Richard Goldstone, which found that both sides had committed war crimes. In May, Israeli naval commanders stormed a flotilla of ships carrying pro-Palestinian activists who were attempting to carry tonnes of aid to the people of Gaza, which has been subject to an Israeli blockade since 2006. At least 10 civilians were killed and many were wounded in the raid, according to a formal statement by the UN Security Council. International condemnation followed, and the UN Secretary-General Ban Ki-moon ordered an impartial inquiry into Israel's actions. In early 2011, Israel issued a report saying its actions were legal under international law. In July 2010, the Knesset stripped Israeli Arab MK Hanin Zuabi – the first female Israeli Arab to be elected to the Knesset on an Arab party list – of three parliamentary privileges because she had taken part in the Gaza-bound flotilla.

At the time of writing, there was deepening

international concern over the increasing instability in Yemen and serious questions over the future well-being of its people. Since 2006, the country has been engaged in a six-year sectarian conflict that has displaced more than 250,000 people. The instability has led to rising lawlessness, and the country has emerged as a base for attacks on civilians elsewhere, including attempted bombings of commercial and cargo flights bound for Germany, the USA and the UK. Over the course of last year, the situation of the Yemeni people became increasingly desperate,

with thousands taking to the streets in January 2011 to demand the resignation of Ali Abdullah Saleh, who has been president for 30 years.

As MRG has noted in its reports, minority women across the region are subject to intersectional discrimination because of both their sex and their minority status. They can also suffer gender-based repression within their own communities. They are particularly vulnerable to certain forms of violence in conflicts. Across the region, they continue to be subject to varying degrees to personal status laws that are based on Sharia law. Such laws privilege Muslims over non-Muslims, and Muslim men over Muslim and non-Muslim women, for example in marriage and inheritance.

Increased legal discrimination and conservatism is not always tolerated or enforced, however. A campaign in 2009 against a revised personal status law in Syria was begun by women's groups in Damascus. Using social media and email, the campaign found support throughout the Middle East and was also backed by international non-government organizations (NGOs). This resulted in the law being 'shelved' by the Ministry of Justice, according to the NGO, Women Living Under Muslim Laws (WLUML). WLUML reported that the law would have made it easier for a man to divorce his wife and nearly impossible for her to do the same, and would have allowed Christian men to marry more than one woman.

This regional update focuses as much as possible on specific incidents and issues faced by women from minorities; however, disaggregated data by sex and religion/ethnicity is very difficult to access, particularly in such a volatile area.

Algeria

According to MRG, about a quarter of the Algerian population self-identifies as Berber. The year 2010 was the 30th anniversary of the 'Berber Spring' in 1980, when students took to the streets to demonstrate against the repression of Berber culture and to demand language rights. Algerian state forces crushed the peaceful protests. Since then, sometimes violent demonstrations have continued to mark relations between Berber communities and the state, and, despite some concessions, the issues are ongoing. For instance, while the Constitution holds that Islam is the state religion and Arabic the official language, the state declared the Berber language Tamazigh a 'national language' in 2002 and has permitted it to be taught in schools. But a 2010 report from a German NGO, the Society for Threatened Peoples (GFvB) said that, despite this, there is still no actual teaching of written or spoken Berber languages in Algerian schools.

In January 2010, Berber activists in Kabylie commemorated the 1980 uprising by repeating demands for autonomy for Berber people. According to the 2010 report on freedom of association by the Euro-Mediterranean Human Rights Network (EMHRN – a network of more than 80 human rights organizations across the region) in 2010 a march was planned in the small city of Aïn Benin to 'demand respect for human rights and commemorate the "Berber Spring"', but was met with force. The report states that although permission to hold the event was formally requested, a response was never given. Police were deployed on the day of the march and around 30 people were arrested. They were held for several hours, questioned and made to sign statements before being released.

The Christian and Jewish minorities in Algeria each make up 1 per cent of the total population. Sunni Islam is the official religion of the state, and non-Muslim religions are subject to restrictions that affect their ability to meet in public to worship. Non-Muslim groups are required to register with the government, and the state also controls the importing of religious texts. Proselytizing has historically been dealt with particularly harshly.

Relations between Christian and Muslim communities were difficult in 2010. The US State Department Report on International Religious Freedom 2010 (IRFR 2010) reported that in January, protesters disrupted a Protestant service being held on the first-floor of an apartment building in Kabylie. A week later, they 'vandalized the building and burned Bibles, hymnbooks, a cross, furniture, and appliances'. The attack took place amid local fears that the Protestant group was trying to convert Muslim children, and concerns that men and women are permitted to worship together in the house, according to the pastor.

In August, two Christian men were arrested for eating and drinking while at work on a building site during the Muslim fasting month of Ramadan. They were charged and detained under a law that bans Algerian citizens from 'causing offence to the Prophet … or denigrating the dogma of Islam'. The trial of the two attracted dozens of protesters, media reports said, with the public prosecutor calling for a three-year jail sentence. However, the two were acquitted in October. In December, Agence France Presse reported that four Christian converts were facing one-year jail sentences for opening a church without state permission. The outcome of the trial is not yet known.

Jews in Algeria continue to suffer discrimination. In June, the government refused requests from

Algerian Jewish associations based in France to visit holy sites in Algeria. Elsewhere, though, the state has made some overtures to religious groups. In February, a symposium entitled 'Religious Worship: A Right Ensured by Religion and by the Law' was held in Algiers by the Ministry of Foreign Affairs and the Ministry of Religious Affairs. According to the IRFR 2010, representatives from Christian and Jewish religious groups in the country and Catholic and Protestant religious leaders from the United States and France were invited, but members of the Jewish community did not participate.

Women, including non-Muslim women, suffer discrimination in Algeria in matters of personal status. As with many of the countries in the region, the Algerian family code draws on Sharia law, and as such Muslim women are prevented from marrying non-Muslim men unless they convert to Islam (although this is not always enforced) Meanwhile, children born to Muslim fathers and non-Muslim mothers are considered Muslim, whatever the mother's religion. Non-Muslim minorities also suffer discrimination in inheritance laws when a Muslim family member lays claims to the inheritance, the IRFR 2010 noted. In this case, widowed non-Muslims whose husbands were Muslim are left particularly vulnerable.

Egypt

Egypt's minority communities include Bahá'ís, Coptic Christians, Nubians and fewer than 200 Jews. In the last few years, experts have noted the rise of sectarian tensions in the country, while a framework of legislation exists that allows minorities to be discriminated against in mainstream society.

Coptic Christians represent between 6 and 9 per cent of Egypt's total population. They are required to list their religion on compulsory national identity cards, a factor which some have noted allows for discrimination to occur against them at the hands of state and private companies, and in access to education and public services. Christians are also under-represented in government at national and local levels. Following the November 2010 elections, Christians held only 2 per cent of seats in the People's Assembly. Christians may freely convert to Islam, but Muslims are prohibited from converting to Christianity or any other religion.

In January 2010, the Coptic minority suffered one of the worst atrocities it has experienced in the past decade, Amnesty International reported. On 6 January, Coptic Christmas Eve, six worshippers and an off-duty police officer were killed in a drive-by shooting that took place as people left a church after midnight mass in the city of Nagaa Hammadi. Amnesty said the attack was reportedly a reprisal for the alleged rape of a 12-year-old Muslim girl by a Christian man in November 2009. The allegation had already resulted in the burning and looting of Christian shops in the nearby town of Farshout by hundreds of Muslim protesters. On 7 January, hundreds of Christian protesters clashed with security forces outside a morgue where the bodies of the dead Copts were being held. The protesters chanted anti-government slogans and were met with tear gas. Clashes also occurred in nearby villages, and 28 Copts and 12 Muslims were arrested.

Officials quickly reported that eight people were being held in connection with the drive-by shooting. One of the perpetrators was sentenced to death, while, a year later, two others are awaiting the conclusion to their trials. This slow access to justice is not uncommon, experts have noted, and adds to the sense that the state is guilty of a long-standing failure to bring to justice those who attack Christians.

In November, Coptic Christians clashed with authorities over the building of a new church in Cairo's Giza district. Hundreds of protesters threw home-made petrol bombs and stones, while security forces fired tear gas into the crowds. The Christians denied authorities' claims that they did not have a proper permit to build the church. One protester was killed and dozens injured. According to the interior ministry, around 100 people were arrested following the clash.

Bahá'ís in Egypt have also historically suffered state-sanctioned repression and persecution. Their faith is not officially recognized by the state, and as such they have been forced to claim they are Muslim, Christian or Jewish on ID cards, or risk not being issued with compulsory documents, including birth certificates, death certificates and passports. Without ID cards, Bahá'ís have limited freedom of movement, and their access to public services, banking services, property rights, education and other key areas is prohibited. In 2009, following years of legal action, the first ID cards which allow religion to be left blank were issued. By mid 2010, the US Committee on International

Religious Freedom (USCIRF 2010) reported that the government had issued around 180 birth certificates and 50–60 national ID cards to Bahá'ís. But the state continues to refuse to recognize Bahá'í marriages, and there is no mechanism for civil marriage in the country. ID documents have been refused to married Bahá'ís unless they specify their status as 'unmarried'. Some Bahá'ís have pointed out that the application form for ID cards includes the provision that any false statements could result in a fine or a prison sentence; therefore, they are reluctant to misrepresent their marital status.

Iran

Iran is home to many ethnic minorities including Arabs, Azeris, Balochis, Fars, Kurds, Lurs and Turkmen. Around 2 per cent of the population are members of religious minority groups, including Christians, Jews and Zoroastrians, all of whom are recognized as religious groups under the Constitution, and Bahá'ís, who have no recognized status. Though Article 14 of the Constitution also charges all Muslims to treat non-Muslims according to the 'ethical norms and the principles of Islamic justice and equity, and to respect their human rights', the situation for Bahá'ís in Iran remained dire in 2010. In a September report on human rights in Iran, the UN said that members of the community faced arbitrary destruction of their homes, arrests, and confiscation and destruction of property. Their access to education and employment is also restricted.

Religious minorities

The trial of seven Bahá'í leaders (including two women), who were arbitrarily arrested in 2008 and held without charge for 20 months, began in January 2010. In August, it was reported that Fariba Kamalabadi, Jamaloddin Khanjani, Afif Naeimi, Saeid Rezaie, Mahvash Sabet, Behrouz Tavakkoli and Vahid Tizfahm – who deny charges of espionage, propaganda activities against the Islamic order, and 'corruption on earth', among other allegations – were given 20-year jail sentences. Independent observers were not allowed to attend the trial. In September, the Bahá'í World News Service reported that lawyers representing the seven were informed that the sentence had been reduced to ten years on appeal. At the time of writing, MRG had received reports that the 20-year sentences were re-imposed in March 2011.

In October, UN Secretary-General Ban Ki-moon issued a report criticizing Iran's use of torture and the death penalty, its discriminatory treatment of women and its failure to protect minority rights. In November, the UN General Assembly approved, for the seventh consecutive year, Resolution A/C.3/65/L.49, expressing deep concern at ongoing human rights violations in Iran, in particular its:

'Continued discrimination and other human rights violations, at times amounting to persecution, against persons belonging to ethnic, linguistic, recognized religious or other minorities.... Increased incidents of persecution against unrecognized religious minorities, particularly members of the Baha'i faith.'

Iran's non-Shi'a Muslim minorities also suffer ongoing persecution. In February 2010, at least 27 members of the Nematullahi Sufi order were arrested, and their place of worship in Isfahan was demolished, according to the report of the UN Special Rapporteur on freedom of religion or belief to the Human Rights Council. The report states that the families of those arrested were denied any information about their fate, and that their lawyers were prevented from meeting with them.

Conversion from Islam is met with harsh state reprisal. Youcef Nadarkhani, who was born to a Muslim family but converted to Christianity, was arrested and sentenced to death under charges of apostasy in 2009. In September 2010, the Gilan province Court of Appeals upheld the sentence. In December, Nadarkhani's lawyer filed an objection with the Supreme Court, and, at the time of writing, the NGO International Campaign for Human Rights in Iran reported that it is not known whether the sentence was overturned or upheld. Elsewhere, two Christian women, Maryam Rostampour and Marzieh Amrizadeh Esmaeilabad, who were accused of proselytizing and apostasy, were cleared of all charges in May 2010. Security forces in Tehran arrested them in March 2009 after they were accused

of handing out Bibles and attending religious gatherings. They were held, initially without charge, in a crowded cell with 27 other women at Evin prison for more than six months, Amnesty International reported. They suffered infections, fever and lack of medical attention.

Ethnic minorities

The Azeri community continues to face restrictions on the use of their language, including in the media, as well as political and social marginalization. In 2010, the case of an Azeri woman, Sakhineh Mohammed Ashtani, who was accused of adultery, attracted international attention when she was sentenced to death by stoning. It was argued that one of the factors that stood against her during her trial was that she did not speak Farsi well enough to be able to understand the proceedings in the case. Ashtani has reportedly been subject to torture. Her previous sentence was revoked, but she continues to face a sentence of death by hanging.

Arabs in Iran's Khuzestan province have faced decades of marginalization and under-development. According to the Ahwaz Human Rights Organization, in its submission for the February 2010 Universal Periodic Review (UPR) of the UN Human Rights Council, the province is rich, and produces 90 per cent of Iran's oil, but one-third of its population lives in abject poverty. They have little access to sanitation, proper housing, and no regular access to clean water or electricity. Access to employment is also limited, and Arabs suffer discrimination in language rights, which impacts on their access to media and other sources of news and information, and to cultural activities. The Ahwaz Human Rights Organization reported that, 'due to discrimination, almost all Ahwazi women living in rural areas are illiterate', and states that 'while the illiteracy rate is about 10–18 per cent in Iran, it is over 50 per cent among Arab men in Khuzestan, and even higher for Ahwazi women'.

For Kurds in Iran, the situation is similar, with the added component of ongoing violent clashes between Kurdish factions and the state. In its recent Iran briefing paper *Seeking Justice and an End to Neglect: Iran's Minorities Today*, MRG reported that in August 2010 the mother of Behmen Mesudi set herself on fire in front of Orumiyeh Prison after her son was tortured and then beaten to death by a prison guard.

Sistan-Balochistan

Sistan-Balochistan, where many Baloch live, is one of Iran's most impoverished provinces, where according to MRG's recent briefing on minorities in Iran, 'human rights have been violated in a way unseen in other parts of the country'. Over decades this has resulted in disproportionate poverty rates, low standards of living, and linguistic and cultural repression. The armed pro-Balochi group Jondallah has engaged in the execution of non-Balochis and government officials, and taken part or expressed support for suicide bombings. This has resulted in an increased militarization of the province and a rise in extra-judicial killings of Balochis by the state.

This cycle of violence looked set to continue past year-end when a suicide attack occurred at the Imam Hussein mosque in Chabahar, in south-eastern Iran. The bombing took place during the Shi'a holy day, Ashura, when worshippers mark the death of the Prophet Muhammad's grandson Hussein. An estimated 39 people were killed. According to the UK's *Guardian* newspaper and other media, Jondallah claimed responsibility. At the end of 2010, 11 Baloch prisoners were reportedly executed for alleged membership of Jondallah following the attack, however all had been imprisoned before the attack took place.

Iraq

Around 3 per cent of Iraq's population is made up of Christians including Armenian, Assyrian, Chaldean and Syriac minorities. Religious and other ethnic minorities include Bahá'ís, Bedouin, Black-Iraqis, Circassians, Kaka'is, Palestinians, Roma, Sabean Mandaeans, Shabaks and Yezidis. There are just eight remaining members of the Jewish community. Sunni Muslim Turkmen are the third largest ethnic group in Iraq, while the Kurdish community makes up 15–20 per cent of the population.

Exact numbers of minorities remaining in Iraq are very difficult to establish due to ongoing displacement, internal migration and violence. In 2010, religious and ethnic minority communities continued to suffer targeted killings and abductions, the destruction of their places of worship, homes and businesses, and, according to the USCIRF 2010, insufficient government protection. A national census that was scheduled to take place in October was postponed for the third time since

1987, re-scheduled for 5 December and then postponed indefinitely. The ongoing dispute over territories in northern Iraq, including the oil-rich city of Kirkuk, that affects Kurds, Arabs, Christians, Turkmen, Yezidis and other vulnerable minorities, is at the centre of this delay.

Political representation

The rising tension in this volatile northern region was also at the heart of disputes over Iraq's electoral law, which was debated in October 2009, delaying the country's parliamentary election, which was scheduled to take place in January 2010. The amended law, which attempts to reach a compromise on how the vote should be conducted in the disputed territory, was passed in November 2009. The new law increases minority representation to eight seats, with Christians allocated five seats, Shabaks and Yezidis one each, and Mandaeans electing their first ever parliamentary representative – Khalid Ahmed Roumi. However, minority representatives criticized the scope of the amended law. The Mandaean seat is restricted to the Baghdad governorate, meaning only those who live in the city, or have proof of residency, can vote for the Mandaean candidate. This does not reflect the fact that Mandaeans have also traditionally lived in Basra and Kirkuk, but have since 2003 been displaced all over the country. Many have fled abroad. Mandaean community representatives in Jordan said that the electoral law should recognize them as one national constituency (as is the case with Iraqi Christians) so they could vote for their chosen candidate, regardless of their governorate of origin. According to the *Jordan Times*, a case was brought before an Iraqi federal court by the Mandaean Council to challenge the amendment in early February.

Yezidi leaders meanwhile pointed out that, given the size of the Yezidi population (estimated at between 300,00 and 400,000, according to MRG sources) and the constitutional provision that there should be one seat for every 100,000 people, the community should have been granted a higher number of seats. Black Iraqis, who number around 2 million according to community estimates, also raised objections. Speaking to Al-Jazeera news in January 2010, activist Tahir Yahya said, 'We want to be like the Christians and Mandaeans and other white minorities who have fixed representation in

parliament – we the black people in Iraq have rights.'

In addition to quotas based on ethnicity, the Iraqi Constitution also holds that parliament should include a 25 per cent quota of female candidates (82 representatives). To ensure this, each party and coalition list must have 25 per cent female candidates.

Elections finally took place on 7 March 2010. However, due to investigations into allegations of fraud and wrangling between parties, it took until November for a power-sharing agreement to be announced, and for Nouri al-Maliki to be reappointed as prime minister. The Council of Ministers includes two Christian ministers (human rights, and industry and minerals), but only one of the 38 ministers is female (Minister Without Portfolio Bushra Hussain Salih)

Attacks on Christian minorities

During this 10-month political vacuum, a period that also saw the end of US combat operations in Iraq, violence against minorities continued. The UK's *Guardian* newspaper called 2010, 'the worst year since 2003 for Iraq's Christians', stating that more Christians fled in 2010 than any other year since the US-led invasion began. In the second week of February, ten Christians were killed in Mosul, in five separate incidents. The USCIRF 2010 reported

Above: A woman from the Sabean Mandaean minority in Iraq. *Ali Abbas/EPA.*

that this caused 43,000 Christians to flee the city for villages in the Nineveh plains, the Kurdistan Regional Governorates and Syria. Christian news websites reported that four people had been arrested for the crimes in early March.

On 31 October, the Christian community suffered its worst atrocity since the conflict began in 2003. According to international media reports, five suicide bombers passed through police and military checkpoints, and attacked the Our Lady of Salvation Syriac Catholic cathedral in Baghdad. The attack took place during a Sunday evening service when about 100 worshippers were at the church. Gunmen held siege to the church for four hours, and witnesses reported hearing explosions and shooting. One hostage reported that worshippers were beaten by the militants. The BBC said many of the worshippers were women. Many were injured, while 56 Christians including two priests were killed, along with 12 others. The al-Qaeda linked group, the Islamic State of Iraq, claimed responsibility for the attack.

International and national political and religious leaders, including Pope Benedict XVI and Grand

Ayatollah Sistani, Iraq's highest Shi'a cleric, condemned the attacks. But in November the group continued to terrorize the minority community, detonating 11 roadside bombs in three Christian areas of Baghdad. Five people were killed. Finally, on 31 December, international media reported that two people were killed and eight injured in bomb and grenade attacks on Christian homes across Baghdad, by militants linked to al-Qaeda.

Numerous Christian and Yezidi businesses, particularly those thought to be selling alcohol, were targeted and attacked during the year. Mandaeans, who are traditionally goldsmiths, reported that their shops continued to be targeted with threats and bombings.

Minority women

Women from minority communities have increasingly reported that they wear Islamic *hijab* for security reasons when they are in public. The IRFR 2010 stated that, regardless of religious affiliation, women and girls are often threatened for wearing 'Western-style clothing, or for failing to adhere sufficiently to strict interpretations of conservative Islamic norms governing public behavior'. According to the report, women from the Mandaean community have told of being 'pressured' from outside to marry outside their faith, which is forbidden according to Mandaean religious practices. (For more information, see special report, below.)

Northern Iraq

Tension in northern Iraq continued to affect minorities. Article 140 of the Iraqi Constitution calls for a referendum to determine whether citizens of territories across parts of five governorates from the Syrian border to the Iranian border east of Baghdad wish to formally join the autonomous Kurdistan region. As a result, Christians, Shabaks, Yezidis and other minority groups living in the region have been subject to pressure from different political groupings seeking to force minorities to identify as either Arab or Kurd, or pledge support for a particular political party. This pressure includes intimidation, arbitrary arrests, political disenfranchisement and the threat of blocking access to employment and resources. Minorities have also reported property being confiscated with no compensation by Kurdish Peshmerga forces.

Targeted and random killings also occurred across the year in the region. In January 2010, Christians and Shabaks were injured in a bomb explosion in the town of Bartellah in Nineveh. Another car bomb was also exploded in Mosul on 10 January, and a Shabak man was shot on the same day. From January to March, MRG reported that more than 13 Christians were killed, with many describing the attacks as an attempt to drive minorities from the region ahead of the elections. Louis Sako, Archbishop of Kirkuk, described the attacks in Mosul as 'ugly and organized'.

The USCIRF 2010 reported that in February, the Iraqi government said it had established an investigative committee into the attacks. The governor of Nineveh ordered increased security and called for an international investigation, the report said, but by the end of 2010, no perpetrators were known to have been arrested or charged. Also in February 2010, church leaders established the Council of Christian Church Leaders of Iraq in an attempt to promote religious acceptance, strengthen their community and engage in dialogue with the state and other religious leaders.

Iraq's Bahá'ís continue to suffer repression, as the faith remains prohibited by Law 105 of 1970. Notwithstanding the provisions of the Iraqi Constitution which allow for freedom of religion, the IRFR 2010 points out that no court challenges have been brought to have Law 105 invalidated, and no legislation has been proposed to repeal it.

Forced returns of rejected Iraqi asylum seekers are occurring despite repeated calls from NGOs and UNHCR not to return people, particularly minorities, who are from high-risk governorates including Baghdad, Kirkuk and Nineveh. UNHCR stated that internal flight was not an option, given access and residency restrictions in other governorates as well as hardship faced by returnees. In 2010, forced returns of rejected asylum seekers including Christians, Shabak and Yezidis took place from the Netherlands, Norway, Sweden and the UK. In December, Sweden forcibly returned around 20 Iraqis, including five Christians from Baghdad. UNHCR condemned the action and expressed its concern at the message forced returns from third countries give to Middle Eastern countries hosting Iraqi refugees. Following a December 2010 seminar in Stockholm, involving NGO representatives including MRG, members of the

Violence against women from Iraqi minorities is rife, but remains poorly addressed

According to NGOs reporting to the UN Human Rights Council Universal Periodic Review (UPR) on Iraq in 2010, women from minorities are 'the most vulnerable section of Iraqi society'. Their minority status and gender identity put them at particular risk in a female population that is already experiencing great trauma.

Violence against women in Iraq has been an increasing problem since the conflict began in 2003. Figures released by the UN Assistance Mission in Iraq (UNAMI) as part of a 2010 campaign against gender-based violence highlighted the scale of the issue. One in five women (21 per cent) in Iraq aged 15–49 has suffered physical violence at the hands of her husband; 14 per cent of women who suffered physical violence were pregnant at the time; 33 per cent have suffered emotional violence; and 83 per cent have been subjected to controlling behaviour by their husbands. The problem is compounded by the sense of shame attached to being exposed to such acts, and the corresponding reluctance to report against family members for fear of reprisals. Where crimes are reported, they are poorly handled by police, medical and judicial authorities, UNAMI said.

Women in Iraq also fear abduction and rape.

Men from all sides of the conflict, including Iraqi and US-led coalition troops and members of security forces, have been responsible for such crimes. MRG has reported that women, including those from minorities, who survive these ordeals can find themselves ostracized from their families and communities; some are punished or killed by their own relatives; and others are pressured to commit suicide by burning themselves.

There are also reports of women from minority groups being forced into marriage outside their faith communities. Minorities including Sabean Mandaeans and Yezidis prohibit marriage outside their religion, and women who do so must renounce their faith. Caught in a politically sensitive situation in the disputed territory in northern Iraq, Yezidi activists have reported that since 2003, there have been around 30 known cases of Yezidi women being abducted and forced to marry members of the Kurdish security force Asayish. In correspondence with the author, a Yezidi activist reported that Yezidi families are threatened with reprisals if women and girls refuse marriage with militia members.

Evidence from the Iraqi Minorities Organization (IMO), an umbrella group that includes members from a range of minorities, confirms that minority women are subject to both domestic and politically -motivated violence. IMO also describes the levels of fear minority women face in their daily lives, and the measures they take to protect themselves; measures which are to the detriment of their religious and cultural identities. For example, in an unstable and increasingly conservative Islamic environment, non-Muslim women feel forced to wear the *hijab* in public to avoid being identified and targeted by extremists. They also refrain from wearing traditional accessories and make-up in public places in certain parts of the country. Christian women in Kirkuk and Mosul reported feeling extremely insecure outside their homes.

Iraq has ratified the UN Convention on the

Elimination of All Forms of Discrimination Against Women (CEDAW). It is also a signatory to the 1993 Declaration on the Elimination of Violence against Women.

However, access to justice for such crimes is a particular problem for women from minorities, as it is for women and minorities in Iraq in general.

The Iraqi Constitution mandates that women are equal to men. However, certain constitutional provisions and other pieces of legislation discriminate against women.

Article 41 of the Constitution allows an individual the right to choose what personal status rules they want to follow based on their 'religions, sects, beliefs, or choices', a provision which potentially forces women to submit to discriminatory personal status codes. According to a 2010 report by the US-based think tank, Freedom House, 'Article 41 is currently suspended after women's advocates, NGOs, members of parliament, legal professionals, and the judiciary protested against the provision, viewing it as a way to increase sectarian divisions and impose undue restrictions on women'. In practice, according to minority activists, disputes relating to marriage and the family are settled inside the family and community itself, rather than being taken to the police or the courts.

Moreover, despite Article 29 of the Constitution, which prohibits violence in the family, schools and in society, under the Iraqi Penal Code a husband is legally entitled to punish his wife 'within certain limits prescribed by law or custom'. The NGO Social Watch has highlighted other provisions in the Penal Code that compound and institutionalize violence against women. Under the code, rape is a private offence; therefore the state cannot take any action without the consent of the complainant or a legal guardian. Article 398 holds that the perpetrator can be excused of

rape and sexual assault if he marries the victim. In the absence of any provision to the contrary, this applies even in cases where the victim is a minor. Sentences for kidnapping and abduction can also be avoided through marriage.

The conditions faced by women, and the particular vulnerability of women from minorities, make it extremely difficult for them to leave the house, access employment and education, or take part in any kind of recreation in public including sports, activists have reported. Access to employment in particular is a pressing concern, given that, in 2009, the Office for the Coordination of Humanitarian Affairs (OCHA) reported that 1 in 10 Iraqi households are headed by women, more than 80 per cent of whom are widows. According to the BBC, this is around one million women, although it is not known how many of these are from minority groups.

Campaigners have highlighted the need to educate women about their rights in order to stem their increasing vulnerability. UNAMI has noted that many women have little or no knowledge about the (limited) options that are available to them. The US Embassy, through its Provincial Reconstruction Team (PRT) in Nineveh, has supported a series of six seminars on minority women's legal rights across the region, attended by 150 participants from communities including Christians, Shabak, Turkmen and Yezidis.

According to UNAMI, the Iraqi authorities are also taking steps towards addressing the situation. A domestic violence bill is being developed at national level and in the Kurdistan Regional Government (KRG) controlled area, while special units in both areas have been established to develop a national database of cases of violence against women. Whatever measures are in place, it is vital that the specific threats facing women from minority communities do not go ignored. ■

Right: A Bedouin family in the unrecognised village of Al Zarnock in the Negev desert, Israel. *Karen Robinson/Panos.*

Swedish parliament and Migration Board officials, the Swedish government instructed the Migration Board to take more care in analysing the claims of asylum seekers from Iraq's religious minorities.

Israel and the Occupied Palestinian Territory (OPT)

Israel

Palestinian Arab citizens make up around 20 per cent of the Israeli population (around 1.2 million people) and include members of three religious communities. MRG has reported that 81 per cent are Muslim, 10 per cent are Christian and 9 per cent are Druze. In 2010, Israeli Arabs continued to experience deeply ingrained institutional discrimination, restricting their political and religious activity, their access to resources and their rights to employment, education and property ownership. A December 2010 report by Adalah, an NGO and legal centre for Arab minority rights in Israel, highlights the multiple forms of discrimination faced by groups such as women and disabled members of the Arab community. It states that the employment rate among Arab women citizens of Israel is around 20 per cent, among the lowest in the world.

Israeli Arab women's lack of participation in the workforce is often ascribed to attitudes they face in their own communities. But this approach was disputed by education expert Fadia Nasser-Abu

Ahija, who became the first Israeli Arab woman in the country to be appointed to a full professorship, taking up her post at Tel Aviv University in March 2010. Professor Nasser-Abu Ahjia told Israel's daily newspaper, *Haaretz* that, 'Arab families are changing – and attributing more importance to educating their girls.' She also pointed out that schools in Arab areas suffer from a serious lack of government investment.

Elsewhere, it has been argued that the obstacles to women's participation are primarily the result of the discriminatory policies of successive governments, rather than family or social attitudes. These include discrimination in hiring policies in the civil service and private companies, and a lack of industrial zones and factories located in Arab areas compared with majority Jewish ones. Israeli Arab women are also affected by a dearth of public transport in their areas, a lack of suitable training courses at national and local levels, and a shortage of state-supported childcare services, compared to those available for Jewish communities. According to a large-scale survey on Arab women's employment in Israel, conducted by scholar and activist Yousef Jabareen, 78 per cent of non-working women said their employment status was due to a lack of job opportunities, and 56 per cent of non-working women said they wanted to work immediately. His survey also found that there were slightly more Arab women at university in Israel than Arab men, but that this did not translate into employment opportunities.

Though Israel's Knesset has highly progressive laws on anti-discrimination and legal protection for women and disabled persons, such legislation does not cover discrimination against the Arab minority on the basis of ethnicity. In fact, the state itself is the largest employer of women in the country, but only 3 per cent of all female state employees are Arab women, according to Hanin Zuabi, Israel's first Arab woman MP to be elected as representative of an Arab party. Because of lack of legislation, women and disabled people from these communities cannot fully access the protection that should be available to them, Adalah noted.

Outside of the Arab community in Israel, this legislated discrimination seems to be widely accepted. A poll released in November 2010 by the independent Israeli Democracy Institute found that only 51 per cent of Jewish citizens of Israel support full equality in rights between Jewish and Arab citizens of Israel, while a March poll by Maagar Mochot, a private Israeli research institute, found that 49.5 per cent of Jewish 15–18-year-olds feel the same, according to *Haaretz*.

The right-wing government elected in 2009 continued to propose legislation to further marginalize the Israeli Arab minority. For example, in October 2010 the government approved an amendment to its Citizenship Law which, if passed, will require all new non-Jewish citizens to pledge allegiance to Israel as a 'Jewish and democratic State'. According to Adalah and other research bodies, the bill was formulated to target Palestinians married to Israelis who may be seeking citizenship. The *Guardian* newspaper noted that it will particularly affect Palestinians from the West Bank who marry Arab citizens of Israel, although in practice since the start of the second intifada there is actually very little possibility for Arab citizens of Israel married to Palestinians from the West Bank or Gaza to provide citizenship or residency rights to their spouses through marriage. Israeli Prime Minister Binyamin Netanyahu subsequently amended that the proposal so that it would apply to all new citizens. However, this did not address the concerns of Palestinians who

face having to take the oath.

In December, a religious ruling signed by a number of Israel's municipal chief rabbis banned the renting and selling of homes to non-Jews, Amnesty International reported. A letter of October 2010, also signed by rabbis, called for action to be taken against Jews renting or selling homes to Israeli Arabs.

Arab Bedouin communities are particularly affected by government actions concerning land tenure and development. In its 2009 report to the CEDAW committee, Israel stated that Bedouin in the Naqab number at least 170,000 people. They have suffered repeated evictions and state appropriation of their ancestral land. According to Adalah's 2010 report on inequality amongst the Palestinian Arab minority in Israel, 'between 75,000 and 90,000 Arab Bedouin in the Naqab live in around 40 unrecognized Arab villages throughout the Naqab, referred to by the state as "illegal clusters".' These villages are extremely precarious living environments, with few basic services. They have little, or no electricity or running water and are cut off from communication; people living in these villages are viewed by the state as 'trespassers'.

On 27 July, the 250 residents of Al-Araqib were woken in the middle of the night by police and given two minutes to leave their homes. Adalah reported that 1,300 police officers began to demolish the town while residents struggled to save their belongings. All the houses were razed to the ground. Attempts to rebuild the village have resulted in the same destruction each time. Amnesty International reported the eighth destruction of the now makeshift village on 23 December 2010.

The West Bank
Aside from the Muslim Palestinian majority, the people of the West Bank include Bedouin, Jews (primarily Israeli settlers), Christian Palestinians and around 400 Samaritans. According to the international news agency Reuters, around 17,000 Catholics live in the West Bank. The number has shrunk as people have left in search of a better quality of life, members of the community have reported. The OCHA has noted that a large proportion (40 per cent in 2007) of land in the West Bank is occupied by Israeli settlements, military bases and tightly controlled areas including nature reserves and roads that are prohibited to Palestinians. An Israeli-controlled separation barrier of around 420 miles exists along and within the

West Bank, limiting the movement of Palestinians into Israel, separating villages from their own land, trapping thousands in closed enclaves and stunting the development of the Palestinian community inside the West Bank.

The occupied West Bank is divided into three administrative areas: A, B and C. Area A is under the control and administration of the Palestinian Authority, while Area B is controlled by Israel but administered by the Palestinian Authority. Area C makes up 62 per cent of the West Bank and is under full Israeli military and planning control. Around 150,000 Palestinians live in this area, alongside approximately 500,000 Israeli settlers. Other minority groups include Bedouin who number around 250,000 people in Area C and 40,000 in the whole of the West Bank.

In 2010, the non-Jewish communities in Area C continued to suffer the demolition of what the Israeli authorities term 'unrecognized' or 'illegal clusters', that is, their homes and villages. In January, the UN Relief and Works Agency for Palestine Refugees in the Near East (UNRWA) reported that the Israeli Defence Forces (IDF) demolished Bedouin homes and part of a school, leaving 50 people homeless. Thirty children were sitting down to complete an exam, and witnessed the partial destruction of their school, the report said.

Palestinians in Area C also faced ongoing devastation of their livelihoods and destruction of their homes. UNRWA reported that in 2010, the military destroyed more than 349 Palestinian structures. Almost 485 Palestinians, half of them children, were left homeless. The number is a 'significant increase' on demolitions in 2009, when around 191 structures were demolished, UNRWA stated. Palestinians also face a number of complex legislative restrictions to their economic, social and cultural rights that keep them in extreme poverty, in stark comparison to their Israeli neighbours.

The United Nations Commission on the Status of Women expressed particular concern in 2010 on the extreme situation faced by Palestinian women in the Occupied Palestinian Territory (OPT), resulting from the impact of the Israeli occupation, the continued construction of Israeli settlements and of the West Bank separation barrier, and the restrictions on movement of people and goods that the community faces. The commission's report noted that this affects their 'right to health care, including access for pregnant women to health services for antenatal care and safe delivery, education, employment, development and freedom of movement', and has led to an increase in 'incidents of domestic violence, and declining health, education and living standards, including the rising incidence of trauma and decline in their psychological well-being'.

Gaza Strip

The Gaza Strip is currently governed by Hamas, and is subject to a blockade and harsh sanctions imposed by Israel, termed 'collective punishment' and in violation of international law by the UN. The area is home to a small minority of Christians (around 3,500), who have suffered sporadic violence and persecution not necessarily at the hands of the state, but from what one priest described to the UK's *Guardian* newspaper as 'vigilante justice'. MRG has noted that over the last decade, the area has become subject to increasing religious radicalization. Many Christians have fled the area's political tensions in the last decade. In 2010, around 500 members of the community were allowed by Israel to cross the blockade and visit Bethlehem for Christmas. In some cases, not all members of a family were issued permits, *The Guardian* reported.

Jordan

Parliamentary elections were meant to follow swiftly after King Abdullah II dissolved Parliament just half way through its four-year term in late 2009, but the polls were delayed by the drafting of a new electoral law. Passed in May 2010, the law is not uncontroversial. Critics note that it increases seats in less populated rural areas that are mostly home to Bedouin and tribes loyal to the king, while decreasing representation in Jordan's urban centres, which are dominated by its large Palestinian refugee community.

The controversy resulted in a boycott of the election by the country's main opposition group, the Islamic Action Front. Notwithstanding this, elections were held in November 2010, with pro-loyalist and tribal-linked candidates filling the majority of the 120 seats. Twelve of these are reserved for women, nine for Christians and three for Circassians, an ethnic group who number between 20,000 and 80,000 people in Jordan.

UNRWA has around 1.9 million Palestinians registered as refugees, and operates 10 long-established refugee camps across Jordan. While most Palestinians in the country are granted full citizenship, around 132,000 refugees from the Gaza Strip are provided only with temporary Jordanian passports and thus have limited access to citizenship rights, including employment, health and education. UNRWA names them among Jordan's 'most vulnerable' people, stating that rates of illiteracy are high, and they suffer from extreme poverty.

Religious minorities in Jordan include Christians, and small numbers of Bahá'ís, Druze and Shi'a Muslims. The IRFR 2010 states that Muslim–Christian relations are generally good, but followers of unrecognized religions and Muslims who convert to other religions face 'societal discrimination and the threat of mental and physical abuse'. The report notes that Bahá'ís in particular face ongoing official discrimination. On official ID cards, their religion can be registered with a dash, a blank space or as Muslim. According to the report, this has implications for the validity of marriages. Since Jordan applies Sharia law, a woman registered as Muslim cannot marry a non-Muslim man. Furthermore, children of non-Muslim fathers and Bahá'í mothers registered inaccurately as Muslim are considered illegitimate under Islamic law, and are not issued birth certificates. Without these documents, they cannot receive citizenship or register for school, the report said.

While the government of Jordan estimates that around 450,000–500,000 Iraqis live in Jordan, only around 31,000 were registered with the UNHCR at the end of July 2010. The IRFR 2010 states that around 61 per cent of Iraqi refugees in Jordan are Sunni Muslim, 25 percent Shi'a Muslim, 11 per cent Christian, and 3 per cent belong to other religious groups, including Sabean Mandaeans. Following the October 2010 attack on Our Lady of Salvation Syriac Catholic Church in Baghdad (see Iraq section), the UNHCR office in Jordan reported an increase of Iraqi Christians registering with them in the second half of 2010.

The IRFR 2010 said that Iraqi Sabean Mandaeans in Jordan continue to report 'extreme societal discrimination and pressure to convert to Islam in the form of harassment and physical threats'. As a result, they find it difficult to attend schools and perform religious rites in Jordan, though the police have provided limited protection for them to perform baptism rituals.

Lebanon

As sectarian tensions continued to increase in Lebanon, for the country's religious and ethnic minorities several key events have marked the year.

An estimated 100–150 Jews live in Lebanon and, in 2010, long-awaited work to rebuild Beirut's Maghen Abraham synagogue (destroyed by shelling in 1982) finally began to bear visible results. Ongoing hostilities between Hezbollah and Israel have contributed to the exodus of Lebanon's Jewish communities, and plans to rebuild the place of worship have been delayed for years. But donations including from Christian and Muslim communities both in Beirut and worldwide have contributed to realizing the project. Work was scheduled to be completed in October 2010, and the synagogue is due to begin conducting services in 2011.

According to UNRWA around 422,000 Palestinian refugees are registered in Lebanon, (around 10 per cent of the population), around half of whom live in 12 recognized refugee camps. The community has been present in Lebanon for over 60 years. They have historically been denied citizenship rights, including access to all but menial employment, thus condemning them to generations of poverty. In August 2010, a new law was finally passed allowing Palestinians to work legally. Though this is a welcome step forward, it does not go far enough. While work permit fees have been waived and workers can now claim cover for work-related accidents, the UK's *Guardian* newspaper reported that a Lebanese employer must still demonstrate to the Ministry of Labour that a Lebanese national cannot perform the job before hiring a Palestinian. Palestinians are still prohibited from accessing more than thirty professions, including medicine, engineering and the law, and they are still unable to access state education and medical facilities, the BBC reported. Proposals to allow Palestinians to buy property were met with 'fierce opposition', according to media reports, and it remains to be seen whether the law will have any real effect. Access for Palestinians to universities and vocational training centres is restricted, with quotas for admitting foreigners under particular courses of study. Palestinian refugees are not entitled to

social security benefits such as family allowance and maternity leave. Around 95 per cent are not covered by health insurance and rely heavily on UNRWA for health services.

In November 2010, Lebanon came under the UN Human Rights Council UPR. The government dismissed recommendations that would promote equality for women, allow Palestinians the right to own property and protect migrants from abuse, HRW reported. Lebanon's personal status law holds that Lebanese women cannot pass citizenship to their spouses or children, and the country's UN delegation rejected recommendations that this be amended. Amnesty International highlighted that this means the children of Lebanese women married to foreign nationals – including Palestinians – are not considered Lebanese citizens and cannot obtain citizenship, and are denied access to free state education. A court case challenging the law was upheld in 2009, based on constitutional provisions on gender equality for all citizens. But the Lebanese Civil Chamber Court of Appeal overturned the decision in April 2010.

Saudi Arabia

Saudi Arabia is a majority Sunni Muslim country. The state's official interpretation of Islam is derived from the teachings of an eighteenth century

Sunni religious scholar, Ibn Abd' Al-Wahhab, and is otherwise known as Wahhabism, a strict interpretation of Islam. The country is a hereditary monarchy, and the kingdom controls more than a fifth of the world's crude oil reserves. King Abdullah wields considerable diplomatic muscle in the Middle East and has been instrumental in peace-building efforts in various countries. But the health of the 86-year-old king remained precarious in 2010, and questions over the succession, which are of international and regional importance, remained rife at the time of writing.

Saudi Arabia's Shi'a minority, who make up about 15 per cent of the country's population, remain subject to systematic discrimination in education, employment and political representation. This includes Shi'a children being taught by Sunni teachers that they are unbelievers. Shi'a are banned from teaching religion and serving as general judges, or taking senior military or security positions, according to a 2010 HRW report, while female Shi'a teachers are prohibited from holding senior positions in schools.

Human rights activists advocating religious equality in Saudi Arabia are subject to ongoing arbitrary arrests and detention without charge. They also experience difficulties expressing views against the establishment. In June 2010, police arrested

Mikhlif al-Shammari, a Sunni journalist and campaigner, who wrote articles criticizing anti-Shi'a statements by clerics. As of the end of the year, he was still in detention.

Shi'as are permitted to mark the religious festival Ashura, which commemorates the death of the Prophet Muhammad's grandson, Hussein. But attacks by militants mean that, for the past few years, the day has been marked by bloodshed. In December 2010, Associated Press reported that extremists attacked the Ashura procession in Medina.

According to the IRFR 2010, the country's Human Rights Commission launched a four-year human rights awareness campaign in January 2010. The Commission worked with the Ministry of Education and provided materials and training to police, security forces, and the Commission for the Promotion of Virtue and Prevention of Vice (CPVPV), Saudi Arabia's 'religious police,' on protecting human rights. The Human Rights Commission, whose mandate is to promote tolerance and awareness, includes no Shi'a or women among its 24 members.

About 10 million people (which is around half the country's population) are expatriates. As well as Muslims, they include Christians, Hindus, Sikhs. These communities are only allowed to practise their religions in private.

Saudia Arabia's prohibitive laws restricting women's rights, including a father's legal right to keep adult daughters captive for 'disobedience', also impact on women from these communities. In May 2010, HRW reported on the plight of a Canadian woman of Indian origin who travelled to Saudi Arabia to visit her father, an Indian citizen who works there. For the last three years her father has refused to let her leave. This is a position supported by Saudi Arabia's 'guardianship' system, which allows a male relative or guardian all rights over women's major decisions, such as leaving the country, attending university, marriage and having certain surgical procedures. Foreign Muslim women are also subject to harassment from the CPVPV for not observing strict Wahhabi dress codes, particularly the wearing of headscarves.

Syria

In the decade since President Bashar al-Assad came to power, Syria's minorities have continued to suffer repression. The country's ethnic Kurdish minority (around 10–15 per cent of the population) has been particularly affected.

The 1962 census stripped around 120,000 Kurds of citizenship, amid state allegations that they had entered the country, settled and registered illegally. HRW and other NGOs have called these allegations false. It is estimated that there are around 300,000 stateless Kurds living in Syria today.

Between August and September, the UN Human Rights Council conducted its first ever mission to the country. Olivier De Schutter, UN Special Rapporteur on the right to food, reported that Kurds continue to be denied Syrian citizenship, and therefore cannot access publicly subsidized food, cannot travel abroad, and cannot access employment and education in the public sector. Many live in the eastern part of the country, and have experienced severe drought and increasing poverty since 2005, his report said. De Schutter called the situation 'unacceptable' and called on the government to grant Kurds nationality so they may access their full economic, social and cultural rights.

In March, a boy was killed and dozens were injured when Syrian police opened fire on a Kurdish New Year celebration, Amnesty Inyernational said. Around 5,000 Kurds had gathered to celebrate Nawrouz, the Kurdish New Year. Some had brought banners protesting the imprisonment in Turkey of Abdullah Öcalan, leader of the Kurdistan Workers' Party (PKK).

A majority Sunni Muslim country, Syria is home to religious minorities including Alawites (a sect of Shi'a Islam), Ismailis and Shi'a, who make up around 13 per cent of the population. Christians form around 10 per cent, and around 3 per cent of the population is Druze. There is a small settled community of Yezidis (around 100,000 people), but the state does not recognize them as belonging to a faith that is distinct from Islam, according to the IRFR 2010. There is also a small population of between 100 and 200 Jews, who are treated with suspicion by the state. They must have government permission to travel, and they are subject to extra state scrutiny and are excluded from employment in the civil service and armed forces.

Though the Constitution provides for freedom of religion, the IRFR 2010 notes that the government continues to impose restrictions on this right, and that Jehovah's Witnesses remained banned and suffer discrimination in accessing employment as a result. The report also notes that though there is no formal legislation forbidding proselytizing in Syria, those who are considered to be doing so risk arrest and detention that can last from five years to life. In May 2010, one American citizen and two Swedish citizens were detained and eventually deported for distributing Bibles in Aleppo.

Under the Constitution, Muslim women in Syria are forbidden to marry Christian men, and Muslim converts to other religions are still regarded by the state as subject to Sharia law. Christian women, who are permitted to marry Muslim men, cannot be buried in Muslim cemeteries unless they convert to Islam. Changes to the law that would have resulted in further discrimination against women were successfully stymied in 2009.

Refugees

Syria is host to a large refugee population including around 500,000 Palestinians, people from Somalia, Sudan, Iran and Afghanistan, and hundreds of thousands of Iraqis. In August 2010, there were 5,102 recognized refugees (not including Iraqis), and 1,103 asylum seekers. Iraqis numbered a total of 151,907.

Iraqi refugees have no legal status within the country, and are considered to be 'guests'. Though they can access basic services such as education and health care, the sheer numbers of refugees have strained Syria's infrastructure and economy, and employment is difficult to access. Many face increasing poverty. Child labour and child sex tourism have been identified as growing problems, and economic imperatives are placing Iraqi refugee women at increasing risk of forced prostitution, kidnapping and sex trafficking, the US State Department Trafficking in Persons Report 2010 noted. Many young girls have been forced by their families to work in nightclubs or forced into *muta'a* marriages, in which the girl's family receives a dowry and the 'marriage' ends at a specified time (effectively prostitution). Refugee families have reportedly abandoned children through economic need, leaving them vulnerable to trafficking and exploitation, the State Department said. In August 2010, UNHCR classified around 8,965 Iraqi women refugees as 'women at risk', a category that can include a number of vulnerabilities. UNHCR has also identified several hundred Iraqi women refugees as survivors of sexual

or gender-based violence.

The Iraqi refugee community includes religious minorities such as Iraqi Christians, several thousand Sabean Mandaeans and Yezidis, all fleeing targeted persecution in Iraq. In Syria, Mandaeans are able to perform religious rituals and ceremonies, including marriage and baptism, that they cannot currently risk in Iraq.

According to UNHCR, around 433 Iraqi Palestinians were living at Al Hol camp in north-east Syria in October 2010. This included a number of people from Al Tanf camp in the desert border between Iraq and Syria, which was closed in February 2010. Iraqi Palestinians were protected under Saddam Hussein's regime but became particularly vulnerable following the US-led invasion in 2003. The UN reported in late 2010 that there is little hope for resettlement in sight for these people, and that they have started living in the camp 'with a sense of permanence'. They have access to basic education, health and recreation services, and women are receiving some vocational training, although this functions as a means of passing time, rather than as a source of income generation.

Western Sahara

Informal talks between the Moroccan government and the Polisario Front (the independence movement of Western Sahara) continued in early 2010 in New York, following an April 2009 UN Security Council Resolution urging the parties to engage in this way. The two sides have been involved in a decades-long dispute over the region, with the Moroccan position being that the Saharawi people should accept autonomy under Moroccan sovereignty. The Polisario Front backs the UN decision calling for a referendum on self-determination, which includes independence as an option. The February 2010 talks ended in impasse.

Before another round of talks began in November, violent clashes occurred when Moroccan security forces attempted to break up a protest camp in the disputed territory. According to the BBC and other media, at least five people were killed, and fighting spread from the camp to the streets of Laayoune, the capital of the territory. Witnesses told the BBC that security forces used 'helicopters and water cannon' to force people to leave. The Gadaym Izik camp held around 12,000 people and was erected in September/October 2010 in protest against Moroccan rule and Saharawis' living conditions. In a November report, HRW said authorities repeatedly beat and abused those they detained after the camp-closing incident, and that civilians had also been attacked.

Thousands of Saharawis also live in refugee camps in Tindouf province, Algeria. Some have been there since the start of the dispute over 35 years ago. The camps are controlled by the exiled government of the self-proclaimed Saharawi Arab Democratic Republic (SADR) which is based in one of the camps. It is estimated that around 150,000 plus people live in the camps, and rely on aid from Algeria and international agencies. A 2010 UN Children's Fund (UNICEF) report states that women and children make up 80 per cent of the camps' population. Because of lack of fresh food, anaemia affects around 1 in 10 women there. NGO reports from the camps have highlighted the entrepreneurial spirit of the women in the camps, who are in charge of the day-to-day running of the camps, and have prioritized education. Many have started micro-businesses despite the harsh conditions they face.

Many in the camps were separated from their families by the conflict in Western Sahara, and have not seen them for many years. UN-facilitated flights seeking to unite people were temporarily put on hold in March 2010 and resumed in early September. But in mid-September, passengers on a flight from Western Sahara were prevented from disembarking by the Polisario Front when the plane landed in Tindouf.

When the November talks between the two sides closed, the UN Special Envoy to the region Christopher Ross said that although both parties continued to reject each others' proposals, they had agreed to meet in December and again in early 2011. One positive outcome was that both sides agreed to resume family visits by air and to speed up visits by road, it was reported.

Despite this progress, HRW, Amnesty International and other NGOs continue to highlight the detention and abuse of Saharawi activists by Moroccan authorities. Women activists have reported being detained and subjected to beatings and torture. In December 2009, when leading Saharawi human rights activist Aminatou Haidar was permitted to return to her home in Western Sahara after a month long hunger-strike in Spain, she was placed under house arrest. She remains under constant surveillance.

Yemen

Although three-quarters of Yemen's income is derived from oil revenues, the World Bank has projected that these will run out by 2017. Sana'a is the world's fastest growing capital city, but it is predicted that the city will run out of water by 2015. Its population is expected to double by 2035. Today, almost half of Yemeni children suffer from malnutrition.

Yemen's problems are made worse by a long-running civil conflict that has displaced over 250,000 people. The armed group al-Houthi claim years of discrimination by the government against the Shi'a community in the north, while the government believes the group wants to establish an autonomous region there. Following armed clashes in 2009 and 2010, a tentative ceasefire was agreed in February 2010, but according to the IRFR 2010, low-level fighting was ongoing in April. According to UNICEF, women and children make up about 70 per cent of those affected by the conflict in the north, where access to basic services including water, nutrition, sanitation, health and education is becoming increasingly limited.

The country has a Jewish population estimated at 370, a number that has dwindled from about 60,000 over the last half century. This tiny minority has continued to face persecution, and were targeted by the al-Houthi movement during the 2009–10 clashes. The UK's *Independent* newspaper reported in April 2010 that, following rising 'hate attacks, murders and forced conversions', Yemeni authorities were in negotiations with the UK to resettle around 20 or 30 Yemeni Jews in Britain. The US had evacuated some 100 Yemeni Jews in 2009.

In 2009, a court ruled that a Muslim man accused of murdering a Jewish man because he refused to convert should pay the family 'blood money'. Following an appeal by the Jewish family, the Yemeni Supreme Court ruled that the perpetrator should be executed by firing squad in July 2010. The case stoked fear amongst the Yemeni Jewish community, according Agence France Press.

Women in Yemen face extreme discrimination, according to a Freedom House report released in June 2010. The US-based research NGO noted that women in some areas continue to be subject to female genital mutilation (FGM), and that the Penal Code gives lenient sentences to those convicted of 'honour crimes'. Muslim women are not permitted to marry outside Islam. Muslim men

are allowed to marry Christians and Jewish women, but not those of any other faith, or women who have renounced Islam.

Yemen is home to around 200,000 Akhdam people, who are the country's largest and poorest minority group. Although Arabic-speaking Muslims, Akhdam are considered servants by mainstream Yemeni society. They suffer deeply ingrained discrimination akin to the caste-based marginalization suffered by India's Dalits. Their situation is harder to address when there is no formal caste system that can be targeted through, say, legislation. Many live in extreme slum conditions with no access to running water, sewerage or electricity. Traditionally, they have been forced to find employment as waste collectors; today they find precarious employment as street cleaners, sanitation workers and rubbish collectors. As such they are viewed as tainted, and some members of the community believe this attitude has become internalized among Akhdam people.

A 2010 report by the US-based Duhur news agency stated that, 'death rates from preventable disease [for Akhdam] are even worse than the nationwide average in Yemen, where overall infant mortality is already an appalling one in nine, and maternal mortality is one in 10'. When they do attend school, children from this community are put to work and experience discrimination and bullying because of the darkness of their skin and

their poverty. Women from this community are also subject to gender-based violence from mainstream society and from the men of their own community, who force them into sex work, according to NGO reports. They have little access to justice because of their marginalized status. Reportedly many are murdered after suffering rape, according to the Yemeni Observatory for Human Rights. Experts have warned that this violence may increase as the security situation in Yemen becomes increasingly volatile.

There were around 171,000 registered refugees in Yemen in late 2009, according to UNHCR. These included people fleeing deadly conflict in Somalia and Ethiopia. According to online news agency Global Post, around 43,000 African refugees and migrants crossed the sea between the Horn of Africa to Yemen between January and October 2010. Rough seas and ill-equipped vessels mean many die at sea. When they reach Yemen, many live in Kharaz refugee camp, an unstable collection of buildings housing around 17,000 Somalis. Women from these communities are often the most vulnerable, having suffered sexual violence, and having been forced to pay smugglers to escape persecution. Once they arrive, they are at further risk of trafficking and sexual exploitation. ∎

Reference

Peoples under Threat 2011

Mark Lattimer

Introduction

The popular uprisings that swept the Arab world in early 2011 have been compared by some commentators to the fall of the Berlin Wall. In an exhilarating push for democratic change, long-term rulers have been ousted and others challenged seriously for the first time. But despite what has been achieved, many voices from the region have urged caution: even in those countries which have seen the greatest changes, the internal security apparatus and other structures of repression have remained largely intact and the struggle for real constitutional reform continues.

Quite apart from the question of the likely outcome of attempted reform is the separate, albeit related, question of the human cost of challenging the established order. Video footage of armed police and in some cases tanks confronting unarmed protestors has graphically demonstrated the dangers attending the 'Arab Spring'. Yet the risks to civilian life, and levels of actual violence, vary widely across the region. The ability of a state to undergo political change without violence is widely considered a hallmark of a mature democracy

(although the record shows that democracies, even very old ones, are hardly immune from violent conflict). Which combination of circumstances, then, makes the onset of mass killing more likely and which conditions lower the risk of a state, even an autocratic one, descending to bloody violence?

It is to help answer such questions that Minority Rights Group International has developed the Peoples under Threat index. Since 2005 Peoples under Threat has pioneered the use of statistical analysis to identify situations around the world where communities are most at risk of mass killing. On numerous occasions since the index was first developed, countries that have risen sharply up the table have later proved to be the scene of mass human rights violations.

Risk factors for mass killing

The Peoples under Threat index is created from a basket of ten indicators, all known antecedents to mass violence. These include indicators of good governance, rule of law, prevailing conflict, international trade risk, and previous experience of genocide or political mass killing. They reflect the fact that communities are more at risk in closed states with poor governance, prone to conflict and with a record of previous killing.

Separate research by MRG has shown that in some three quarters of recent conflicts, much of the killing has been targeted by ethnicity or religion.

Major risers since 2010

Rank	Rise in rank since 2010	Country	Group	Total
3	1	Afghanistan	Hazara, Pashtun, Tajiks, Uzbeks, Turkmen, Baluchis	21.77
10	9	Côte d'Ivoire	Northern Mande (Dioula), Senoufo, Bete and Guéré, newly-settled groups	17.63
15	5	Yemen	Zaydi Shia, 'Akhdam'	15.89
20	3	Nepal	Madheshis (Terai), Dalits, linguistic minorities	14.09
21	3	Uganda	Acholi, Karamojong, Basongora, Batwa	13.81
25	4	Guinea	Fulani (Peul), Malinke	13.48
36	19	Kyrgyzstan	Uzbeks, Russians	12.21
46	10	North Korea	Political/social targets, religious minorities	11.54
50	New entry	Kosovo	Serbs, Roma/Ashkali/Egyptians, Bosniaks, Turks, Gorani	11.40
64	New entry	Libya	'Black' Libyans, migrant workers, political/ social targets, Berbers	10.51

Leading studies concur, however, that the degree of ethnic diversity in a state is not itself positively correlated with risk of conflict. This apparent paradox resolves when we note that risks rise sharply when socio-political divisions in society fall on ethnic or religious lines. Ethnicity and religion have also proved powerful mobilising factors once conflict begins, and are typically reflected in patterns of human displacement. Peoples under Threat thus also includes indicators of group division. Many – although not all – of the specific communities listed as under threat will be minorities, whose smaller numbers and relative degree of marginalization will increase their vulnerability. More information on the methodology of Peoples under Threat is given below.

Among those states that have risen significantly in the table since last year are two from the Arab world, Yemen and Libya. The threat level in Yemen has now risen sharply every year for the last five years, as the population faces at least four separate patterns of political violence: the renewed conflict with al-Houthi rebels in the north of the country; a separate campaign by the Southern Movement which has taken control of four districts in Shabwa; bombing and violent clashes in Abyan between government forces and Al Qaeda in the Arabian Peninsula; and finally, popular demonstrations against the government in Sana'a, Aden, Taiz and other major cities which have met with violent repression leading to over 80 deaths. The greatest humanitarian toll has to date been suffered by the Zaydi Shi'a population in the north where some 300,000 people have been displaced, many repeatedly, but as the state begins to fracture other communities are also at risk, including the 'Akhdam', a group who are historically marginalized in Yemen and live without tribal protection.

The situation in Libya has dominated news headlines around the world as US- and NATO-led forces have carried out aerial bombing in support of UN Security Council Resolution 1973 which mandated a no-fly zone and other measures to protect civilians and civilian-populated areas under threat of attack. Civilian deaths have increased since the start of international military action, particularly in Misrata and towns on the central coast as troops loyal to Colonel Gaddafi have launched fierce attempts to regain control. There were also casualties in the mainly Berber town of Zuwara, west of

Tripoli, which was retaken by the government in mid-March, and at least 500 Berbers have fled Libya to Tunisia. Since the early days of the Libyan uprising there have also been reports of organized racist attacks on so-called 'Black' Libyans and foreign workers, particularly in rebel-held areas. Officials of the UN High Commissioner for Refugees related that refugees arriving from eastern Libya at the Egyptian border reported that armed Libyans had been going from door to door, forcing sub-Saharan Africans to leave. Tens of thousands of refugees arriving at camps in both Tunisia and Egypt have said they were accused of being mercenaries hired by the government, and told of racist killings and beatings. In all, some 500,000 people have fled the country, a large proportion of them foreign workers. Libya has a long history of discrimination against its large population of sub-Saharan migrants, including racially-motivated killings, previously earning the censure of the UN Committee on the Elimination of Racial Discrimination.

Other Arab states also occupy relatively high positions in the Peoples under Threat index, including Syria which rose in the table this year and which has a history of violent repression of both Kurds and Palestinians.

The most notable riser in the table this year, however, is Côte d'Ivoire, which jumped nine places to enter the top ten. Following disputed Presidential elections in November, the incumbent President Laurent Gbagbo refused to cede power, despite international calls for him to resign. The conflict that ensued saw the onset of mass killings driven by ethnic factors that have divided the country for the last decade. By the end of March 2011 (the make-up date for Peoples under Threat) over 1,000 people had been killed, included hundreds of Guéré civilians in the western town of Duékoué. Even with the departure of Gbagbo and the installation of President Alessane Ouattara, the risk of further killing remains high, with over one million internally displaced, and armed militias on both sides threatening revenge attacks. A recent mission for the UN High Commissioner for Human Rights found evidence of extra-judicial killings, enforced disappearances, torture and sexual violence in the capital Abidjan and the rest of the country. The UN Security Council has called on President Ouattara to form an 'all-inclusive, broad-based government', and to implement his promise to investigate human rights violations and initiate a justice and reconciliation process, but the level of cooperation across the north-south divide is poor and inter-community trust largely absent.

The dangers of transition

Recent events in both Côte d'Ivoire and in the Arab world underline that political transitions – even from authoritarianism towards democracy – carry inherent dangers. For those spearheading protest or revolution, the most immediate danger may come in the form of violent repression from a threatened regime. But in many situations, minorities have the most to fear from political instability itself, or from the negative side of popular movements. This was perhaps most tragically demonstrated in recent history by the series of ethno-nationalist conflicts that were sparked by the fall of the former Eastern Bloc, and a number of the situations that figure prominently in Peoples under Threat this year are still marked by that legacy.

In Kyrgyzstan, following the overthrow of President Bakiyev in April 2010, MRG warned that political tension could take on an ethnic character and called on the interim government to prevent an escalation of violence against minorities. Unfortunately in June widespread rioting broke out in the southern cities of Osh and Jalalabad. Although both Kyrgyz and Uzbeks were involved in the violence, Uzbeks were disproportionately affected, with 'groups of ethnic Kyrgyz attack[ing] ethnic Uzbeks in a systematic manner, killing, looting and burning, sometimes provoking counter attacks', in the words of the OSCE High Commissioner on National Minorities. Some 500 people were killed, mostly Uzbeks, and 2,000 buildings destroyed. An official inquiry into the events released in January pinned much of the blame for starting the violence on local Uzbek politicians, reflecting the reluctance of the Kyrgyz authorities to accept responsibility for their failure to protect the Uzbek community during the June events, itself a dangerous precedent.

Figures are included on Kosovo, as a separate entity from Serbia, for the first time this year, and it has jumped into the table at number 50. With Kosovo's unilateral declaration of independence in 2009, the Kosovo Serbs became at a stroke Europe's newest minority. In practice the community, heavily concentrated north of the River Ibar, became highly segregated after 1999 when Kosovo became an international protectorate, with separate systems for education, healthcare and policing. The community still looks to neighbouring Serbia for security. Serbs living elsewhere fear a repeat of the anti-Serb violence of March 2004, when over 4,000 were displaced. Complaints of lack of effective protection and forced assimilation are also voiced by smaller minorities, including Bosniaks, Turks, Gorani, Roma, Ashkali and Egyptians.

However, Kosovo is not the highest placed part of the former Yugoslavia in the table; that unwelcome distinction falls to Bosnia and Herzegovina which remains stuck at number 28 after a difficult year in which attempts at constitutional reform to improve minority participation were blocked and political deadlock worsened further. A year ago Bosnia's senior politicians and representatives of the international community agreed that despite the country's political problems, a return to inter-ethnic violence was impossible; now, some are not so sure.

Accomplishing successful political transition is always partly about managing popular expectations and in Nepal a series of stalemates in the constitutional reform process is turning high expectations into rising frustration. After the end of the war in late 2006, prospects for the country improved but Nepal has remained relatively high in the Peoples under Threat table, and rose again this year. Entrenched discrimination against Dalits, marginalization of the Janajati and unaddressed grievances of Madhesis in the Terai are all factors contributing to deep divisions in Nepalese society.

Two other states that have risen in the table this year, Uganda and North Korea, could hardly be more different, but both have long-term, ageing rulers facing the prospect of inevitable transition. North Korea is the most closed society in the world, but everything we know about it indicates that the calculus of mass repression is highly systematic. In Uganda, which saw mass ethnic killing before the coming into power of the National Resistance Movement, human rights violations and communal tensions have both risen again in the last years of Museveni's Presidency. In both states, the exact form that transition will take is hard to predict, but it is a dangerous time.

Where the killing is ongoing

Peoples under Threat is designed to identify at the earliest possible stage those situations where communities are at risk of future killing, but the sad reality is that in many of those states at the top of the list the killing is ongoing. Somalia, Sudan, Afghanistan, Iraq, Burma, the Democratic Republic of Congo, and Nigeria have remained over time at the head of the list, joined in recent years by Pakistan and Ethiopia.

This year Somalia marks 20 years without an effective government, since the fall of Siad Barre in 1991. The situation deteriorated once again during 2010, with heavy fighting in Mogadishu. Clashes in Somaliland, generally considered the most peaceful part of the country, displaced more than 3,000 people in Sool, Sanang and Cayn this February. In November a new report from MRG detailed the appalling situation of the country's minorities: Bantu, Benadiri and the 'caste' groups which together are estimated to constitute up to a third of the population. The traditional clan structure of Somali society excludes minorities from any but the most low-status employment, denies them proper education and meaningful

political participation, and prevents inter-marriage with members of majority clans. Outside the clan protection system, minorities live a precarious existence where they can be attacked or dispossessed with impunity. However, as the situation in Mogadishu demonstrates, it is not just the minority communities who are at risk: the ongoing conflict has repeatedly fractured society on clan lines, and inter-clan rivalry has touched every region of the country.

Afghanistan tops the list of major risers in the table this year, rising to number three. Civilian deaths have climbed every year for the past five years, totalling nearly 3,000 in 2010 according to the UN Assistance Mission in Afghanistan. Over 75 per cent of these the UN attributes to anti-government forces, including the Taliban, while government forces, NATO and the US were together responsible for 440 civilian killings, nearly half in aerial bombing. The continued weakness of the central government, internal disunity and systemic corruption contribute to the poor prognosis, as does the fact that the Taliban now appear able to carry out complex, coordinated attacks in the capital. Any further escalation of

Peoples most under threat – highest rated countries 2011

Rank	Country	Group	Total
1	Somalia	Minorities incl. Bantu, Benadiri and 'caste' groups (Gabooye etc.); clan members at risk in fighting incl. Hawiye, Darod, etc.	23.66
2	Sudan	Fur, Zaghawa, Massalit and others in Darfur; Dinka, Nuer and others in the South; Nuba, Beja	21.89
3	Afghanistan	Hazara, Pashtun, Tajiks, Uzbeks, Turkmen, Baluchis	21.77
4	Iraq	Shia, Sunnis, Kurds, Turkmen, Christians, Mandaeans, Yezidis, Shabak, Faili Kurds, Bahá'is, Palestinians	21.31
5	Burma/Myanmar	Kachin, Karenni, Karen, Mons, Rakhine, Rohingyas, Shan, Chin (Zomis), Wa	20.99
6	Pakistan	Ahmadiyya, Baluchis, Hindus, Mohhajirs, Pashtun, Sindhis, other religious minorities	20.70
7	Dem. Rep. of the Congo	Hema and Lendu, Hutu, Luba, Lunda, Tutsi/Banyamulenge, Batwa/Bambuti, other groups	19.67
8	Ethiopia	Anuak, Afars, Oromo, Somalis, smaller minorities	19.37
9	Nigeria	Ibo, Ijaw, Ogoni, Yoruba, Hausa (Muslims) and Christians in the North	18.26
10	Côte d'Ivoire	Northern Mande (Dioula), Senoufo, Bete and Guéré, newly-settled groups	17.63

the conflict or major re-alignment of power in Kabul carries the risk of large-scale bloodshed in a country still split between the Pashtun-dominated south, heartland of the Taliban, and the largely Tajik-Uzbek strongholds of the former Northern Alliance.

Sudan rose in the table last year in advance of a nationwide referendum on the future of South Sudan. The vote went ahead in January, resulting in a strong mandate for secession, but the region has been scarred by inter-communal violence and clashes between militia groups and the Sudan People's Liberation Army (SPLA) of the southern government. Over 100 people have been killed and 20,000 displaced in the disputed territory of Abyei, where a separate referendum on whether to join the north or south of Sudan was prevented by failure to agree the ground rules. In a situation with uncomfortable echoes of the continuing violence in Sudan's Darfur region, Misseriya pastoralists in Abyei are confronting Ngok-Dinka communities, while the Sudan Armed Forces (SAF) and the SPLA have both sent deployments. In a joint statement in March, the UN Special Advisers on the Prevention of Genocide and the Responsibility to Protect warned that 'Given the perception that the SAF supports the Missireya Arabs and the SPLA supports the Ngok-Dinka, a standoff between the two armies is very dangerous... [and] could easily trigger further ethnic-based violence in Abyei.' ∎

How is *Peoples under Threat* calculated?

Since the genocide in Rwanda in 1994, our ability to identify those situations most likely to lead to genocide or mass killing has improved. A number of comparative studies of the factors preceding historic episodes of political mass killing had been undertaken since the 1970s, including by Helen Fein and Ted Robert Gurr, but it was not until the 1990s that researchers such as Rudolf Rummel and Matthew Krain pioneered quantitative longitudinal analysis of a wide range of such factors, enabling the testing of different causal hypotheses. Rummel, for example, showed the very strong relationship between concentration of government power and state mass murder; Krain demonstrated the correlation between existing armed conflict or political instability and the onset and severity of mass killing.

Following the early work of the Clinton administration's policy initiative on genocide early warning and prevention, Professor Barbara Harff, a senior consultant with the US State Failure Task Force, constructed and tested models of the antecedents of genocide and political mass murder and her results were published in 2003 ('Assessing Risks of Genocide and Political Mass Murder since 1955', *American Political Science Review* 97, February 2003). Her optimal model identifies six preconditions that make it possible to distinguish, with 74 per cent accuracy, between internal wars and regime collapses in the period 1955 – 1997 that did, and those that did not, lead to genocide and political mass murder (politicide). The six preconditions are: political upheaval; previous genocides or politicides; exclusionary ideology of the ruling elite; autocratic nature of the regime; minority character of the ruling elite; and low trade openness.

MRG has drawn on these research findings to construct the *Peoples under Threat* table, although responsibility for the final table is exclusively our own. *Peoples under Threat* is specifically designed to identify the risk of genocide, mass killing or other systematic violent repression, unlike most other early warning tools, which focus on violent conflict as such. Its primary application is civilian protection.

Indicators of conflict are included in the table's construction, however, as most, although not all, episodes of mass ethnic or religious killing occur during armed conflicts. War provides the state of emergency, domestic mobilization and justification, international cover, and in some cases the military and logistic capacity, that enable massacres to be carried out. Some massacres, however, occur in peacetime, or may accompany armed conflict from its inception, presenting a problem to risk models that focus exclusively on current conflicts. In addition, severe and even violent repression of minorities may occur for years before the onset of armed conflict provides the catalyst for larger scale killing.

The statistical indicators used all relate to the state. The state is the basic unit of enquiry, rather than particular ethnic or religious groups at risk, as governments or militias connected to the government are responsible for most cases of genocidal violence. Formally, the state will reserve to itself the monopoly over the means of violence, so that where non-state actors are responsible for widespread or continued killing, it usually occurs with either the complicity of the state or in a 'failed state' situation where the rule of law has disintegrated. Certain characteristics at the level of the state will greatly increase the likelihood of atrocity, including habituation to illegal violence among the armed forces or police, prevailing impunity for human rights violations, official tolerance or encouragement of hate speech against particular groups, and in extreme cases, prior experience of mass killing. Egregious episodes of mass killing targeted principally at one group have also seen other groups deliberately decimated or destroyed.

However, some groups may experience higher levels of discrimination and be at greater risk than others in any given state. MRG has identified those groups in each state which we believe to be under most threat. (This does not mean that other groups or indeed the general population may not also be at some risk.) It should be noted that although these groups are most often minorities, in some cases ethnic or religious majorities will also be at risk and in relevant cases

are therefore also listed in the table. In some cases, all the groups in the country are at risk of ethnic or sectarian killing.

One indicator that has been tested and discarded by a number of studies is the general level of ethnic or cultural diversity in a society. Krain did not find any correlation between 'ethnic fractionalization' and the onset of genocide or political mass killing. Similarly, neither of the patterns of ethnic diversity tested by Harff had any effect on the likelihood of mass killing (although she did find the minority character of the ruling elite to be significant). These findings are supported by research on the relationship between diversity and conflict.

The overall measure is based on a basket of ten indicators. These include indicators of democracy or good governance from the World Bank, conflict indicators from the Center for Systemic Peace and other leading global conflict research institutes, indicators of group division or elite factionalization from the Fund for Peace and the Carnegie Endowment for International Peace, the State Failure Task Force data on prior genocides and politicides, and the country credit risk classification published by the Organization for Economic Cooperation and Development (as a proxy for trade openness). For citations and further information, see the notes to the table. For a fuller discussion of the methodology, see *State of the World's Minorities 2006*.

Based on current indicators from authoritative sources, *Peoples under Threat* seeks to identify those groups or peoples most under threat in 2011. ∎

Right: Two Uighur women living in Norway protest in front of the Chinese Embassy in Oslo. *Fredrik Naumann/Panos.*

Country	Group	A. Self-determination conflicts	B. Major armed conflict	C. Prior genocide/politicide

Table 1
Peoples under Threat 2011

Country	Group	A. Self-determination conflicts	B. Major armed conflict	C. Prior genocide/politicide
Somalia	Minorities incl. Bantu, Benadiri and 'caste' groups (Gabooye etc.); clan members at risk in fighting incl. Hawiye, Darod, etc.	4	2	1
Sudan	Fur, Zaghawa, Massalit and others in Darfur; Dinka, Nuer and others in the South; Nuba, Beja	5	2	1
Afghanistan	Hazara, Pashtun, Tajiks, Uzbeks, Turkmen, Baluchis	4	2	1
Iraq	Shia, Sunnis, Kurds, Turkmen, Christians, Mandaeans, Yezidis, Shabak, Faili Kurds, Baha'is, Palestinians	5	2	1
Burma/ Myanmar	Kachin, Karenni, Karen, Mons, Rakhine, Rohingyas, Shan, Chin (Zomis), Wa	5	2	1
Pakistan	Ahmadiyya, Baluchis, Hindus, Mohhajirs, Pashtun, Sindhis, other religious minorities	5	2	1
Dem. Rep. of the Congo	Hema and Lendu, Hutu, Luba, Lunda, Tutsi/Banyamulenge, Batwa/Bambuti, other groups	2	2	1
Ethiopia	Anuak, Afars, Oromo, Somalis, smaller minorities	5	2	1
Nigeria	Ibo, Ijaw, Ogoni, Yoruba, Hausa (Muslims) and Christians in the North	5	2	1
Côte d'Ivoire	Northern Mande (Dioula), Senoufo, Bete and Guéré, newly-settled groups	5	2	0
Israel/OPT	Palestinians in Gaza/West Bank, Israeli Palestinians	5	2	0
Zimbabwe	Ndebele, Europeans, political/social targets	2	0	1
Chad	Black African' groups, Arabs, Southerners	3	1	0
Iran	Arabs, Azeris, Baha'is, Baluchis, Kurds, Turkomen	5	0	1
Yemen	Zaydi Shia, 'Akhdam'	0	2	0
Central African Republic	Kaba (Sara), Mboum, Mbororo, Aka	0	2	0
Sri Lanka	Tamils, Muslims	4	1	1
Philippines	Indigenous peoples, Moros (Muslims), Chinese	5	2	1
Russian Federation	Chechens, Ingush and others in North Caucasus; indigenous northern peoples, Roma, Jews	5	2	1
Nepal	Madheshis (Terai), Dalits, linguistic minorities	2	1	0
Uganda	Acholi, Karamojong, Basongora, Batwa	1	1	1
Burundi	Hutu, Tutsi, Batwa	0	0	1
Angola	Bakongo, Cabindans, Ovimbundu, Pastoralists, San and Kwisi	4	0	1

Indicators of group division			Democracy/governance indicators				Total
D. Massive movement – refugees and IDPs	E. Legacy of vengeance – group grievance	F. Rise of factionalized elites	G. Voice and accountability	H. Political stability	I. Rule of law	J. OECD country risk classification	
10	9.7	10	-1.99	-3.31	-2.53	7	23.66
9.8	9.9	9.9	-1.59	-2.65	-1.34	7	21.89
9.2	9.7	9.4	-1.39	-2.75	-2.04	7	21.77
8.7	9.3	9.6	-1.17	-2.33	-1.83	7	21.31
8.3	8.7	8.2	-2.17	-1.72	-1.52	7	20.99
8.9	9.4	9.5	-1.00	-2.76	-0.93	7	20.70
9.6	8.6	8.9	-1.45	-2.13	-1.70	7	19.67
7.8	8.6	9.0	-1.26	-1.73	-0.77	7	19.37
5.8	9.5	9.4	-0.85	-1.95	-1.22	5	18.26
8	8.9	8.5	-1.16	-1.53	-1.33	7	17.63
7.8	9.5	8.2	-1.01	-1.98	-0.37	8	17.61
8.6	8.8	9.5	-1.55	-1.44	-1.91	7	16.76
9.5	9.8	9.8	-1.40	-1.75	-1.53	7	16.66
8.3	8.1	9.5	-1.49	-1.52	-0.90	6	16.48
8.3	8.2	9.2	-1.27	-2.31	-1.150	7	15.89
9.3	8.9	9.1	-0.98	-2.03	-1.32	7	15.76
9.4	9.6	9.4	-0.50	-1.33	-0.07	6	15.63
6.7	7.6	8.0	-0.12	-1.42	-0.53	4	15.29
5.4	7.1	7.6	-0.95	-0.72	-0.77	3	14.67
7	9.2	8.5	-0.58	-1.81	-0.96	7	14.09
8.9	8.5	8.6	-0.49	-1.06	-0.43	6	13.81
8.4	7.8	7.9	-0.73	-1.42	-1.20	7	13.74
6.9	5.9	6.8	-1.14	-0.24	-1.19	6	13.59

Table 1
Peoples under Threat 2011

Country	Group	A. Self-determination conflicts	B. Major armed conflict	C. Prior genocide/politicide
Lebanon	Druze, Maronite Christians, Palestinians, Shia, Sunnis	2	1	0
Guinea	Fulani (Peul), Malinke	0	0	0
Equatorial Guinea	Bubi, Annobon Islanders	2	0	1
Georgia	Adzhars, Abkhazians, South Ossetians	5	1	0
Bosnia and Herzegovina	Croats, Bosniac Muslims, Serbs, Roma	3	0	1
Colombia	Political/social targets, Afro-descendants, indigenous peoples	3	2	0
Syria	Kurds, Palestinians	0	0	1
Algeria	Berbers, Saharawi	2	1	1
Laos	Hmong, other highland peoples	4	0	0
Rwanda	Hutu, Tutsi, Batwa	0	0	1
Indonesia	Acehnese, Chinese, Dayaks, Madurese, Papuans	4	1	1
Thailand	Chinese, Malay-Muslims, Northern Hill Tribes	5	2	0
Kyrgyzstan	Uzbeks, Russians	1	1	0
Eritrea	Afars, Saho, Tigre, religious minorities	0	0	0
Kenya	Borana, Kalenjin, Kikuyu, Luyha, Luo, Muslims, Turkana, Endorois, Masai, Ogiek, other indigenous groups	0	1	0
Niger	Djerema-songhai, Hausa, Tuaregs	3	0	0
Turkey	Kurds, Alevis, Roma, Armenians and other Christians	5	2	0
Haiti	Political/social targets	0	1	0
Bangladesh	Ahmadiyya, Hindus, other religious minorities; Chittagong Hill Tribes	3	0	0
Uzbekistan	Tajiks, Islamic political groups, religious minorities, Karakalpaks, Russians	1	0	0
China	Tibetans, Uyghurs, Mongols, Hui, religious minorities	5	0	1
Cambodia	Cham, Vietnamese, indigenous hill tribes (Khmer Leou)	0	0	1
North Korea	Political/social targets, religious minorities	0	0	0
Azerbaijan	Armenians	4	0	0
Tajikistan	Uzbeks, Russians	0	0	0
Venezuela	Indigenous peoples, Afro-descendants	0	0	0
Kosovo	Serbs, Roma/Ashkali/Egyptians, Bosniaks, Turks, Gorani	4	0	0
Cameroon	Westerners	2	0	0
Serbia	Bosniaks, Ethnic Albanians, Croats, Roma	2	0	1

Indicators of group division			Democracy/governance indicators				Total
D. Massive movement – refugees and IDPs	E. Legacy of vengeance – group grievance	F. Rise of factionalized elites	G. Voice and accountability	H. Political stability	I. Rule of law	J. OECD country risk classification	
8.9	9.0	8.8	-0.33	-1.51	-0.64	7	13.56
7.5	8.2	9.3	-1.43	-1.90	-1.61	7	13.48
2.3	6.8	8.4	-1.82	-0.02	-1.27	7	13.40
7.8	8.4	9.1	-0.18	-0.99	-0.17	6	13.06
7.1	8.7	9.2	-0.05	-0.57	-0.39	7	13.05
9	7.2	8.0	-0.21	-1.67	-0.44	4	12.85
8.9	8.3	7.8	-1.63	-0.68	-0.47	6	12.70
6.5	8.2	6.8	-1.04	-1.20	-0.73	3	12.68
5.9	6.8	8.5	-1.71	0.00	-0.94	7	12.56
7	8.5	8.0	-1.29	-0.33	-0.51	7	12.42
6.5	6.3	7.1	-0.05	-0.64	-0.56	4	12.32
6.7	7.8	8.0	-0.40	-1.11	-0.13	3	12.27
5.2	7.4	7.4	-0.96	-0.50	-1.29	7	12.21
7.2	6.1	7.9	-2.16	-0.80	-1.24	7	12.11
8.7	8.9	8.7	-0.32	-1.30	-1.07	6	12.07
6.5	8.0	7.6	-0.70	-1.17	-0.64	7	12.07
6.3	8.0	7.8	-0.12	-0.88	0.12	4	12.06
5.6	7.3	8.4	-0.60	-0.87	-1.34	7	11.99
6.7	8.9	8.9	-0.37	-1.55	-0.72	6	11.97
5.1	7.4	9.0	-1.93	-0.91	-1.22	6	11.89
6.6	8.0	7.2	-1.65	-0.44	-0.35	2	11.82
5.3	6.9	7.7	-0.88	-0.63	-1.05	6	11.63
5.6	7.2	7.8	-2.24	-0.24	-1.25	7	11.54
8.1	7.9	7.9	-1.20	-0.39	-0.81	5	11.51
6.2	6.9	8.4	-1.33	-1.00	-1.22	7	11.51
5.1	6.8	7.5	-0.79	-1.41	-1.59	7	11.40
6.9	7.8	8.0	-0.08	-0.68	-0.48	7	11.40
7.6	7.5	8.7	-1.03	-0.41	-1.07	6	11.23
6.9	7.8	8.0	0.32	-0.50	-0.41	6	11.12

Table 1
Peoples under Threat 2011

Country	Group	A. Self-determination conflicts	B. Major armed conflict	C. Prior genocide/politicide
Mauritania	Haratins ('Black Moors'), Kewri	0	0	0
Djibouti	Afars	3	0	0
Ecuador	Afro-descendants, Indigenous peoples	2	0	0
Timor Leste	'Westerners', 'Easterners', Muslims, Chinese	0	0	0
Moldova	Trans-Dniester Slavs	4	0	0
Vietnam	Montagnards (Degar), other highland peoples, religious minorities	2	0	1
Nicaragua	Indigenous peoples, Creoles	3	0	0
India	Assamese, Bodos, Nagas, Tripuras, other Adivasis; Kashmiris, Sikhs, Muslims, Dalits	5	2	0
Guinea Bissau	Balanta,Fula (Fulani), Manjaco (Manjack or Mandyako), Mandinga (Mandinka), Papel (Pepel), Ejamat (Felupe), Jola (Diola), Susu , Cape Verdeans	0	0	0
Liberia	Dan, Krahn, Ma, other groups	0	0	0
Congo (Rep.)	Lari, M'Boshi, Aka	0	0	0
Libya	Black' Libyans, migrant workers, political/social targets, Berbers	0	2	0
Guatemala	Indigenous peoples, Garifuna	0	0	1
Bolivia	Indigenous Highland, Indigenous Lowland, Afro-Bolivians	2	0	0
Armenia	Armenians, Yezidi Kurds, Russians, Assyrians, Kurds, Ukrainians, Greeks	4	0	0
Turkmenistan	Uzbeks, Russians, Kazakhs, religious minorities	0	0	0
Fiji	East Indians, Fijians	0	0	0
Togo	Ewe, Kabre	0	0	0

Notes to Table
Sources of the indicators are as follows:

- *Conflict indicators*: The base data used was Monty G Marshall, 'Major Episodes of Political Violence 1946-2010' (Center for Systemic Peace, 2010) and, for self-determination conflicts, Monty G Marshall and Ted R Gurr, 'Peace and Conflict 2005' (CIDCM, University of Maryland, 2005) updated for 2010 using figures from Center for Systemic Peace, MRG and the Heidelberg Institute for International Conflict Research.
Self-determination conflicts in 2010 were ranked on a scale of 0-5 as follows: 5=ongoing armed conflict; 4=contained armed conflict; 3=settled armed conflict; 2=militant politics; 1=conventional politics. Major armed conflicts were classified as 2=ongoing in late 2010; 1=emerging from conflict since 2006 or ongoing conflict with deaths under 1,000.
- *Prior genocide or politicide*: Harff, US Political Instability Task Force (formerly State Failure Task Force). 1=one or more episodes since 1945.

	Indicators of group division			Democracy/governance indicators				Total
	D. Massive movement – refugees and IDPs	E. Legacy of vengeance – group grievance	F. Rise of factionalized elites	G. Voice and accountability	H. Political stability	I. Rule of law	J. OECD country risk classification	
	6.4	8.0	7.9	-1.01	-1.17	-0.84	7	11.11
	6.8	5.9	7.1	-1.11	0.48	-0.65	8	11.08
	6.1	6.4	7.8	-0.26	-0.75	-1.28	7	11.05
	9.1	7.5	8.7	0.09	-0.48	-1.25	8	10.86
	4.3	6.9	8.0	-0.31	-0.50	-0.45	7	10.84
	5.2	5.3	7.0	-1.52	0.19	-0.43	5	10.80
	5	6.3	7	-0.49	-0.51	-0.83	7	10.76
	5.2	7.8	6.2	0.47	-1.19	0.05	3	10.75
	6.8	5.8	8.9	-0.76	-0.49	-1.38	7	10.59
	8.2	6.3	8.1	-0.32	-0.99	-1.09	7	10.54
	7.7	6.3	7.1	-1.04	-0.41	-1.19	7	10.53
	4.3	5.8	7.1	-1.89	0.62	-0.75	5	10.51
	5.6	6.8	6.3	-0.33	-0.73	-1.12	5	10.42
	4.7	7.7	8.3	-0.08	-0.82	-1.22	6	10.32
	6.9	6.0	7.0	-0.82	0.09	-0.40	6	10.20
	4.6	6.3	7.7	-2.06	0.18	-1.37	6	10.10
	4.2	7.4	8.2	-0.72	-0.22	-0.76	8	10.00
	6.2	5.6	7.6	-1.04	-0.21	-0.90	7	9.76

- *Indicators of Group Division*: Failed States Index, Fund for Peace and the Carnegie Endowment for International Peace, 2010
- *Democracy/Governance Indicators*: Annual Governance Indicators, World Bank, 2010
- *OECD country risk classification*: Organisation for Economic Cooperation and Development, 'Country Risk Classifications of the Participants to the Arrangement on Officially Supported Export Credits', January 2011. Where no classification is given, a value of 8 was accorded.

Indicators were rebased as necessary to give an equal weighting to the five categories above, with the exception of the prior geno-/politicide indicator. As a dichotomous variable this received a lesser weighting to avoid too great a distortion to the final ranking. Resulting values were then summed.

The full formula is:

$$(A/2) + (Bx1.25) + (Cx2) + (D+E+F)/6 + (G+H+I)/-1 + (Jx0.625)$$

Status of ratification of major international and regional instruments relevant to minority and indigenous rights

as of 1 February 2011

■ Ratification, accession or succession.

□ Signature not yet followed by ratification.

■▶ Ratification of ICERD and Declaration on Article 14.

■▷ Ratification of ICERD and Signature of Declaration on Article 14.

■● Ratification of ICCPR and Optional Protocol.

■○ Ratification of ICCPR and Signature of Optional Protocol.

□○ Signature of ICCPR and Optional Protocol.

	International Convention on the Prevention and Punishment of the Crime of Genocide 1948	International Convention on the Elimination of All Forms of Racial Discrimination 1965	International Covenant on Civil and Political Rights 1966	International Covenant on Economic, Social and Cultural Rights 1966
Africa				
Algeria	■	■▶	■●	■
Angola			■●	■
Benin		■	■●	■
Botswana		■	■	
Burkina Faso	■	■	■●	■
Burundi	■	■	■	■
Cameroon		■	■●	■
Cape Verde		■	■●	■
Central African Republic		■	■●	■
Chad		■	■●	■
Comoros	■	■	□	□
Congo		■	■●	■
Côte d'Ivoire	■	■	■●	■
Democratic Republic of the Congo	■	■	■	■
Djibouti		□	■●	■
Egypt	■	■	■	■
Equatorial Guinea		■	■●	■
Eritrea		■	■	■
Ethiopia	■	■	■	■
Gabon	■	■	■	■
Gambia	■	■	■●	■
Ghana	■	■	■●	■
Guinea	■	■	■●	■
Guinea Bissau		□	□	■
Kenya		■	■	■
Lesotho	■	■	■●	■
Liberia	■	■	■○	
Libyan Arab Jamahiriya	■	■	■●	■
Madagascar		■	■●	■
Malawi		■	■●	■
Mali	■	■	■●	■
Mauritania		■	■	■
Mauritius		■	■●	■
Morocco	■	■▶	■	■
Mozambique	■	■	■	
Namibia	■	■	■●	■
Niger		■	■●	■

Convention on the Elimination of All Forms of Discrimination against Women 1979	Convention on the Rights of the Child 1989	ILO 111 Discrimination (Employment and Occupation) Convention 1958	ILO 169 Convention Concerning Indigenous and Tribal Peoples in Independent Countries 1989	International Convention on the Protection of the Rights of All Migrant Workers and Members of Their Families 1990	ICC Rome Statute of the International Criminal Court 1998	African Charter on Human and Peoples' Rights 1981	African Charter on the Rights and Welfare of the Child 1990
■	■	■		■	□	■	■
■	■	■			□	■	■
■	■	■		□	■	■	■
■	■	■			■	■	■
■	■	■		■	■	■	■
■	■	■			■	■	■
■	■	■		□	□	■	■
■	■	■		■	□	■	■
■	■	■	■		■	■	□
■	■	■			■	■	■
■	■	■		□	■	■	■
■	■	■		□	■	■	■
■	■	■			□	■	■
■	■	■			■	■	□
■	■	■			■	■	□
■	■	■		■	□	■	■
■	■	■				■	■
■	■	■			□	■	■
■	■	■				■	■
■	■	■		□	■	■	■
■	■	■			■	■	■
■	■	■		■	■	■	■
■	■	■		□	□	■	■
■	■	■			■	■	■
■	■	■		■		■	■
■	■	■		□		■	■
■	■	■				■	■
■	■	■			■	■	■
■	■	■			■	■	■
■	■	■		■	■	■	■
■	■	■		■		■	■
■	■	■			■	■	■
■	■	■		■	□	■	■
■	■	■			□	■	■
■	■	■			■	■	■
■	■	■		■	■	■	■

Status of ratification of major international and regional instruments relevant to minority and indigenous rights

as of 1 February 2011

■ Ratification, accession or succession.

□ Signature not yet followed by ratification.

■▶ Ratification of ICERD and Declaration on Article 14.

■▷ Ratification of ICERD and Signature of Declaration on Article 14.

■● Ratification of ICCPR and Optional Protocol.

■○ Ratification of ICCPR and Signature of Optional Protocol.

□○ Signature of ICCPR and Optional Protocol.

	International Convention on the Prevention and Punishment of the Crime of Genocide 1948	International Convention on the Elimination of All Forms of Racial Discrimination 1965	International Covenant on Civil and Political Rights 1966	International Covenant on Economic, Social and Cultural Rights 1966
Nigeria	■	■	■	■
Rwanda	■	■	■	■
Sahrawi Arab Democratic Republic				
São Tomé and Príncipe		□	□○	□
Senegal	■	■▶	■●	■
Seychelles	■	■	■	■
Sierra Leone		■	■	■
Somalia		■	■	■
South Africa	■	■▶	■●	□
Sudan	■	■	■	■
Swaziland		■	■	■
Togo	■	■	■●	■
Tunisia	■	■	■	■
Uganda	■	■	■●	■
United Republic of Tanzania	■	■	■	■
Zambia		■	■●	■
Zimbabwe	■	■	■	■
Americas				
Antigua and Barbuda	■	■		
Argentina	■	■▶	■●	■
Bahamas	■	■	■●	■
Barbados	■	■	■●	■
Belize	■	■	■	□
Bolivia	■	■▶	■●	■
Brazil	■	■▶	■●	■
Canada	■	■	■●	■
Chile	■	■▶	■●	■
Colombia	■	■	■●	■
Costa Rica	■	■▶	■●	■
Cuba	■	■	□	□
Dominica			■	■

Convention on the Elimination of All Forms of Discrimination against Women 1979	Convention on the Rights of the Child 1989	ILO 111 Discrimination (Employment and Occupation) Convention 1958	ILO 169 Convention Concerning Indigenous and Tribal Peoples in Independent Countries 1989	International Convention on the Protection of the Rights of All Migrant Workers and Members of Their Families 1990	ICC Rome Statute of the International Criminal Court 1998	African Charter on Human and Peoples' Rights 1981	African Charter on the Rights and Welfare of the Child 1990
■	■	■		■	■	■	■
■	■	■		■		■	■
						■	□
■	■	■		□	□	■	□
■	■	■		■	■	■	■
■	■	■		■	■	■	■
■	■	■		□	■	■	■
	□	■				■	□
■	■	■			■	■	■
	■	■			□	■	■
■	■	■				■	□
■	■	■		□		■	■
■	■	■				■	□
■	■	■		■		■	■
■	■	■			■	■	■
■	■	■			■	■	■
■	■	■			□	■	■

Convention on the Elimination of All Forms of Discrimination against Women 1979	Convention on the Rights of the Child 1989	ILO 111 Discrimination (Employment and Occupation) Convention 1958	ILO 169 Convention Concerning Indigenous and Tribal Peoples in Independent Countries 1989	International Convention on the Protection of the Rights of All Migrant Workers and Members of Their Families 1990	ICC Rome Statute of the International Criminal Court 1998	American Convention on Human Rights 1969	Additional Protocol to the American Convention on Human Rights in the area of Economic, Social and Cultural Rights 1988
						*	
■	■	■			■		
■	■	■	■	■	■	■	■
					□		
■		■		■	■		
■	■	■		■	■		
■	■	■	■	■	■	■	■
■	■	■	■		■	■	■
					■		
■	■	■	■	■	■	■	□
■	■	■	■	■	■	■	■
■	■	■	■		■	■	■
■	■					■	
■	■	■	■		■	■	

Status of ratification of major international and regional instruments relevant to minority and indigenous rights

as of 1 February 2011

■ Ratification, accession or succession.

□ Signature not yet followed by ratification.

■▶ Ratification of ICERD and Declaration on Article 14.

■▷ Ratification of ICERD and Signature of Declaration on Article 14.

■● Ratification of ICCPR and Optional Protocol.

■○ Ratification of ICCPR and Signature of Optional Protocol.

□○ Signature of ICCPR and Optional Protocol.

	International Convention on the Prevention and Punishment of the Crime of Genocide 1948	International Convention on the Elimination of All Forms of Racial Discrimination 1965	International Covenant on Civil and Political Rights 1966	International Covenant on Economic, Social and Cultural Rights 1966
Dominican Republic	□	■	■●	■
Ecuador	■	■▶	■●	■
El Salvador	■	■	■●	■
Grenada		□	■	■
Guatemala	■	■	■●	■
Guyana		■	■●	■
Haiti	■	■	■	
Honduras	■	■	■●	■
Jamaica	■	■	■●	■
Mexico	■	■▶	■●	■
Nicaragua	■	■	■●	■
Panama	■	■	■●	■
Paraguay	■	■	■●	■
Peru	■	■▶	■●	■
Saint Kitts and Nevis		■		
Saint Lucia		■		
Saint Vincent and the Grenadines	■	■	■●	■
Suriname		■	■●	■
Trinidad and Tobago	■	■	■●	■
United States of America	■	■	■	□
Uruguay	■	■▶	■●	■
Venezuela	■	■▶	■●	■
Asia				
Afghanistan	■	■	■	■
Bangladesh	■	■	■	■
Bhutan		□		
Brunei Darussalam				
Cambodia	■	■	■○	■
China	■	■	□	■
Democratic People's Republic of Korea	■		■	■
India	■	■	■	■
Indonesia		■	■	■
Japan		■	■	■
Kazakhstan	■	■▶	■●	■
Kyrgyzstan	■	■	■●	■
Lao People's Democratic Republic	■	■	■	■

Convention on the Elimination of All Forms of Discrimination against Women 1979	Convention on the Rights of the Child 1989	ILO 111 Discrimination (Employment and Occupation) Convention 1958	ILO 169 Convention Concerning Indigenous and Tribal Peoples in Independent Countries 1989	International Convention on the Protection of the Rights of All Migrant Workers and Members of Their Families 1990	ICC Rome Statute of the International Criminal Court 1998	American Convention on Human Rights 1969	Additional Protocol to the American Convention on Human Rights in the area of Economic, Social and Cultural Rights 1988
■	■	■	—	—	■	■	□
■	■	■	■	■	■	■	■
■	■	■	—	■	—	■	■
■	■	■	—	—	■	—	—
■	■	■	■	■	—	■	■
■	■	■	—	□	■	—	—
■	■	■	—	—	□	■	□
■	■	■	■	—	—	■	—
■	■	■	—	—	□	■	—
■	■	■	■	■	■	■	■
■	■	■	■	■	—	■	□
■	■	■	—	—	■	■	■
—	—	—	—	—	■	■	—
■	■	■	■	■	■	■	■
■	■	■	—	—	■	—	—
■	■	—	—	—	■	—	—
■	■	—	—	—	■	—	—
■	■	—	—	—	■	—	—
■	■	—	—	—	■	■	■
■	■	■	—	—	■	■	—
□	□	—	—	—	□	□	—
■	■	■	—	■	■	■	■
■	■	■	—	—	■	■	□
—	—	—	—	—	—	—	—
■	■	■	—	—	■	—	—
■	■	■	—	□	■	—	—
■	■	—	—	—	—	—	—
—	—	■	—	□	■	—	—
■	■	■	—	—	—	—	—
■	■	—	—	—	—	—	—
■	■	—	—	□	—	—	—
■	■	■	—	—	—	—	—
—	—	—	—	—	■	—	—
■	■	■	—	■	□	—	—
■	■	■	—	—	—	—	—

Status of ratification of major international and regional instruments relevant to minority and indigenous rights

as of 1 February 2011

■ Ratification, accession or succession.

□ Signature not yet followed by ratification.

■► Ratification of ICERD and Declaration on Article 14.

■▷ Ratification of ICERD and Signature of Declaration on Article 14.

■• Ratification of ICCPR and Optional Protocol.

■○ Ratification of ICCPR and Signature of Optional Protocol.

□○ Signature of ICCPR and Optional Protocol.

	Genocide 1948	Racial Discrimination 1965	ICCPR 1966	ICESCR 1966
Malaysia	■			
Maldives	■	■	■•	■
Mongolia	■	■	■•	■
Myanmar	■			
Nepal	■	■	■○	■
Pakistan	■	■	■	■
Philippines	■	■	■•	
Republic of Korea	■	■►	■•	■
Singapore	■			
Sri Lanka	■	■	■•	■
Tajikistan		■	■•	■
Thailand		■	■	■
Timor Leste		■	■	■
Turkmenistan		■	■•	■
Uzbekistan	■	■	■•	■
Viet Nam	■	■	■	■
Europe				
Albania	■	■	■•	■
Andorra	■	■►	■•	
Armenia	■	■	■•	■
Austria	■	■►	■•	■
Azerbaijan	■	■►	■•	■
Belarus	■	■	■•	■
Belgium	■	■►	■•	■
Bosnia and Herzegovina	■	■	■•	■
Bulgaria	■	■►	■•	■
Croatia	■	■	■•	■
Cyprus	■	■►	■•	■
Czech Republic	■	■►	■•	■
Denmark	■	■►	■•	■
Estonia	■	■►	■•	■
Finland	■	■►	■•	■
France	■	■►	■•	■
Georgia	■	■►	■•	■

Top section

Convention on the Elimination of All Forms of Discrimination against Women 1979	Convention on the Rights of the Child 1989	ILO 111 Discrimination (Employment and Occupation) Convention 1958	ILO 169 Convention Concerning Indigenous and Tribal Peoples in Independent Countries 1989	International Convention on the Protection of the Rights of All Migrant Workers and Members of Their Families 1990	ICC Rome Statute of the International Criminal Court 1998
■	■				
■	■				
■	■	■			■
■	■	■	■		
■	■	■			
■	■	■		■	□
■	■	■			■
■	■	■		■	
■	■	■		■	■
■	■				□
■	■			■	■
■	■	■			
■	■	■			

Lower section

Convention on the Elimination of All Forms of Discrimination against Women 1979	Convention on the Rights of the Child 1989	ILO 111 Discrimination (Employment and Occupation) Convention 1958	ILO 169 Convention Concerning Indigenous and Tribal Peoples in Independent Countries 1989	International Convention on the Protection of the Rights of All Migrant Workers and Members of Their Families 1990	ICC Rome Statute of the International Criminal Court 1998	European Charter for Regional or Minority Languages 1992	Framework Convention for the Protection of National Minorities 1995
■	■	■		■	■		■
■	■				■		
■	■	■			□	■	■
■	■	■		■	■	■	■
■	■	■			□		■
■	■	■			■		□
■	■	■		■	■	■	■
■	■	■			■	■	■
■	■	■			■	■	■
■	■	■			■	■	■
■	■	■	■		■	■	■
■	■	■			■	■	■
■	■	■			■	□	
■	■	■			■		■

Status of ratification of major international and regional instruments relevant to minority and indigenous rights

as of 1 February 2011

■ Ratification, accession or succession.

□ Signature not yet followed by ratification.

■▶ Ratification of ICERD and Declaration on Article 14.

■▷ Ratification of ICERD and Signature of Declaration on Article 14.

■• Ratification of ICCPR and Optional Protocol.

■○ Ratification of ICCPR and Signature of Optional Protocol.

□○ Signature of ICCPR and Optional Protocol.

	International Convention on the Prevention and Punishment of the Crime of Genocide 1948	International Convention on the Elimination of All Forms of Racial Discrimination 1965	International Covenant on Civil and Political Rights 1966	International Covenant on Economic, Social and Cultural Rights 1966
Germany	■	■▶	■•	■
Greece	■	■	■•	■
Holy See		■		
Hungary	■	■▶	■•	■
Iceland	■	■▶	■•	■
Ireland	■	■▶	■•	■
Italy	■	■▶	■•	■
Latvia	■	■	■•	■
Liechtenstein	■	■▶	■	■
Lithuania	■	■	■•	■
Luxembourg	■	■▶	■•	■
Malta		■▶	■•	■
Monaco	■	■▶	■	■
Montenegro	■	■▶	■•	■
Netherlands	■	■▶	■•	■
Norway	■	■▶	■•	■
Poland	■	■▶	■•	■
Portugal	■	■▶	■•	■
Republic of Moldova	■	■	■•	
Romania	■	■▶	■•	■
Russian Federation	■	■▶	■•	
San Marino		■	■•	■
Serbia	■	■▶	■•	■
Slovakia	■	■▶	■•	■
Slovenia	■	■▶	■•	■
Spain	■	■▶	■•	■
Sweden	■	■▶	■•	■
Switzerland	■	■▶	■	■
The former Yugoslav Republic of Macedonia	■	■▶	■•	
Turkey	■	■	■○	■
Ukraine	■	■▶	■•	■
United Kingdom of Great Britain and Northern Ireland	■	■	■	■
Middle East				
Bahrain	■	■	■	■
Iran (Islamic Republic of)	■	■	■	■

Convention on the Elimination of All Forms of Discrimination against Women 1979	Convention on the Rights of the Child 1989	ILO 111 Discrimination (Employment and Occupation) Convention 1958	ILO 169 Convention Concerning Indigenous and Tribal Peoples in Independent Countries 1989	International Convention on the Protection of the Rights of All Migrant Workers and Members of Their Families 1990	ICC Rome Statute of the International Criminal Court 1998	European Charter for Regional or Minority Languages 1992	Framework Convention for the Protection of National Minorities 1995
■	■	■	■		■	■	■
■	■	■			■		□
	■						
■	■	■			■	■	■
■	■	■			■	□	□
■	■	■			■		■
■	■	■			■	□	■
■	■	■			■		
■	■	■			■	■	■
■	■	■			■		□
■	■	■			■	□	■
■	■				□		
■	■	■		□	■		
■	■	■	■		■	■	■
■	■	■	■		■	■	■
■	■	■			■		■
■	■	■			■		■
■	■	■			■	□	■
■	■	■			■	■	■
■	■	■			□	□	■
■	■	■			■		■
■	■	■		□	■	■	■
■	■	■			■		■
■	■	■	■		■	■	■
■	■	■			■	■	■
■	■	■			■		■
■	■	■			■	□	■
■	■	■		■			
■	■	■			□	■	■
■	■	■			■	■	■
■	■	■			□		
	■	■			□		

	International Convention on the Prevention and Punishment of the Crime of Genocide 1948	International Convention on the Elimination of All Forms of Racial Discrimination 1965	International Covenant on Civil and Political Rights 1966	International Covenant on Economic, Social and Cultural Rights 1966

Status of ratification of major international and regional instruments relevant to minority and indigenous rights

as of 1 February 2011

■ Ratification, accession or succession.

□ Signature not yet followed by ratification.

■▶ Ratification of ICERD and Declaration on Article 14.

■▷ Ratification of ICERD and Signature of Declaration on Article 14.

■● Ratification of ICCPR and Optional Protocol.

■○ Ratification of ICCPR and Signature of Optional Protocol.

□○ Signature of ICCPR and Optional Protocol.

	Genocide 1948	ICERD 1965	ICCPR 1966	ICESCR 1966
Iraq	■	■	■	■
Israel	■	■	■	■
Jordan	■	■	■	■
Kuwait	■	■	■	■
Lebanon	■	■	■	■
Oman		■		
Qatar		■		
Saudi Arabia	■	■		
Syrian Arab Republic	■	■	■	■
United Arab Emirates	■	■		
Yemen	■	■	■	■
Oceania				
Australia	■	■▶	■●	■
Cook Islands				
Fiji	■	■		
Kiribati				
Marshall Islands				
Micronesia (Federated States of)				
Nauru			□	□
New Zealand	■	■	■●	■
Niue				
Palau				
Papua New Guinea	■	■	■	■
Samoa			■	
Solomon Islands		■		■
Tonga	■	■		
Tuvalu				
Vanuatu			■	

Compiled by Marusca Perazzi

Sources:

http://www2.ohchr.org/english/bodies/docs/RatificationStatus.pdf
http://www.unhchr.ch/tbs/doc.nsf/Statusfrset?OpenFrameSet
http://www.iccnow.org/?mod=romesignatures
http://www.achpr.org/
http://www.oas.org/juridico/english/Sigs/b32.html
http://www.cidh.oas.org/
http://conventions.coe.int/

Convention on the Elimination of All Forms of Discrimination against Women 1979	Convention on the Rights of the Child 1989	ILO 111 Discrimination (Employment and Occupation) Convention 1958	ILO 169 Convention Concerning Indigenous and Tribal Peoples in Independent Countries 1989	International Convention on the Protection of the Rights of All Migrant Workers and Members of Their Families 1990	ICC Rome Statute of the International Criminal Court 1998		
■	■	■					
■	■	■			□		
■	■	■			■		
■	■	■			□		
■	■	■					
■	■				□		
■	■	■					
■	■						
■	■	■		■	□		
■	■	■			□		
■	■	■			□		
■	■	■			■		
■	■				■		
■	■	■	■		■		
■	■	■					
■	■				■		
■	■						
	■				■		
■	■	■			■		
	■						
	■						
■	■	■					
■	■	■			■		
	■				□		
	■						
■	■						
■	■	■					

Who are minorities?

Minorities of concern to MRG are disadvantaged ethnic, national, religious, linguistic or cultural groups who are smaller in number than the rest of the population and who may wish to maintain and develop their identity. MRG also works with indigenous peoples.

Other groups who may suffer discrimination are of concern to MRG, which condemns discrimination on any ground. However, the specific mission of MRG is to secure the rights of minorities and indigenous peoples around the world and to improve cooperation between communities.

Selected abbreviations

ACHPR – African Commission on Human and Peoples' Rights
AHRC – Asian Human Rights Commission
AU – African Union
CEDAW – Convention on the Elimination of All forms of Discrimination Against Women
CERD – UN Committee on the Elimination of Racial Discrimination
CRC – UN Convention on the Rights of the Child
ECHR – European Convention on Human Rights
ECtHR – European Court of Human Rights
EHRC – European Human Rights Commission
EU – European Union
FCNM – Council of Europe Framework Convention for the Protection of National Minorities
FGM – female genital mutilation
HRW – Human Rights Watch
IACtHR – Inter-American Court of Human Rights
ICC – International Criminal Court
ICCPR – International Covenant on Civil and Political Rights
ICERD – International Convention on the Elimination of All Forms of Racial Discrimination
ICESCR – International Covenant on Economic, Social and Cultural Rights
IDP – internally displaced person

ILO – International Labour Organization
IOM – International Organization for Migration
LGBT – lesbian, gay, bisexual and transgender
MDGs – Millennium Development Goals
NGO – non-governmental organization
OAS – Organization of American States
OCHA – UN Office for the Coordination of Humanitarian Affairs
OECD – Organisation for Economic Co-operation and Development
OHCHR – Office of the High Commissioner on Human Rights
OSCE – Organization for Security and Co-Operation in Europe
UDHR – Universal Declaration on Human Rights
UN – United Nations
UNDM – UN Declaration on the Rights of Persons Belonging to National or Ethnic, Religious and Linguistic Minorities
UNDP – UN Development Programme
UNDRIP – UN Declaration on the Rights of Indigenous Peoples
UNIFEM – UN Development Fund for Women
UNRWA – UN Relief and Works Agency
UNHCR – UN High Commissioner for Refugees
UPR – Universal Periodic Review
USCIRF – US Commission on International Religious Freedom

Contributors

Sumit Baudh *(Contributor – case study, South Asia)* is a lawyer, and has a decade of experience in the development and the corporate sector combined. Presently located in Delhi, he works as a consultant.

Maurice Bryan *(Americas)* is a Caribbean-born writer and communications consultant with a special focus on the use of information technology in a rights-based approach to social and economic development and cultural processes. He has worked in over 25 countries in Latin America, the Caribbean, Asia and Africa, and currently spends most of his time in Central America.

Michelle Carnegie *(Co-author – Violence against women in indigenous, minority and migrant groups)* is a Lecturer in the Development Studies and Culture Change Program at Macquarie University, Sydney. Her research interests include investigating social, environmental and political change processes in remote, rural places of the global South.

Joshua Castellino *(South Asia)* is Professor of Law and Head of the Law Department at Middlesex University, London. A former journalist in India, he has written several books and journal articles on issues concerning minority rights, indigenous peoples, comparative constitutional law and international law.

Deborah Eade *(Co-author - Women and armed conflict: from victims to activists)* has worked in the international development and humanitarian fields for 30 years, including a long-term senior assignment in Mexico and Central America. She was Editor-in-Chief of the journal *Development in Practice* from 1991 until 2010 and her many publications include *The Oxfam Handbook of Development and Relief* (3 vols.) and *Development, Women and War: Feminist Perspectives* (co-edited with Haleh Afshar).

Yakın Ertürk *(Preface)* served as a faculty member at the Department of Sociology, Middle East Technical University in Ankara, Turkey (Sept.1986 – Oct 2010). In addition to her academic career, Yakın also served as Director of the International Research and Training Institute for the Advancement of Women (INSTRAW) Director of The Division for the Advancement of Women (DAW) and as UN Special Rapporteur on Violence against Women (2003 – 2006). In November 2009 she was elected to the European Committee for the Prevention of Torture (CPT) for a term of four years.

Katalin Halász *(Europe)* is a researcher, writer and activist with expertise in anti-discrimination legislation, minority rights, Roma rights and racism as a crime. Over the last decade she has worked for national and international human rights organizations in Hungary, Germany, India, Belgium and the UK, and at the European Court of Justice in Luxembourg. She is currently undertaking a PhD research in Visual Sociology at Goldsmiths College, University of London, on the representation of race and ethnicity in contemporary visual arts

Rahnuma Hassan *(Southern Africa)* is an aspiring writer with a background in international development. She is interested in issues of identity and can be found on the internet writing about the intersections of race and gender in the context of development interventions.

Joanna Hoare *(SWM editor)* worked as Commissioning Editor at MRG in 2010/2011. Prior to this, she worked in editorial roles on the journals *Gender & Development* and *Feminist Review*, and as a freelance editor, writer and consultant on gender and development issues for a variety of NGOs and intergovernmental organisations.

Anna Horvai *(Co-author – Somalia)* has an MSc in Comparative and International Education from the University of Oxford, where she completed her dissertation on the obstacles surrounding the integration of Roma children into the Hungarian education system. She recently completed a Publications internship at MRG, which broadened her understanding of minority issues throughout the world.

Nurçan Kaya *(Turkey)* is a lawyer specializing in international human rights law, in particular anti-discrimination law and protection of minority rights. Currently she works as Cyprus/Turkey

Coordinator at MRG and Director of Turkey Fund at Global Dialogue.

Mark Lattimer *(Peoples under Threat)* is the Executive Director of Minority Rights Group. Formerly he worked with Amnesty International. Recent publications include (as editor) *Genocide and Human Rights* (Ashgate 2007).

Corinne Lennox *(Minority and indigenous women and the MDGs)* is a Lecturer in Human Rights at the Institute of Commonwealth Studies, University of London. Her research focuses on minority and indigenous rights protection and on human rights and development. She has worked as a human rights practitioner and consultant, including for MRG, UNDP and the UN Office of the High Commissioner for Human Rights.

Irwin Loy *(East and South East Asia)* is a multimedia journalist and editor based in Phnom Penh, Cambodia, where he focuses on human rights and development issues. He has filed news and feature reports from around the South East Asia region for international media.

Morna Macleod *(Co-author - Women and armed conflict: from victims to activists)*, with an MA and doctorate in Latin American Studies, is an independent consultant and invited researcher at the Centre for Research and Higher Studies in Social Anthropology (CIESAS) in Mexico City. She worked for Oxfam for almost a decade and has worked in human rights, aid and research on Guatemala since 1983.

Gay McDougall *(Foreword)* was appointed in July 2005 by the High Commissioner for Human Rights as the first UNs Independent Expert on Minority Issues. A human rights lawyer, Gay McDougall was Executive Director of the US based international NGO Global Rights from 1994 through 2006. As Special Rapporteur on the issue of systematic rape and sexual slavery practices in armed conflict, she presented a groundbreaking study calling for the international legal standards for the prosecution of such acts.

Bobbie Mellor *(Co-author – Somalia)* was a Publications Intern at MRG in 2010/11. A recent graduate of French and Dutch at University College London, her research interests include constitutional challenges to linguistic rights and the development of regional language legislation in France. She also works with the Routes into Languages scheme to promote foreign language teaching in the UK curriculum.

George Mukundi Wachira *(East and Horn of Africa)* is a Member of a Panel of Legal Experts to the African Commission on Human and Peoples' Rights Working Group of Indigenous Populations/Communities in Africa, and the Africa Regional Coordinator for the Transitional Justice Programme, Centre for the Study of Violence and Reconciliation, South Africa.

Matthew Naumann *(Central Asia)* is a freelance researcher and writer with seven years of experience on human rights, social development and humanitarian issues in Central Asia, including periods with the UN and International Crisis Group. He holds degrees in Development Studies (BA), International Human Rights Law (LLM), and Politics and Security in Central Asia (MA).

Marusca Perazzi *(China and Mongolia)* is Programmes Coordinator at MRG. Her areas of specialization are Chinese language and culture, international relations and global governance. She works in Africa and Asia and has lived and worked with ethnic minority communities in northwest China.

Claire Rowland *(Co-author – Violence against women in indigenous, minority and migrant groups)* has been working with local and international NGOs in Asia and the Pacific for over seven years in a variety of roles. Increasingly interested in research, and passionate about women's activism and gender equality, Claire has recently been involved in two multi-year research projects exploring the gendered outcomes in water and sanitation initiatives in the Pacific and the gendered impacts of economic development projects in Melanesia.

Kathryn Ramsay *(Why focus on minority and indigenous women?)* is Gender Coordinator at MRG, managing programmes supporting minority women in Asia and Africa to work on a range of human rights issues. She holds an MA in the

Theory and Practice of Human Rights from the University of Essex.

Tanya Saroj Bakhru (*Reproductive rights: a long way to go*) holds a PhD in Women's Studies from University College Dublin, Ireland (2007). She is currently an Assistant Professor of Women's Studies in the Department of Interdisciplinary Social Science at San Jose State University, California.

Preti Taneja (*Middle East and North Africa*) is a writer and film maker whose previous work for MRG includes (as editor) two editions of *State of the World's Minorities and Indigenous Peoples*, and (as writer/ co writer) *Assimilation, Exodus, Eradication: Iraq's Minority Communities since 2003* (2007) and *Uncertain Refuge Dangerous Return: Iraq's Uprooted Minorites* (2009). As a documentary maker with ERA Films, she directs and produces campaign films for local charities and international NGOs.

Paige Wilhite Jennings (*Central and West Africa*) has worked with inter-governmental and non-governmental organisations in Central Africa, Central and South America and the Caribbean.

Jacqui Zalcberg (*Oceania*) is an Australian human rights lawyer who has worked on a range of international human rights cases in a variety of international and domestic forums, focusing on the rights of indigenous peoples. This has included working for the UN OHCHR Indigenous Peoples and Minority Unit, and the US based NGO EarthRights International. She currently works as a legal adviser to the United Nations Special Rapporteur on Indigenous Peoples, as well as teaching and coordinating the Human Rights Law Clinic at the Law Faculty of the Humboldt University, Berlin.

Acknowledgements

With thanks to Carl Soderbergh for considerable editorial input, Kristen Harrison for production coordination, Publications interns Anna Horvai, Charlie Hoyle and Bobbie Mellor for research and admin support, MRG gender experts Kathryn Ramsay and Claire Thomas for advice and comments on the thematic chapters, Sophie Richmond for copy editing and Tom Carpenter for design.

In addition to the MRG staff who provided their feedback on earlier drafts, we would like to thank and acknowledge the following individuals who have contributed their thoughts, comments, advice and expertise to this edition of State of the World's Minorities and Indigenous Peoples:

Daniel Alberman, Alan Barnard, Gretchen Bauer, Gwendolyn Beetham, Bruce Bennett, Treva Braun, Sandra Brunnegger, Rowan Callick, Kamala Chandrakirana, Nicholas Cheesman, June Dreyer, Amani El Jack, Yakın Ertürk, William Fierman, Judith Gardam, Geoff Gilbert, Laura Hammond, Rita Manchanda, Fiona McCallum, Eugina McGill, Roberta Medda, Erik Mobrand, Ian Neary, Francisco Panizza, Vijayan Pillai, Scott Radnitz, Richard Rathbone, Mervat Rishmawi, Claudia Seymour, Chayanika Shah, Declan Walsh.

Minority Rights Group International

Minority Rights Group International (MRG) is a non-governmental organization (NGO) working to secure the rights of ethnic, religious and linguistic minorities and indigenous peoples worldwide, and to promote cooperation and understanding between communities. Our activities are focused on international advocacy, training, publishing and outreach. We are guided by the needs expressed by our worldwide partner network of organizations which represent minority and indigenous peoples. MRG works with over 150 organizations in nearly 50 countries. Our governing Council, which meets twice a year, has members from 9 different countries. MRG has consultative status with the United Nations Economic and Social Council (ECOSOC), and observer status with the African Commission on Human and People's Rights. MRG is registered as a charity and a company limited by guarantee under English law. Registered charity no. 282305, limited company no. 1544957.

Discover us online:

MRG website
Visit our main website for news, publications and more information about MRG's work:
http://www.minorityrights.org

Minority Voices Newsroom
An online news portal that allows minority and indigenous communities to upload multimedia content and share their stories:
http://www.minorityvoices.org/

World Directory of Minorities and Indigenous Peoples
The internet's leading information resource on minorities around the globe:
www.minorityrights.org/Directory